Republican Rome,
the Army and the Allies

Emilio Gabba

REPUBLICAN ROME, THE ARMY AND THE ALLIES

Translated by P.J. Cuff

UNIVERSITY OF CALIFORNIA PRESS

Berkeley and Los Angeles 1976

UNIVERSITY
OF CALIFORNIA PRESS
Berkeley and Los Angeles,
California

ISBN 0-520-03259-4

Library of Congress
Catalog Card No. 76-14307

© *Basil Blackwell 1976*

Translated by arrangement from
Esercito e società nella tarda Repubblica Romana
© Nuova Italia Editrice 1973

Set in Castellar (display)
and Monotype Fournier (text)
Made and printed in Great Britain by
Richard Clay (The Chaucer Press) Ltd
Bungay, Suffolk

Contents

Preface

The school of Ancient History which flourished in the University of Pavia after the last war and which was bred and nurtured by Professor Fraccaro, needs no introduction. From this small town in northern Italy which had already made a substantial contribution to learning in the past (to mention only Alessandro Volta) there came a stream of papers on ancient history which gave fresh illumination to old problems and unique insight into new ones; the work of (Prof.) G. Tibiletti on the newly-discovered *Tabula Hebana* (*Athenaeum* N.S. XXVII 1949, 210 f.) was matched by his re-examination of the problems of Republican agrarian politics (*Athenaeum* N.S. XXVI 1948, 173 f.; *ibid.* XXVII 1949, 3 f.; *ibid.* XXVIII 1950, 183 f.) and of the *repetundae* courts (*Athenaeum* N.S. XXXI 1953, 5 f.). Each article is an original and lasting contribution to the study of Roman History.

To this school (Prof.) Gabba had the honour to belong. His work, like that of his contemporary Tibiletti, immediately displayed that quality of freshness and originality which distinguishes the best in scholarship. Gabba would be the first to attribute any talent he may possess to the guidance of his teacher Fraccaro, but as one who was fortunate enough to be present in Pavia soon after the papers began to appear I can testify that the bulk of his achievement is none other than the product of his own flair for sensitive judgement, disciplined imagination and clear argument.

Gabba's articles have recently been collected in *Esercito e Società nella tarda repubblica romana* (Florence 1973) and I have selected the most important of them for translation. His earliest inquiry was into the Roman army of the Republic. The first article which appears in this translation ('The origins of the professional army at Rome . . .') sets out to show how the

vii

so-called reform of Marius in 107 BC was no more than the last stage in a process which had been going on for over a hundred years and was therefore in itself worthy of little remark; it was later propaganda which set out to paint Marius' levy of that year in sombre colours.

The purpose of the next article ('The Roman Professional Army from Marius to Augustus') is to describe the significance of that force in the political history of the last century of the Roman Republic, concentrating in particular on its role as a medium for the advancement of the lower classes of Italy to important posts in the state's service, and on the problem of the veterans.

This important contribution to Republican history (and in particular to the analysis of the origins of the Principate) was soon followed by a substantial but more controversial essay on the Social War ('The Origins of the Social War . . .'). Here Gabba examines the causes of that war and sets it in the political context of the period, relying principally on the account to be found in Appian. The second part of the article deals with Sertorius and his struggle in Spain.

These are the major works I have translated. In addition I have included the article on 'M. Livius Drusus and Sulla's Reforms', which analyses the programme of the tribune of 91 BC and draws an interesting parallel between his policy and that of Sulla (it also contains some useful commentary on Cicero's *pro Sex. Roscio Amerino*); also 'The Equestrian Class and Sulla's Senate', which is concerned with problems of recruitment to the Senate and with Sulla's attitude to the Equites; and finally 'The *lex Plotia agraria*', a valuable note on the provisions made for Pompey's Spanish veterans. The collection is completed by two reviews, both of classics (Toynbee's *Hannibal's Legacy* and Badian's *Foreign Clientelae*) and both in their own way excellent examples of the author's ability to criticize sympathetically and constructively in the best tradition of review-discussions. They are, in my view, outstanding among all the assessments of these two works which have appeared.

I hope that this translation will be of service to those students of Roman history who do not read Italian but who wish to supplement their reading of standard English interpretations by recourse to works which have made a considerable impact on world scholarship and which should continue to be basic studies for many years to come. The text I have used is that in *Esercito e Società*, which has incorporated some useful amendments and additions to the original articles. Its page numbers are set in italic figures within brackets, in the headlines of this book. Where an article has appeared in *Esercito e Società* and has not been translated by me, I have given full references. Square brackets in the translation indicate my own addenda. All notes are to be found on p. 171 ff.

There are debts to acknowledge. I am grateful to Professor E. Badian who made some useful comments. My University and my College gave me the leave which enabled me to write this translation and financial assistance which helped me to make it suitable for publication. The University of Western Australia, where most of it was written, provided that quiet hospitality which it is no longer easy to find in the northern hemisphere. I am indebted to my colleague, Mr. G. W. Bond, who read the proofs and to Miss S. Robb who did most of the typing. The debit side of my personal account with my wife and family has substantially increased during the last eighteen months. But my principal obligation – and it is a very substantial one – is to Mr. M. W. Frederiksen and Mrs. Ursula Hall (formerly Ewins); the former has read most, and the latter all, of the translation. Without their generosity, their unfailing ear for the Italian language and their sensitive appreciation of Professor Gabba's thought, this book would not have been possible.

The memorial which follows comes from both the author of *Esercito e Società* and his translator.

Pembroke College, Oxford   P. J. CUFF
  September 1975

PLINIO FRACCARO
H. M. LAST
ABSENTES ADSUNT

I

The Origins of the Professional Army at Rome: the 'proletarii' and Marius' reform[*]

I

My object in this inquiry is to investigate Marius' reform of the levy in 107 BC and to assess how far it was responsible for that proletarian character of the Roman legions which is the basis of the professional armies of the first century BC. Without wishing to belittle the importance of the 107 *dilectus* both for Roman military history and, more crucially, for the crisis which overtook the Republican system, I think my study shows that the new type of enrolment practised by Marius was only the final stage of a process which had lasted for a century and which had led to the entry of more and more *proletarii* into the Roman citizen militia. This process can, at least in part, be reconstructed by a careful examination of the progressive reductions which were made in the census minimum qualification of the fifth class in the 'Servian' system.

As a result, the *dilectus* of 107, as Delbrück had already tentatively surmised, takes on a meaning somewhat different from that which has been commonly accepted, and seems less of a revolution or an innovation. Hence it becomes necessary to re-examine both its actual significance and the reactions it produced in the contemporary political scene. This reassessment will involve *inter alia* a rejection of the view which sees 'social' significance in the Marian levy although this is the interpretation which almost every source offers us.

I do not, in fact, intend here to reconsider the professionalism of the proletarian army and its political consequences which gave rise to the posthumous attacks by the oligarchy on Marius' *dilectus*. I shall try only to show

how the professional army, whose birth modern scholars usually date to 107 BC, had origins of another kind, more complex and more remote.

In order that what follows may be the more easily understood, it is worth summarizing the principles on which the Roman military system was based down to the end of the second century BC, even if they are to a large extent familiar.

The citizen militia originated in the so-called 'Servian' constitution; under this system legionary service was compulsory for citizen *adsidui*, those enrolled in the five classes into which the Roman people was divided according to census qualifications. The first three classes supplied soldiers of heavy armour, the last two those of light armour. All the citizens had to arm themselves at their own expense.

However, those who did not belong to the five classes, that is to say, those who could not declare to the censors the minimum census qualification for enrolment in the fifth class, were excluded from military service. This was not because they were under no obligation to serve (all citizens had a duty to share in the defence of the state) but because they were in practice exempted from service as they lacked the means to provide arms. These citizens were called *proletarii* or *capite censi*.[1]

However, even these did military service at times of especial danger, and on these occasions they were armed at public expense and served in non-regular units, quite separate from the legionary order of battle.

II
The proletarii *and the citizen militia before 107 BC*

I. THE MINIMUM CENSUS QUALIFICATION
OF THE FIFTH 'SERVIAN' CLASS

First some chronological points concerning the census qualifications of the 'Servian' system.

It is not possible to say with certainty in what period the census figures which are preserved for us as Servian were actually in force in view of the fact that, expressed as they are in sextantal asses,[2] they share the uncertainty which attends the origin of the silver denarius, itself intimately connected with the sextantal as.

It is, however, undeniable that the figures were already in force during the Second Punic War, for some of them are found in the well-known *S.C.* dealing with the fitting-out of the fleet for Sicily in 214 BC.[3] The figures which the *S.C.* records are not explicable unless they are treated as expressed in sextantal asses, and therefore we should reject the view of Mattingly who, in line with his own dating of the silver denarius to 187 BC,[4] has sought to

explain them as reckoned in libral asses.[5] This leads to absurd and unacceptable consequences (the capital qualification of the first class alone would
require excessively high figures) and so those who rely on Mattingly's
numismatic researches for their study of the 'Servian' system at this point
take a different course and maintain that the figures in the *S.C.* are false –
without any just cause.[6]

Such figures, however, coincide at two points with those of the 'Servian'
scale, exactly with the census figures for Class III (50,000 asses) and for
Class I (100,000 asses), while the other figures which the *S.C.* mentions and
which are higher than those for Class I are not census figures but serve for
this one occasion to define precise categories into which the citizens of Class I
were divided for the purpose of their contributions; these contributions
rightly weighed especially heavily on the richest citizens. Furthermore, the
fact that Class II of the 'Servian' scale (75,000 asses) is not specifically mentioned is easily explained by the fact that it was impossible to fix a fair
contribution for those assessed between 75,000 and 100,000 asses and another
for those assessed between 50,000 and 75,000 asses, so that contributors in
the classes between 50,000 and 100,000 asses had to be treated together in a
single group.

To sum up, it is my view that the 'Servian' scale with its traditional figures
was already in force during the Second Punic War, but it is impossible to
determine at what precise point it was introduced, and anyway the matter is
not in the present case of any great importance.

If this scale was perfectly attuned to economic conditions in Rome in the
last decades of the third century BC, then certainly by the second century on
the other hand it was already beginning to look like a relic of a past and
economically more backward age. It did not, for example, properly reflect the
increased wealth of the first class and especially of the equestrian order. This
fact should be sufficient to rebut the view of those who have accepted the
dating of the denarius provided by Mattingly and proposed that the 'Servian'
scale came into force only in 179 BC in a reform of the *comitia centuriata* at
which Livy seems to hint in an obscure passage.[7] In fact, we should also note
that the dating of the denarius given by Mattingly is anything but certain.
Rather I think it probable that J. G. Milne is nearer the truth in placing the
first minting of the silver denarius about 218 BC.[8] This date would fit well
with my own conclusions.

In the 'Servian' scale the minimum census qualification required for
membership of the fifth class was 11,000 asses.[9] We know, however, that in
Polybius' time service in the legions required property worth 400 drachmae
(= 4,000 asses).[10] Finally, Cicero mentions 1,500 asses as the census qualification which distinguished the *adsidui* from the *proletarii*[11] and Gellius, with
one modification, also follows this view.[12]

The problem is, what do these figures (11,000, 4,000, 1,500 asses) represent?

Are they to be taken as contemporary one with each other, indicating different categories of citizens for different purposes, or do they all represent variations which occurred at different times in one and the same figure, namely the census minimum of the fifth class?

The first view depends principally on Mommsen's statement[13] that the organization of taxation had no connexion with the census classes and that therefore two figures must have existed, one (1,500 asses) to represent the dividing-line between *adsidui* who paid *tributum* and the *proletarii* who were exempt from it, and another (11,000 and subsequently 4,000 asses)[14] to indicate the census minimum required for the performance of military service.[15]

There are various reasons why this statement can be challenged. First of all we do not find in the sources any such distinction between the census minimum required for military service and that for taxation; on the contrary, it is absolutely clear in the case of the 1,500 asses qualification that they were identical, as can be seen from the passages of Cicero and Gellius already cited,[16] and it must clearly be so also in the other cases. Secondly, even if it is true that *tributum* was not paid in varying proportions according to the class to which one belonged[17] and that the graded class system of the centuriate organization was therefore irrelevant to its operation,[18] it would still appear odd that in a timocracy in which taxation and military service were imposed on the citizens in proportion to their property these two imposts had no common base-line to indicate those who were subject to them and those who were not.[19]

Furthermore, although the various authors to whom I have referred cite different figures one from another, in doing so they do suggest that they believed there were no other categories or classes of citizens below them.[20] If various figures had co-existed there would have been duplication of the census divisions of the Roman people, all the more improbable in so far as it would have been precisely the poorer citizens who would have been subjected to these very fine subdivisions and classifications.[21] Such a view also leads to other incongruities, for example the position of those citizens between 4,000 and 1,500 asses.[22]

There can, then, be no doubt that the various figures have to be seen as successive reductions of the original 'Servian' census rating of the fifth class.[23] This is surely the most natural explanation; indeed, the other 'Servian' figures, especially that of the first class, must have been brought up to date on successive occasions in an attempt to match inevitable economic and social developments.[24]

On the one hand, then, the progressive lowering of the census minimum offered the *proletarii* (now artificially converted into *adsidui*) the political advantages of the fifth class,[25] yet on the other it was a response to a definite policy for levy purposes in that it replenished the diminished ranks of citizens subject to military service. These reductions of the census minimum

qualification, therefore, marked the stages in the proletarianization of the
Roman citizen militia. Even an approximate dating of these reductions will
throw more light on the phenomenon.

2. THE REDUCTION OF THE CENSUS MINIMUM
OF THE FIFTH CLASS TO 4,000 ASSES

The first reduction of the census minimum of the fifth class is clear from
Polybius VI 19, 2, who, as I have said, records a figure of 400 drachmae as
the minimum requirement for legionary service.

This qualification must have been in force in the period in which Polybius
wrote (mid-second century BC).[26] It cannot, however, have been introduced
before the Second Punic War; the figures of the 'Servian' scale, including
that of the fifth class amounting to 11,000 asses, were in force at the time of
that war and since they were connected, as I have already said, with the silver
denarius they cannot antedate that war by more than a very short period.
This is adequate to refute hypotheses which attribute the reduction to an
earlier period.[27]

In my view the reduction in question took place a few years after the
beginning of the Hannibalic War, since only in this way can we explain the
fact that our sources fail to mention explicitly enrolments of *proletarii*. Such
enrolments during that war there must have been if for no other reason than
that we cannot believe that the Romans would not have had recourse to
citizens, even the poor, before they resorted to slaves and criminals. In fact
the old system of calling the *proletarii* to arms by declaring a *tumultus*,[28] which
we may infer from some accounts to have been applied after the battle of
Trasimene and Cannae,[29] must soon have been abandoned; it was ill-suited
for the purpose of any systematic exploitation of the manpower reserves of
the *proletarii* since, among other reasons, Rome was practically the only
place where it could be put into effect. Since immediately afterwards the
census minimum was reduced to 4,000 asses and substantial numbers of
proletarii were thus qualified for regular service, memories of the old system
must soon have grown dim.

The census reduction is to be dated between 214 and 212 BC, for we may
see its effects in the changes which it brought about in the military organization: I refer to the creation of the corps of *velites*. Livy, XXVI 4, 9 (*institutum
ut velites in legionibus essent*) is too often treated as a worthless gloss which
has crept into the text.[30] However, sandwiched as it is inside extensive
passages from a source which is clearly annalistic,[31] it seems to attest a
genuine historical fact, namely the complete reorganization of the light-armed
troops and their integration into the legionary order of battle, following
upon the reduction of the census minimum qualification.[32]

It is probable, however, since we see the *proletarii* (now transformed into *adsidui*) already serving at Capua in 212–211 BC in the formation of *velites*, that the actual reduction of the census minimum is to be dated a few years prior to that. In 214 BC a *S.C.* was passed authorizing the use of slaves provided by private citizens for manning the fleet[33] and we know that three years before, in 217 BC, *libertini* and *proletarii* had been levied to form the ships' crews.[34] It is natural to suppose that the enrolment of slaves in 214 BC had been undertaken precisely to provide a substitute for the *proletarii*. Because of the lowering of the census minimum these had from that time onwards to serve as land troops.[35]

The connexion between the reduction of the census minimum to 4,000 asses and the *S.C.* of 214 BC is perhaps confirmed by the fact that according to Polybius, VI 19, 3 citizens with property below 4,000 asses served only in the navy. This does not seem ever to have happened after the Second Punic War,[36] and it takes us back precisely to 214 BC when the need for ships' crews may have led to the rule recorded in Polybius.[37]

3. THE REDUCTION OF THE CENSUS MINIMUM OF THE FIFTH CLASS TO 1,500 ASSES

As I have suggested above, a second reduction of the census minimum of the fifth class is attested in the figure of 1,500 asses which marked off the *adsidui* from the *proletarii* according to Cicero, Gellius and Nonius. While the last two authorities give us no help on the period during which this figure could have been in force, Cicero seems to refer it directly to the age of Servius Tullius. As is well known, however, Chapter XXII of his *de Republica* II contains the description of the reformed centuriate organization,[38] and it seems probable that the mention of the 1,500 asses must also be referred to that. More precisely, it may be dated to around 129 BC, the dramatic date of the dialogue given in the *de Republica*. At any rate there is no doubt that this figure of 1,500 asses is a reduction from the 4,000 asses of the Polybian period.[39]

Moreover, the reduction must be both prior to 107 BC[40] and also be post-Polybius; it must post-date not only the first edition of his Histories, to which the chapters of Book VI that deal with the Roman military organization belong,[41] but also the second edition, since Polybius would be bound to have corrected his earlier narrative on a matter of such obvious importance. Since the second edition apparently alluded to events after 133 BC,[42] we might say that the reduction to 1,500 asses took place between this date and 107 BC, but an even more precise date may be possible given the extraordinary social impact such a measure would have had in that period and given the consequences which were bound to follow.

During his first tribunate (123 BC) C. Gracchus had a military law carried and Plutarch has preserved its drift: the state was to provide equipment for the soldiers without making any deductions from their *stipendium*, and the enrolment of *iuniores* below the minimum legal age (17) was prohibited.[43] I have referred to 'a' military law but it is possible that there was more than one seeing that various authors speak of νόμοι in reference to Gracchus' military measures.[44]

In this law the clause which forbade the state to deduct from a man's *stipendium* its expense of providing military equipment (Plutarch's ἐσθῆτα must certainly be interpreted in this broad sense) is of far-reaching importance, not only with regard to the history of the well-known principle concerning private armour but principally because, as Last has shrewdly observed,[45] it indicates the existence of a serious social crisis. With the progressive lowering of the census minimum of the fifth-class citizens had come to be enrolled who were too poor either to provide their own equipment or to afford to bear the cost of this equipment at all when it was provided by the state and debited against their modest *stipendium*.

We may, then, infer that 123 BC reflects the consequences of a measure by which citizens of reduced means had been introduced into the Roman army.[46] The measure must be none other than the reduction of the census minimum to 1,500 asses which on other grounds has been seen to be later than 133 (or 146) BC.[47] It fits well with what is known of the Roman military situation of the period; it was one method by which the Romans tried to find new manpower for their armies. The Gracchi wished to provide it in another way, by creating large numbers of small proprietors.

The admission of many *proletarii* into the ranks of the *adsidui*, brought about by the reduction of the census minimum and coming at a time when the proletarian class was very numerous, was bound to affect the citizen census lists and therefore the total numbers of those qualified to bear arms. In fact the reduction has left an even more positive trace in our tradition than that which appears from the provisions of C. Gracchus' military law: I refer to the striking increase in the number of citizens in the census of 125 BC when compared with the census returns of 131 BC.

In order to be certain, however, that this increase resulted from the admission to the census lists of citizens with a minimum qualification of 1,500 asses, we must also show that the census totals recorded only the *adsidui* and did not include the *proletarii*. This, I think, it is possible to do.

4. THE SIGNIFICANCE OF THE CENSUS FIGURES[48]

First a word of caution: we must distinguish between the registration of citizens by the censors and their drawing up of lists of *civium capita* whose totals have in many cases been preserved in our sources. In fact, although the lists of *civium capita* were necessarily based on returns by individuals to the censors, they differed essentially from them in that the censors also registered the names of persons who were not recorded in the final list of *civium capita*.[49]

The formula by which the census figures are introduced is *civium capita praeter orbos orbasque tot*.[50] What kind of citizen-list was it which contained *orbi* and *orbae*? and, in consequence, what was the purpose of the published list if *orbi* and *orbae* were omitted from it?

The only purpose in listing *orbi* and *orbae* officially was that of taxation; as far as the state was concerned, they were only taken into consideration in that they were subject to payment of *aes equestre* and *aes hordearium*.[51] Alongside them in the censors' list we should expect to find only the *adsidui*, those citizens subject to the payment of *tributum*.[52]

This conclusion is confirmed by another point. The part-formula *cives qui arma ferre possunt*[53] can refer only to the *adsidui*; the capacity to bear arms can be understood only as an economic capacity ($\chi\rho\acute{\eta}\mu\alpha\sigma\iota$), and this only the *adsidui* possessed. It cannot be maintained that the formula refers to their physical condition since this was not a matter for the censors to decide; it was scrutinized later at the time of the levy.[54] In short, the meaning of the formula *cives qui arma ferre possunt* must be the same as that of the well-known Greek phrase οἱ τὰ ὅπλα παρεχόμενοι and it is used therefore to indicate those in a position to provide their own arms.[55]

A list of *civium capita* which excluded orphans and widows could therefore equally well serve for the levying of *tributum* and for military recruitment;[56] the *adsidui* were subject to both these imposts, in accordance with timocratic principles. But such a list must surely have excluded the *proletarii*, exempt both from *militia* and from *tributum*.[57] There are other arguments which also demonstrate this.

The *proletarii* as such were called to arms only in cases of a *tumultus* when the levy was applied *en masse* and it is clear that their enrolment as individuals was not in question; this shows that no other procedure was possible, that is to say, the names of the *proletarii* were not to be found in any list.[58] Yet when the Romans finally decided to make regular and continuous use of *proletarii* in their armies, they employed the device of lowering the census minimum of the fifth class, thus transforming some of the *proletarii* into *adsidui*. This is most naturally explained as a legal fiction which, while it preserved outwardly the terms of a timocratic order, afforded the possibility of increasing the list of eligible citizens by adding those who up to that time had not been so. This is supported by the fact that after 214–212 BC there was never again any need to enrol *proletarii* by means of a *tumultus*.[59] If the *proletarii* had already been members of a list, the lowering of the census minimum could have had only a symbolic significance.[60]

5. THE PROLETARIANIZATION OF THE 'ADSIDUI'
IN THE SECOND CENTURY BC

The reduction of the census minimum to 1,500 asses[61] and the large number of *proletarii* who thus joined the fifth class[62] are two extremely important pieces of evidence for our view of social conditions at Rome in the second century BC. They are pointers to that gradual proletarianization of the middle class *adsidui* and they explain the deterioration which ensued in the social status of the citizen militia.

The second century witnessed not only a marked decline in population compared with the preceding century,[63] but also alongside it a not un-expected general increase in poverty.[64] There was a progressive decline on the part of those who belonged to the middle classes, either into the lowest class of the census or still lower into the ranks of the *proletarii*.[65]

Although this phenomenon had already appeared at the time of the Hannibalic War and reflected the economic crisis caused by the Carthaginian occupation, it had been slowly increasing in the course of the second century BC. The gravity of the situation finally became clear after 159 BC, the year when the numbers of *adsidui* started to diminish and in contrast the ranks of the *proletarii* necessarily to increase. This is the state of affairs with which the Gracchi were concerned, with all its political and especially military consequences.

Indeed, in military terms (which alone concern us here) the injury to the state was extremely grave; most of the *adsidui* were such only in name, not in fact (that is to say, in terms of wealth). The state was thus obliged to take upon itself a burden which could only grow heavier with time; it had to arm at public expense an ever-increasing proportion of citizen-soldiers.[66] At the beginning of the Second Punic War there were about as many *adsidui* as there were in the second half of the second century BC but at least they were for the most part genuine *adsidui* and able to provide their own armour; as a result the army of the period was sounder and more efficient. It was, in other words, a true militia of a timocratic state.

That this was no longer the situation in the second century BC emerges from the important information supplied by Polybius. Indeed, when he tells us [67] that of the classes which provided the heavy-armed soldiers (I, II and III) only I in his time was distinguished from the rest by wearing its own cuirass while II and III no longer wore distinguishing armour, we can only conclude that the citizens of these two classes, for whom the census was no longer related to the style of armour, were armed for the most part at state expense and that the same arms were supplied for all.[68] This is confirmed in another passage where Polybius gives a general account of Roman military equipment. He says (VI 39, 15): τοῖς δὲ ῾Ρωμαίοις τοῦ τε σίτου καὶ τῆς ἦεσθτος, κἄν τινος ὅπλου προσδεηθῶσι, πάντων τούτων ὁ ταμίας τὴν τεταγμένην τιμὴν ἐκ τῶν ὀψωνίων ὑπολογίζεται. This means that the quaestor deducted a fixed sum from the pay of the Roman soldier for his food and clothing and a further sum if a man needed any arms.[69] This distinction (κἄν τινος ὅπλου προσδεηθῶσι) confirms that, although in theory arms had to be obtained by the individual, in practice the state provided them.[70] One may therefore accept that most of the *adsidui* enjoyed this benefit if, as I would think, only the first class at that time served at their own expense.

The reduction of the census minimum to 1,500 asses, as the census statistics of 125 BC show, had introduced some 76,000 *proletarii* into the ranks of the *adsidui* but the latter tended to suffer a still further decline in economic status while the former did not really make any economic advance. So the need arose for that clause in C. Gracchus' military law (123 BC) which I have already discussed. In prohibiting deductions from a man's *stipendium* it was certainly intended to include all deductions and not just those for ἐσθῆτες as Plutarch says; our author has possibly abridged his material, for deductions for clothing would have been the least onerous.

In fact, however, in the last decades of the second century BC these deductions from pay ceased to represent genuine reimbursements by the soldier of the state's cost of equipping him but were bound to take on merely a symbolic character. By continuing them the state asserted, in a sense, that the old principle of private armour was still in force. Even when the citizen militia ceased to exist and was replaced by a professional army, equipped entirely at public expense, the deductions from pay were still retained,[71] one of the links, surely, by which the theory of the new army remained tied to the old military system and its timocratic principle. There would have been only one way of swimming against the tide and of restoring not simply the name but the reality of a strong class of *adsidui*. This, as is well known, the Gracchi tried; their efforts foundered on the opposition of the oligarchs.

So it can be seen that the innovation of Marius in 107 BC was in fact inevitable and necessary.

6. CONCLUSION: THE ROMAN MILITIA ON THE EVE OF MARIUS' 'DILECTUS'

It is not necessary to set out in detail the development of Rome's military crisis after the Second Punic War and its political consequences. Suffice it to say that all those extraordinary military expedients which had been necessitated by the Hannibalic War were destined not to remain temporary in effect. The reasons which led to their adoption turned out to be permanent; repetition of the same measures continued to be the only feasible response to difficulties that allowed no other possible solution.

To this situation were added the demands arising from overseas armies. Troops sent outside Italy could no longer be discharged annually as the traditions of a citizen militia required when men had been called up to fight a summer campaign in the neighbourhood of Rome. The long terms of service and the protracted loss of economic livelihood gave rise to the demand that the citizen soldiers should be rewarded on discharge after service which had been extended continuously for many years. The conflict so created between the political and military citizen institutions on the one hand and the new demands of imperialism on the other had first appeared during the Second Punic War and then later, in more strident fashion, during the Spanish War.[72]

At the same time voluntary enlistment and *evocatio*, already attested during the Hannibalic War,[73] take on new importance during the wars in the East and clearly exemplify the birth of militarism in a soldiery emerging from a long war.[74]

These two tendencies permit the deduction that the citizen militia was moving towards a form of military professionalism of which the chief characteristics may be defined as continuity of service and a mercenary outlook. From the conclusions reached above it can be maintained with some confidence that in the course of the second century BC the citizen militia underwent progressive modifications, not only in its external appearance but also in its very nature and composition, and that these modifications went hand in hand with changes in social conditions attested at Rome in that period and the political demands they evoked.[75]

The proletarianization of the middle class *adsidui* was bound to have its effects on the militia, drawn as it principally was from the middle class of small proprietors. It is an evident conclusion that simultaneously with the disappearance of the middle classes there must have occurred a proletarianization of the militia.

In 214–212 BC the *proletarii* became eligible for entry to the legions, although at first they were limited to the corps of *velites*, having been reclassified as *adsidui* by the reduction of the census minimum from 11,000 to 4,000 asses. Subsequently the decline of the regular *dilectus* and the habit of relying on tumultuary levies must have suggested the dropping of the restriction on the use of the former *proletarii*; the new *adsidui* were presumably also admitted to the other units of the legion. This is all the more likely because, as already mentioned, the tripartite division of the legion had become a formality[76] and the arms used were by that time the same for all.

The decline of the *adsidui* in the censuses after 159 BC and the opposition to the levy, especially for the Spanish War, became so serious that in 134 Scipio Aemilianus took with him to Spain an army of volunteers which featured a large number of his clients.[77] After a serious attempt by the Gracchi to cure the evil at its source had failed, the Romans were compelled to have recourse once again to a lowering of the census minimum for service from 4,000 to 1,500 asses.

This measure, although undoubtedly dictated by military needs, led to a weakening of the census basis of the citizen militia: that is to say, a weakening in fact – so much is clear from the military measure of C. Gracchus – but not in law since the soldiers nominally came, as always, from the *adsidui*!

If, then, by 107 BC all that remained of the citizen militia was only an external appearance of its original character, it is perfectly legitimate to pose the question, to what extent the Marian reform of the levy was an innovation. Delbrück had long ago set it in its true form:[78]

The essential distinction is whether in the second century the composition of the Roman army was fundamentally restricted to the sons of the middle class, or whether it was already in essence a professional army which only in practice (in so far as the *proletarii* would have gone into the fleet if there were recruitment to it)[79] retained a certain peasant-proprietor character. In the former case Marius' reform would have set the army on a quite different basis and would have introduced something quite new; in the latter it would have provided only the form to correspond with the reality which already existed, for whatever remained of the peasant-proprietor character was not completely removed even by Marius but can only have gradually died out.

Since it is clear from what has been said so far that the second alternative posited by Delbrück meets the truth in its essentials, it remains to show what significance we should attribute to Marius' reform.

In my view the new method of enrolment used by Marius in 107 BC may be seen as the logical and inevitable result of the process of proletarianization of the citizen militia which began with the Second Punic War. Marius' 'reform' did not make important or substantial innovations in the Roman army; the proletarian army of the years following 107 BC, a professional and voluntary one, differed little in composition or outlook from the army that preceded it. The only point was that it now finally lost that purely formal link with the census classes which until then it had preserved. To repeat the words of Delbrück and to sum up, the Marian reform of the levy 'provided the form to correspond with the reality which already existed'.

Hence the political consequences which attended the establishment of an army based on *proletarii* and which appeared in the first century BC cannot be derived solely from the reform of Marius as the Optimates insisted was the case. Rather they should be seen as originating in the more general condition of Rome in that period of transition which spans the decline of Republican institutions and the rise of the Empire, a transition in which the Marian reform itself finds its natural place.

III
The Marian reform of the levy[80]

I. DATE AND CAUSES

Marius' enrolment of the *capite censi* took place, according to Sallust,[81] in 107 BC, the year of his first consulship, and this date is that commonly accepted by the ancient sources.[82] However, Gellius says:[83] *capite censos autem primus C. Marius, ut quidam ferunt, bello Cimbrico difficillimis rei publicae temporibus vel potius, ut Sallustius ait, bello Iugurthino milites scripsisse traditur . . .*, and ps.-Quintilian ascribes the enrolment of the *proletarii* to the period of the Cimbric War.[84]

There are two possible reasons why, besides the Sallustian date which Gellius himself considered to be more likely (*vel potius*), there arose another which assigned the levy a later date by some years. *Prima facie* one might suppose that the authors to whom Gellius refers confused their data and connected all the innovations introduced by Marius in matters of armour, the baggage-train and the tactical organization of the legion (which belong to the Cimbric War, 104 BC and the years which followed)[85] with his reform of the levy some years earlier.

But a different explanation is more likely, that the redating was wilfully invented. As I shall show more fully later, towards the middle of the first century BC there were evidently discussions at Rome concerning Marius' enrolment of the *proletarii* and its social effects; the arguments of the pro-Marian *populares* in answer to the objections of the nobility are preserved for us, leaving aside the clear rhetorical distortions, in the passage of ps.-Quintilian which has been cited. The pro-Marians thus had every interest in maintaining that only the severe peril of the German invasion could have produced such a serious measure as the voluntary enrolment of the *capite censi*. The *declamatio* accordingly stresses the need to match *hostibus prope humanas vires excedentibus parem dilectum*, and Gellius, in reporting this view as against Sallust's, tells of the *difficillima tempora* through which the state passed at the time of the Cimbric War.

It should, of course, be recognized that the systematic levying of the *proletarii* must have assumed increasing proportions from the time of the Cimbric War onwards;[86] yet in 107 the lack of manpower must have been making itself felt in an alarming fashion and to this extent confirmed the view of those who explained the enrolment of the *proletarii* by *inopia bonorum*.[87] Losses of men in these years were very heavy: in 113 BC there was the defeat of Papirius Carbo in Noricum, in 109 that of Iunius Silanus in Gaul, in 107 again that of Cassius Longinus. The advantages derived from the lowering of the census minimum to 1,500 asses must have dwindled in a short space of time, for it was in 109 BC that the restrictions on the length of military service imposed years before by the Gracchi were abrogated.[88] Furthermore, we know that during the Jugurthine War, though it was not fought with large forces, it was considered necessary to ask allied kings and peoples to send troops,[89] while of the total forces employed the Latins and the allies must have formed the majority, to judge from their frequent mention in Sallust;[90] this cannot, in my view, be explained solely by the general tendency of Rome to use allied forces rather than her own.

It was thus for purely military reasons – principally to remedy the *inopia bonorum* – that Marius was inspired to enrol the *capite censi*, and these reasons must have been almost universally acknowledged since, as will be seen, almost no objections were raised to what he did.

Sallust, recording the anti-Marian point of view, says that some held that the measure had been taken *per ambitionem consulis*.[91] However, it is incredible that Marius or his contemporaries saw in the enrolment of the *capite censi* the chance of expanding personal power based on the army; apart from the reasons already advanced this is contradicted by the subsequent course of events.[92] The term *ambitio* should rather be understood in the narrower sense that Marius profited from the voluntary enrolment by not offending the city Plebs which was notoriously hostile to military service.[93] The nobility would be bound to see it as a part of the general attitude of the anti-*nobilis* from Arpinum, displayed especially during his election campaign for the consulship, an attitude which Sallust says was dominated by *ambitio*.[94]

This is the only political consequence – clearly a very minor one – seen by the nobility in the enrolment of the *proletarii*. The enrolment was an expedient adopted to overcome temporary difficulties; it had no long-term aim and it lacked, as we shall see, any particularly revolutionary character. It would probably have passed without notice, as did many similar cases, if the crisis which followed had not made it assume in the eyes of the oligarchy responsibility for many evils; this is how it is presented in almost all our sources. When the political role of the proletarian army became clear, then men began to reflect on the *dilectus* of Marius, its far-reaching significance and the harmful effects it had had on the state. It was easy for the oligarchy to attribute to Marius all the blame for the enrolment of the *proletarii*. If seen in its purely formal aspect there was some logical basis for this, but with such criticisms we are already in a period subsequent to the Sullan civil war.

2. THE NEW METHOD OF ENROLMENT

According to Sallust, Marius enrolled citizens in 107 *non more maiorum neque ex classibus, sed uti quoiusque lubido erat, capite censos plerosque*.[95] Of the two terms which pinpoint the new levy the first, *uti quoiusque lubido erat*, shows that it was based on the criterion of voluntary enlistment, whereas the normal *dilectus* was carried out on a tribal basis; the second, *capite censos plerosque*, indicates the type of citizen which went to make up the legions, in contrast to the traditional composition of the citizen militia which took account – nominally at any rate – of a citizen's census, and which came to comprise *adsidui*.[96]

The Marian *dilectus* did not actually abolish the cardinal principle of the citizen militia – the levy *ex classibus* – but simply dispensed with its application, given that the soldiers were volunteers. A voluntary enlistment was not actually an unusual occurrence in Roman military organization; without going back to the volunteers and *evocati* of the Eastern wars one can say that the case of Aemilianus, who in 134 BC set out with 4,000 volunteers for Numantia, is typical and suggestive, given the short period which separated it from 107.

If, then, the army which was enrolled in that year was almost totally composed of *capite censi*, this was due to the fact that those who were well-off were doubtless content not to be compelled to perform military service and glad to let its weight fall completely on the *proletarii*. On the other hand, the legions' new character was not to be seen as something extraordinary since the lowering of the census minimum a few years before had in fact already reduced the economic status of the army. It would thus seem that the Marian *dilectus* cannot be held to be a revolutionary act even in a formal sense – very important as this was for the Romans – despite the fact that Sallust refers to *mos maiorum* and Plutarch says it was παρὰ . . . τὴν συνήθειαν. In form it displays an important affinity with the old-style enrolment of *proletarii* in time of a *tumultus*.[97] This practice, which involved the arming of the *proletarii* at the state's expense if not their actual service in the legions, was quite usual and therefore unobjectionable, and anyway the case of Aemilianus cited above constituted an undeniable precedent in Marius' favour. Since, moreover, the causes which had inspired Marius to undertake voluntary enlistment continued in existence, his measure was bound to be more than a single episode and to become a regular usage although at the same time – owing to the well-known Roman respect for appearances – the traditional *dilectus* was never abrogated;[98] this surely provides the clearest proof that it was only military need, not political ambitions of whatever kind, which made its adoption necessary.

All this goes to show that, both formally and in fact, the Marian *dilectus* of 107 was not a genuine reform of the Roman military system but the outcome of developing tradition, and it becomes still clearer why there was no contemporary concern over its long-term significance.

3. THE MARIAN 'DILECTUS' AND ITS
POLITICAL SETTING

We must now consider the origin of the *proletarii* enrolled by Marius. That they were Roman citizens can clearly be inferred from Sallust, who distinguishes the *dilectus* conducted in Rome from the requests to the Latins and Italian allies for fresh contingents of troops, and is supported by general considerations; the *dilectus* of a Roman consul could affect only Roman citizens. The fact that Marius asked Latin and Italian veterans to volunteer to go with him to Numidia[99] cannot be generalized into a basis for a belief that the allied military organization was, as at Rome, now based on a principle of enrolment different from the normal one. On the contrary, we know that on this occasion the allies also provided Rome with the usual contingents *ex formula*.[100] Marius' allied volunteers must have been isolated cases.[101]

We must now determine how it was that the Roman Plebs, on whose antipathy to military service the Optimates counted in order to frustrate Marius' plans,[102] succumbed so quickly to *lubido cum Mario eundi*. In fact, a whole range of evidence makes it certain that it was not the city Plebs that supplied the real strength of Marius' proletarian army, but the country Plebs who had already attracted the attention of the Gracchi; the former was bound by ties of *clientela* to the nobility and was more inclined to enjoy the *frumentationes* at Rome than to risk their lives in battle. Their attitude must have been what I have indicated above.

Marius' candidature for the consulship of 107 had been favoured by the *agrestes*,[103] and the same people are found in 100 BC as supporters of Marius and Saturninus in their struggle with the Senate and the oligarchy. It is well-known that in the year of his second tribunate (100 BC) Saturninus proposed the distribution of land to Marius' veterans, thus continuing a programme already begun in 103 BC.[104] Various sources tell[105] how the intervention of Marius' soldiers was decisive in getting the demagogue's proposals approved; it is most significant that in Appian, our most accurate source in this connexion, Marius' veterans are consistently shown as coming from the countryside and that their claims encounter opposition from the city Plebs.[106] Our view must be that in the mass enrolment of the years prior to 100 BC the greatest number of volunteers had come from the rural Plebs; otherwise the peculiar passion with which the veterans returning from their campaign fought for their rewards, a passion natural to men directly involved, becomes hard to explain.

Finally we must examine the reasons why the rural Plebs volunteered for service at the levy of 107 BC. Marius left for Africa only *cum aliquanto maiore numero quam decretum erat*;[107] it would appear from this that the *dilectus* of 107 BC had not produced large numbers of volunteer *capite censi* and that the really large-scale enrolments came after the Numidian War and probably after 103 BC as well. In that year Saturninus proposed that 100 *iugera* of land should be given to the veterans of Marius' African army. A very powerful incentive to enrolment must have been offered to the *proletarii* who saw realized the promises of rewards Marius had made earlier in 107 BC,[108] and this is confirmed by the energy the veterans employed in 100 to have their rights enforced.

This argument, together of course with the military reasons for the reform which I have detailed above, disposes of the alternative view that the timocratic principle was abandoned in the levy of 107 BC and a system of voluntary service introduced to meet the wishes of the *proletarii*;[109] on this view the latter aimed at recapturing, through the medium of military service, their original legal, political and economic position. Rather, it is probable that the promises of the new consul suggested to the ruined rural classes a way of escape from the economic difficulties against which they were struggling. As I have said, after 103 BC the prospect of rewards in the shape of land would have assumed a definite, concrete form. There is no doubt that in the first century BC a return to the land was an aim that inspired the large majority of the soldiers who came from the rural poor, and that Sulla, Pompey, Caesar, the Triumvirs and Augustus sought to meet this need with grants of land to time-expired veterans.[110] But it is difficult if not impossible to believe that at the time of the 107 levy, over and above the rather general idea of increasing the number of citizens who could perform military service, Marius was aware of any link in social terms between the Gracchan attempt (itself the outcome of serious thought about the causes of Roman military decadence and its most effective cure) and his own voluntary enrolment of the *proletarii*. To this enrolment nothing is more alien than a social purpose; in intention at least it could have had no more than incidental importance.

The *proletarii* themselves, in fact, both then and later looked on military service as a profession. For them it was not a step towards self-improvement in the state, except in so far as the status of the soldier during the period of the civil wars was itself of great importance and thence the *proletarii* could find a secure place in political life.

It remains to show how not even the Optimates foresaw the consequences that would automatically follow from the new type of levy and how, therefore, they mounted no serious opposition to it. Sallust says that the *ambitio consulis* was the explanation Marius' opponents offered of his act; this, however, like the *invidia* which the *dilectus* aroused and to which, as we have noted, ps.-Quintilian alludes, is no more than a general objection based on prejudice and need not presuppose any more coherent vision of the future.[111] We would not be in a position to make such statements as these if the Optimates had really voiced that 'social interpretation' of Marius' *dilectus* found in various sources; this has made some[112] believe that in 107 BC there already existed a state of tension between rich and poor, such that the former thought the enrolment of *proletarii* could produce a social disaster. We find such fears in a passage of Val. Max. II 3: *laudanda enim populi verecundia est, qui impigre se laboribus et periculis militiae offerendo dabat operam, ne imperatoribus capite censos sacramento rogare esset necesse, quorum inopia suspecta erat, ideoque his publica arma non committebant.*[113]

In fact, this 'doctrinaire theory'[114] derives from Greek thinkers who had long been accustomed to the nightmare of a class revolution,[115] and it can only have appeared in Rome when the arming of the *proletarii* had revealed its harmful effects in social terms, that is to say, in a period certainly later than the dictatorship of Sulla (82–81 BC). We cannot exclude a possible connexion with the Catilinarian conspiracy which witnessed a new bitterness in social conflicts.[116] Certainly the theory which was clearly oligarchic in sentiment and therefore anti-Marian attracted disagreement, for the pro-Marian tradition, known to us from ps.-Quintilian, met its opponents' objections with the assertion: *cum scires* (Marius) *non ex censu esse virtutem, praeterita facultatium contemplatione vires animosque tantum spectasti.* This seems to show that the account of the *dilectus* of 107 in social terms also commended itself to those who were favourable to Marius, and must therefore stem from an erroneous political and social interpretation of his whole position; this can be detected in various views adopted by Caesar and the *populares* in general.[117]

Since the process of proletarianization of the army had already gone a long way by 107 BC, the abandonment of enrolment by census qualification could not have justified any beliefs that there was a social danger inherent in the new type of *dilectus*. In fact the knights, who favoured a vigorous policy towards Jugurtha, may well have welcomed the Marian *dilectus*; it avoided making the war unpopular in so far as it did not involve calling up Rome's urban citizens.[118]

Finally, from a political point of view it should be said that the Optimates in 107 did not understand – just as Marius did not – the importance which an army of *proletarii* could assume once it became, as it was bound to do, a professional army. Worse still, they were not completely aware of it even after Saturninus' rioting had given a clear warning that an extra-constitutional use of the army had now become inevitable. Men, perhaps, could delude themselves that in the future, as in 100 BC, the army's intervention in politics would be limited to the legal field of assembly-proceedings and that there would be no direct recourse to violence. Certainly a few years later the chance was lost of remedying what was a serious situation when the proposals of Livius Drusus were rejected; following the lines laid down by the Gracchi they involved distribution of *ager publicus* and aimed at reconstituting the rural middle class, and were the only way for the Romans to free themselves of the necessity, otherwise unavoidable, of continually resorting to levies of *proletarii*.[119] It was left to Sulla's attempt to establish a supremacy based on his troops to make clear to everyone the army's importance in Roman political life.

If, then, there were no serious or valid arguments which could have been brought against Marius' *dilectus*, and if therefore one should conclude that in the contemporary political context it was no more than a manoeuvre of passing importance, it remains no less true that the new levy system completed a process (the proletarianization of the Roman militia) and established a military organization which later is to be found dominating the political history of the first century BC.

II

The Roman Professional Army from Marius to Augustus[*]

A. The Army in the period of the Revolution

1. The fundamental principle of a timocracy is that the higher one's census qualifications the greater are one's military obligations and the wider one's political rights.[1] This principle never in theory disappeared from the Roman scene. However, in the third and second centuries BC its practical application was so restricted that it essentially forfeited any value.

In this connexion we need do no more than consider the history of the provision of armour at private expense (*privato sumptu*), itself an example of the timocratic principle at work. First came payment of *stipendium* to soldiers; this was intended as the state's contribution to *adsidui* to meet the losses they incurred when the usual summer campaign was extended into winter.[2] There was also the provision, again by the state, of rations, necessitated by the ever-growing distance of theatres of war from Rome;[3] after these came the supply of armour at public expense for citizens of low means, found for the first time in 281 BC.[4] As a result – and I am not concerned with more than the military side of the question – the citizen militia was progressively stripped of its class character,[5] and the *centuria* became an anachronism; the latter had had its tactical significance diminished by the introduction of the new manipular formation (end of the fourth century BC) and now became useless even for the purposes of the levy.

The new type of levy, which was probably already in operation at the time of the First Punic War, was based on the tribe, with the requirement that the soldiers had to come *ex classibus*. This qualification kept at first a particular significance of its own in the distinction which was observed between the fourth and third classes (soldiers with hoplite armour being distinguished from the light-armed)[6] but in the course of the second century BC, when only a detail distinguished the equipment of the first class from the others,[7] the qualification *ex classibus* became a purely formal one.

It may not be possible to establish with certainty how this came about, but it may help to recall that the new type of levy was a response to the need, or wish, to lighten the burden of military service on the upper classes at Rome by making it fall more heavily on those citizens who had in more recent times obtained the Roman citizenship. Indeed, if the *dilectus* by centuries weighed proportionately more severely on the first class with its smaller centuries than those of the other classes,[8] it is certain that the new citizens who were gradually incorporated in the citizen body had great difficulty in acquiring a census rating which entitled them to be enrolled in the highest class.[9] The levy by tribes, on the other hand, permitted a fairer distribution of military burdens and thus achieved the object of sparing, at least in part, the wealthier Roman classes; it offered a better use than previously of the poorer citizens for military purposes.

Previous substantial changes in the military system, which was for obvious reasons more likely to reflect a new and changing situation, had not been without influence, sometimes decisive, on the political organization of the state.[10] So it was in the case of this change. The loss by the century of its fundamental military significance stripped it also of any political importance (which sprang from its military role); this is shown by the reform of the *comitia centuriata* which took place in the second half of the third century BC. Here too, perhaps, the object was to safeguard the interests of the oldest and most solid nucleus of the Roman citizen body,[11] and so the organization of the *comitia centuriata* came to embody a connexion between tribe and century which resulted in the latter ceasing to have any real existence of its own.[12]

The Roman governing class displayed great aptitude for introducing changes in the constitution which reduced the class basis of the *comitia* to a mere form but left untouched the major political rights of the upper classes. These rights, in so far as they derived from more onerous military duties, ought to have suffered a substantial if not total reduction. However, it now happened, as a result of the reform, that not only did the greater burden of military duty fall no longer on the wealthier classes, but also the needs of war obliged the state to provide, without distinction and almost universally, the armour of all citizens. Only some deductions from pay were a formal reminder for the Romans of the ancient timocratic base of their society.[13]

Clearly it follows that the fundamental principle, to which I have earlier referred and which had a basis in reality, gave way – even though practically speaking the two coincided – to a totally different political concept: the census qualification *per se* gave a man the right to hold power. Cicero makes this concept go back to King Servius Tullius[14] and we shall see how a theory arose which was designed to explain thus the absence of the *proletarii* from military service, although the real reason for this was the fact that they could not equip themselves from their own resources. This is clearly shown by the fact that in times of crisis the state had taken steps, as I have said elsewhere, to arm them at public expense.[15]

It has been shown how the levy based on the tribe did not affect the soldiers' membership of the five classes (*adsidui*). No one in the middle of the third century BC could have anticipated the crisis which a century later was to hit the social structure of Rome as a result of an increase in empire and a change in the nature of the economy. What had been a clever political manoeuvre on the part of the governing class – the distinction between rich and poor in the field of political rights – in practice acquired economic and political shape, and contributed to a serious and ever-growing breach between the wealthy oligarchs and the ever-increasing mass of the poor.

As far as the military sphere was concerned, the *adsidui* began progressively to decline in number, either as a result of a natural decrease in population or because of the fact that those who belonged to the census middle class came to be relegated to the ranks of the *proletarii*. As a corollary the latter – those citizens who did not belong to the five census classes and were not reckoned in the numbers of those who were able, under the constitution, to bear arms[16] – enjoyed an ever-increasing numerical superiority[17] and this, in the long run, could no longer be ignored for the purpose of the levy.

The difficulties of the Second Punic War had already made necessary a reduction from 11,000 to 4,000 asses in the census minimum qualification required for membership of the fifth class,[18] so that a greater use could be made of the *proletarii*. This figure was still valid when Polybius wrote, towards the middle of the second century BC.[19] By this manoeuvre, which clearly did not provide a solution to the problem but merely dealt with a particular situation at a particular time, many *proletarii* were legally transformed into *adsidui* and thereby qualified for regular service in the army. The continuous worsening of the situation in the course of the second century BC – it is from 159 that the census figures begin decisively to decline – made necessary a further recourse to the same sort of measure about 133–125 BC and the census minimum of the fifth class was yet again lowered, from 4,000 to 1,500 asses.[20] Seventy-six thousand *proletarii* were transformed into *adsidui* as among other things the census returns of 125 show when compared with those of 131. However, this could not affect the real situation, the gravity of which was now appreciated by the governing classes who were in varying degrees concerned about it.[21]

At about the same time as the minimum census qualification was reduced to 1,500 asses, attempts were made by the Gracchi to remedy the economic and social situation. This they saw first and foremost, if not exclusively, as a military problem, and their solution was to reconstitute the middle class of small peasant proprietors. Although this policy was not totally out of touch with social and political reality, it had one serious weakness which fundamentally invalidated it: the solution proposed was still within the city-state framework at a time when the territorial limits of the Republic were being extended across continents. This was the main factor in the grievous situation in which the Roman state found itself: to match the constant increase of territory and of the political and economic demands which followed, there had been no corresponding progress in Rome's structural organization which continued to be that of a city-state.[22]

Military organization, on the other hand, as is always the case, had had to adapt itself to new needs. The continued service of soldiers under arms for long periods was fundamental here in that this was irreconcilable with the organization of an army on the basis of a citizen militia. There were serious consequences over and above those of an economic order. These consequences were moral in so far as they sowed the seed for the birth of militarism, as we have already seen, in the aftermath of the Hannibalic War.[23] This state of affairs became evident principally during the long years of the Spanish wars which, in their final period, compelled a reduction to only six years (but of continuous service) of the period soldiers should serve in Spain.[24] For this reason the Spanish army can be considered the Republican prototype of the standing armies in the provinces during the Principate.[25]

The citizen militia was being decisively transformed into a professional army, and at this point the inherent anachronism of the Gracchi's efforts becomes clear: a citizen militia consisting of a revived class of small peasant proprietors could not meet the demands which the situation imposed except on the basis of a fresh annulment of the really fundamental characteristic of short-term service, with all its economic and social consequences. The composition of the citizen militia was radically altered in so far as its economic status declined along with that of the middle class *adsidui* (although in theory the soldiers always came *ex classibus*) when, as I have already mentioned, the census minimum was reduced.

The status of the soldiers of the Gracchan period can easily be ascertained either from the well-known statement of Ti. Gracchus,[26] that those who were considered the masters of the world did not actually have even what the animals had, a lair in which to rest their heads, or from the character of the military law of C. Gracchus (123 BC) which forbade the state to make deductions from their *stipendium*, naturally enough granted the precarious circumstances of the soldiers.[27]

When, however, in 107 BC C. Marius felt himself impelled by the demands of the Numidian War to eliminate the traditional system of levy by tribe and to resort to voluntary enrolment, the composition of the army was already, for all practical purposes, proletarian. Marius' measure, which had a link with the institution of *tumultus* and for which there was a precedent, for example, in the levy of 134 BC,[28] did not appear revolutionary in character and actually only confirmed the state of affairs which already existed.[29]

However, the particular solution of the military problem devised by Marius provided at the same time, perhaps unconsciously, the right lines for resolving the general political situation; it went some way towards restoring that link between the governing class and social reality which had in the course of the second century BC been considerably weakened.

2. The nucleus of the Roman citizen militia had been, as is well known, represented by the class of small rural proprietors who for the great majority comprised the middle class *adsidui*. It is of interest to note that, even after the proletarianization of the farmer middle class which I have already described, the soldiers of the professional army still continued to come principally from the countryside.

The evidence is particularly plentiful and precise for the period of the Marian consulships (107–100 BC). Marius' candidature for the consulship of 107 was championed by the *agrestes*,[30] and also, of course, by representatives of such truly political groups as the Equites. Later, in 100 BC, the *agrestes* were the most active supporters of Appuleius Saturninus' opposition to the coalition of oligarchs and urban Plebs. Appian, whose account brings out the contrast particularly well, adds that Saturninus relied mainly on the peasants because they had fought for Marius.[31] It is clear that the enthusiasm displayed by the rural Plebs on that occasion was a result of their direct interest in the rewards they hoped to be given.[32]

The fact that the professional soldiers came from the rural population has nothing to do with the ancient formation of the army from country sources; it is the absolute abandonment of every timocratic principle in the levy and the introduction of voluntary enrolment which offer the decadent agrarian class the chance of escape from their recent economic distress.

We know, even if the evidence is not all it should be, that the conditions of the agrarian class did not change substantially in the course of the first century BC (the theme of the exclusion of the poor from the land, common in the literature of the period from the Gracchi to Augustus,[33] is certainly something more than a rhetorical commonplace lacking any reference to the contemporary scene) and it is therefore legitimate and logical to conclude that the equation 'decadence of the agrarian class = rural origin of the soldiers' certainly holds beyond the period of the late second century BC for which, as we have seen, there is direct evidence.[34]

The fact that the social origins of the soldiers were what they were must have been to a great extent influenced by the type of levy which came into use in the first century BC, especially after the extension of the citizenship to the allies. The levy was by this time carried out through *conquisitores*[35] who conducted their business in specified districts without, of course, being governed by rigid criteria; at the same time, probably, they tried not to disturb the upper classes of the population. As a result the levy was arbitrary[36] and military service for all practical purposes voluntary.[37] Naturally these volunteers represented the poorest or the worst elements of society.

At this point it is worth emphasizing a very important factor, that we cannot deduce from the conclusion that has just been reached a further conclusion, that an actual desire of the rural proletariat had initially led to the abolition of the levy *ex classibus* and, afterwards, military service was considered not so much as a profession but rather as a means of recovering its primitive legal, economic and political position.[38] This would be at variance with the fact that there was no precise relationship between the objectives of the Gracchan proposals and the purposes of the Marian levy (demonstrated above all by the immediate aims of the levy of 107 BC) and it is also at variance with a generalization, but a most important one, which from this time onwards must always be borne in mind, namely the non-political nature of the post-Marian army. Finally it conflicts with the objectives as conceived by the various champions of benefits for the disbanded armies; with the exception of Caesar and Augustus these objectives never went beyond ephemeral issues of contemporary politics.

In fact, the impulses and sentiments of the masses must have been influenced only by considerations of an economic kind: *stipendium*, the booty which followed a war, and finally a plot of land as a reward for service. The last, though, was regarded not only and not always as a means of returning to a comfortable life in the country but as a piece of capital which could be readily realized. All these economic considerations would have exercised the strongest attractions for the masses.

These common demands which are at the root of the voluntary levy of the proletariat explain the homogeneity of outlook that is a feature of the Roman army in the first century BC. This is true, despite the existence of ties based either on *clientelae* or on regional interests which seem sometimes to create differences. This homogeneity increased in depth when the dynasts, representatives of opposing political views, drove their troops to take up positions in favour of their specific interests.

As a result of the political importance that these interventions afforded the army in the life of the state, the proletariat acquired a stronger and more elevated position, but the demands which the army personified remained for all that purely economic in content.

On the other hand, this homogeneity which was, so to say, part of the army's structure was continually being reinforced by an *esprit de corps*; this was bound to go hand-in-hand with the formation of a professional army and was in its turn not uninfluential in cementing a sense of indifference towards problems of a political character which were considered alien to a soldier's true nature and his occupation.[39] This, of course, led to a distinction in outlook and approach, and introduced a gap between military and political life, as is clear in the last century of the Republic.[40]

3. I have referred above to the existence of *clientela*-relationships in the field of military activity. In view of the primary importance which this phenomenon is to assume it is necessary now to show in greater detail its development and consequences.

The phenomenon of military *clientela* developed *pari passu* with the proletarianization of the citizen militia and with the extension of continuous military service. As early as the period after the Hannibalic War, which had for the first time exacted continuous service, there had been clear signs of a birth of militarism when veterans of the Second Punic War presented themselves in large numbers to serve in the East under generals of high reputation and individual personal magnetism (for example, Scipio Africanus and Flamininus).[41]

A supreme example, far more important than its predecessors, is the case attested in 134 BC when Scipio Aemilianus set out for Numantia with an army composed entirely of his clients;[42] although it has much in common with the old example of clients fighting for their family *patroni* when the Plebs refused to serve,[43] it is worth noting that in this period *clientela* had long ceased to carry with it an obligation to perform military service on the patron's behalf.[44]

Indeed, continuous military service and the proletarian make-up of the army, together with the fact that generals changed less frequently, began to create bonds which were either tighter than before or of a completely unprecedented nature, and these bonds joined the general and his soldiers together[45] in a relationship which was now inseparably connected with the military career of the client.

It is, of course, undeniable that between military and, so to say, 'civil' *clientela* there was an organic connexion, brought about by the double transformation which took place (clients serving their patron, soldiers joining the *clientela* of their general);[46] it is, however, equally unquestionable that military *clientela* introduced a new element into the conception of *clientela* and therefore into politics itself.

Personal *clientela* was based on the *fides* of the *patronus*, under whose protection the client placed himself; this was solely a moral bond, for all that the dependence of one on the other had often, as an essential part of the background, an economic cause. For his part the client maintained *pietas* towards his patron, was aware of his dependence and appreciated his obligation to repay the benefits received.[47] From the beginning of the first century BC the establishment of more binding ties between client and patron can be detected, especially when the client comes to perform his appropriate activity *qua* client in a political and military field.[48] The origins of this development are to be found in the changed relationships between patrons-military dynasts and clients-soldiers; these relationships, no longer based on the old moral constraints, were now embodied in a strictly formal act, represented by the oath of allegiance.[49]

In this lies the fundamental relevance of military *clientela*: it introduces into the political struggle, which on the surface continues to lie between families, groups or individuals, forces of men who are, as I have said, homogeneous in their social condition and their outlook. These men, as we should note for future developments, have a heightened consciousness, either individually or collectively, of their own ability and their own rights which they have derived from their lives as soldiers and from their military experience. These client-soldiers, who more or less unconsciously personify and entertain very profound social demands, do not represent precise political movements. They can therefore be hooked indiscriminately by the political bait of either a Marius or a Sulla.[50]

From one point of view this makes it difficult for us to think of military *clientela* simply as an extension of 'civil' *clientela*[51] – the bond of *clientela* established with provincial circles falls, however, into this category – and from another point of view we should conclude that revolutionary interventions brought a powerful and radical change in politics, and not only in its external aspects.

The old political structure which had formed the moral basis of the citizen militia no longer presented the professional soldier with a problem, either because he was not personally interested in it or because he came from that social class of peasants which, as we shall see more clearly later, is completely without influence in Roman political life. As a result the soldier ends up by being considered simply as a *miles Caesaris* or a *miles Cn. Pompei*,[52] and the army thereby ceases to be the state's army but becomes in practice a private army.[53]

A characteristic example of the soldier's indifference to questions which could have brought about a revival of patriotic sentiment can perhaps be provided by the ease with which Sulla in 88 BC could persuade the legions to challenge, for the first time in Roman history, the state's authority and to march on Rome. All the officers, with only one exception, refused – a typical example of a divergence of outlook which subsequently, however, completely disappeared.[54]

Until now only the disregard of the general-patron for the interests of his soldiers can make them change their political allegiance.[55] Otherwise, the bond established between general and soldier continued to survive even after service was over, especially if the intervention of the general obtained for his demobilized soldiers the provision of rewards,[56] and that bond could be taken over by the descendants of the general himself.[57]

Of course, as I have already shown, military experience gave the client a position of greater substance in his relationship with his patron, and as a result it was necessary to bind him with a formal act. This set of circumstances came to acquire ever greater significance in the course of the first century BC with the progressive decline of the central authority of the state, until the soldiers came to be conscious of their indispensability and there resulted a general state of anarchy. This led in its turn to a slackening of the ties of *clientela* between general and soldiers, for the most part when the latter, for whatever motive, came to believe that the reasons for which it had previously suited them – especially from an economic point of view – to undertake service no longer existed.[58]

4. The following factors have to be borne in mind. The continued survival of a city-state structure while Rome was acquiring an ever-growing empire had the consequence that the urban Plebs was bound to grow in political importance, while the rural Plebs was bound to decline. The former was a notoriously treacherous element because of its very close ties with the nobility and its *clientelae*, and on it devolved all real political activity; the latter formed the conservative basis of the state, then as always. Hence participation in the *comitia*, whether legislative or electoral, of those who came from districts far away from Rome caused deep astonishment, for example in the time of Cicero,[59] astonishment which could produce the bitter reflection that what ought to have been the rule had now become only an exception.

Alongside such men from the *municipia* we also find frequent mention of the intervention – sometimes decisive – of soldiers, whether as serving men or veterans. They might be used to intimidate, certainly, but more often just took their legitimate part in the voting.[60]

The army was composed principally of men from the countryside. As a result, its interventions in politics and, in more general terms, the fact that the rural proletariat gained promotion through military service must be considered as the countryside's revenge, however unconscious it may have been, on the city, and thereby of the various Italian races on Rome. For them the grant of Roman citizenship had represented, in the field of politics, an advantage that was without practical effect.

It seems undeniable that the unification of the various races of the peninsula had originated and developed primarily in the composition of the army, even in the period prior to the Social War and, in part, prior to the so-called reform of the levy in 107 BC;[61] it preceded and prepared the way for the political unity of Italy and, once this had been achieved, strengthened and consolidated it.[62]

The existence of the proletarian, Italian army as the plainest expression of the outmoding of city-state principles has its context and setting in the way in which those opposed to the oligarchs had long looked at the structure and functions of the state. This view expressed itself in a series of confrontations which aimed – for different reasons at different times but for practical purposes all of the same kind – at forcing the Roman state to go outside its own citizen body. It has already been shown how profoundly significant was the hostility of the senatorial oligarchy to the attempts of M'. Curius Dentatus to colonize the *ager Sabinus* and of C. Flaminius to colonize the *ager Gallicus* and Picenum, to the *lex Rubria* of 123 BC which proposed a transmarine colony at Carthage, and to the foundation of Narbo Martius between 118 and 115.[63] All these episodes represented stages in the conflict between popular leaders and the senatorial oligarchy concerning the essential nature of the Roman state, a conflict which reached its peak in the problem of the allies.[64]

The result of such a process of evolution was what was to be expected: while the army saw an accelerated trend towards the fusion of various Italian races, the Roman *populares* on the other hand, operating in a strictly political sphere, collaborated closely with the rebel Italian peoples and went so far as to participate, in times of their weakness and that of the state, in residual separatist tendencies, aiming at the independence of regional political groups.[65]

The role which the army played in late Republican politics in the end made this contrast of attitudes stand out still more sharply. It is worth noting that this contrast did not arise from fundamental differences of a formal, theoretical nature but, as I have said above, expressed itself in practical terms in the different reactions of rival political groups to concrete problems of the day.

It is, however, understandable that a number of factors combined to produce in the minds of the oligarchy the conviction that the professional army of volunteers represented a danger to the stability of the Roman state. These included the composition of the army from the lowest social elements of society; the concept of military service as a profession which the new recruits came to entertain;[66] the economic and social demands which as a result the army – more or less consciously – inspired; and finally the political power which it could assume under the guidance of a leader and, conversely, the power of a leader who found himself at the head of a large following of soldiers, as became particularly evident for example in 61 BC when Pompey returned from the East and approached the coast of Italy.[67] To the governing class which, as I have said, continued even after the late third-century BC reform of the *comitia centuriata* always to be represented by the wealthy orders,[68] the army now appeared as an army based on the class system.

The Optimate tradition presents the enrolment of the *proletarii* in 107 BC as a manoeuvre which threatened the utmost danger to the state and which all generals before Marius had always avoided with the utmost care. Indeed, *quoniam res pecuniaque familiaris obsidis vicem pignerisque esse apud rem publicam videbatur amorisque in patriam fides quaedam in ea firmamentumque erat, neque proletarii neque capite censi milites nisi in tumultu maximo scribebantur, quia familia pecuniaque his aut tenuis aut nulla esset.*[69]

For various reasons,[70] however, one can confidently maintain that in this passage we are confronted with a shallow *post eventum* interpretation, put forward at a time when the army could have assumed a class-based character. This interpretation is based on an erroneous, abstract view of what had been the basis of the Roman citizen militia of the Golden Age; although this interpretation undoubtedly held good for its own time, the Golden Age was a period when the form of the militia was dictated by nothing more than practical considerations.[71]

In fact, this interpretation of the *dilectus* of 107 BC, which reflects the political interests of the oligarchy, attributes to Marius the chief responsibility for the extra-constitutional activity of the army, and must draw its real origin from Greek political thought. It is not, perhaps, hazardous to assume that it found its first formulation in the historical work of Posidonius. Athenian politicians, and those who concerned themselves with Athenian political history, had been able to perceive without undue difficulty the intimate connexion between the ever-growing power of the δῆμος and the creation of a fleet at Athens.[72] They thus developed a theory which, on the broadest interpretation – and that is the only way it should be considered – recognized that the services rendered by the proletariat in military defence or, on a more general level, in boosting the military power of the state, constituted for the proletariat themselves a means of acquiring power.

It must have been easy to apply this historical and political rule to the situation at Rome in the first century BC. The oligarchy restored by Sulla was able to count the existence of a proletarian army among the causes of instability affecting its system of government. This oligarchy was always committed to a superannuated conception of the timocratic city-state[73] and had lost any real connexion with those who were at that time the dominant classes in the social order.[74] It could not therefore fail to point to Marius as the man responsible for the enrolment of *proletarii* and therefore, by implication, for those policies which had long aimed at removing the upper classes from the control of government; these policies were in some cases given concrete form as proposals to modify the structure of the *comitia* that then existed.[75]

It may be impossible to solve the problem with certainty but it is necessary here to point out that the highly revolutionary character of the provision of rewards to ex-soldiers in the first century BC must have influenced the sort of attitude which the oligarchs adopted towards the professional army and which I have just sketched.

The passage of Cicero, *de Officiis* II 73–85, is well-known. Here he sets out the basic principle that those who try to bring about changes in the sphere of *res agraria* or of debts undermine the very foundations of the state: *qui . . . aut agrariam rem temptant . . . aut pecunias creditas debitoribus condonandas putant, labefactant fundamenta rei publicae.*[76] It is certain that in essence this passage is derived from the Stoic themes elaborated by Panaetius in the face of the Gracchan revolution,[77] but it is significant that Cicero wrote it in the aftermath of Caesar's agrarian and debt legislation – the *de Officiis* dates to 45/44 BC – which put private property rights at risk.[78] In this passage of Cicero there is clear emphasis on the contemporary crisis, for example the opposition to the collection of *tributum* that was in effect proposed by Caesar at that point.[79]

Finally the phrase in II 83: *sic par est agere cum civibus* (as Aratus had done) *non, ut bis iam vidimus, hastam foro ponere et bona civium voci subicere praeconis* clearly alludes to the examples of Sulla and Caesar.

We may now mention a factor which may help us to understand more clearly Cicero's thought on the subject. It is a commonplace that the logic of Panaetius when applied to the proposals of the Gracchi – a logic whose essentials are re-echoed by Cicero – contains a weakness in that it wrongly represented them as an attack on private property;[80] this has been clearly shown by Pohlenz.[81] In the passage of Cicero we have considered the contradiction is less obvious, not to say totally absent, when we concentrate our attention on the time which for Cicero was obviously the most important. This is not the time of Gracchus; this, like the proposal of L. Marcius Philippus, has no more than the validity of a historical *point d'appui*, for all that it had been the central point in Panaetius' account. Rather it is with Cicero's own period that the comparison with Aratus' activity (a comparison already in Panaetius' account) fits much better than with the Gracchan period. Concerning the Sullan and Caesarian (46 BC) proscriptions and allotments, it is certainly right to talk here of violation of private property, and it is therefore clear that Cicero's arguments take on a real character of vigorous polemic, like that attending the views of Panaetius on the period of the Gracchi. Cicero's position, then, is at the centre of the general trend of opposition which the revolutionary allotments of land to the veterans, regarded by many in effect as a social cataclysm, aroused among the propertied classes during the fifty-year period from Sulla to the Triumvirate.[82]

To return to our problem, it seems that this fear of an *aequatio bonorum*,[83] fed by the payment of rewards to the army, can and ought to be connected with the view that the poor were a source of danger, and this view – as I have tried to show above – was the moving force behind the oligarchs' opposition to the professional volunteer army.

The political assumptions behind the oligarchs' interpretation did not escape those who were their enemies. The collusion in 88 BC between Marius and the main groups opposed to the oligarchs, which resulted in their winning control of the government with Cinna's supremacy, had already helped to bring into being the concept of Marius the democrat. This aimed at investing with reality what had only been a dream, quite at variance with the true personality and activity of Marius;[84] this interpretation was reinforced by the fact that the democratic factions after Sulla were supported by old elements or by Marian traditions.[85]

The explanation offered by the oligarchs of the 107 levy fitted in well with this view. To their claims on the social and political danger of the enrolment of the landless one could reply that a man's worth was not tied to wealth and that Marius concentrated on the strength and courage of his soldiers in 107 BC.[86] Even in this respect the *populares* by justifying the practical need to supersede the timocratic military organization (*praeterita facultatium contemplatione*) superseded as well – even though it was in the context of a particular problem – the whole concept of a city-state structure.[87]

Naturally this 'democratic' interpretation of Marius' political activity does not confine itself to the difference in attitude adopted by Optimate and *popularis* factions when confronted with the reality of a professional army. On the contrary, it is part of the general political situation of the first century BC in so far as it can, in a certain sense, be regarded as the final expression of that phenomenon which appeared in the period subsequent to the Gracchi, namely the identity of *populares* and military leaders. The progressive assimilation of the two has its basis in the common anti-oligarch position which the democratic groups and the military leaders adopted. It was promoted by the rigidly organic nature of the ancient state and by the fact that the state was consequently identified with the political groups which held power; as a result the oligarchs were unable to make clear distinctions among those movements or policies which, because they were against the oligarchs' interests, appeared at times to involve the disintegration of the state.[88] To solve the problems which his brother had earlier raised C. Gracchus had probably relied on attempting to introduce the popular classes to a more effective participation in government. Moreover, this attempt no longer followed the practice of former times but was made by more direct methods, after the example of Greek democracy.[89] This line failed with Gracchus and was not in practice resumed; there was substituted for it another, and this, for whatever reason it appeared – the fact is that at that time and for some time in the future those who adopted it, of all ranks or positions, were unconscious of it – produced a conclusion not very different from that at which Gracchus had consciously aimed. The professional army was now a permanent feature, and this could only consolidate the position of the proletariat in Roman politics, as we have several times observed.

The democratic view of Marius and the oligarchs' fears concerning the danger of military professionalism entitle us, therefore, to say that in the period after Sulla men already realized that the object of the Gracchi and the result which the professional army showed how to achieve were substantially one and the same.

On the other hand, the actual gains which the military chiefs had been able to achieve in politics through the army – not properly understood during the interventions of the soldiers in 100 BC but clear to all after 88 BC – decisively transferred effective political action to another level altogether. This especially applies to the methods which the opposition had employed until that time and hence the contrast with the Gracchi, for example, was particularly noticed when the 'democrats' seized power, even if it was only for a few years (87–82 BC).[90]

From another point of view the popular faction took advantage of the unification of the different elements of the various Italian regions, a unification brought about through the medium of the army. It made its own concern the defence of those common social and economic needs which, as I have already said, the army personified. However, in this connexion it is important to note that the absence of political interests to go side by side with actual economic needs within the framework of the army makes it impossible to say categorically that the *populares* exclusively represented the interests of the army proletariat, in so far as those very needs could be met by the opposition faction, as in effect they sometimes were; Sulla's example, however it can or will be explained, is significant.[91]

This point does not undermine the observation from which we started, that in the first century BC popular and military leaders were one and the same, nor does it rule out the claim that this identity must not be considered purely a matter of accident. On the contrary – and this is what I have sought to show – it drew its *raison d'être* from a very profound cause, more or less understood by contemporaries but seldom clearly distinguished: with the organization of the masses against the oligarchy, or with the use of these masses when they were organized as they were already in the army, it was implicit in the situation that there should come into being a formula of compromise between the needs of the Empire and the structure of the ancient city-state. Military service had already brought this about in its own sphere when the army was transformed in the course of the second century BC under the pressure of absolute necessity into a professional fighting force. The struggle begun by the Gracchi in the name of the restoration of the ancient city-state of peasants ended with the remodelling of that state.[92]

5. The conclusion which we have reached is this: the soldiers came now from classes which did not entertain sincere and clearly defined political views. This, together with the fact that their demands as soldiers were purely of an economic nature, had drained the army of all political character. This conclusion must now be integrated with another important question

which we must examine and which will help to clarify the matter still further: what was the relationship that existed between the outlook and demands of the soldiers on the one side and the body of officers on the other? The problem is particularly interesting in that it is connected with, and contributes points of unique importance to, the central problem of our study: we have to explain the way in which military service brought the lowest classes of the population into politics.

It is well-known that in the Roman army there was a rigid class distinction which prevented the centurion from reaching the ranks of *tribunus militum* or of *praefectus equitum*, i.e. officer status.[93] The establishment of the professional army meant the introduction of changes and exceptions to the general rule. It is no accident that it is after Marius that cases appear, historically documented, of soldiers being subsequently admitted to the ranks of officers: L. Petronius, in the time of C. Marius, *admodum humili loco natus ad equestrem ordinem et splendidae militiae stipendia P. Coeli beneficio pervenerat;*[94] L. Fufidius, a *primipilaris* of Sulla, later enjoyed a higher career and was even governor of Baetica;[95] L. Septimius, mentioned as a *tribunus militum* by Caesar, *bello praedonum* (67 BC) *apud eum (Pompeium) ordinem duxerat.*[96] These cases which are, in our present state of knowledge, isolated ones must have led to the practice which developed, perhaps from the time of Caesar and certainly attested during the early Principate of Augustus, whereby the highest centurionate opened the door to *militia equestris.*[97]

Even more interesting are the qualifications to the rule mentioned above which stem from the observation not of single cases but of a general phenomenon: the wealth which the soldiers acquired could often lead to their enjoyment of an equestrian census and therefore to the possibility of their joining the body of officers. There is no need to dwell on the ease with which men enriched themselves during the civil revolts.[98] As examples of soldiers who gained equestrian status we should note those whom Sulla introduced into the Senate,[99] a model for Caesar later,[100] and the ex-centurions who sat on juries.[101] Sometimes the equestrian census of the father allows the son to begin a military career and subsequently enter the magistracies. This is the case with the father of the well-known jurist Ateius Capito who was *praetorius* but who was also the son of a Sullan centurion;[102] it is also the case with M. Petreius, praetor in 63 BC and well-known Pompeian legate, son of a Volscian centurion of Atina,[103] and with T. Flavius Petro, a Pompeian veteran and father of a knight.[104]

It is not extravagant to speak of an absorption of the other ranks by the officer class, and this is a significant factor in so far as it is clear that the soldiers and centurions who subsequently joined the corps of officers brought with them their own outlook and their own especial demands. Even if we allow that the possibility of promotion is confirmed only by a very few, random cases – though, of course, that is not the case; it is just not possible for us to exemplify this promotion except in a restricted way – is it permissible to agree with Seel that 'the officers did not belong to the Plebs bound to the land but came from those Roman citizens who always had their thoughts firmly fixed on the future of Rome'?[105] That is to say, can we postulate that a different social origin produced a different outlook for the officers from that of the soldiers or the centurions?

The fact of the matter is that military professionalism had long been responsible for levelling out differences in the outlook of officers and men.[106] If, as we have said, high pay and hopes of booty induced members of equestrian families to enrol in the ranks of centurions, it is quite credible, and indeed more logical, that this held for the class of officers, and therefore one should conclude that at an early stage they too looked on military service as a career. An officer career, in other words, also became a profession, and the term *homo militaris*,[107] which is frequently applied to many people in the first century BC, is an indication of this; this term is used to refer to a distinctive type, in contrast to the ancient practice of considering military service as a civic duty. In the old days the Romans did not know how to distinguish, nor could they, man in his political and military role.

It is perfectly true that Seel's assertion mentioned above could be taken to refer to the well-known and very significant episode of 88 BC which concerned Sulla: καὶ αὐτὸν (Sulla) οἱ μὲν ἄρχοντες τοῦ στρατοῦ, χωρὶς ἑνὸς ταμίου, διέδρασαν ἐς ῾Ρώμην, οὐχ ὑφιστάμενοι στρατὸν ἄγειν ἐπὶ τὴν πατρίδα.[108] However, the situation is really quite different, in so far as we cannot generalize from the example of Sulla; its character is unique for it was the first occasion of its kind in Rome's history! It may be enough to contrast what we know about Caesar in 49 BC; only Labienus went over to Pompey's side, and even in his case his motives were far removed from patriotism.[109]

In fact, soldiers as well as officers displayed indifference towards problems of a political nature, important and obvious though they were (for example, the *libertas* of the *respublica*). When Appian in a famous passage[110] analyses the psychology of the army in the face of the greatest political question of the time, where true patriotism lay, he not only does not distinguish officers from soldiers but, for obvious reasons, insists on the fact that the outlook of the soldiers, whole armies and famous generals was always the same and based on what would make a profit for themselves. With some important reservations[111] this psychology is the same as that which Drexler inferred from an analysis of *Bell. Hisp.* 17. It is characteristic that the author of this work was in fact an officer of Caesar's.[112]

Furthermore, we are not in a position to be able to assert that officers and soldiers came consistently from different social classes. We have seen how the equestrian census was required for entry to officer status and how it could be acquired with a certain ease by other ranks. The cases set out above show that the social origin was in many cases the same.

The well-known Asculan inscription of Pompeius Strabo shows[113] that at the siege of Asculum there was a legion composed entirely of Picenes, officers and men. Without doubt all came from the rural class. We must remember that the Picenes provided a true class of professional soldiers.

Also the officers of the Marian party whose names betray an Etruscan origin would certainly not always have belonged to the upper classes of the region; these latter, as is well-known, were clearly connected with the Roman oligarchy. Some Marian officers would have come from economically inferior classes, perhaps even from tenants *(coloni)*.[114] This is still more probable in the case of those officers who did not come from Italy; in *Bell. Afric.*28 two *tribuni militum* are sons of a Spanish senator.[115] Their patriotism, incidentally, could not have been that of the Roman *nobiles*. All of these points support and illuminate my interpretation of the period.

In fact, the improved position which the *proletarii* came to enjoy in Roman politics in the first century BC thanks to their military service cannot be regarded simply as reflecting the importance of organized armed interventions in Roman political struggles, and this improvement in their position must therefore be something more than mere confirmation of the decisive influence of professional military service.[116] On the contrary, the progress of the *proletarii* appears to transcend such incidental considerations and must be assessed in the light of its impact on the social and political life of contemporary Rome.

What I have said above shows, I think, that those of the oligarchs who were far-sighted did not fail to observe how the granting of arms or, to put it in more general terms, of the means of defence to the *proletarii* had led to a breakdown of that balance which was essential to the Roman state, and that from this period dated the collapse of the timocracy. Today this episode appears to us as the first link in a chain of events which saw a progressive abdication on the Romans' part of their own defence and which was to end with making the barbarians defenders of the Empire, thereby ensuring its eventual collapse.[117]

The army brought the Italians into a closer contact with politics – this process, already begun in the second century BC, was developed and completed by the Social War – and set in still greater relief (if that were possible) the inadequacy of the restricted Roman governing class, the patrician-plebeian *nobilitas*. This had lost all contact with the social structure of the nation from the time when the rural class of small proprietors, whose supreme representative was originally the *nobilitas*, became submerged in the huge sea of the urban and rural proletariat.

Military service represented the ladder by which the proletariat, particularly the rural proletariat, reached the position that was due to it, even though its progress took different forms and even though it was not fully conscious of what was happening. The Empire is the product of those sections of society which had been denied any direct participation in political interests and activity by the continued existence of the city-state constitution and thereby of the anti-democratic *comitia*; it marks at the same time the doom of the Roman oligarchy which in its capacity as the governing class had traditionally stood its ground for the whole of the first century BC.

It is true that the advance of the Italians towards a more extensive and more direct share in government had already made itself felt through the ever-growing admission to politics during the first century BC of members of the municipal aristocracies and, in general, of the wealthier local elements.[118] However, only service in the army could bring such participation within the reach of the poorest classes of Italian society, and it did this by promoting people of low origin to the Senate and to the magistracies through factions which were now largely based on military elements;[119] it was military service also which guaranteed in the political field effective expression for that equality of rights which was ratified by the extension of the Roman citizenship after the Social War.

In the Senates of Sulla and Caesar the army certainly played a large part, side by side naturally with members of the local aristocracies and the city oligarchy. There is no need to dwell on the few cases known directly to us of simple soldiers or centurions who reached the Senate, for prosopographical research in this period is unavoidably restricted by the fact that we have to confine ourselves to the principals in the action; the intervention of the masses, which is the most significant factor, is basically beyond the reach of prosopography.[120]

With Caesar the Italian character of the Senate was extended and augmented, for representatives of those peoples who had followed the democratic and Marian line and who had therefore been gravely weakened by Sulla were admitted to the Curia. At the same time Italians reach the highest positions in the army.[121]

The Augustan Principate, directed as it was to the formation of a national Italian state, made for further steps in that direction while the area from which soldiers were drawn was widened in Italy and extended, sometimes on a vaster scale, to the provinces.[122] The case of the Emperor Vespasian, grandson of a Reatine veteran of Pompey's who had had a son of equestrian rank,[123] is the best example of the way in which the professional army had become the chief means in the course of the first century BC of promotion for the rural proletariat and of securing an improved position for the Italians in Rome's political and social life.[124]

B. *The Veteran Problem*

1. With the end of the second century BC traditional Roman agrarian and colonial policy gave ground; this was a theme which throughout that century had been worked out on a scale of undeniable magnitude, even though it was sporadic in its operation on account of the faint interest it aroused in the minds of the public and of the ruling class.[125]

There must have been two main reasons for this development. Alongside the indifference of public opinion towards colonial expansion went the growing demands of the actual colonists who were increasingly reluctant to abandon the pleasures of the metropolis in return for a plot of land in far-away, disagreeable places.[126] Secondly, the proposal of Ti. Gracchus to resolve the economic and social crisis of Italian society by breaking up the *latifundia* on *ager publicus* had substantially changed the traditional basis of agrarian politics and had aroused demands and interests which made it still more difficult to satisfy the new potential colonists.

Even after the Gracchi, however, proposals to found colonies on a reduced scale continued down to the turn of the century, and in the traditional way: the colony of Dertona probably dates to 120,[127] Narbo Martius between 118 and 115,[128] and Eporedia to 100.[129]

After Velleius has mentioned the settlement of Eporedia in his famous list of colonies founded *post Romam a Gallis captam*,[130] he adds: *neque facile memoriae mandaverim quae, nisi militaris, post hoc tempus* (100 BC) *deducta* (*colonia*) *sit.*[131] Velleius' view is still perfectly acceptable today; all the long series of colonies founded from the end of the second century BC is based on a principle completely independent of that followed earlier and, what is more important, has in practice no connexion with the Gracchan policy which merely supplied, and then not on a regular basis, the instrument for practical action, namely the *lex agraria*.

In an earlier passage[132] Velleius had indicated clearly the points which distinguished the colonies prior to 100 BC and those (of the military type) which came later: *nam militarium et causae et auctores et ipsarum praefulgent nomina.*[133]

I turn now to a brief consideration of these three factors, and especially the *causae*. Velleius has included in his account the list of colonies from the invasion of Rome by the Gauls, and rightly maintains that no more than a bare list of names can show Rome's expansion in the Italian peninsula and elsewhere. However, when he arrives at the military colonies he stops; to list them would not serve his purpose. The object of these colonies, that is to say the fundamental object over and above any incidental motives there might be, was quite different and distinct from the purpose of propagating the Roman name. It was to reward time-expired soldiers: *erat tunc praemium terra et pro emerito habebatur.*[134]

Next the *auctores*. Non-military colonies derived their foundation *iussu Senatus* and in reality – except for a few cases of senatorial opposition (for example to the colonization of M'. Curius on the *ager Sabinus* and that of C. Flaminius on the *ager Gallicus* and *ager Picenus*)[135] – this had been the normal practice for all colonization down to 100 BC. Then the opposite happened: from that time it is only rarely that the Senate makes a proposal and, when it does, it seems almost as if it acts in the firm knowledge that other factors would prevent anything being done.[136] Usually it is a general who takes the initiative, more or less legally, and his objects are quite explicit.[137] From this the *nomina* follow; they are no longer the fine, propitious names which set out to predict a happy outcome for the foundation or invoke divine aid for the new city.[138] The names now posit a strict connexion between the colony and the *auctor*, as if to record or to emphasize the personal character of the foundation.[139]

However, the fundamental distinction is represented by the *causae*. From what date had it been necessary to reward soldiers on discharge? Of course, there had never been any necessity to make provision for soldiers at the end of their campaigns in times when the timocracy's military system was flourishing and when even the distribution of part of the booty was only a concession, which had become a common practice, varying in degrees of flamboyancy with the generosity of the general. On the other hand, the allocation of conquered territory between Roman citizens, even if the beneficiaries may have been chosen by the use of criteria which gave weight to military service,[140] was very far from representing a reward for that service; it was on the contrary all part of the general framework of Roman politics which attended colonization. Given the military character (defensive or offensive) of the settlements, it was perfectly proper to take account of the military capacity of the colonists to be settled.

On the other hand, it became necessary to reward soldiers when the traditional principles of the citizen militia weakened[141] and when the prolonged absence of soldiers from their homes and hearths – and therefore from all civil activity – began to have severe consequences for the economic status of many families. Hence came the attempt to re-establish the diminished economic freedom of the citizen with distributions of land, an obvious method given the pre-eminence of agriculture in the economy of that period and given perhaps, in my view, the precedent already in fashion of offering land to individuals as a reward for extraordinary acts of individual valour.[142]

These distributions, which of course took account of the length of a citizen's military service, occurred first[143] in the years following the Hannibalic War, 201–199 BC.[144] The connexion with continuous military service appears undeniable when one considers that the provisions applied to soldiers who had fought in Africa, Spain, Sardinia and Sicily, that is, only to those citizens who had served outside Italy and therefore had not been able to enjoy leave, even for a spell.[145]

The allocations of land centred on those parts of Samnite and Apulian territory confiscated after the defections of the Hannibalic War;[146] two *iugera* for every year of campaigning were awarded. It has been calculated that not less than 30,000–40,000 soldiers would have qualified for participation in the allotments;[147] even if the whole of this huge number of ex-soldiers did not benefit from the provisions of the scheme, it is certain that the work of dividing the land must have been exacting seeing that for the first time it was thought necessary to operate with *Xviri*.[148]

These arrangements at the end of the Hannibalic War were clearly not the result of a concerted plan but were perhaps conceived in their initial stage by Scipio only for the veterans of Africa and Spain if, as has been said, they are connected with the beginnings of the professional army. On the other hand, they came to be part of the context of the Roman government's attempts to reconstruct the class of small peasant proprietors which had been destroyed by the war,[149] and therefore to assume a particular significance in the Roman timocracy. This is, in my opinion, of the greatest importance for the way in which this phenomenon later developed.

Although in the course of the second century BC military professionalism gathered speed and established itself as part of Rome's military institutions,[150] wars even remotely comparable with the Hannibalic War did not recur, and as a result there was never the need to arrange for the reward of soldiers on discharge; colonial politics in the second century BC does not concern itself with that.[151]

However, the contemporary situation in Spain is quite a different matter. I have already emphasized how the conflict between the political and military organization at Rome and the new demands of imperialism (including the need for continuous military service) manifested itself in the clearest fashion in the formation of senatorial policy in Spain,[152] and how the military situation in those provinces required the creation of a real standing army, the prototype of those found in the Principate. It should therefore not be surprising that the Spanish provinces saw the origin of a phenomenon which we can search for in vain elsewhere during that period and which became a commonplace during the Empire, the voluntary settlement of Roman or allied soldiers. These for the most part formed a new 'family' *in loco*.

All this led to the foundation of numerous and thriving cities, inhabited by Italians and linked to the natives although the legal position is not very clear; these cities provided a useful means of Romanizing the country. It is typical that the Senate, which was notoriously hostile to transmarine colonialism, not only was not opposed to these foundations, much less did it just ignore them, but it even participated in them through some of its influential members.[153]

Although these settlements should not be regarded simply as military colonies, it is of interest to refer to them, besides the fact that they represent a foretaste of conditions which marked a later age. The military provincial colonies of the Principate are not dissimilar to these settlements both as regards causes and consequences. Also the presence of a large number of Romano-Spanish citizens (*Hispanienses*) helps us to understand the decisive importance assumed by the Spanish provinces in the first century BC and especially the ease with which such sections of the population there came to be affiliated to Pompeian and Caesarian *clientelae*.[154]

2. After the so-called reform of 107 BC had set its seal on the proletarian composition of the army and thereby on professional military service, the veteran problem naturally became urgent and from time to time demanded a solution. If the case of the veterans of the Second Punic War seems to exemplify the inevitable connexion of the phenomenon with the professional army, the phenomenon, as Velleius saw, is fully developed only after 100 BC. Thereafter it will persist in its fundamental, revolutionary form down to the time of Augustus.

In the period we can call 'Marian' (107–100 BC) the veteran phenomenon becomes important for the first time; it also acquires an added significance in that it cannot now be considered as a problem on its own but is only an aspect of problems which have a far wider range. It firmly takes its place in the struggle between the political factions, and hence it may be claimed that its importance both then and in the future was in direct proportion to the role played by the army in the political struggle.

In fact, it is impossible to claim that the first provisions for the veterans of Marius, which aimed at the foundation of colonies in Africa (103 BC),[155] were seen solely or principally against a political background. It is quite probable that the equestrian class even on this occasion maintained its earlier approval of the measures taken by Marius and his partisans,[156] but it is highly significant that the Senate not only did not register objections – so far as we know – but even participated with its own members in the agrarian Xvirate set up to give the allotments effect.[157] This can be explained by the fact that Saturninus' measure left quite untouched the more serious political problems of the time (there is no difficulty in the fact that Latins and allies were included among the veterans) and was part and parcel of that form of colonial policy in Africa which had been triggered off by C. Gracchus and which had been continued in the post-Gracchan period.[158]

The potential political significance of the rewards offered to the veterans appeared more clearly in 100 BC, the year of Saturninus' second tribunate, when the legislation of the popular party allowed the development of a longer-term objective which went beyond the solution of the problem affecting Marius' veterans.[159] It was clear that Appuleius' object was to bring over to him the rural Plebs,[160] to give him support in his struggle against the ruling oligarchy. He had no wish to raise the two principal problems of the time – Italian *ager publicus* and the allies – which the Gracchan precedent had shown carried with them enormous difficulties, but he knew how to make use of the presence of large numbers of rural *proletarii* in the army and he hoped in due course to arrange a good settlement.

The undeniable enthusiasm with which the rural Plebs received the proposals of Saturninus seems all the more noteworthy in the light of the fact that his proposals[161] provided for the sending of colonists overseas. This appears explicable only in the context of that migratory movement of commercial and agrarian interests which developed towards the end of the second century BC in the Roman West.[162]

Consequently the Senatorial opposition which at once made itself very strongly felt and which succeeded in drawing over to its view the urban Plebs, and, albeit temporarily, the equestrian class, must not be interpreted as aimed at preventing the passing of measures for the veterans; this would not in any way have damaged its interests. Neither is there any question of an opposition whose basic principle was to bar the sending of citizens outside Italy so as to avoid the expansion of the city-state's territory,[163] since too many concessions had already been made on this point. On the contrary, the Senate was motivated only by a desire to oppose the general anti-oligarchic tendency of Saturninus' proposals, a tendency made clear in the means and methods used to get the laws approved. It was obvious that this general outlook of the Senate must have involved opposition also to the measures for the veterans although we may surmise that these, like the earlier ones of 103 BC, could not by themselves have inspired any specific disapproval.

More interesting is the position of Marius since it shows clearly how rewards for veterans, although they had become a political weapon, had not in any way come to acquire for the benefactor the particular significance of which they were certainly capable. Marius not only did not appear to exhibit special sympathy for the arrangements for settling his own soldiers[164] but also found it easy later to abandon his *popularis* allies, thereby siding with the forces of law and order – though his attitude here was probably the product of a shrewd political calculation.[165] This seems all the more noteworthy in so far as it was Marius himself who would, not many years later, personally experience the usefulness of his own soldiers settled in Africa by the *lex Appuleia* of 103 BC.[166]

Saturninus' laws of 100 BC were subsequently rendered ineffectual in a period of triumphant reaction and with them, of course, the provisions for the veterans.[167] It does not appear that the latter made good their claim to a reward and we should therefore conclude that they had not yet acquired that consciousness of their rights which characterized the army of the first century BC. The precedent provided by the events of 100 BC must have shown the impossibility of finding a solution to the veteran problem by legal means and must have led the army (that is to say, the military chiefs) to take upon themselves the responsibility for solving it.

3. The 'veteran phenomenon' of the first century BC, whose fundamental characteristic was the granting of land to soldiers, has to be seen, as I have said above, in the context of the army's political importance and of the establishment by its leaders of extra-constitutional power.[168]

If we set the problem of rewards for the veterans in the context of the civil wars and their consequences (proscriptions, confiscations, etc.), it is true on the one hand that the significance of these rewards in the contemporary political and social atmosphere seems to increase. On the other hand, it is clear why it became absolutely impossible to introduce schemes of rewards by the use of legal methods without resort to any form of revolutionary solution. With this in mind we must examine the attempts made to reward the veterans of Pompey, and it is as well to say something of these now since, unconnected as they were with a time of civil war, they do not appear to have anything to do with the veteran problem of the first century BC, as I have pointed out above and as I shall re-emphasize below.[169]

Pompey, in conformity with his general attitude towards the senatorial government, never dared – as Sulla had already done and Caesar did later – to assume directly and illegally the responsibility for making provision for his own veterans. He preferred, without success, to follow the practice of getting a *lex agraria* proposed, and this of course left the final decision to the discretion of an assembly which was easily swayed by forces hostile to him.

Indeed, rewards for Pompey's and Metellus' soldiers who had returned from the war against Sertorius were proposed by the tribune Plotius in 70 or 69 BC[170] and easily succeeded in winning the approval of the Senate, thanks perhaps to the presence of a Metellus among the interested military leaders; it was only the disastrous state of the treasury which prevented the law from taking effect. However, as I have said above,[171] it is possible to take a less optimistic view of the Senate's attitude on this occasion.

On the other hand, senatorial opposition was, and showed itself to be, invincible in 60 BC when Pompey, through the tribune L. Flavius, proposed rewards for his Asian veterans[172] with a law whose substance is partly known to us from a letter of Cicero's.[173] The oligarchy's attitude, dominated as it largely was by personal motives,[174] is, as our research shows, all the more interesting when one reflects that Flavius' proposal followed closely on the demobilization of the army which had been ordered by Pompey at the time when he set foot in Italy.[175] That episode could not have banished all the fears of the oligarchs if Cicero can emphasize the increase in power which could have come to Pompey on the law being approved.[176] This shows very clearly the difficulty of using legal means to provide for the veterans; given the contemporary attitude to the state such measures always had a revolutionary character. Hence even Cicero attacked the law, except for the clause on the acquisition of land. Despite the background of violence engineered by the tribune, Pompey was forced in the end to have the proposal withdrawn.[177]

An attempt was made again the next year (59 BC) to settle the veterans and succeeded, since Pompey was able to enjoy the support of Caesar as consul and of Crassus who united with him in the private agreement known as the First Triumvirate. Although the provisions (*leges Iuliae*)[178] were cloaked in constitutional orthodoxy, it is not to be believed either that the colonies which were founded had anything in common with the Gracchan tradition[179] or that, with certain reservations, one is dealing here with the last agrarian proposals in which party interests were at stake.[180] In fact, to distinguish the legislation of Caesar from the Gracchan provisions it is sufficient to consider that the confirmation of *possessiones*[181] left intact the problem of *latifundia* and that secondly it is not the *proletarii* – in so far as they were such – but the veterans who are in question, and it is their intervention in the assemblies which had to be invoked, just as it was forty years before in the time of Saturninus.[182] Furthermore, it is a hard fact that we are no longer talking of measures taken through constitutional channels (as strictly one can describe the Plotian and Flavian proposals); the extra-constitutional position of the Triumvirate in the political scene (the interventions of the soldiers are an aspect of this) is sufficient to make one consider the proposals purely formal, lacking real significance but within which it seems the provisions of Caesar in 59 BC operated. Henceforth Sulla's example admits no exceptions.[183]

4. We can now try to judge the political and social significance of the land distributions to demobilized soldiers[184] in the context of their economic and political promotion in society. To do this we must establish the true significance of the distributions: that is to say, we have to be able to claim with a fair measure of certainty that the allotments themselves had more than a passing significance.

To start with some considerations on the Sullan allotments, these were[185] principally in the regions where there had been the strongest opposition from the Marians, i.e. Campania, Etruria, Latium, and Umbria and Picenum. Although Strabo's famous statement on Sulla's massacres of the Samnites cannot be accepted in its entirety,[186] it is, however, certain that even in Samnium a large amount of land must have been confiscated. Moreover, it is no accident that we do not know of colonies or any kind of Sullan allotment in that region. Large-scale acquisitions of land by private individuals are, however, recorded.[187]

We have more detail about the situation in Campania since economic and social research on Pompeii, a Sullan colony, permits us to form a quite clear impression of the importance which Sullan colonization had in that Campanian town. Furthermore, given the nature of the district, the results of this research do allow a generalization, albeit a cautious one. Modern scholarship[188] favours the conclusion that the year 80 BC did not introduce a break in continuity in the system of *villae rusticae* – enterprises conducted on a planned basis, of about 100 *iugera*[189] – and that the Sullan colonization cannot be regarded as something which forced the pre-Sullan upper class to undertake new activity and therefore changed the class-structure of the rural proprietors.[190] There are two possibilities, not mutually exclusive but complementary: either the amount of land given to the veterans was around 100 *iugera*[191] or the fragmentation of the enterprises was of such short duration as not to allow the formation of a stable class of medium-scale or small rural proprietors, and the colonists at once disburdened themselves, for whatever reason, of the parcels of land assigned to them.[192] The emigration to Africa which became established at that time ought probably to be a reflection of the two possibilities I have mentioned, given that those who emigrated from Pompeii to the African colonies were in part Roman and in part Samnite; this allows us to suppose that the emigration was supported by more than veterans.[193] However, if we bear in mind that the differences at Pompeii between colonists and citizens were exclusively of a political nature,[194] a general observation seems possible that the colonization was not very ambitious from an economic or social point of view but was in fact somewhat limited in scope. This, we can say, was its fate in the whole of Campania.

In Latium the example of Praeneste, where the plots assigned to the colonists were at once re-sold to private citizens,[195] is likely to be typical and certainly proves that the view which I have just been considering is correct.[196]

Characteristic differences present themselves in the situation in Etruria (and perhaps in Umbria and Picenum). Here there is direct evidence of expropriations on a huge scale and of allotments to veterans. Even if the territory confiscated from the pro-Marian towns is not always divided subsequently[197] – and the old owners continued to retain possession – it is certain that sometimes, for example at Fiesole,[198] the settlement of veterans was sizeable and led to a change in the class of landowners, a change which was moreover complicated by the social make-up of the district where those who lost their land would have been primarily owners of large estates which were now divided.[199] However, even in Etruria, as we have already seen evidenced at Praeneste and probably in Campania, there are signs (and we know it was on a large scale) of progressive purchase by a few latifundists of the land-parcels which had been allotted,[200] so that we can safely assume that even in Etruria *res agraria* did not in general suffer any significant change. Beyond that we cannot go. However, even here, alongside the allocations of land, we find evidence of direct acquisition by private individuals of the property confiscated from their Marian opponents.[201]

What has been said so far does not, of course, justify more general conclusions to take into account the different forms of Sullan colonization assumed in the different regions. We may, however, accept the view that the economic and social consequences must have been less significant than those which could be expected to follow from a figure of 120,000 veterans settled.[202]

Above all, a clear distinction should be drawn between confiscation and colonization. The former must certainly have been present on a huge scale,[203] but the cases of Volaterrae and Arretium, where the existing owners largely retained possession of their land, can probably be multiplied on a grander scale.[204] Furthermore, we must take into account the so-called *Sullanae possessiones*,[205] in whose number are included the land of Volaterrae and Arretium, and the *venditiones*, which from the evidence of the sources seem to have accounted for most of the confiscations.

As for the actual *assignationes* which made up the colonization, we have already seen how widespread was the tendency on the part of the veterans to dispose of the land-parcels which were made over to them, either immediately – as probably happened in many cases where perhaps those very people who had their property confiscated sometimes redeemed it – or at a time when the new holders' incompetence in their strange métier and their natural tendency to squander their advantage brought them to the brink of ruin.

That part of the land allotments which was not subject to this fate[206] must have been only a small fraction of Sulla's whole colonization scheme, since neither in Campania nor in Etruria, as we have seen, are we able to find any economic change which resulted from it. We must therefore reject the observations of those[207] who see the Sullan colonies as bringing with them a revival of the Italian countryside; on the contrary, we must maintain that the agricultural wealth of Italy attested in Varro's day,[208] in so far as it is not a rhetorical commonplace,[209] does not date from Sulla but marks a state of affairs which had matured over many decades if not centuries.

As a further step in a thorough examination of this problem it is singularly interesting to spend some time considering the way in which Sulla came to found his colonies. It is, in fact, important to note that in the majority of cases, and certainly in the most significant ones, colonization gave birth to the existence of two communities side by side, the one containing the old citizens and the other the new colonists, separated administratively the one from the other even if they co-existed. This state of affairs, even if it cannot be considered to be the general rule,[210] is certain for Interamnia Praetuttianorum, where inscriptions attest a (Sullan) colony and a *municipium* existing at one and the same time.[211] It also holds for Arretium,[212] Clusium,[213] Nola[214] and Faesulae.[215] The case of Pompeii is, however, extremely dubious; here, judging from the tone of some of Cicero's remarks,[216] a single community seems to have been formed.[217]

Various points arise from all this: first and foremost, the formation of a new, autonomous community alongside an existing one encourages the

belief that subordination of old citizens to new colonists in the administrative field – and therefore, with certain reservations, in the economic field
as well – did not take place. This could not have failed to occur if the new
colonists had been imposed directly on the old community where they
would, of course, have assumed a privileged and dominant position. This
appears to confirm what I have said above about the view that a change took
place in the upper classes at Pompeii, all the more so because, given their
small numbers, the colonists were in some cases absorbed by the older community,[218] so restoring the situation to what it had been before the foundation, in favour of the existing community.

Secondly, co-existence of the kind I have mentioned is all the more noteworthy in so far as it is attested in, for example, localities such as Nola, one
of two cities which resisted Sulla longest[219] and which probably, like
Arretium and Volaterrae, had its right of citizenship restricted.[220] However,
the presence of Nola and Arretium among places with a double community
makes one think that even the *ademptio civitatis* did not have a ruinous effect
on the existing inhabitants, as could have happened with a direct confronta-
tion with the Sullan colonists if the latter had been settled in one and the
same community with a prominently privileged position.[221] Furthermore, it
is known that at Arretium and Volaterrae the territory which was confiscated was never, at least in part, assigned. Equally, the continued existence
of the *municipium* at Interamnia tells strongly against the well-known phrase
of Florus[222] on the *municipia Italiae splendidissima* sold up by Sulla.

In short, from what has been said so far it does not seem hazardous to
maintain that not even in the other places where Sullan settlements are
attested without a new community being established alongside that which
already existed[223] must these settlements be regarded as a calamity and a
catastrophe for the original inhabitants; this contrasts with the general tone
of the evidence which clearly reflects traces of the horror felt by those who
for the first time witnessed the consequences of civil war. This conclusion is
confirmed by what I have said above when considering the problem from
another point of view.[224]

Such are the limitations we should impose on the actual effects of Sulla's
colonization. From these we should try to establish what significance it
could have had for the preferment of proletarian soldiers in Italian society of
the first half of the first century BC. There is above all one point which confirms what I have said above,[225] that the soldiers looked on military service
as a career in itself. Despite their rural origins the soldiers who were settled
in colonies, at least in the majority of cases, were not interested (as they
would have been if their object in enrolling had been to return to their old
social position) in renewing their life in the countryside in a new and respectable position. They preferred to sell the parcels of land allotted to them. I do
not, of course, wish by this to deny that the extensive movement of wealth

in the period after the first civil war was reflected also in the sphere of land ownership, but the fact is that generalizations such as that of Taylor,[226] that the allotments were of extreme importance for promoting the entry of proletarian ex-soldiers into the landed classes of the rural tribes, have for this period to meet this objection.

It is more probable, in my view, that the acquisition of wealth through war booty, the civil wars and the sale of land obtained in allocations represented the chief means by which soldiers were able to rise to those higher economic and social positions which are attested by the substantial entry of people of low origin into the equestrian class and thence into the Curia.[227]

In fact, one gains the impression that only indirectly (through wealth acquired by land-sales) did the allotment of land in the country confer a new position in society on the veterans; as we shall see, it was otherwise in the Augustan period. Clearly this indirect connexion is enough to show that the Sullan colonies brought with them a more positive and historically more important consequence than that which Sulla himself intended when he settled his soldiers. In fact, despite the clause in the law on the inalienability of the land-parcels allotted which can encourage one to see in the Sullan colonization programme a purpose which was totally alien to it,[228] it is clear that Sulla did not go beyond a strictly provisional view of the situation, as we can see from the location of the allotments. The colonies had to be $\phi\rho o\acute{v}\rho\iota\alpha$[229] to suppress the peoples who had sided with the popular faction.[230]

After Sulla these themes of petty politics became less important. On the one side the developed consciousness of the soldiers demanded systematic provision of benefits on discharge as a right, and they regarded this reward, of course, as the last payment for service;[231] on the other, as far as the founders of colonies were concerned, colonial policy came more and more to be part of a general view of the state rather than the purely police function adopted by Sulla's colonization. Naturally, various political contexts make one or other of the two themes dominant from time to time. For example, the provision of rewards by the Triumvirate was worked out almost entirely under the assault which the soldiers delivered by their haughty and persistent demands,[232] and it is natural that in these cases the strongest desire of the founders of colonies should have been to achieve the object of offering rewards with the least damage to the rural class.[233] A more ambitious conception, however, had already dominated the colonizing activity of Caesar in 46–44 BC[234] as it is presented to us by Caesarian propaganda. This deliberately emphasized the 'Romulean' identity of peasant and soldier, and we should not write off this harking back to a fundamental principle of the city-state simply as a piece of propaganda designed to soften the impression of a violent opposition between social classes caused by the allotment of land, but rather look on it as the reflection of a felt need of social politics.[235] The two particular points (consciousness on the part of the soldiers of their right to settlement and a political view of the veteran problem taken by the founders of colonies) can be definitively resolved in the more general observation that in various degrees and under different guises the allotments themselves led to a consciousness of a higher social purpose. Hence it seems legitimate to draw the conclusion that the colonization of veterans, for example by Caesar and Augustus, came to play a relevant role in the process I have already described of upgrading the Italian *proletarii*, greater in fact than that of the Sullan colonization scheme, significant as the latter was.

This is all the more so in that the 'Romulean' theme of Caesarian propaganda, which might appear to some extent to contradict the imperialistic policy of Caesar[236] (but the contradiction disappears if we follow the (Sallustian) interpretation of the colonial problem),[237] came to acquire a more concrete significance with the 'nationalism' of Augustus. He made a great effort to establish in hard reality the well-publicized principle that a return to the land was the fundamental basis for the strongest and most genuine virtues of patriotism and civic responsibility.[238]

Here too, however, we should dwell briefly on the economic and social significance of the measures before drawing political consequences from them.

The Triumvirate's measures, dictated as I have said by the need to make instant provision for the veterans since their demands could no longer be passed over, are intimately connected with the proscriptions which were a consequence of the Triumviral pact.[239] Unlike the case of Sulla – it is worth repeating this – the allotments could not be effectively confined within the limits of the anti-Caesarian towns but had to extend, given the large number to be placed,[240] even beyond the eighteen cities[241] whose territory, according to the original plan, should have been confiscated and divided.[242] The scale of the allocations was such that it is proper to describe what happened as the violent substitution of a new social class for the agrarian class then existing, and the loss fell not so much, of course, on the highest Roman and Italian classes[243] as on the small proprietors and tenants. Leaving aside the various political interests involved with the problems of the allocations (hence the *Bellum Perusinum*), the economic upset which the measures brought with them led directly in most cases to conflicts between civilians and soldiers[244] and generally to an all-round upheaval in the countryside. It is well-known that not only the historical sources but also the poets have left us an account charged with horror at these unjust measures of confiscation and allocation.[245]

The agricultural emigration from Italy, already begun for other reasons in the Gracchan period and, at least as regards Africa, perhaps accelerated by Sulla's measures,[246] was given further impetus by the transfer to the provinces of the Italian peasantry which had been driven out of the fields.[247]

Of course, this gives rise to a number of doubts on the question whether the Triumviral allocations exercised a positive social and economic influence, and these doubts are reinforced when one considers that the instability of the political situation was reflected also in the foundations themselves; for example, the Antonian colonies were disbanded after Actium and the colonists were sent to the East to make room for the veterans of Octavian.[248]

Augustan colonization after Actium had different consequences. Above all, it was able to develop in a changed political climate. Furthermore, followed as it was by a long period of peace, it was able to establish itself in a way which was of necessity impossible for the Triumvirs' colonization schemes. However, the principal reason for its success was that it operated in accordance with criteria which were applied with great discretion and not devoted to the satisfaction of such selfish interests as the veterans' were, for all their undoubted importance. A survey of the Augustan measures in this field shows at once how their purpose was to bring prosperity to a much wider range of population by reconciling the soldiers' demands with the peace and tranquility which now obtained once again in the countryside. In fact Augustus, as is clear from evidence which he himself provides in the *Index*,[249] aimed first at substituting allotments of acquired land[250] for colonies and then cash donatives instead of land, finding the money initially from his own private purse and then, after AD 5, from the *aerarium militare*.[251] This was an innovation; the state came to be clearly established as the source of the indispensable provision of rewards for demobilized soldiers which hitherto had been left to the private responsibility and initiative of an individual general. In this way the soldiery came to be reintegrated in a truly effective way in society, where it made its weight felt and where its own respectable economic status produced a balancing and conservative function, forming the link between army and people, the two fundamental elements which are the basis of the new Augustan regime.[252]

In order to define more closely the economic status of the colonists we should mention a problem of great interest although its solution, whatever it may be, can in no way undermine our conclusions. The problem is whether the Augustan measures – and, with the limitations on their actual execution which have often been mentioned, one can say this for all the colonial measures of the first century BC – created a class of small peasant proprietors[253] or instead a class of urban owners of rural properties.[254] Our research must, of course, start from the available evidence concerning the size of plots assigned in the course of the first century BC. What little we know does not seem to warrant the assertion[255] that the size of the holdings was always growing. The 100 *iugera* (NB of provincial land) fixed in 103 BC by Saturninus are never matched in the course of the first century in Italian allocations.[256] We do not know the size of the Sullan plots[257] but from a phrase of Cicero's[258] it seems that they were not such as to allow an excessively easy existence. In 59 BC Caesar allocated 10 *iugera* apiece in Campania, an extremely fertile region.[259] At Volaterrae, on the other hand, whether the evidence refers to the allocations of Caesar or the Triumvirate, the *Gromatici* mention plots of 25, 50, 35 and 60 *iugera*,[260] and the variations certainly refer to the *gradus militum*, given that under-officers and officers received half as much again or double what the ordinary soldier received.[261] This evidence shows that the size of plot remained far below that allocated in the last known colonies founded in the second century BC in the traditional fashion.[262]

Furthermore, donatives for veterans, which at a certain time came to be substituted for land allocations,[263] were certainly not very generous and it has been calculated that they would have permitted the acquisition of 10–20 *iugera* according to rank.[264] It is impossible to believe that the plots of land acquired by the Emperor were greater in size than those of public or confiscated land.[265] In my opinion it is more likely that the first solution is correct: that is to say, the allocations to soldiers gave rise to a class of small proprietors. This, of course, is only a generalization; examples of large estates which arose in times of revolution (for example, those mentioned by Cicero with reference to Antony's measures[266] or those already referred to from the period of Sulla) have no general significance and are irrelevant to our inquiry.

Syme[267] has enlisted in support of Rostovtzeff's theory the well-known inscription of the *trib. mil.* C. Castricius.[268] We do not know, however, whether Castricius' properties derived from allocations or whether they just happened to be an ancestral inheritance; anyway, Castricius, even if he is represented as a small capitalist, appears to have direct links with his own land, and therefore his case is difficult to reconcile with the concept of an urban owner who was inevitably absent.

Because of the limited extent of land generally assigned it is also difficult to accept the thesis of Rostovtzeff[269] that the veterans leased out the allotments which had been assigned to them, although this probably happened in the second century BC in those cases where the plots were on a much greater scale.[270]

This new set of circumstances had its first effects on municipal life. We can easily understand the prestige acquired by the veteran who left his native country a *proletarius* and returned a wealthy man. We can also appreciate the respect he engendered if only for his soldier's rank. This phenomenon, which began to develop in the course of the first century BC,[271] reached maturity in the Triumviral period when centurions received on discharge the rank of decurion in their *municipia*.[272] At the same time the settlement of soldiers reunited in their military units – a custom which began with Caesar[273] – automatically transformed the military tribunes and centurions of the legion into magistrates and decurions of the new military colony.[274] Light seems to be thrown on this by epigraphic evidence, from the beginning of Augustus' principate, of municipal magistrates who mention their officer rank, and we may note especially those of Interamna Nahartium where out of 14 names of *IVviri* left to us 9 are *tribuni militum*.[275] This case should not be used as evidence of military activity on the part of middle class citizens in that period[276] but rather to illustrate the importance of military service in municipal politics; it became in the present instance the vehicle for transporting citizens of low origin to supreme municipal offices. We should remember that even in the Augustan period Umbria and Picenum preserved the tradition of providing a class of professional soldiers.[277] Furthermore, the political influence of the military factor transcended the limits imposed by the narrowness of municipal life and made itself felt in the wider sphere of the nation, principally because in the crisis involving the Roman governing class the men from the *municipia* saw their own importance grow in the first century BC through a natural and spontaneous development.[278] This seems to be confirmed by the privilege granted to the magistrates of the new Augustan colonies to participate in voting in Rome even in absence.[279]

Given all the reservations which scholars feel in considering this measure – and the fact that no one knows whether it was put into effect seems to be of less importance in the light of the pessimistic view we must take of the real value of the vote in that period – the principle is still valid; clearly the chief obstacle to an effective participation in politics of men from the *municipia* was appreciated and the measure represents an attempt to overcome it, even if it was conceived in the interests of a limited, privileged class.

5. Our inquiry into a specific problem (that of the veterans) has brought us back to points we made earlier arising out of a more general observation on the entire nature of first century BC Roman politics.

We can formulate our conclusion in this way: the Roman professional army in the second and first century BC consistently represents, in its social make-up and the demands for which it is the vehicle, the personification of those economic themes which are widespread among the masses and which during this period assume growing importance in Roman political life.

The profound importance of military professionalism consists in its having introduced to a new and extremely powerful position, both in political and social terms, those Romans and Italians who until then had been kept out of political life by the sheer survival of the city-state structure.

This improved position which non-political classes enjoyed as a result of army service led to the disappearance of those 'traditional contests of noble families' which had always in practice represented Roman politics, and in consequence to the realization of the Principate.[280]

APPENDIX I

The Tribal Levy and the Equestrian Census

In Polybius' description (VI 19–20) the operations of the levy are based exclusively on the tribe,[1] and the division of the Roman people according to the census (i.e. the century)[2] no longer has any part to play except in so far as the soldiers were recruited among the *adsidui*, that is to say, *ex classibus*.[3]

When was this system introduced? Most historians believe that even before the time of Polybius the levy had been based on the tribe,[4] and this should be agreed, though with important reservations: for example, that hypothesis is unacceptable which sees the institution of territorial tribes as having the purpose of creating an efficient recruitment system in place of that which was based on the *curiae*. This view involves denying that the fundamental purpose of the centuriate organization was military,[5] and on that there can be no doubt when one reflects that soldiers were armed according to their census class and that there was a structural identity between the Servian organization and the Roman legion.[6] These last points confirm the view (based on Dion. Hal. IV 19) that the centuries of the census were the levy-units for those of the army, all the more so since the century had only a limited tactical importance in the legionary phalanx and it was therefore in the levy that its fundamentally military nature appeared.[7]

Dionysius in the passage I have cited says:

. . . τὰς μὲν τῶν στρατιωτῶν καταγραφὰς κατὰ τὴν διαίρεσιν ἐποιεῖτο (Servius Tullius) τὴν τῶν λόχων . . . ὁπότε γὰρ αὐτῷ δεήσειε μυρίων ἢ δισμυρίων εἰ τύχοι στρατιωτῶν, καταδιαιρῶν τὸ πλῆθος εἰς τοὺς ἑκατὸν ἐνενηκοντατρεῖς λόχους, τὸ ἐπιβάλλον ἑκάστῳ λόχῳ πλῆθος ἐκέλευε ἕκαστον λόχον . . . συνέβαινεν οὖν τοῖς τὰς μεγίστας ἔχουσιν οὐσίας ἐλάττοσι μὲν οὖσιν, εἰς πλείονας δὲ λόχους μεμερισμένοις, στρατεύεσθαί τε πλείους στρατείας οὐδέποτε ἀναπαυομένους . . . τοῖς δὲ τὰ μέτρια καὶ μικρὰ κεκτημένοις πλείοσιν οὖσιν ἐν ἐλάττοσι λόχοις στρατεύεσθαί τε ὀλιγάκις καὶ ἐκ διαδοχῆς . . .

In this passage, in addition to the explicit testimony that the levy took place according to the division of the people by centuries, it is worth noting the author's very proper comment that the frequency of military service came in practice to be varied according to a man's census class.[8]

In fact, Dionysius' statement on the levy by centuries is in contradiction with what he himself says at IV 14, that, after the division of Rome into 4 tribes, Servius had carried out the levy in accordance with this new sub-division.

Attempts have been made to reconcile these two passages by assuming that a relationship existed between tribe and century[9] which, for some scholars, later fell into disuse until it was resumed again at the time of the reform of the *comitia centuriata*.[10] But this sort of hypothesis is not only explicitly contradicted by a passage of Livy[11] but is also in itself highly improbable,[12] given that the numerical relationship between tribe and century would have had to change continually with the progressive increase in the number of tribes.[13]

The truth is that in Dionysius there are two discordant versions, and it is not even necessary to choose between them, given that they refer to different situations in two different periods. The evidence of IV 19, which describes a levy system no longer in use in the second century BC, goes back probably to an excellent antiquarian source, while the passage of IV 14 must come from an annalist, possibly Calpurnius Piso cited at IV 15, who may have transferred back to the regal period that system of the *dilectus* which had long been in force before his own day (the end of the second century BC).[14]

It is important to try and fix the point at which the levy system changed and the tribe came into use as the basis of the *dilectus*.[15] A unique episode attested in the levy of 275 BC can throw light on the problem and suggest its solution. The passages which mention the event[16] are: Varro, *apud* Non. p. 28 Lindsay: *Manius Curius consul, Capitolio cum dilectum haberet nec citatus in tribu civis respondisset, vendidit tenebrionem*; Livy, *Per.* XIV: *Curius Dentatus cos. cum dilectum haberet, eius, qui citatus non responderat, bona primus vendidit*; Val. Max. VI 3, 4: *id factum imitatus M'. Curius consul, cum dilectum subito edicere coactus esset et iuniorum nemo respondisset, coniectis in sortem omnibus tribubus, Polliae, quae prima exierat, primum nomen urna extractum, citari iussit neque eo respondente bona adulescentis hastae subiecit. quod ut illi nuntiatum est, ad consulis tribunal cucurrit collegiumque tribunorum appellavit. tunc Manius Curius praefatus non opus esse eo cive rei publicae, qui parere nesciret, et bona eius et ipsum vendidit.*

These passages are not easy to interpret. In Valerius Maximus the levy seems to be quite distinct from the successive drawing of lots for tribes and members of tribes[17] and this is the way in which Cagnat[18] has interpreted it, not even accepting, apparently, the principle of enrolment by tribes prior to the time of Polybius.[19] A similar interpretation has also been given of the passage from Varro.[20]

In my view, however, the connexion in this episode between the levy and the tribes must be admitted, for Marquardt[21] is probably right in saying that what we have here is a special case, possibly a *tumultus*: see Val. Max. *cum dilectus subito edicere coactus esset.*

Marquardt's view seems to me to throw light on the origin of the levy by tribes: it came from tumultuary enrolment. This speeded up the mechanism of the levy in moments of need and at the same time allowed a wider use of manpower. It is in fact in 281 BC that the first enrolment of *proletarii* during a *tumultus* is attested. The partial levy of ten tribes recorded by Livy in 418 BC can well be regarded as an example of *tumultus* since it seems logical that to repel a sudden attack by the enemy the Romans had recourse in the crisis to tribes nearer the scene of danger.[22]

I have said above that the levy by tribes, like the tumultuary levy to which the Romans resorted in emergencies, allowed the more wealthy classes to be spared and a more intensive use to be made of human resources. It is probable that the change in the levy system took place about the middle of the third century BC when the demands of the first overseas wars called for a more speedy and more profitable type of *dilectus*. Its background lies in the general development of the military structure which I have described above, and it is closely related to the diminished importance of the century which was due to the introduction of manipular tactics from the end of the fourth century BC.[23]

It is interesting to note how the *dilectus* by tribes is closely related to the *census equester*. We know that as long as the legionary cavalry was entirely and solely drawn from the eighteen centuries of *equites equo publico*, the enrolment of cavalry followed on that of the infantry, just as the *census equitum* followed the *census populi* in the censors' lists.[24] Later, when there was a recurring need to resort to citizens whose private means allowed them to meet the requirements of cavalry service (*equites equo privato*), the *dilectus* began with the enrolment of those *iuniores* of the first class who were so qualified and who, if not chosen for the cavalry, could be chosen for the infantry. While in the period of the *dilectus* by centuries it was easy to have recourse to a fixed number of centuries (those of the *iuniores* of the first class) for the selection of cavalry, matters became more complex when the levy by tribes was introduced and the *adsidui* took to presenting themselves at the levy without distinction of centuries or classes (except that the differentiation between the fourth and third classes was perhaps maintained for a while). Hence a list or a classification already drawn up by the censors on the basis of wealth had to be used for this levy of *equites* and this involved the separation from the first class of a category of citizens in possession of a given property qualification.[25]

It is certain, of course, that the levy of *equites* (*equo privato*, later also *equo publico* after an equestrian census was required of them,[26] although the enrolment of the latter continued to be based on the eighteen centuries) had precedence over that of the infantry. Since the levy by tribes came into force about the time of the First Punic War, the establishment of an equestrian census must have occurred at about the same time.

So it is certain that at the time of the Second Punic War the equestrian census was already in force and we must reject those arguments which have been developed by H. Hill, *AJPh* LX 1939, 361 f., whether based on the passage of Polybius which I have cited or on Livy, XXVII 11, 15.[27] Moreover, the conclusions of Hill – that the equestrian census was introduced in the Gracchan period – have not been generally accepted.[28]

My view is further confirmed by a feature of the constitution of the Latin colonies which has seldom been considered. There the timocratic distinctions which, in spite of their purely military terminology, reflected the actual economic conditions of the settlers, were between *pedites, equites* and sometimes *centuriones*.[29] The fact that one of the highest classes of the colony was called *equites*, together with the point that the constitution of the Latin colonies was modelled, *mutatis mutandis*, on that of Rome, shows that the word *equites* was already a technical term in the metropolis and that it meant a class defined in economic terms, superior to the others. The first Latin colonies, at least those where we know this census qualification appears, are Placentia and Cremona in 218 BC.[30]

APPENDIX II

The colony of Capua (83 BC) and the Marians of Campania

Our only evidence that in the period of Cinnan ascendancy at Rome a colony was founded at Capua is in some passages of Cicero's *de lege agraria* II,[1] and since in one of these[2] it is explicitly stated that the founder was M. Iunius Brutus, the father of the man who later assassinated Caesar,[3] it is generally held that the foundation took place in 83 BC, the year in which Brutus was tribune.[4]

However, the causes which modern scholars assign to this foundation are unsatisfactory. According to some the object would not have been substantially different from that of the Gracchi,[5] though there is the reservation that the ultimate purpose was really to attach the rural proletariat to the popular regime.[6] But all this is hardly convincing; the gap which separates the *populares* of the period of Marius and the Gracchi is too great, and it is incredible that colonists should have been established in a region as predominantly anti-Sullan as Campania was, while it would have been much more fitting to apply such a measure to those regions where it was evident that the authority of the popular government was weakening, for example in Picenum.

A military purpose has been put forward by other historians, from Drumann to Last, and it is undeniable that this thesis seems to receive strong support from the fact that Campania was the battlefield chosen by Marian generals on which to fight Sulla, and from a passage in Cicero, *de leg. agr.* II 90: ... *omnibus domesticis externisque bellis Capua non modo non obfuit, sed opportunissimam se nobis praebuit et ad bellum instruendum et ad exercitus ornandos et tectis ac sedibus suis recipiendos.*

However, if on all those occasions mentioned by Cicero Capua had been as useful for the Roman armies as it was, we must ask ourselves what greater advantage could accrue to Rome's military operations by raising it to the status of a colony. For, it should be carefully noted, Cicero does not in fact speak either of colonists settled there or of lands divided among them.[7]

The fact is that modern scholars have not taken account of what Cicero says in the speech which I have mentioned. Too common is the view that the speech is 'the most perverse that Cicero ever produced',[8] and that only sophistic arguments were used by the orator against 'the excellent law, wisely conceived', of Rullus.[9]

Cicero goes to great lengths to insist on the following point:[10] as formerly Brutus, so now Servilius Rullus with his proposal to found a colony at Capua is aiming to raise the Campanian city from the decline into which it had fallen after its defection during the Second Punic War and in which our ancestors in their political wisdom had left it. He aims, in fact, to set it up in opposition, perhaps, to Rome itself.

I think there is no doubt that for Rullus the foundation of a colony at Capua was part of the function of dividing the *ager Campanus*, but it seems undeniable that Cicero's statement has a ring of truth about it when referred to the object of Rullus' model, i.e. to the colony of M. Brutus.[11]

That Cicero's assertion is true is, I think, proved by a review of the role which the Campanians played in the anti-oligarchic movement from the Gracchi to Cinna. One example of this has already been seen. Despite the fact that only recently has it been authoritatively reaffirmed that in the Gracchan period one witnessed the curious fact that both the party of reform and the party of the *boni* were supported and sustained by the teaching of Stoic philosophy, personified respectively by Blossius and Panaetius,[12] it seems to me that D. R. Dudley, *JRS* XXXI 1941, 94–9, has completely succeeded in demonstrating that Blossius of Cumae did not draw his democratic principles from Stoic sources but from his Campanian origin. Stoicism in that period was conservative in tendency, as exemplified by Panaetius and Scipio.

This is not an isolated fact but is part of a general phenomenon: the upper classes of Campania, in the majority of cases, do not make common cause – as those of Etruria, Umbria and Picenum do – with the Roman oligarchs but line up against them alongside the *populares*.

This alignment which is all part of the general phenomenon of the union that existed between the Marians and the Italian rebels – but note[13] that at Capua, from which most of the Marians in Campania come, no anti-Roman movement is attested during the *Bellum Sociale*, and this is to be explained by the presence in the city of Roman armies – exercises a profound influence; it becomes hard reality when Campanians participate in the Roman political struggle.

It is possible to illustrate, if not in any great detail at least with some very characteristic examples, Campanian participation in the Marian faction and their support of its cause. In 88 BC, after his march from Nola on Rome, Sulla had declared public enemies twelve Roman citizens of whom, however, only ten are known by name.[14] Among these, four, either certainly or very probably, are Campanians: Cn. and Q. Granius,[15] a noble family from Puteoli, who resisted Sulla later as well and maintained allegiance to their own anti-oligarchic principles down to the Caesarian period;[16] Q. Rubrius Varro,[17] whose family already boasted an intimate connexion with the Gracchi if Quintus' father is the tribune of 123 BC;[18] and finally M. Laetorius,[19] probably connected with the P. Laetorius who was a friend of C. Gracchus.[20] It is interesting to reflect that among the twelve *hostes* there was a Iunius Brutus, praetor in that year; we do not know the nature of his relationship to the founder of the colony at Capua in 83 BC.[21]

The list of examples should not stop here; other Campanians played a role of prime importance in the Marian faction. The famous Capuan family of the Magii[22] is represented by P. Magius, tribune in 87 BC[23] and, above all, by that L. Magius who worked for the conclusion of a pact between Sertorius and Mithridates,[24] an interesting point for our inquiry since it shows how the political views of these Campanian *populares* drove them to oppose not only the oligarchy but also Rome itself.

Furthermore, Gutta was a Capuan;[25] he commanded an army for the *populares* against Sulla at the Colline Gate. L. and C. Insteius were also certainly Campanian; they were Sertorius' companions in Spain, and the former appears with the description *Fal (erna tribu)* in Pompeius Strabo's *consilium* at Asculum.[26] Finally, from Formiae came that Helvius Mancia who many years later defended the Marian *populares* against Pompey, among them Brutus the founder of the colony at Capua.[27]

This Campanian support for the *popularis* faction must be interpreted in the light of Cicero's explanation of the foundation of the colony at Capua and can, therefore, fit straight into the tradition of an independent Campanian nobility, well-known since the pre-Hannibalic period; the attitude of Magius, the Mithridatic sympathizer, provides the clearest of examples. Not without reason did Cicero call to mind the Blossii, Magii and Vibellii when he visited Capua after the creation of the colony.[28] We should, I think, note here that the conflict of interests between the senatorial oligarchy at Rome and the upper classes in Campania must have been an obstacle to their assuming a common political stand of the kind which came into being between the Etruscan and Umbrian aristocracy and Rome.[29] This is confirmed by the fact that families belonging to the industrial class (i.e. the Equites) such as the Cossutii and the Pedii[30] were connected with the Marian faction. We know that the Italian commercial class, for example on Delos, were largely of Campanian origin.[31] A concentration of economic interests, represented by the Italian commercial and industrial classes in general and the Campanians in particular, is very probable within the Marian faction.[32]

In conclusion, I think it is clear that the re-establishment of an autonomous community at Capua must have been the direct result of the widespread support given by the upper classes of Campania to the Marian faction (in Etruria, on the other hand, the Marians were generally the socially depressed classes). This Marian faction must have been able to impose this measure on the popular government after the death of Cinna when the political and military crisis would have enabled the extremists, as always, to gain the upper hand. Certainly such men as L. Magius whom I have mentioned were extremists; in his hatred for the oligarchy he did not hesitate to ally himself with the worst enemy Rome had at that time.

Cicero will surely have exaggerated in painting the scene which presented itself to him at Capua in 83 BC.[33] In my opinion, however, it is certain that the promotion of Capua to colonial status, representing perhaps the first stage in a programme of Roman reorganization after the grant of citizenship to the allies and presaging the transformation of Roman territories hitherto directly dependent upon Rome into autonomous communities, must have appeared to Campanian pride as revenge, even if rather belated revenge, for the notorious measures of 211–210 BC.

Sulla, on the other hand, used his victory to restore the *status quo ante* and with massive settlements of veterans made his position secure against possible new attempts at autonomy by Campania.[34]

Appendix III

Sullan Senators[1]

It is well-known that the sources are divided on the origins of the senators appointed by Sulla in 81 BC. According to Appian, I 100, 468, and Livy, *Per.* LXXXIX, they were members of the equestrian class, while Sallust, *BC* 37, and Dion. Hal. V 77, say they were men of low origin. It is also well-known that the views of modern scholars repeat the disagreement of the ancient writers.[2] Hill has tried to resolve the problem, in so far as agreement can be reached on the evidence at our disposal, by researching into the individual senators themselves.

Before discussing the conclusions he reached after such an inquiry I have thought it necessary to retrace some of the ground he has covered, trying to correct in so far as I can the inevitable imprecisions of his account. The criteria which he adopted[3] are correct and acceptable; only the first – marked (*a*) by Hill – needs some comment here.

Hill's assertion that those are probably Sullan senators 'who held the praetorship, aedileship or consulship after 81 BC without having been quaestors' is valid only in so far as Sulla would not have compelled those new senators of his who had not yet begun their political career to go through the whole *cursus*.[4] However, that assertion – in the sense intended by Hill, which can only refer to exceptional situations – cannot make sense unless we remember that the proviso ('without having been quaestors') is valid only with the rider 'after 81 BC'; we know that from that year, by reason of the Sullan legislation, ex-quaestors would have acquired the *ius sententiae* in the Senate.[5] Curule magistrates for whom the quaestorship is attested after 81 BC cannot be considered Sullan senators.[6] But that proviso, of course, is irrelevant for *quaestorii* prior to 81 BC. In their case, it is clear, one must maintain that the Sullan measure mentioned above granted them entry into the Senate; hence the large majority of the praetors, aediles and consuls post-81 BC are for this reason to be considered Sullan senators in that they had held the quaestorship before 81 BC.

Hill is right to leave out of the reckoning praetors post-70 BC and consuls post-66 BC. Although Sulla's *lex annalis* required an interval of two years to be observed between praetorship and consulship and of nine years between quaestorship and praetorship,[7] it is clear that the majority of magistrates would not have been elected *suo anno*, and a criterion which leaves such a wide margin in the computation is therefore justified.

The list of senators which follows – I have thought it convenient to separate the Sullan senators into two groups, depending on the degree of probability with which they can be identified – differs from Hill's list only in a few cases, and these are for the most part additions. I have thought it right to give my reasons in detail for the more important alterations to Hill's list.

The first of the five categories into which Hill distributes the Sullan senators comprises those men who had been expelled from the Senate by the Marians and who had been readmitted by Sulla. As a matter of logic[8] they cannot be classified as Sullan senators. Furthermore, at least four of the names given by Hill seem to have been placed wrongly in that category. One example does for all, L. Licinius Lucullus[9] who was not in fact a senator before 81 BC. He was quaestor in 88, curule aedile in 79, praetor in 78 and consul in 74,[10] and was certainly made a senator by Sulla in 81.

Among those included in the second category[11] it is hardly possible that M. Caecilius Metellus can be properly included as a Sullan senator. In fact it seems odd that a Caecilius Metellus had not held the magistracies *suo anno*; praetor in 69, he would certainly have been quaestor in the previous decade and as *quaestorius* would have entered the Senate.[12] In the same category is included P. Sulpicius Galba,[13] but from what we know of his *cursus*[14] he appears to have kept quite precise intervals between the offices: curule aedile in 71, praetor between 68 and 66, and candidate for the consulship in 63. His quaestorship is therefore to be placed in the decade 80–70 and he too will have entered the Senate as *quaestorius*. Hill[15] is wrong to maintain that

Sulpicius Galba entered the Senate before he had held the quaestorship; Verres' *iudex* in 70, quaestor designate for 69,[16] is another P. Sulpicius,[17] who must have been a Sullan senator.

Finally, concerning the nine names in the fifth category, besides some other doubtful cases it seems that T. Aufidius[18] should not be considered a Sullan senator. It would be odd if Sulla had introduced into the Senate the brother of that M. Vergilius, *qui tribunus plebis* (87 BC) *L. Sullae imperatori diem dixit*.[19] If we bear in mind his age and his brother's political views, we may assume that he entered the Senate in 86 BC. To the same year certainly dates the entry into the Senate of the Samnite Statius.[20] On the other hand, I have included in my list other magistrates of the decade 80–70 BC whom Hill excluded without, in my view, adequate reason.

Although the discrepancies between Hill's list and my own are relatively few, the conclusions which I think may be drawn are different. In Hill's view the list proved that, in the context of the disagreement between the ancient sources to which I have referred, those authors (Livy and Appian) were right who maintained that Sulla drew his new senators from the equestrian class and that these equestrians were the *equites equo publico* of the eighteen centuries. This latter hypothesis was proposed by Hill himself after an initial examination of the passages from Livy and Appian. His former conclusion was in substance accepted also by Syme who accordingly advised caution in accepting the traditional evidence on the composition of Caesar's Senate which is quite similar in tone to that of Sallust and Dionysius in the present instance.[21]

In my view the problem must be posed in a different way. By 81 BC the Roman Senate must have been reduced to not more than 150 members,[22] especially after the murders of the civil war. After Sulla the statutory number was six hundred.[23] It is of course true that we are not in a position to decide with certainty whether this figure was reached at once with Sulla's nominations or whether it was rather the case that the dictator confined himself to nominating three hundred new senators,[24] leaving it to the successive annual intake of twenty ex-quaestors to achieve the total number.[25] However, it is not in my opinion permissible to generalize from a batch of ninety cases, with not a few of them far from certain, to the original social background of all the new Sullan senators, whether they were 450 in number or, on a more limited view, 300.

This observation is self-evident and such as to prejudice Hill's conclusions; it acquires even greater weight when one reflects on the criteria which were bound to govern Hill's and my own classification of Sullan senators. In fact, the overwhelming majority of the names admitted to the list is provided by magistrates and only in the case of P. Sulpicius and of L. Fufidius, *primipilaris*, are we in a position to assert that they were in the Senate before they held the quaestorship.

Hence it is obvious that there is of course a much greater possibility of knowing the names of Sullan senators who held magistracies than there is of those who entered the Senate through Sulla's agency and proceeded no further in their political career or did not even begin it.

To this it may be added that, following Hill, I have entered in the list almost all the curule magistrates post-81 BC who fall within the chronological limits I have indicated above. Given that the magisterial lists of the Ciceronian period are in a reasonable state when compared with other periods, it does not seem credible that, along with the other magistrates of the same period who were probably Sullan senators though their names have not come down to us, our total can be much extended, far less reach Appian's figure of three hundred (to keep the lower total).

All the other Sullan senators (a figure more than double those comprised in my list if we limit ourselves to Appian's number) must have been quaestors before 81 BC who held no further offices after that year or, for the most part, people who were nominated without ever having occupied any magistracy. With the exception of P. Sulpicius and L. Fufidius who are known to us, and of others whom we can only imagine, they did not make it their business later to enter upon a political career.

On their social origins we are, of course, only in a position to venture hypotheses. Certainly it is no longer legitimate with the aid of the list to reject the tradition of Sallust and Dionysius in favour of Livy's and Appian's account.

If they really were members of the *equester ordo*[26] it is worth noting the serious reduction the *ordo* had suffered during the civil war and the inclusion in it of newcomers of various origins. They came both from low social orders so enriched by the war and the proscriptions that they acquired the equestrian census,[27] and from the aristocracies or rather, in more general terms, pro-oligarchic elements in the Italian cities;[28] some of their original members are already present in the list which follows.[29]

It also seems right to accept Willems' conjunction[30] of the evidence that people of low origin entered the Senate with the evidence that the censors of 70 BC excluded some 64 senators. It is not a question of a *petitio principii*[31] but of two pieces of data which can support one another. It is worth mentioning that other scholars when considering the favourable attitude of the censors of 70 BC towards Pompey[32] attribute to their activity a more decisively political character. Those who were expelled would have been largely Pompey's enemies.[33]

Another conclusion drawn from the list is that Sulla chose a great many of his senators from the Roman *nobilitas*. Therefore it is no longer possible to accept Carcopino's view which is precisely the contrary.[34]

Sullan Senators

A. MORE CERTAIN

1. M'. Acilius Glabrio Willems, I² p. 436; *RE* no. 38; Hill, p. 175, n. 5. Pr. 70, cos. 67.
2. M'. Aemilius Lepidus Willems, p. 437; *RE* no. 62; Hill, p. 175, n. 5. Cos. 66.
3. L. Afranius Willems, p. 440; *RE* no. 6; Hill, p. 176. Leg. 77, cos. 60. Picene? See Syme, *JRS* XXVIII 1938, 118; *contra*, Pais, *Dalle guerre puniche* II 680, n. 3. Nicolet, p. 582, would exclude him.
4. C. Antistius Vetus Willems, p. 455; *RE* no. 46. Pr. 72, procos. 69–8. Nicolet, p. 582, would exclude him.
5. M. Antonius Creticus *RE* no. 29; Hill, p. 175, n. 5. Pr. 74.
6. Aquinus *RE* no. 1; Hill, p. 176. Legate against Sertorius. See Nicolet, p. 582.
7. Q. Arrius Willems, p. 454; *RE* no. 7. Pr. 73. Campanian? See *RE* s.v. col. 1251. Cf. Cic. *Brut.* 242. See Nicolet, p. 582; Wiseman, p. 214.
8. Cn. Asinius Willems, p. 451; Wehrmann, *Fasti praetorii* 34. Pr. 78(?). Nicolet, p. 583, would exclude him.
9. M. Atilius Bulbus Willems, p. 414; *RE* no. 34; Hill, p. 175.
10. Cn. Aufidius Orestes Willems, p. 433, n. 5; *RE* no. 32; Hill, p. 175, n. 5. Pr. 77, cos. 71.
11. M. Aurelius Cotta Willems, p. 432, n. 1; *RE* no. 107; Hill, p. 174, n. 3. Cos. 74.
12. L. Caecilius Metellus Willems, p. 435, n. 5; *RE* no. 74. *Monet.* 89, pr. 71, cos. 68.
13. Q. Caecilius Metellus Creticus Willems, p. 435; *RE* no. 87; Hill, p. 174. Pr. 75, cos. 69.
14. M. Caesius Willems, p. 455; *RE* no. 9. Pr. 75. Campanian. Cf. *RE* no. 5; Nicolet, p. 583.
15. C. Calpurnius Piso Willems, p. 436; *RE* no. 63; Hill, p. 175, n. 5. Cos. 67.
16. C. Cassius Longinus *RE* no. 58. Cf. Willems, p. 433. *Monet.* 83, cos. 73.
17. C. Claudius Glaber *RE* no. 165; Hill, p. 175, n. 5. Pr. 73.
18. C. Claudius Marcellus Willems, p. 450; *RE* no. 214. Pr. 80.
19. C. Claudius Nero Willems, p. 449; *RE* no. 247; Hill, p. 175, n. 5. Pr. 81, procos. 80.
20. P. Coelius Willems, p. 454; *RE* no. 2. Pr. 74.
21. Q. Considius Willems, p. 502; *RE* no. 7; Hill, p. 177. Senator 74. See Nicolet, pp. 583–4; Wiseman, pp. 225–6.

22. Cn. Cornelius Dolabella Willems, p. 449, n. 6; *RE* no. 135; see Hill, p. 174, n. 3. Pr. 81.
23. Cn. Cornelius Lentulus Clodianus Willems, p. 428; *RE* no. 216; Hill, p. 174. Cos. 72.
24. L. Cornelius Sisenna Willems, p. 451, n. 6; *RE* no. 374; Hill, p. 175. Pr. 78.
25. M'. Curius Willems, p. 453. Pr. 76(?), procos. 75–4; excluded by Nicolet, p. 584.
26. M. Domitius Calvinus *RE* no. 44; Hill, p. 175. Pr. 80.
27. L. Faberius Willems, p. 503; *RE* no. 2. Senator 78. See Nicolet, p. 584; Wiseman, p. 230.
28. M. Fannius Willems, p. 451; *RE* no. 15. *Monet.*, pleb. aed. 83–2, pr. 80.
29. M. Fonteius Willems, p. 452; *RE* no. 12. Quaestor 85, pr. 76.
30. L. Fufidius *RE* no. 4; Hill, p. 170; Gelzer, *Nobilität* 3 [= Seager, p. 3]; Syme, *JRS* XXVII 1937, 127 and *id. PBSR* XIV 1938, 13; see Willems, p. 450. Campanian (Dubois, *Pouzzoles antique* 48, n. 1) or from Arpinum (Münzer, *RE* s.v. col. 200)? See Nicolet, p. 584; Wiseman, p. 232.
31. L. Furius Willems, p. 452; *RE* no. 18; Hill, p. 175, n. 5. Pr. 76.
32. A. Gabinius Willems, p. 503; *RE* no. 10; Hill, p. 175, n. 5.
33. Q. Hortensius Hortalus Willems, p. 435; *RE* no. 13; Hill, p. 174. Quaestor 87 or 86, cur. aed. 75, pr. 72, cos. 69.
34. M. Iuncus Willems, p. 452; *RE* no. 4. Pr. 76(?).
35. M. Iunius Silanus Willems, p. 452; *RE* no. 170. Quaestor 84/81, pr. 77, procos. 76; see Wehrmann, p. 36.
36. M. Licinius Crassus Hill, p. 174; Garzetti, *Athenaeum* N.S. XIX 1941, 21.
37. L. Licinius Lucullus Willems, p. 432, n. 1; *RE* no. 104. See Hill, p. 174, n. 3.
38. C. Licinius Sacerdos Willems, p. 454; *RE* no. 154; Hill, p. 175. Pr. 75.
39. Cn. Manlius Willems, p. 455; *RE* no. 21. Pr. 72.
40. L. Manlius *RE* no. 30 (= 29 or =79). Procos. 78.
41. Q. Manlius *RE* no. 34; Hill, p. 175, n. 5.
42. T. Manlius Torquatus *RE* no. 95; Hill, p. 175, n. 5. See Willems, p. 540.
43. Q. Marcius Rex Willems, p. 435, n. 5; *RE* no. 92; Hill, p. 175, n. 5. Cos. 68.
44. C. Memmius *RE* no. 6 (= no. 7), not = no. 9, *pace* Hill, p. 176.
45. L. Minucius Basilus *RE* no. 37; Hill, p. 176. Picene: Syme, *JRS* XXVIII 1938, 124, n. 74; excluded by Nicolet, p. 585.
45a. M. (Minucius) Basilus Nicolet, p. 587; Wiseman, pp. 241–2.

46. M. Mummius Willems, p. 456; *RE* no. 9. Pr. 70.
47. Cn. Octavius Willems, p. 432, n. 1; *RE* no. 22. Cos. 76.
48. L. Octavius Willems, p. 432, no. 1; *RE* no. 26. Cos. 75.
49. (Octavius) Balbus *RE* no. 43 (= 46?); Hill, p. 176.
50. Oppius Willems, p. 455; *RE* no. 4. Pr. 72(?).
51. Sex. Peducaeus Willems, p. 452; *RE* no. 5; Hill, p. 175, n. 5. Pr. 76.
52. Q. Petilius Willems, p. 504; *RE* no. 6; Hill, p. 175, n. 5. Senator 78. See *RE* no. 5, and *CIL* I² 709.
53. P. Popillius Willems, p. 418; Hill, p. 177; *RE* no. 10. See, however, Mommsen, *SR* III 859, n. 4.
54. M. Pupius Piso Frugi Willems, p. 440; see Hill, p. 174, n. 3. Quaestor 83, pr. 73 (or 72), cos. 61 (*RE* no. 10).
55. M. Servilius *RE* no. 19; see Willems, p. 540, and Hill, p. 174, n. 3. *Monet.* 89.
56. P. Sulpicius Willems, p. 411 and n. 3; p. 504; *RE* no. 15; Hill, p. 173, is in error. See *Es. e Soc.* 162 [= 60 above]. Cf. Nicolet, p. 585.
57. A. Terentius Varro Willems, p. 451; *RE* no. 82; Hill, p. 175, n. 5. Pr. 78(?).
58. M. Terentius Varro Willems, p. 453; *RE* no. 84 in *Supplb.* VI 1175; Hill, p. 175; see Münzer, *N. Jahrbb.* LI–LII 1923, 36.
59. M. Terentius Varro Lucullus Willems, p. 433; *RE* s.v. 'Licinius', no. 109. Quaestor, cur. aed. 79, pr. 76, cos. 73.
60. L. Titurius Sabinus Willems, p. 505; *RE* no. 2. *Monet.* 87, legate 75.
61. L. Turius Willems, p. 456; *RE* no. 2; Syme, *The Roman Revolution*, Oxford 1939, 81, n. 1.
62. C. Valerius Triarius Willems, p. 455; Hill, p. 175, n. 5. Legate 73 (*RE* no. 363).
63. P. Varinius Glaber Willems, p. 455; Hill, p. 176, n. 13; Wehrmann, p. 42. Pr. 73 (*RE* no. 1).
64. C. Verres Willems, p. 454, n. 5; see, however, M. Gelzer, *Caesar*³ 1941, 31. Pr. 74. Cf. Nicolet, p. 585; Wiseman, p. 272.

B. LESS CERTAIN

65. C. Anneus (Brocchus) Willems, p. 508; Mommsen, *Hermes* XX 1885, 281 = *GS* V 507; *RE* no. 3. Senator 73. Sicilian: Cic. II *Verr.* 3, 93. Nicolet, pp. 585–6; Wiseman, p. 212.
66. M'. Aquilius Willems, p. 418; Hill, p. 175, n. 5.
67. Q. Axius Willems, p. 516; Mommsen, p. 281 = p. 507; *RE* no 4. Senator 73. Cf. Nicolet, p. 586; Wiseman, p. 216.
68–69. C. and L. Caepasius Willems, p. 502; *RE* s.v.; Syme, *PBSR* XIV 1938, 23.

70. CALIDIUS Willems, p. 506; Hill, p. 177; see *RE* no. 2. Senator 73–71.
70a. L. CASSIUS J. Suolahti, *The Junior Officers* . . ., Helsinki 1955, 93, n. 3; Nicolet, p. 587.
71. M. CASSIUS Mommsen, p. 282 = p. 508; *RE* no. 18. Senator 73.
72. CASSIUS BARBA Willems, p. 506; Hill, p. 176. Leg. 73.
73. L. CASSIUS LONGINUS Willems, p. 461, n. 5; *RE* no. 64; Hill, p. 175, n. 5. *Monet.* 78, pr. 66.
73a. L. CAULIUS MERGUS Broughton, II 489; Nicolet, p. 587; Wiseman, p. 223.
74. L. CLAUDIUS Mommsen, p. 282 = p. 508; *RE* no. 23. Senator 73.
75. P. CORNELIUS SULLA *RE* no. 386; Hill, p. 175, n. 5.
76. Q. CORNIFICIUS Willems, p. 460; *RE* no. 7; Hill, p. 175, n. 5. Senator 70, pr. 67 or 66.
77. C. COSCONIUS Willems, p. 451; see *RE* no. 3, col. 1668. Pr. 79, procos. 78/76.
78. L. CRITONIUS Willems, p. 450; *RE* no. 2. *Monet.*, pleb. aed. 83 or 82. He should be removed from this list because he was a Marian; see Broughton, II 63; Wiseman, p. 228, no. 147.
79. EGNATIUS *RE* no. 2; see Willems, p. 503. If he were *RE* no. 27, he would not be a Sullan senator.
80. C. FIDICULANIUS FALCULA Willems, p. 503; *RE* s.v.; Syme, *PBSR* XIV 1938, 23; Nicolet, p. 586; Wiseman, p. 23.
81. C. FONTEIUS Willems, p. 506; *RE* no. 7; Hill, p. 175, n. 5. Legate 73.
82. TI. GUTTA Willems, p. 418; *RE* s.v. Senator 74. Campanian. Cf. Nicolet, p. 586; Wiseman, p. 234.
83. CN. HEIUS Willems, p. 504; *RE* no. 3. Senator 74. Sicilian. Cf. Wiseman, p. 234.
84. C. IUNIUS Willems, pp. 413–4; *RE* no. 15. Senator 74.
84a. M. IUVENTIUS PEDO Broughton, II 492; Nicolet, p. 587.
85. L. LARTIUS Mommsen, p. 283 = p. 509; *RE* no. 1. Senator 73.
85a. LICINIUS BUCCO Münzer, *RE* no. 39; Broughton, II 492.
86. T. MAENIUS Mommsen, p. 284 = p. 510; *RE* no. 16. Senator 73.
87. SEX. NONIUS SUFFESAS Willems, p. 450; *RE* no. 53; Hill, p. 175, n. 5. Pr. 81.
88. M. OCTAVIUS LIGUS Willems, p. 504; *RE* no. 69. Senator 75.
89. M. PETREIUS Willems, p. 463; *RE* no. 3; Hill, p. 176. Pr., leg. 63/2. From Atina: see *RE* no. 4.
90. POMPTINUS Willems, p. 464; Hill, p. 176. Leg. 73/1, pr. 63.
91. C. POPILIUS Willems, p. 414; *RE* no. 3.
92. M. PORCIUS CATO Willems, p. 451, n. 6. Cur. aed., pr. 78(?). *RE* no. 11; different chronology in Broughton, II 13 and n. 2.
93. M. PUBLICIUS SCAEVA Mommsen, p. 284 = p. 510. Senator 73. *RE* no. 25.

The Roman Professional Army (pp. 171–173) 67

94. Q. RANCIUS Mommsen, p. 284 = p. 510; *RE* s.v. Senator 73.
94a. P. SATURIUS Broughton, II 496; Nicolet, p. 588.
95. M. SEIUS Willems, p. 455; *RE* no. 3; Hill, p. 177. Cur. aed. 74. For the name see *RE* s.v. col. 1120 and Syme, *RR* 358. Cf. Nicolet, p. 586; Wiseman, p. 259.
96. P. SEPTIMIUS SCAEVOLA Willems, p. 414; *RE* no. 51. Senator 74.
97. SORNATIUS Willems, p. 507; *RE* s.v.; Hill, p. 176. Leg. 73/68.
98. P. TADIUS Willems, p. 508; *RE* no. 17; Hill, p. 177. Leg. 73/71.
99. Q. TITINIUS Willems, p. 508; *RE* no. 17; Hill, p. 177. Senator 70; excluded by Nicolet, p. 586; Wiseman, p. 266.
100. VOCONIUS Willems, p. 463; Hill, p. 176; Wehrmann, p. 59. Legate 73. *RE* no. 1; Broughton, II 113.
101. L. VOLCATIUS TULLUS Willems, p. 437. Cos. 66. *RE* no. 8.
102. L. VOLUSCIUS Mommsen, p. 285 = p. 511; Syme, *PBSR* XIV 1938, 23; *RE* no. 1.

APPENDIX IV

List of Sullan Colonies

Lists of Sullan colonies appear in Zumpt, *Comm. Epigr.* 250 f.; Mommsen, *art. cit.* (see *Es. e Soc.* 117, n. 184 [= 44, n. 184 above]) p. 161 = p. 202 f. (used by E. De Ruggiero, *Diz. Epigr.* s.v. 'colonia', and Kornemann, *RE* s.v. 'coloniae'); also in Pais, *AAN* N.S. VIII 1924, 313–31, and *Serie cronolog.*, *MAL* VI, I, 1925, 352 f. and in Beloch, *RG* 511–2 (used by T. Frank, *ESAR* I 220). See also Commentary,[2] *Appiani Bell. Civ. Lib.* I Florence 1967, 260–1; P. A. Brunt, *Italian Manpower* 300 f. NB also what has been said *Es. e Soc.* 126, n. 218 [= 47, n. 218 above].

I distinguish the colonies from those localities where all that is known is that there were allotments there, and I distinguish also the names into categories of those that are certain and those that are uncertain. I do not propose to examine the large number of localities where, on the basis of insufficiently discriminatory criteria (such as lie behind Zumpt's list), Sullan veterans are supposed to have been established. In the case of Puteoli it is sufficient to refer to Dubois, 'Pouzzoles antique' (*Bibl. Éc. franç. d'Athènes et de Rome* XCVIII), 1907, 27 f. The extremely informative article of A. Degrassi, *MAL* VIII, II 6, 1949 = *Scritti vari di antichità*, I 99 f., has been useful on various points and has allowed me to exclude Paestum from the list of Sullan colonies in which it has generally been included.

Colonies

A. CERTAIN

1. ALERIA (in Corsica) see Gabba, *Athenaeum* N.S. XXIX 1951, 20 and n. 4.
2. ARRETIUM Zumpt, p. 251; Mommsen, p. 165; Pais, *Stor. Coloniẓ.* 168 f.; Beloch, p. 611. For the evidence see *Es. e Soc.* 122, n. 197 [= 45, n. 197 above] and *Es. e Soc.* 125, n. 212 [= 46, n. 212 above].
3. CLUSIUM Zumpt, p. 257; Mommsen, p. 165, n. 1; Beloch, p. 511; *CIL* XI 2102. For the evidence see *Es. e Soc.* 125, n. 213 [= 46, n. 213 above].
4. FAESULAE Zumpt, p. 253; Mommsen, p. 166; Pais, *Stor. Coloniẓ.* 166; Beloch, p. 511 and p. 611. The best discussion is in A. Degrassi, *art. cit.* 292. For the evidence see *Es. e Soc.* 122, n. 198 [= 45, n. 198 above] and 125, n. 215 [= 46, n. 215 above]; see also my article in *SCO* XIX–XX 1970–1, 462 = *Es. e Soc.* 362.
5. FLORENTIA Flor. II 9, 27–8; see Degrassi, p. 292 and notes with bibliography; see also *SCO loc. cit.* = *Es. e Soc. loc. cit.*
6. INTERAMNIA PRAETUTTI(AN)ORUM Zumpt, p. 253 f.; Mommsen, p. 166; Pais, *Stor. Coloniẓ.* 189; Beloch, p. 512. See Flor. II 9, 28. For the evidence see *Es. e Soc.* 125, n. 211 [= 46, n. 211 above]. See also *SCO art. cit.* 463 = *Es. e Soc.* 363.
7. NOLA Zumpt, p. 254; Mommsen, p. 185; Pais, *Stor. Coloniẓ.* 240 f.; Beloch, p. 512 and *id. Campanien²* 391. For the evidence see *Es. e Soc.* 125, n. 214 [= 46, n. 214 above] and 126, n. 218 [= 47, n. 218 above]; see Lib. col. p. 236, 3 Lachmann.
8. POMPEII see *Es. e Soc.* 120 f. [= 44 f. above] and 126, n. 218 [= 47, n. 218 above]; Mommsen, p. 167.
9. PRAENESTE Zumpt, p. 254; Mommsen, p. 167; Fernique, *Études sur Préneste* 55; Pais, *Stor. Coloniẓ.* 243; Beloch, p. 512. See Cic. *de leg. agr.* II 78; Strabo V 3, 11; Flor. II 9, 28. See also Cic. *in Cat.* I 8.
10. URBANA Zumpt, p. 252; Mommsen, p. 168; Pais, *Stor. coloniẓ.* 218 f.; Beloch, p. 512 and *id. Campanien²* 309. Cf. Plin. *NH* XIV 6(8), 62, and Lib. col. p. 232, 8 Lachmann, which certainly refers to Urbana.

B. UNCERTAIN

1. ABELLA Mommsen, p. 164; Beloch, p. 511 and *id. Campanien²* 411 f.; *CIL* X p. 136. Colony in 73 BC; Sall. *Hist.* III 97 Maur.
2. HADRIA Mommsen, p. 194; Beloch, p. 512. Called Veneria in *CIL* IX 5020. Colony in the Augustan period.

Allotments

A. CERTAIN

1. VOLATERRAE Zumpt, p. 261; Mommsen, p. 165; Pais, *Stor. Coloniz.* 267.
For the evidence see *Es. e Soc.* 122, n. 197 [= 45, n. 197 above]; not
improbable that it was a colony.

B. UNCERTAIN

1. FORUM CORNELII see *Es. e Soc.* 121, n. 196 [= 45, n. 196 above].
2. SPOLETIUM Zumpt, p. 254; Pais, *Serie cronol.* 355. See Flor. II 9, 27.
3. SUESSULA Zumpt, p. 255; Pais, *Stor. Coloniz.* 244. See Lib. col. p. 237,
   5 Lachmann.
4. TUSCULUM Zumpt, p. 255; Pais, *Stor. Coloniz.* 269. See Lib. col. p. 238,
   10 Lachmann. For the districts of Latium collected together in the Lib.
   col. under the name of Sulla (Aricia, Bovillae, Capitulum, Castrimoenium,
   Gabii) see *Es. e Soc.* 121, n. 196 [= 45, n. 196 above] and Mommsen,
   pp. 174–5.

III

The Origins
of the Social War
and Roman Politics
after 89 BC*

I
The extension of the Roman citizenship to the allies
and the tribunate of M. Livius Drusus (91 BC)

In the problem concerning the extension of the Roman citizenship to the Latins and Italians there is one point that can be regarded as certain: its origin is linked with the question of *res agraria* raised by the Gracchi at the end of the second century BC.[1] Yet we can see that it later became so deeply and inevitably involved with the other political problems of the age that the real cause of the revolt in 91 BC has been obscured. The ancient tradition tells of the allies' desire to obtain the *civitas*[2] but does not clearly explain what gave rise to this demand. Cicero indeed explains the revolt by referring to the *metus iudiciorum*:[3] that is, he relates it expressly to the most urgent political problem of the time. But while we may acknowledge the important connexion between the Social War and the Roman political struggle,[4] it is not possible to treat an event so vast in extent and so significant as the *Bellum Italicum* in terms of a single, specific question. In any case Cicero is here influenced by a special purpose of his own and finds it useful to avail himself of such an agreement, which in fact originated earlier at the time of the outbreak of the revolt, as the explanation contrived by the equestrian class and later reflected in the drafting of the famous *lex Varia*.[5] Another ancient author, Appian, although aware that the question of the allies was necessarily part of the general context of Roman politics, nevertheless expressly insists on the desire of the *socii* to obtain the *ius civitatis*, and his motivation for it, while admittedly generic, seems to give a better interpretation of the situation as a whole.

In order to resolve the problem it will help to consider why the Roman citizenship was wanted in 91 BC and above all by whom. It is as well to state at once – I shall try later to prove its truth – that the demand for Roman citizenship by the allies took a different form in 91 BC from that which it had taken in 125 BC. In that year, as we know, the proposal of the consul M. Fulvius Flaccus to grant the citizenship contained an alternative offer: for those allies who did not wish to accept the Roman citizenship the concession of the *ius provocationis* was envisaged.[6] The alternative is indeed used in the formula for rewarding non-Romans who prosecuted successfully in a trial *de repetundis*;[7] this broader use of the privilege may perhaps be responsible for an underestimation of its true significance when first it appeared in Flaccus' proposal. Yet, as has been rightly emphasized,[8] its occurrence is a significant proof of a widespread reluctance on the part of allied public opinion to surrender the substantial advantages they enjoyed under their traditional alliances in exchange for other advantages (the *ius civitatis*) which at that time were either not seen as so important, or at least not decisively so.

This indifference to the acquisition of Roman citizenship as an end in itself is a sign that the problem had arisen solely from outside causes (that is, the operation of the Gracchan *lex agraria*) and the passage in Appian which refers to the proposal of Flaccus and mentions that the *socii* wanted to share power,[9] should be seen simply as an attempt to link these events with the later phases of the problem. In other words, this passage reveals that the allies desired the citizenship and desired it for a particular reason, but this recognition itself dates from a time later than that of Flaccus' proposal. However, there is no logic in the argument that the origin of this desire must be attributed to the proposal of Flaccus, especially since in the period after 125 BC – with the exception of Caius Gracchus' policy which was again linked with the agrarian problem – we hear nothing more of the allied question, not even when there would have been every occasion for it (as in the *seditio Appuleiana* of 100 BC). Furthermore, the clause found both in Flaccus' proposal and in the *leges repetundarum* granting *provocatio* was clearly designed to meet a felt need of the allies, that they should be protected from the authority of Roman magistrates which was proving excessive and uncontrollable.[10] We may conclude that, if the allies did wish to gain the citizenship, this aim was rather limited and anyway arose from external factors that had nothing to do with the citizenship itself.

This conclusion holds for the events of 125 BC[11] but ceases to apply to the demand for citizenship in 91 BC. Then the concern of the *socii* to acquire Roman citizenship, a concern which had grown appreciably in the interim, becomes clearly explicit. It is no immediate objection to this that in 89 BC discussions took place at Heraclea and Naples on the question whether the allies should or should not accept the *civitas*,[12] since these were Greek cities whose *foedera* of alliance apparently granted specially privileged terms.[13] In 91 BC the demand for the citizenship appears in a form divorced from the agrarian question even though this had been revived by Drusus, and it is to this period that the situation suggested by the earlier passage of Appian refers.[14] What expressly marks this situation is the allies' demand to participate in the life of the ruling power by holding offices and by carrying out administrative duties.[15]

To demonstrate this we must examine the problems connected with Drusus' agrarian proposal. In Appian I 36, 162 the 'Ιταλιῶται are afraid of the law on the colonies;[16] in this passage there is no doubt that the name is used to designate the allies.[17] Bernardi,[18] relying on Appian's evidence, rightly emphasizes that Drusus' agrarian law was really a colonial law and so excluded individual allotments; he holds that it was devised in such a way as to safeguard the interests of the oligarchic latifundists. In order to maintain this Bernardi has to make a famous passage of Florus[19] refer to a threat by Drusus to propose a 'radical agrarian reform' at a point shortly before he was assassinated (and in any case after the repeal of this law) and accordingly he has to date to the same point of time the opposition by the Etruscans and Umbrians to Drusus which Appian mentions.[20] These peoples, because they were pro-oligarchic, would have been spared by the first law.

Carcopino[21] had also asked the question: 'was an exception made in favour of the *trientabula* (in the hands of the senatorial oligarchy) and of Campania?' and answered, citing the passage of Florus, 'very unlikely', though he held that the senators, being at odds with Drusus, would have been able to impede the operation of the law at a suitable moment. Yet Bernardi's view that the opposition to Drusus by the pro-oligarchic Etruscans and Umbrians arose later since they had been spared by the first Livian agrarian law with its oligarchic bias and were threatened only by the radical law which succeeded it, has a basic assumption in common with Carcopino's interpretation of the Social War. For the latter the rebel peoples were those whose territory had been used for the Gracchan allotments[22] and so the Etruscans and Umbrians, since they did not revolt (at least in the initial phase of the struggle), must have been spared earlier by the Gracchi[23] and did not anticipate any threat from Drusus either. This conclusion, which could not be valid for Arretium, Ferentinum and Tarquinii,[24] is unlikely on more general grounds; it would be very odd if Etruria, the very region whose desolation had suggested to Ti. Gracchus the initial idea of agrarian reforms, had been excluded when the reform was later put into effect.[25] The infertility of the Etruscan land can hardly have been a cause for excluding it since it is well-known that Etruria later saw allotments by Sulla, Caesar, the Triumvirs and Augustus.

It seems that we must give up the attempt to decide how or where the agrarian law of Drusus was put into effect,[26] and to see in this the cause of the opposition by the Etruscans and Umbrians. Yet this last event – which is decisive for what I wish to show – requires further investigation. Bernardi's argument is based on the fact that Appian I 36 mentions the Etruscans and

Umbrians coming to Rome at the invitation of the consuls to protest against the law (the *lex agraria*, one must understand) and to await τὴν τῆς δοκιμασίας ἡμέραν, and that this appears immediately before the passage recording Drusus' death. Although I agree that Appian's narrative is the most intelligent we possess for any evaluation of Drusus' activity,[27] it is clear that he has heavily abbreviated his source after the mention of the Etruscans and Umbrians. Suffice it to say that in the Greek historian we find not a word on the repeal of Drusus' laws; its mention ought to have come at this point and it could not, in my view, have been missing in Appian's source.[28] Furthermore, his statement that the Etruscans and Umbrians complained of the (agrarian) law and awaited the day of the δοκιμασία shows that they intervened after the voting on the agrarian (and jury-court) laws but before the repeal of the whole Livian legislation, since by δοκιμασία he must refer to the *rogatio de sociis*.[29] It is worth adding that in all probability the arrival of the Etruscans and Umbrians in Rome added new forces to the opposition to Drusus and, to take one example, made possible the election to the tribunate of certain violent enemies of Drusus like Varius.[30]

Finally, any idea that Drusus revolted against the Senate once his laws had been repealed, as is presupposed by Bernardi's reconstruction, is contradicted by a passage of Diodorus which there is no reason to challenge and which is, in fact, generally accepted.[31]

Given the argument so far, it follows that, if the words of Florus refer to the *lex agraria* of Drusus, we can understand the reasons which led the Senate, or that part of it which had been allied to Drusus, to change its own attitude. The law would have re-opened discussion on all the senatorial agrarian legislation passed after the Gracchi.[32] However great the selfishness and factious spirit of individual senators at the time,[33] it is incredible that the Senate abandoned Drusus only when he decided the Roman citizenship must be granted to the *socii*.[34] Such a development must have been easily foreseeable in view of the Gracchan precedent, and Drusus from the beginning of his tribunate must have made his own intentions clear – if we follow Appian's version which I believe to be preferable.

But a further conclusion of still greater importance is to be drawn. From Appian we learn that all the Italians without distinction were opposed to the agrarian law,[35] while the *rogatio de sociis* aroused the opposition of only the Etruscans and Umbrians.[36] What is more important, this difference of attitude appears not only in Appian's account but in the facts of the situation; the repeal of Drusus' legislation and hence of the *lex agraria*[37] did not dispel the opposition as one would have expected had it been the only or the principal cause of the evils (as was the case with the Gracchi). Rather it was only for the Etruscans and Umbrians that the crisis had passed and with it the need, for them, for a *rogatio de sociis*; meanwhile the other Italian allies turned to armed insurrection.[38]

For some time the basic reasons for this distinction have been understood to lie in the peculiar structure of Etrusco-Umbrian society; the rigid oligarchy on which it was based and the position of 'feudal' supremacy which the great landowners enjoyed would have been finally overthrown by any equality with the economically and socially inferior classes that might have resulted. It was natural, therefore, on the one hand that the consul L. Marcius Philippus in leading the opposition should have battened on to the discontent felt by the upper classes in Etruria and Umbria, and on the other that, once the *lex agraria* and the *rogatio de sociis* had failed, these regions should have taken no part in the revolt. In confirmation it is to be noted that these areas suffered disorders of a purely social nature when the grant of the citizenship was finally decided on by the Senate itself; parity of political rights brought with it the possibility of seizing power in some cities, and the lower classes sought to join the ranks of the rebels but were quickly suppressed.[39]

Clearly, then, the allies' interest in the Roman citizenship – we must exclude the special motives of the Etruscans and Umbrians – was no longer exclusively connected with *res agraria*, as it had been in the Gracchan period, but was directed to obtaining definite political advantages. The exasperation felt by the allies on the news of Drusus' death and the collapse of the *rogatio de sociis* shows that they saw more in the acts of the tribune than the simple reformer of the *quaestio de repetundis* or a man who tried to gain the support of the urban Plebs and the allies with laws of a demagogic character in order to play his own political hand from a position of strength. Since this is the picture that most of the tradition gives of Drusus,[40] it is perhaps as well once more to insist on the conception of his tribunate that we find in Appian where the problem of the allies predominates. The contacts between Drusus and the Italian leaders confirm this.[41]

Before we turn to examine the thirty-year period between C. Gracchus and the tribunate of Drusus, and to inquire why this change in allied opinion came about whereby the citizenship was henceforth to be seen as a means of sharing in Roman political life – a problem to be clarified by considering the growth of Roman imperialism in this period and its effects on the social structure of Rome and Italy – we must first define the class of allies that would gain from the *ius civitatis* a concrete advantage and not merely an *imago sine re*.

II
The upper classes in rebel Italy

The Roman state's structure at the end of the second century BC was of such a kind that even to the allies one point must have been clear: an extension of citizenship, when eventually made, could guarantee to the majority of the new citizens only limited advantage in that sphere where the benefits of the *ius civitatis* could be most directly exercised, that is to say in participation in the political assemblies.

From the middle of the second century BC it is clear that Roman citizens living in outlying districts were prevented, by force of circumstances, from intervening often in the life of the state, and that their political concern was consequently weakened. Hence it is impossible to see what advantages, in terms of practical politics, the majority of the allies could have expected from a grant of the citizenship; their situation was very like that of Roman *cives* from country districts. Furthermore, it does not seem very evident what meaning or importance the civil rights contained in the *civitas* could have had for them.

To a large extent the opposite is true of the allied upper classes.[42] There are some points which will show that it was really they who were agitating for the *civitas*. In its first phase the revolt of the *socii* was certainly not popular in character even if it was not actually aristocratic, as was already observed by Mérimée,[43] and, despite the outburst of popular anti-Roman hatred witnessed at Asculum,[44] it was only in a second phase that the revolt took on a popular aspect. This was no doubt stimulated by means of a propaganda that dwelt mainly on themes of regional separatism and independence, and these themes naturally had little relevance to the central problem of the Roman citizenship.[45] In any case, the conduct of political and military affairs seems to have remained in the hands of upper class leaders; the exceptions are the attempted insurrections of the Etruscans and Umbrians which, as I have suggested above, fall into a different and special category. That this thesis is correct is shown by the names of rebel leaders recorded in the sources. These, so far as we can judge, belonged to the upper classes.[46]

We must define, however, what we understand by 'upper classes'. It was Mommsen's view[47] that in the regions of the Abruzzi and neighbouring areas the rural middle class survived in greater cohesion and greater strength than elsewhere in Italy and that this middle class started the rebellion; the municipal aristocracy, on the other hand, kept on good terms with the Roman government. In fact, the first part of this hypothesis has already been shown by Carcopino[48] to be unsupported by evidence, and is difficult to accept; what we know of the social structure of the allied communities in the second century BC points to the conclusion that the changes which are better attested for the organization of *cives Romani* were taking place among the allies also.[49] What we do know, with sufficient supporting evidence, is that Campania, and to a lesser degree Apulia and Lucania and still less Picenum, show the presence of a social class actively pursuing commercial operations, and acquiring wealth thereby, alongside the old landed aristocracy. In short, the process is to some extent analogous to what was happening at Rome in the same period; as far as we can see, however, it was both more marked and more diffuse since the Italian commercial element, by inheriting the role of its predecessors from the Greek cities of the south, held in its hands the small, medium and large-scale trade both with East and West.

In the West the connexions between southern Italy and the Spanish provinces during the second century BC took the form of migration of Oscan-speaking groups;[50] in Africa substantial business contacts are known to us in the period of the Jugurthine War, and these in turn explain the emigration of the Sullan period for which the causes were often political.[51] Finally, the *negotiatores* present in Sicily in Cicero's time originated largely in southern Italy, as is evident from the nomenclature recorded in the Verrines.[52]

It is in the East, however, that the Italian *negotiatores* held a monopoly of trade during the second and first centuries BC. Dubois first stressed the predominance of the Campanians on Delos but his suggestions have been greatly extended and developed by the researches of Hatzfeld:[53] men from Campania, Apulia and Samnium are either specifically attested or can be inferred from their *gentilicia*, and are to be found alongside a small minority of Latins, Etruscans and others from central and northern Italy in general. This widespread commercial activity had two inevitable results, equal in their extreme significance but different in effect. The first was that this class of *negotiatores* acquired a socially dominant position in their home cities – as the Equites did at Rome – for traders tended either to return to their native city or to keep up connexions with it which varied in individual circumstances. The involvement with the class of landed proprietors is especially noteworthy; it derived on the one side from various motives of self-interest and on the other from the direct investment in land of the wealth obtained in trade.[54]

The economic impetus given to their cities by this group, dedicated to commerce but not reluctant to invest in property, finds a conspicuous expression in the programmes of building and renovation which seem to be a feature of the Italian towns in the late second century BC and of which we are well-informed through Pompeii and Capua.[55] The natural political consequence was that members of the commercial class very often held the highest magistracies.[56]

Secondly, it followed that the commercial class had of necessity to concern itself with Roman foreign policy and, as a result of this, to assume a more definitive attitude towards the events of Roman domestic politics where the successes and defeats of opposing political groups were tending more and more to determine policies abroad. It is customary to accept the view to which Rostovtzeff added his *imprimatur*,[57] and assert that the Italian upper classes had little interest in interfering in Roman politics and hence in influencing decisions of policy. Their horizons were still confined to the narrow and restricted worlds of individual towns. As will be argued more fully later,[58] the truth is probably the exact opposite. In fact the Italian *negotiatores* must have been struck by the contrast between their positions in the East and in Italy. In their commercial activities they could be considered men of high repute and be generally identified with the great political power which in truth they represented; the Greek world could not distinguish between *cives Romani* and allies, and called them all 'Ρωμαῖοι.[59] At home precisely the opposite was the case. Apart from professional contacts between the Italian commercial class and the Roman capitalists – admittedly close but with little real effect in practical politics – the *negotiatores* must have been well aware that their whole way of life was at the mercy of the Roman ruling classes who as oligarchs naturally saw the interests of the Italian commercial class as mere side-issues in the game of politics. Roman indifference will have become especially clear (and perhaps, indeed, became so for the first time) in the last decades of the second century BC as the policies of the Roman business class took shape and as the chances of conflict between political and economic interests became more apparent. *Cives Romani* and allies were on the same level in the trading areas in East and West, and indeed the latter might have been in a stronger position there because of their greater numbers; in Italy, on the other hand, the allies must, as Appian says, have felt that they were ὑπήκοοι. Hatzfeld[60] has already shown that the centre of the allied revolt corresponds in general terms to the areas from which Italian *negotiatores* came; perhaps they wished to win at home the equality they could freely enjoy in their Eastern communities? Here the modern historian may find himself agreeing with that ancient writer who saw the Italian allies conceiving at a particular moment a desire to share in the ἡγεμονία.

In view of what has been outlined above we should expect that the feelings and wishes of the commercial class would soon be adopted as the common demands of all, even of those whose positions were less directly concerned with business but were based mainly on landed estates. They, the jealous custodians of the autonomy of individual districts of Italy, had long resented their state of inferiority and subservience, the more so as the centralization of the Roman government increased.[61] Commercial classes and landowners, already united by economic ties, shared a common sentiment by 91 BC and display to the historian a single front which fully justifies the use of the general term 'upper classes' to refer to them.

At this point an inquiry into Roman foreign policy in the thirty years between C. Gracchus and M. Livius Drusus becomes necessary; even though limited to the larger perspectives it will serve to show how the Italian upper classes began their pressure to join the citizenship body, a pressure which eventually became the cause of a bloody struggle.

III
The principles of Roman foreign policy from the Gracchi to the Social War

In the historical literature of the first century BC it became a common theme to regard the middle of the preceding century as the point when the Roman state began to decline. The causes of the decline were sometimes seen in the destruction of Carthage, which political leaders of the time had resented on the grounds that Carthage represented the one deterrent capable of allaying the latent dissensions in society;[62] sometimes the moralizing vein was stressed of a disintegration of the virtue and *mos maiorum* which had guided the rise of the Republic, a disintegration produced by Rome's victories in the East.[63] At all events one can see a breakdown in internal equilibrium, and most modern historians would interpret it as part of a more general problem, of the transition from city-state to Empire. However, to the politicians and historians of the end of the Republic it seemed in many ways to be a revival of the traditional theme of the earliest history of Rome, the Struggle of the Orders; the conflict had been healed by combining the patrician families and new plebeian *gentes* who had experience of government into a *nobilitas*, but now it seemed to re-emerge as the struggle of an inferior part of the citizen body against the *boni cives*.[64]

In this struggle we see the increasing gap between the ruling class and social reality, and the pressure from new classes powerfully thrust into public life by the changing political conditions; at the same time a fracture began to appear even within the class which held power, between the senatorial *ordo* and the Equites, a ruinous development (so it was regarded) at the very time when it was essential rather to unite the upper classes against the irruption of hostile forces. The *concordia ordinum*, the *consensus omnium bonorum* came therefore to represent for Cicero not simply an ideal but a genuine goal to be achieved at all costs and pursued continuously and purposefully in his political career.[65]

In this situation the conflict between Senate and Equites became a *leit-motif* – at least for those who were inclined to support the oligarchs in their politics and historiography. The entire history of the post-Gracchan age could be seen in terms of the struggle, although it took different forms and the nature of the conflict was not the same before and after Sulla. C. Gracchus is commonly presented as the *iniquus* creator of the conflict: *equestri ordini iudicia tradidit ac bicipitem civitatem fecit, discordiarum civilium fontem.*[66]

Certainly the conflict which existed in the late second and early first centuries BC must have seemed extraordinary and extremely grave. Attitudes had been acquired and ideas formed in a political context where such dis-agreements as there had been were quite different in kind from those we have seen existing between Senate and Equites. Disagreements had arisen only within the same closed circle and usually spent themselves within it, without flowing over into other areas. However, we should not accept this point of view of the ancient politicians and historians in its entirety. The more we look at this conflict, the stronger becomes the impression, at least to my mind, that the exchanges of political trials retailed in the tradition as a sort of manifestion of the struggle and by their very nature fleeting, isolated moments involving a variety of interests, are indeed the conflict itself; this *is not* so much to reduce the conflict to, as to *identify* it with, particular disagreements about specific problems or about an individual's actions, and with the play of political forces at a given moment. In other words, one cannot speak of a conflict of social classes, struggling to gain the upper hand, nor of two groups formed along the lines of party politics; this carries with it the risk of implying the existence of alternative governments when in fact there was no choice.

The conflict was certainly profound but mainly because the interests of the two *ordines* were different in kind rather than simply opposed – political on the one side and economic on the other. However, it took place in an established framework that both sides accepted and on a few occasions jointly defended when they deliberately tempered the clash of ideals and basic positions.[67]

Of course we shall understand the nature of this conflict better if we consider how it arose. This question is connected with another, the formation of the equestrian class as we know it from the time of the Gracchi onwards. Ancient tradition emphasized that C. Gracchus was responsible for the opposition of Senate and Equites. Yet it is obvious that, however great this responsibility may have been, the ground must have been already prepared or, to put it a different way, Gracchus must have known how to seize the opportunity to play upon a latent hostility or on struggles already existing. Gracchus' ability, therefore, lay in translating into a concrete political programme (albeit in foreign policy, for differences about provincial administration really belonged here) what until then had been an obscure and spasmodic theme; with the concession of the *iudicia* to the Equites the struggle found both a permanent cause and a lasting source of friction.

We should, then, reject the theory that Gracchus created the equestrian order or even the alternative that, by the simple and arbitrary instrument of fixing a *census equester* as the necessary requirement in choosing the new *iudices* in the *quaestio de repetundis*, Gracchus united the scattered groups hitherto engaged in commerce and so produced the equestrian class of the post-Gracchan and Ciceronian periods; this theory can be seen as both too abstract and historically ill-founded. It rests on too rigid a conception of social changes and above all it mistakes political aims and trends for real changes in the social order. It is one thing to see Gracchus as revealing a political situation, as acutely detecting real differences of underlying motives, and so as giving political form to hitherto vague purposes of the equestrian class by setting it at odds with the governing *nobilitas*; it is another to imagine that Gracchus by his actions had created a new social class – the equestrian order – which must indeed have existed already, for it is presupposed by his actions and their effects as we have indicated them above.

It is clear that the equestrian class as we know it in the post-Gracchan period, with its particular attitudes and policies fairly well defined, can only have come into being at a time when circumstances were such as to allow this development. In this case the economic and commercial foundations of the equestrian class and the growth of their power were related to a process which can be precisely defined and, within somewhat broad limits, dated as well: Rome's expansion and the consequent opportunities (which became immediately clear) of milking the provinces. The process obviously belongs to a period before the Gracchi. Of course this does not mean that there were no social groups engaged in business activity before that time, but their interests, in the context of politics, must have taken a different form. The point to emphasize is this: so long as business life and economic interests observed the traditional limits of the city-state, or at least so long as the city-state was considered to be fundamental for them, no conflict of principle on two different levels, the one economic and the other political, could emerge.

But when business and economic activity began to expand more widely and contacts were established with foreign powers – the result of Rome's increase beyond limits compatible with its city-state structure – the first examples of friction necessarily started to make themselves felt. Indeed, under the promptings of the profit motive, an attitude dictated by economic and commercial considerations spread very rapidly, if not immediately, in these new conditions, and so automatically came into conflict with the outlook of the governing class whose traditional ideas still prevailed and who still continued to think in purely political terms.

Before we consider, albeit briefly, when this conflict began and when, as a consequence, economic considerations started to enter, although irregularly, into political decisions, it is of the highest importance to remember what has clearly emerged so far. The struggle between the political and commercial classes, from that time and almost continually thereafter, has as its setting those issues of foreign policy that could provoke a real conflict of different views, whereas it is as well always to bear in mind that in domestic policy the position of the two opposing social groups was regarded, in practice, as fixed. Differences in this field did not endanger the more important concept of upper class unity. This comes out clearly on those occasions when it was thought there was a threat to the whole social order (Saturninus, Catiline). These are our terms of reference for evaluating the sporadic support given by the equestrian class to the *populares* in their attempts to win power.

If the second half of the third century BC shows us the importance of groups dedicated to commerce and business in Roman life,[68] it is only with the second century BC that we can be sure of their political influence. Modern historians are not unanimous in their assessment of the extent and importance of Roman commercial interests in the East in this period nor do they all recognize that some of the more important events of the middle of the second century BC show economic factors at work.[69] It seems, however, difficult to deny that considerations other than those of pure politics lay behind the punitive measures taken against Rhodes after the Third Macedonian War (167–166 BC) and in the choice of Delos as a free port[70] and also in the taking of such extremely serious decisions as the destruction of Corinth and of Carthage.[71]

On the other hand, one should not forget that the activity of equestrian *societates* in the exploitation of the Spanish mines dates from 179 BC[72] and this activity must have been a topic of much discussion if we can trust Livy; he says that in 167 BC the Senate ordered the Macedonian mines to be closed to avoid the evil consequences resulting from the letting of contracts to companies of *publicani*.[73] In any case it is at the very least worthy of note that the transformation of Macedonia into a province (148 BC) was preceded by the institution of the *quaestio de repetundis*.[74]

In the Gracchan period economic factors came to be ever more important in Roman politics and at the same time they were more clearly defined; as a natural corollary points of friction between the Senatorial governing class and the capitalists, who had now become a very important element in Roman society, could emerge more clearly. They came to represent, as I have said, one of the most common features in Roman life. The organization of the province of Asia (129 BC) probably represents the victory of Senatorial policy, which aimed at maintaining the traditional structure of the state and was therefore opposed to any increase in territory subject to the Roman government. Its policy was to limit provincial territory to the basic minimum by granting to allied monarchs the remoter districts of the ex-kingdom of Pergamum.[75] The displeasure of the capitalists at seeing their zone of influence restricted perhaps inspired the trial of M'. Aquilius in 125 BC.[76] It was appeased a little later (123 BC) when C. Gracchus had a law passed which reorganized the administration of Asia;[77] as a result capitalist activity in the province increased.[78] It is difficult to regard this outcome as accidental when one thinks of the relationships, however obscure to us they may be, of C. Gracchus with the Campanian business class.[79] It should in fact be viewed as part of a general programme which contained the famous *lex iudiciaria* that made over the jury-courts in the *quaestio de repetundis* to the knights and which belongs to Gracchus' first tribunate.[80]

Without suggesting that this episode has the epoch-making character which has been attributed to it by the ancient tradition, it certainly represents the central point of Gracchus' policy of giving political expression to the Equites' economic interests. Henceforth we really are in a position to see in the development of Roman foreign policy the alternating flow of two currents which seek to shape and direct Rome's approach to her relationship with other states. These two currents can, in general terms, be traced back to two sources: on the one hand the conservative policy of safeguarding the state's structure and therefore of restricting any extension of the Empire's boundaries, and on the other the Equites' desire for a policy of expansion and intervention, in line with their views on economic growth. Clearly the difference of principles and outlook vindicates, or rather explains, the bitterness of trials used to hit at the representatives of ideas they opposed; it also explains why they ended frequently in trivial feuds and as outlets for personal vendettas.

As a result, a temporary victory in Roman domestic politics for those opposed to the oligarchs led at once to an equally transitory success of the capitalists in foreign policy. It is wrong, however, to think in terms of clear-cut positions in Roman politics which was always conducted on a rather restricted stage. Indeed in 123 BC we find a settlement of Roman citizens in the Balearics, the work of Q. Caecilius Metellus, and the absence on this occasion of senatorial opposition to transmarine colonization cannot simply be explained by the fact that the colonists were Romans from Spain.[81] A little later, indeed, the founding of a colony at Narbo Martius in 118 BC sees the popular party in alliance with the commercial class and opposed to the conservative-minded oligarchs.[82]

The conflict becomes significant politically in the context of the Numidian question (111–103 BC). Although scholars have argued in this case also against an equestrian policy of aggression, or at least of expansion,[83] the evidence is all too explicit and leads to the clear conclusion that behind the anti-oligarchic activity of the popular faction and the pressure of Marius definite economic interests are at work.[84] Among this evidence perhaps the most important is that which Frank thought supported his own view, the organization of Numidia.[85]

However, in 106 BC Q. Servilius Caepio, unquestionably taking advantage of a political situation at Rome which eludes us, succeeded in restoring to the senators, perhaps only in part, the jury-courts in the *quaestio de repetundis*.[86] They retained this privilege down to 100 BC, even – and it is a point which at first sight seems astonishing – during the years of Marius' consulships. Probably the danger posed by the Cimbri and Teutones counselled moderation and solidarity in domestic politics. However, if the African colonization of 103 BC did not arouse opposition among the oligarchs,[87] some of whom took part in the commission which was established, the *lex Appuleia de maiestate* of the same year provided the legal instrument by which Servilius Caepio could be attacked for his responsibility for the defeat at Arausio.[88] It is true that the condemnation of the other general, Cn. Mallius, may encourage us to think of these trials as resulting rather from a general agreement to assign blame than from purely party motives.[89] We should also remember that in 102 BC[90] Appuleius Saturninus attempted – though the evidence records only the violence to which he resorted – to oppose that conservative foreign policy which was resigned to non-intervention *vis-à-vis* Mithridates; the latter begins to loom up on the Eastern horizon.[91] This episode seems to represent the start of a period in which Eastern problems come to receive more attention, and it is not, to be sure, pure coincidence that in these same years, as the wealth of inscriptional evidence attests,[92] one can see Roman and Italian commercial expansion flourishing as never before in the East. These are the years in which the Italian community on Delos reaches a position of great wealth, as is attested by the construction of the agora; this position is never reached again in the future. These closing years of the second century BC witness Marius' victories over the Cimbri and Teutones, and, as a result, the supremacy of those opposed to the oligarchs; they assume, especially in 100 BC, an exceptional concentration of power. It therefore follows that the growth of Eastern interests has a close connexion with the political situation at home.

The measures taken in 102–101 BC against the pirates may have represented a concession to the commercial class who had suffered losses in their trading;[93] what is at any rate certain is the intervention of the vested interests of this class in the measures taken in 101–100 BC. I would like to mention here the well-known Pirates Law preserved at Delphi in the monument of Aemilius Paulus;[94] we must try to evaluate its significance without exaggerating it. Even though the arguments of Passerini[95] rule out the possibility that this text can prove, as Carcopino wished to argue,[96] the intention of the *populares* in 101[97] to confer an Asiatic command on Marius in 99 BC, the preoccupation of the Pirates Law with safeguarding the free movement of sea-trade does attest the atmosphere in which it came to be passed. It is the very atmosphere in which a further law was successfully proposed that the knights should be restored to the jury-courts in the *quaestio de repetundis* (the *lex Servilia Glauciae* of 100 BC) and in which Marius' Eastern tour was launched. From certain points of view this tour symbolized official approval of the role played by the *populares* and by Marius himself in favour of the interests of the capitalists and the business class.[98] At that time Marius' brother-in-law, C. Iulius Caesar, was govenor of Asia.[99] It is probable that Marius represented to the Senate the gravity of the situation in the East, even if it is difficult to be certain whether his views had any practical effect;[100] the alleged connexions between the senatorial class and Mithridates on which the opposition's propaganda delighted to dwell and which must belong to this period (99–91 BC) are significant and show that the governing class continued to entertain ideas opposed to any policy of offensive action. These accusations, which are closely connected with the trials launched against members of the senatorial aristocracy,[101] implicated the *princeps senatus*, M. Aemilius Scaurus; in view of the well-known connexions of that oligarchic leader with the capitalists and with Marius himself,[102] one may deduce that personal considerations played a large part, as often in Roman political life.[103]

Coinciding with the Social War came Mithridates' invasion of Asia. Its immediate cause was the rash provocation offered by M'. Aquilius, egged on by commercial interests.[104] The interference of the *negotiatores* is clearly attested by Appian who says that King Nicomedes of Bithynia, even though he had only just been restored to his throne, was forced to make forays into the territory of Mithridates by Roman pressure; they had lent him large sums and hoped for restitution from a policy of pillage and conquest.[105] The results of the war were disastrous and Roman losses in men and money enormous.[106] Inscriptional evidence allows us to get some idea of the destruction, and of the slow and no longer resplendent restoration, of the commercial colony of Delos.[107] What we know of the financial provisions of 85 BC can be attributed to the collapse, albeit temporary, of the fortunes of the capitalist and commercial class[108] in Asia.

All this serves to explain how the Equites wanted to push Sulpicius in 88 BC[109] into his well-known anti-Sullan policy. Since Sulla, presumably as the Senate's champion, could not provide adequate guarantees that his policy would be carried out with vigour and decision, men turned to a man like C. Marius, whose interests were well-known, and chose him to put a definite end to the threat offered by Mithridates.

In these last few pages I have tried to summarize the foreign policies of Roman political groups in the period 123–91 BC and, as a consequence, the interests and inspirations behind these policies which bring out their true nature for us. There are two different policies here: the first, a policy of favouring military expansion as a basis for economic and commercial expansion, and secondly a policy of conservatism, aiming as far as possible at maintaining the traditional structure of the state and therefore opposed to a policy of intervention. These policies are the product of different categories of interest, one economic, the other political. I have tried at the same time to show how these two policies, first one then the other, and in association with factors of domestic politics, influenced the course of action adopted by the Roman government; they robbed it of stability and power of decision. I have also emphasized the way in which questions of foreign policy interacted with the political situation at home.

We must now consider – again for the period 123–91 BC – how these

conflicts in Roman foreign policy affected the problem of the allies, since it
is precisely in the field of foreign affairs that the allies' demand for the
Roman citizenship came to fruition.

IV
The Italian allies and Roman foreign policy

The Italian allies found themselves confronted with changing policies in
Roman foreign affairs, depending on the amount of influence exercised by the
two parties engaged in the Roman political struggle or on the victory of one
over the other. As a result they must have maintained an attitude of vigilance
and followed with rapt attention the slightest development in events. When
we refer to 'the capitalist class' or 'the commercial class' we must remember
that while the class of Roman Equites was for the most part interested in the
contracts concerning provincial taxes, all small and medium-sized business
and most of the large-scale enterprises were in the hands of *negotiatores* of
Italian origin.[110]

It is therefore highly probable that the policy of political and economic
expansion pursued by the Roman capitalist class, at least from the second
half of the second century BC onwards, found support from the class of
Italian *negotiatores* because of their common interests.[111] In any event it is
no accident that, when we speak of Italian traders anywhere in the Mediterranean world, we cannot point to even the minutest privilege which distinguished those who were *cives Romani* from those who were *socii*.[112] This
shows above all that in business the two must have worked hand in hand,
so much so that any difference at law was of minor importance; we may
conclude from this that connexions founded on common interests were
established in politics as well. This seems beyond argument even if, of
course, it is difficult to support with precise evidence. All we can do is
adduce individual cases, but these are extremely significant: for example, the
massacre of the Italian *negotiatores* at Cirta and the pro-war policy of the
Roman capitalists.[113] Likewise the Italians dedicating a statue to Marius on
Delos would have included more than citizens, and the significance of the
dedication certainly extends beyond a feeling of gratitude to the conqueror
of the Cimbri; it attests recognition that Marius' political activity promoted
their common interests.

Roman capitalists and Italian *negotiatores*, then, shared common political
ground. This is shown by the fact that in the struggle between Marius and
Sulla the Italian businessmen, and especially those from Campania, chose to
range themselves alongside the *populares* and therefore alongside the Equites.
I have tried elsewhere to explain this by examining the composition and outlook of the Campanian upper classes;[114] many of the people I have mentioned there would possibly have been Roman citizens already before 91 BC,

like the Granii of the colony of Puteoli. But others (e.g. the Pedii) were not,[115] and we can trace no difference in their political attitudes.[116]

In the provinces there was a close business connexion between *cives* and *socii*, and the latter's relationship with the Equites reinforced their interest in foreign affairs. Given all this, they were bound to regard it as proportionately all the more serious that their status in their native land should be one of subjection. The very fact that the upper class rebels were largely involved in the Marian faction and played a decisive part in it, together with the fact that the rest of the rebels supported the Marians,[117] shows how strongly they felt the need, contrary to what is usually believed, to acquire more influence in Roman politics and, above all, in foreign policy decisions. This need must be seen against the background of the post-Gracchan period, i.e. the last years of the century, the time when expansion of Italian trade in the Mediterranean basin was at its height and when the most acute differences of political principle were to be seen at Rome. This was a period when Italian aspirations could not be denied.

This Italian influence in Roman affairs, the need to make their voices heard in those decisions which concerned them intimately, could only be achieved, and then in a partial and insignificant way, through the agency of the Roman capitalist class, the Equites. The allies must have seen how firmly entrenched the oligarchic government of the Senate was, with its traditionalist ideas in domestic policy and its consequently limited perspective in foreign policy (this was proved by the way the composition of the jury-courts in the *quaestio de repetundis* chopped and changed). They saw also that, when faced with an urgent domestic crisis, this very conflict of Senate and knights could resolve itself, and they saw finally that the equestrian order had not succeeded in imposing a coherent and lasting programme of its own to solve problems of foreign policy. The collapse of the 'democratic' movement after 100 BC and the oligarchic reaction which followed (NB the *lex Licinia Mucia* of 95 BC) were both clear signs of what was happening.

For the Italians to achieve a decisive influence in Roman politics only one solution offered: they must take a direct part in politics itself. To do this, of course, they needed to possess the Roman citizenship. Only in this way could they be κοινωνοὶ τῆς ἡγεμονίας. In fact it was the upper classes of those districts which later rebelled who sought the Roman citizenship; only they were truly interested in it.

The difference between the Gracchan proposals, offered and accepted purely in the context of the agrarian problem, and Drusus' tribunate in 91 BC is profoundly important. The latter was the last occasion when the Italians could hope to see Roman political groups taking decisions to accept their demands. But it was only an illusion. For on that occasion they found ranged against them not only the senatorial oligarchs but also the Equites themselves. The latter opposed them, not, as was the case with the senators, because they felt a principle was at stake and reacted accordingly (after 89, as we shall see, the Equites looked favourably even on the admission of new citizens to all the thirty-five tribes) but because the grant of citizenship to the *socii* was tied to a provision which transferred the courts in the *quaestio* back to the senators, even if the latter were not to have a monopoly. This could under no circumstances win the approval of the equestrian class.[118]

In this context it is legitimate to emphasize, as some have done, the fact that the political struggle at Rome and the revolt of the *socii* are connected in so far as they have similar aspirations. However, if we are to limit our inquiry to the causes of the *Bellum Sociale*, the political conflict at Rome and the tribunate of Drusus are only pretexts, they are not the decisive factor. The real, substantial cause of the war lies in the long and complex process which produced in the allies a new kind of need and a new kind of outlook. If we examine the *lex Varia*, an illustration of the Roman political struggle in these closely-packed years in one of its most typical aspects, we shall find a new proof that the connexions between the Social War and Roman politics as it existed on the eve of that war are fortuitous by nature and not an essential part of the story; the *lex Varia* can also throw light on the Equites' attitude towards the allies' demands.

V
The lex Varia *and the relations of the Italian rebels with Mithridates*

The ratification of the *lex Varia* in the early months of 90 BC[119] represents the culminating point of the Equites' counter-offensive, in league as they were with that section of the Senate which had as its leader the ex-consul, L. Marcius Philippus, and in opposition to the followers of Livius Drusus. The law aimed at smashing those senators who had championed Drusus' efforts in favour of the Italians.[120] We must be clear that we are not dealing with a measure directed, principally or uniquely, against the demand of the *socii* for the citizenship; its purpose must be interpreted in a much broader sense if we are to understand its meaning and significance. In particular we should remember that only by using such a charge could any move stand a good chance of influencing the popular assembly, and also Drusus' own supporters had begun to detach themselves from him as soon as the agrarian law was approved; the *rogatio de sociis* had been proposed effectively on Drusus' own initiative, and this must have been well-known.[121] In fact, the Equites were basing their action on those Livian proposals which had a pro-Senate flavour and principally that which concerned the *quaestio de repetundis*; these proposals, by a chain of circumstance, certainly produced the allied revolt and this, at the time when the *lex Varia* was approved, was the most glaring fact for everyone to see. This is clear to Appian and, in the passage I have cited which lists the benefits the knights were promised by the law, he does not mention a final refusal of the allies' demands but speaks instead of the possibility of breaking the Senate's supremacy and, above all, of winning control of the jury-courts *de repetundis* (δικάσειν μὲν αὐτοί).[122]

Later, of course, as the names of the accused reveal, the *quaestio ex lege Varia* was transformed and became a sort of special tribunal. The connexions with what was alleged to be the original cause weakened still more, and free play was made with the possibility of bringing down that part of the senatorial class which governed Rome. This explains how even M. Aemilius Scaurus could come to be accused; there is good evidence on his relationships with the provincial capitalists and *negotiatores* as well as on his hostility to the allies' demands.

In any event Scaurus' case shows, perhaps, that one cannot use the Mithridates affair to connect Varius' law and the allied problem. In fact the evidence of Val. Max. III 7, 8: *quod ab rege Mithridate ob rem publicam prodendam pecuniam accepisset* (Scaurus), which refers to an accusation of Varius against Scaurus after the installation of the former as tribune on December 10th, 91 BC,[123] has wrongly been rejected;[124] it can perfectly well stand as an example of harking back to a type of complaint traditionally favoured by the equestrian class[125] and employed against the same Scaurus on two other occasions, first by Servilius Caepio in a trial *de repetundis ex lege Servilia Glauciae*, apropos a rather obscure *legatio Asiatica*,[126] the second by the same Caepio in another trial launched against Scaurus in 90 BC on the basis of the *lex Varia* when Scaurus was accused of *proditio*.[127]

The fact that this theme occurs in a charge brought under the *lex Varia* seems to rule out the possibility that the law dealt in practice with the problem of the allies, and therefore it confirms that the Equites, for whose attitude we have other evidence, looked kindly on the demands of the *socii*. This is all the more true because we cannot follow those[128] who hold that in the charges laid by Varius and Caepio (the latter's second charge) against Scaurus, to the effect that he had been bribed with gold from Mithridates, there were hints, more or less spelled out, of the relationships which we know from other sources to have prevailed between the rebel Italians and Mithridates.[129] In fact these overtures for alliance (which made no progress; a solid pact had to await Sertorius) are attested at least two years after the *lex Varia*, in 88 BC, both by Posidonius[130] who placed them after the massacre of the Italians in Asia, and by Diodorus,[131] who dated them to a time when Mithridates did not yet control the whole of Asia[132] but when the rebel Italians were fighting in the last ditch. Since there is no reason to accept the view[133] that these negotiations dragged on over the years, they were clearly the work of those extremist and independent elements which reappeared later, for example in 83 BC and alongside Sertorius, and equally clearly there is no connexion with the charges laid under the *lex Varia*. These negotiations in any event must have been conducted by people familiar with the East and with Mithridates, and to some extent reconfirm that the class of *negotiatores* played a leading role in the revolt; they were the only class which had the necessary qualifications.

The *lex Varia* represents, then, the climax in the dispute between Senate and Equites, and the gravity of the situation engendered by the allied revolt succeeded only to a limited extent in composing this dispute, at least on the surface. The civil struggle which followed the insurrection of the *socii* provided an opportunity for those extremists opposed to the oligarchs, that is the Marian 'democrats', to take over the government of the state by force. The Equites quickly saw that this 'democratic' government was inclined to look more favourably on their own interests and their own demands, and gave it their support.

The problem of the allies dominates these years also but obviously its nature and appearance change. The oligarchy sought in fact to 'contain' the gains which the allies had snatched from them by resorting to an old expedient which earlier had yielded good results, although the circumstances were completely different: they confined the enrolment of the *novi cives* to a limited number of tribes. It was over the question of maintaining this distinction that the last battle came to be fought by the defenders of the old Roman city-state.

VI

The extension of the Roman citizenship to the socii

Confronted with the outbreak of the revolt the Senate had no alternative but to accept, albeit gradually, the petition of the allies; that is to say, realizing that the object of the revolt had always been the grant of the *civitas*, this they conceded. The preliminaries to the armed struggle and the way in which the tide of battle ebbed and flowed show clearly that the majority of the allies were glad to welcome Roman recognition of their demands, however belated it was. Their attitude is summed up in a source paraphrasing a conversation between one of the principal rebel chiefs and the Roman leaders: 'They struggled to gain admission to the Roman citizenship, not to snatch it from the Romans.'[134] The laws which granted the *civitas* were the *lex Iulia* of 90 BC and the *lex Plautia Papiria* of 89. While the evidence of the sources, especially Cicero's *pro Archia* and *pro Balbo*, combines to give us a clear idea of the two laws and their content, so much so that there is no need to stress it here,[135] we cannot be sure what actual mechanism was set up to control the admission of the *socii* to the citizenship. This is a point of exceptional interest since the problem *de novorum civium suffragiis* was the really vital one in the years stretching from the end of the Social War down to Sulla's landing in Italy; if we can find the right interpretation a flood of light will illuminate the different themes of the Roman political struggle in those years.

The passages which come up for discussion in this problem are: Appian, I 49, 214 and 53, 231;[136] Velleius, II 20, 2, and Sisenna, fr. 17 Peter. I begin by examining the Sisenna passage. Fragment 17 reads: *L. Calpurnius Piso ex senati consulto duas novas tribus.*

On the basis of the chronology established for the books of Sisenna it is generally maintained that this fragment, which comes from Book III, dates to the year 89 BC,[137] and scholars hold that the Calpurnius mentioned here was tribune in that year.[138] Some, however, connect this fragment with Sisenna fr. 120, which reads: *milites ut lex Calpurnia concesserat virtutis ergo civitate donari*, and without question connect the *lex Calpurnia* recorded there with the measure of fr. 17, maintaining that the law under discussion regulated both the admission of the allies to the ranks of citizens and the grant of citizenship for military services.

This reconstruction contains, however, some points which are not clear: if the *lex Calpurnia* dates to 89, it would be later than the *lex Iulia* of 90 which already envisaged the possibility of grants of citizenship for military service, and extensively too; indeed, it was on the basis of the *lex Iulia* that a grant was made in November 89 as the famous inscription of Pompeius Strabo from Asculum shows.[139] The *lex Calpurnia*, at least on this point, would have been unnecessary. It was certainly to meet this difficulty that Carcopino held that the *lex Calpurnia* was passed before the *lex Iulia*[140] and that Schur[141] made Calpurnius tribune in 90 BC instead of 89.

We could dispense with this line of argument if we accepted Niccolini's view[142] that the *lex Calpurnia*, as far as grants *virtutis causa* were concerned, limited the operations of the *lex Iulia*. This view is supported by a description of the way in which the power granted to magistrates *cum imperio* to award the citizenship developed, which we may summarize as follows: although Pompeius Strabo's decree was perfectly legal, the grant of the *civitas* to whole groups of *peregrini* would not have secured approval, and the *lex Calpurnia* would in fact have regularized the position by allowing grants of the citizenship only *viritim* or *singillatim*. The *lex Gellia Cornelia* of 72 BC would have been the final stage in this process.

This reconstruction is open to some weighty objections. In Sisenna's text there is no hint that the measure was one which imposed restrictions. Furthermore, the formula of the *lex Gellia Cornelia*, that the *civitas* had to be granted *singillatim* and *de consilii sententia*, was not designed to restrict grants but must be considered tralatician, and we must recognize that it was in the *lex Iulia* as well. In fact, the grant of the citizenship in Pompeius Strabo's decree is made *singillatim* in so far as the soldiers are named one by one.[143] It matters little whether there was more than one man involved and whether they belonged to only one *turma*. But Niccolini's other premiss, which aims to show that the *lex Calpurnia* was subsequent to the *lex Iulia*, also does not convince; the latter, on his view, would have contained little by way of practical provisions, and was modified by the *lex Calpurnia*.[144] This view is accepted also by Biscardi,[145] who says that the *lex Iulia* would not have provided for the enrolment of the *socii* in the tribes. That *per se* seems very difficult to credit, but is contradicted anyway by Appian, I 49, 214, which Biscardi tries to invalidate by arguing (erroneously) that it does not refer to the *lex Iulia*. It seems improbable that in this passage Appian was condensing his material for the sake of brevity and was referring here to two measures, the *lex Iulia* and the *lex Calpurnia*.

Carcopino's view, therefore, stands; the *lex Calpurnia*, as it is conceived by him and others, cannot be later than the *lex Iulia*. But is it the case that the contents of the *lex Calpurnia* were as is generally supposed? In other words, is it proper to connect the two fragments of Sisenna, 17 and 120?[146] This objection seems to have been foreseen by Niccolini[147] who refers to Cicero, *pro Balbo*, 55. This passage (*cognoscite nunc iudicium senatus quod semper iudicio est populi comprobatum*) does not, however, in fact prove that fr. 17 must be connected with fr. 120, since Cicero is clearly referring to grants of the citizenship (and in this case his claim is absolutely justified),[148] not to the creation of two new tribes.

In my view, subject to proof to the contrary, the connexion of the two fragments is arbitrary. Fr. 120 seems to assign the *lex Calpurnia* a very restricted range; it must have been the sort of law which authorized individual generals to grant the *civitas* (cf. the *lex Gellia Cornelia*). This had already been observed by Mommsen,[149] and it seems to be confirmed also by a passage of Diodorus[150] which shows the consul L. Iulius Caesar, at a point of time prior to his *lex de civitate*, offering the *civitas* to a Cretan. This power very probably derived from the *lex Calpurnia* of Sisenna's fr. 120, which would therefore date to the first months of 90 BC.

This law was superseded by the *lex Iulia* which was of a general nature. The clause on the grant of the citizenship to *peregrini* can be deduced only from the mention of the law in the Asculan inscription, but it is well-known that the literary sources refer to important laws only by their principal points and disregard their minutiae.

Fr. 17 must therefore be considered as standing by itself. In it Sisenna does not speak of a law but of a *S.C.* and we may suppose that the Senate had taken the initiative and that L. Calpurnius Piso had put the *S.C.* into practice.[151] This Calpurnius, as Lange tentatively proposed,[152] could have been praetor and not tribune.

We can now turn to examining the passages of Appian. The first problem is to what law I 49, 214, refers. The position which the passage occupies in the context of the narrative fixes the chronological reference to 90 BC. There can be no doubt that the passage reproduces the general drift of the *lex Iulia*. It is necessary to mention this because the view of M. A. Levi,[153] that the number of 10 newly created tribes – based on Appian's δεκατεύοντες – into which the *novi cives* were drafted results from the 2 of Sisenna and the 8 of Velleius, presupposes that the measure referred to in Appian, I 49, 214, is the one which settled the question of the *civitas* and is therefore the *lex Plautia Papiria*.

Another view, which also denies that Appian is referring to the *lex Iulia*, has been advanced by Biscardi.[154] He maintains that in Appian, I 49, 212, there is a reference to the *S.C.* preceding the *lex Iulia*, but that 49, 214, describes the criteria of the *lex Calpurnia*. As I have said, not only is it impossible that the *lex Iulia* would have left vague a point as important as the position of the new citizens *vis-à-vis* the established body of old citizens, but also this reconstruction is contradicted by a proper interpretation of the Appian passages. Although these are clear, it will be as well to show more precisely just how clear they are.

Appian knows a measure of 90 BC, which is clearly the *lex Iulia*, which granted the *civitas* and which established a fixed number of tribes in which the new citizens had to vote. It is only prejudice which can see different parts in a measure of this organic unity. The change of subject – βουλή at 49, 212, and 'Ρωμαῖοι at 49, 214 – is of very little importance. Appian next explains why the new citizens were to be admitted to a restricted number of tribes. Another measure (the *lex Plautia Papiria*) which awarded the citizenship to the rest of Italy, is mentioned for 89 BC in 53, 231. Appian adds that the citizens were admitted to the tribes on the same terms as before (that is to say, as in 49, 214, and as under the *lex Iulia*). Here, too, as in 49, 214 (and 64, 287), we are given the reason for this arrangement: the Romans did not wish to give the new citizens a majority in voting.

Appian does not say how many the new tribes were, or rather, if he does, the number is concealed in the formula δεκατεύοντες of 49, 214, on which historians have argued furiously for a long time. Most maintain[155] that there is a reference here to the number 10, others – such as Carcopino[156] – maintain that the passage is corrupt and emend it in various ways. For those who accept the number 10 the difficulty consists in reconciling this passage with that of Velleius who, as we shall see, speaks of 8 tribes.

The new interpretation of Biscardi which I have just mentioned sets out to save the number 10 drawn from Appian by connecting it with the 2 tribes of Sisenna. Biscardi entirely accepts the explanation which Tibiletti[157] has given of the reformed *comitia centuriata* with the aid of the *Tabula Hebana* and refers the Appian passage to the reformed assembly, translating: 'but granting the new citizens ten votes in the *comitia centuriata*' (literally: 'dividing them into 10 groups or centuries') 'they' (that is, the Romans) 'constituted some supernumerary new tribes'. The new tribes would have been two according to Sisenna's evidence, each one corresponding to 5 centuries.[158] This view is impossible, both because it encounters insuperable difficulties in the passages of Appian, and because of a factor which is really a political one.

Biscardi himself is perhaps aware of the former problem:[159] how can one explain Appian's statement, repeated three times, that the new tribes voted last? Fortunately, one thing is certain in the *comitia centuriata*, reformed or not, and, so far as I know, admitted by all scholars no matter what their theory: it is that the citizens voted each in his own class according to his census qualifications. Now, if Appian is taken to refer to the *comitia centuriata*, neither he nor his source would have been able to say that the *novi cives* voted last, since either one would have to suppose they voted last within their own classes – and in that case the vote of many new citizens, voting last it may be but for example among the Equites or the first class, was not in fact ἀχρεῖος[160] – or one would have to believe that in their case the census qualification was dispensed with and they were relegated to the class of *proletarii*. There is none of this in Appian and it is difficult to believe that anyone except Biscardi would accept such a muddle. Biscardi himself[161] seems to acknowledge that Appian's terms ἔσχατοι (49, 214) and τελευταῖοι (64, 287) can only refer to the tribes in the *comitia tributa*, and he concluded that it is possible that the supernumerary tribes voted last both in the *comitia centuriata* and in the *comitia tributa*. He does not, however, explain how this was managed in the former case.

The political factor I have mentioned is of the utmost importance both for understanding the problem under discussion and for the general theme of our inquiry, and it is this: it is not in fact true, as Biscardi claims,[162] that there was no reason why the Roman government – and the historian who records their decisions – should concentrate on the *comitia tributa*;[163] on the contrary, there was a fundamental reason.

It is a well-known fact, which is made quite clear by the ancient sources, that in the *comitia centuriata* the traditional influence of the wealthy classes was represented by the greater weight their votes carried. With minor modifications the reformed assembly kept this feature. It is equally well-known – and again Taylor has recently called attention to it[164] – that the *comitia tributa* had a more democratic character because the influence which the upper classes could exercise there was less.

Hence we can understand the fears of the Roman oligarchy and their preoccupation with the position of the *novi cives* in the *comitia tributa*. In fact, in the *comitia centuriata* only the wealthy among the *novi cives* would have acquired a position of importance;[165] Rome would have known that she need not expect revolutionary activity from them. I have already shown the various sorts of relationships which existed between the allied and Roman upper classes, and from this it must obviously and inevitably follow that, once the *socii* had entered the citizen body, these relationships would have continued and would have deepened. On the other hand, as the city-state declined, that policy of exclusiveness which operated in favour of a very limited nucleus of Roman citizens weakened; it was that policy which had, so it seems, dictated the reform of the *comitia centuriata* in the third century B.C.[166]

Much of the history of Roman domestic policy after the Social War is dominated by the conservatism of the municipal classes.[167] Let me mention here only what Cicero said about a proposal by the jurist Ser. Sulpicius Rufus.[168]

To sum up: from the presence of new citizens in the *comitia centuriata* the governing oligarchy at Rome had very little to fear. Not so in the *comitia tributa*; with the *novi cives* distributed in the thirty-five tribes it would have been easy, whatever the motive and whatever the occasion, to transport to Rome groups of men from the *municipia*, and by sheer force of numbers, as Appian and Velleius say, to turn everything upside down.[169] Here was the danger, and it was here that the Romans tried to protect themselves by restricting the enrolment of new citizens to a limited number of tribes, created especially for the purpose. A parallel in principle and method is provided by the Roman policy of restricting the vote of the *libertini* to four urban tribes. Furthermore, the tribes of the new citizens had to vote last; Appian notoriously concentrates here on the legislative *comitia* in which the voting of the tribes took place one after the other.[170]

I do not know whether Appian indicated the number of tribes appointed by the *lex Iulia*; if this lies behind δεκατεύοντες in 49, 214, it is a desperate undertaking to ascertain it.

We do know, however, the number of tribes created by the *lex Plautia Papiria*. In fact Velleius, II 20, 2, says: *itaque cum ita civitas Italiae data esset, ut in octo tribus contribuerentur novi cives, ne potentia eorum et multitudo veterum civium dignitatem frangeret* . . . Two points need to be emphasized: Velleius takes this to be the end of the *socii* problem (*cum civitas Italiae data esset*) and therefore the number of 8 tribes is that precisely sanctioned by the *lex Plautia Papiria*.[171] Even if Velleius does not say so in so many words, with the help of passages from Appian we may suppose that the 8 tribes were not already in existence[172] but were created specially for the purpose. When one thinks that these tribes lasted only a few years and then disappeared without any trace, and that Velleius mentions them only incidentally in the context of Cinna's proposals of 87 BC, his failure to emphasize this point becomes clear.[173] It is not necessary therefore to posit a conflict here with Appian's evidence.

All that remains is to see how the figure of 8 tribes, mentioned by the *lex Plautia Papiria*, was reached and in particular what was the relationship of these tribes to the two tribes of the *S.C.* mentioned by Sisenna. Biscardi, considering the increase in the number of citizens which must have resulted between the *lex Iulia* and the *lex Plautia Papiria*, objected to the view that there was a shift from an original 10 tribes to 8;[174] the passage of Sisenna would in that case indicate a reduction. With this one might agree, although I think that if the Senate did not hesitate to confine *c.* 350,000 citizens to a few tribes, it is of little importance whether these numbered 10 or 8, and also whether 10 later gave way to 8. However, I am unable to decide on this point, and for my part it is enough to be certain that the final number was 8, as Velleius says.

It would appear that complete parity for the *novi cives* at Rome, with the possibility of enrolment in all thirty-five tribes, was in the years after the Social War more a weapon in the hands of the democratic party than a real demand by the new citizens. Or at least this issue was such an integral part of the Roman political struggle that the Italian side of it seems to fall into second place. But this is only a superficial view and arises from the fact that the new citizens immediately assume their own positions in the Roman political line-up and the rebel elements play a decisive part in the popular faction.[175] Sulpicius' attempt in 88 BC to distribute the *novi cives* among the thirty-five tribes is closely related to the proposal to make over the command against Mithridates to Marius.[176] The most important feature of this relationship, which I have emphasized above, is that the demand of the commercial classes of southern Italy, those that were most widely represented among the Marian faction, to exercise their influence in bringing about a more decisive policy in Asia was now being given practical expression. However, a solution of the problem was subject to the vicissitudes of the Civil War. After Sulla's armed intervention (88 BC) had restored the previous distinction between old and new citizens, the proposal was renewed by Cinna in 87 BC but with little success. Finally, in 84 BC enrolment in the thirty-five tribes was granted, apparently, by *S.C.*[177] It may not be possible to believe[178] that this was an Optimate move, since it is probable that after the *lectio* of 86 BC the Senate had been filled up with those who favoured the *popularis* cause, but in any event it is characteristic of the period that even those who, like Sulla, had previously held and practised opposite views had to accept that full concession was inevitable. Probably it did not escape attention that a fair number of the new citizens interested in voting at Rome (that is, the upper classes) had the same political views as those Romans who were totally disinclined to extremism, and that these Italians could be useful in maintaining a policy of law and order. In fact, as many new citizens aligned themselves with the Sullan faction as did with the Marians. Sulla had already accepted the opposite side's view on the matter when he met the consul L. Cornelius Scipio at Teanum in 83 BC,[179] and undertook, apparently, in treaties[180] with the Italian peoples not to take away from them their recently acquired rights to vote in the thirty-five tribes. Without this parity of citizen rights, obtained in the course of shifts of power, the energies of the new citizens could not have been deployed in the new life of the Roman state. We must now see how they interpreted their new position in a resurgent Rome and in what direction they developed their political activity.

VII

The new citizens in first century BC politics

Modern scholarship, in my opinion, has not properly interpreted the question of municipal participation (after 89 BC largely from the ex-allies) in first century BC Roman politics. The most commonly held view is that of Rostovtzeff,[181] who believed that the municipal upper classes, businessmen and urban bourgeoisie, would have been basically uninterested in general political questions since their sole concern would have been problems connected with their own material interests or, at most, the political life of their cities. For the rest they would have adopted the traditional attitude of their Roman counterparts.

On this basis W. Schur[182] put forward the view that Sulla had a policy of profound importance, and this was to bolster up the positions of the conservative, oligarchic classes at Rome by bringing in fresh reserves from the *municipia* whose interests and outlook were bound up with those of the classes of law and order. On the other hand, R. Syme[183] has emphasized Caesar's role in advancing also those elements which had belonged to districts or circles opposed to Sulla and had therefore not been able to play their part in Roman political life, and he has given us a detailed documentation with examples. In my view, the premiss is in the main erroneous, and therefore the results drawn from it largely questionable. It is clear that the Italian upper classes had a very lively interest in the Roman political struggle, even though they had differing aims and even though their interest assumed different forms. It is certain – and here Rostovtzeff's view is undoubtedly right – that the Etruscan and Umbrian oligarchs, for social reasons particular to their districts as I have said above, were happy to support the Roman Optimates' policy in their firm championship of the *status quo*. On the other hand, the upper classes from the regions that later rebelled, those groups who were politically active in their own districts, had shown by their demand for the *civitas* that they wanted to take a direct part in Roman political life.

This demonstrates quite clearly that the entry of *municipales* into Roman political life after the Social War was only the natural corollary of those demands which had led to that war. It was implicit in the purpose of the allies that insurgent Italy should Romanize itself, not vice versa. Consequently it follows that Sulla and Caesar, to confine ourselves to the statesmen selected by Schur and Syme, did no more than support and maintain this historical process which was inevitable and which developed beneath their eyes; dictated as it was by a mood that was widely felt and by vast, practical demands, it far outweighed the purpose and decisions of a single administrator, however important he may have been.[184] It is another question, which we shall examine later, whether these men from the *municipia,* once they participated in Roman politics, generally assumed the outlook of the Optimate faction.

My point is proved *inter alia* by the fact that the *novi cives* did not wait for Sulla to take the initiative before they assumed their place in Roman life.

The support of the ex-rebel elements for the Marian and democratic faction[185] confirms that on common interests in foreign policy were built clear and intimate relationships even in the field of domestic politics. It is especially in the circle of Sertorius that these new elements of the Roman community assumed, albeit in a *factio,* powers of responsibility and leadership.[186] The coalition around Sulla, therefore, which consisted of those in politics who embodied interests or opinions opposed to what had gone before, instead of representing a deliberate attempt at reform of the governing class, takes on the appearance of a partisan manoeuvre which only in part was due to the necessity of the civil war. It was natural enough that every new citizen entering the new state had to choose his own path.

The *lectio Senatus* of 86 BC[187] took place in a period of full democratic control. Very probably it acknowledged the need to admit representatives of new citizens to the supreme assembly without distinction of origin if, as seems likely, it is to that year that we should date the entry into the Senate of the Samnite Statius[188] and admission as senators of the two sons of Minatus Magius of Aeclanum who held magistracies at Rome in later years.[189] We should remember that in the controversy which followed at once on the laws *de civitate* dealing with the allocation of the *novi cives* to the tribes (a controversy fostered by those who wanted to enjoy to the full the rights won by armed force and indicative therefore that men were directly interested in political life), the democrats, to a certain extent represented by ex-rebel elements,[190] showed no hesitation whatsoever in championing the most radical solution. But still more significant is the fact that those who entertained traditional political views, who would be less disposed to grant concessions and who in fact opposed those who upheld such concessions, saw that this demand for equality in the practical exercise of rights which went with the *ius civitatis* was both right and important. Among the first acts carried out by Sulla when he landed in Italy was to recognize the legitimacy and absolute necessity of the demand of the *novi cives* by distributing them among the thirty-five tribes. It is a fact that Sulla, both explicitly and implicitly, legitimized everything the allies had done to achieve what they wanted against the view of the Senate: that is, the war itself.

What happened as a result was first of all that in revising the Senate – the centre as before of the new governing class – Sulla had to (and he probably wished to do so anyway) take the new situation into account. Syme recognized the importance of Schur's view[191] on the admission to the Senate of representatives of the municipal aristocracies, and posed himself the question what regions specifically had contributed to it:[192] 'Surely not, save for rare exceptions and renegades, the Italia that fought against Rome. Presumably Campania, Umbria, Etruria and the Sabine land, which already had produced senators – and which had been strongly on the side of Marius.'[193]

It is, of course, difficult to answer such a question and therefore to confirm or deny Syme's hypothesis, since an examination of the social make-up of Sulla's Senate can be based only on thin, fragmentary material.[194] However, it is certain that the Senate included men from Picenum (3. L. Afranius: 45. L. Minucius Basilus), Campania (7. Q. Arrius; 14. M. Caesius; 30. L. Fufidius; 82. Ti. Gutta) and Sicily (65. C. Anneus; 83. Cn. Heius); for others a district of origin, although we can be sure it is not Rome, is difficult to pinpoint with precision or even with probability.[195] Among these – and it is an important example of individuals holding views different from those generally prevailing – leading representatives of business were not apparently lacking.[196]

Obviously these newcomers to the Roman governing class were assimilated by it, and the fact that they became members of political factions is a very clear token of this. In this direction great progress was made by the Sullan reform of the Senate. By introducing into that body in one way or another members of the *equester ordo* who were in large part from the *municipia*,[197] Sulla lessened the friction between the Equites and the senatorial class, at least in its more violent external aspects.[198] One should not forget that it was very probably only a revival of Livius Drusus' proposal.[199] It is only by keeping this fact in mind – it produced important changes in the post-Sullan political struggle at Rome compared with the period before the Social War – that one can understand the phenomenon (an undeniable one even if it perhaps was not as general as Rostovtzeff and Schur maintain) whereby the municipal classes, introduced into the political arena at Rome, lent their support by preference to the Optimate *factio*. This phenomenon depends especially on a factor common to all periods, that social classes which, even by using revolutionary methods, have acquired in a state a position of supremacy over, or simply parity with, the existing governing class become forces of conservatism in the new order of affairs which they have helped to create.

This goes against any conception of municipal classes dragged against their will, as it were, beyond their circle of limited civic interests and confronted with problems beyond their compass. This, it should be said at once, is impossible for the commercial class of ex-allies which fed the equestrian order after the time of Sulla. This class was well-used to rising above the petty interests of the individual community in order to tackle very large-scale commercial and political problems. There is, without doubt, more truth in the assertion with regard to the Campanian oligarchy (or rather nobility); in Campania a traditionally conservative outlook was super-seded with great difficulty or else, as certainly happened in the majority of cases, did not in fact disappear.[200] But one should make a distinction here, one which it may not be possible to support with examples from prosopo-graphy but which still has an undeniable validity of its own.

We should distinguish in the *municipia* those classes which had a political interest in the life of the state, even if their views were conservative, and those upper classes which cannot be considered as 'politically' orientated. What influence, if we wish to form a general picture, is to be attributed to the attitude of unconcern and crass materialism which appears to dominate certain bourgeoisies in municipal Italy in the Caesarian period?[201]

A considerable one, and this answer still holds even if it is undeniable that from a certain point in time – when a kind of depression descended over the fortunes of state and society during the greatest crisis of the civil war – the demand for *otium* and *pax*, peculiar to these classes, got a foothold even within the circle of the old Roman governing class.[202] It is impossible to maintain that such sections of the Caesarian faction (I exclude the lower classes from Etruria and Umbria, Marian to a man) as those victims of the Sullan reaction, the Campanian and Samnite aristocracies, were poorly endowed with political ideas or interest.[203]

In short, one should always bear in mind the distinction between those who wanted to exercise the political rights which the *civitas* had given them and those who, even when they had obtained the citizenship, remained involuntarily or otherwise removed from the life of the state. The latter found their realization, when they wanted to, in the professional army. In any event this interweaving of motives in which particular causes came to affect attitudes adopted by various regional and family groups and, more so, by individuals, tends to confirm that, whether Optimate- or *popularis*-in-clined (depending on the pressure of differing opinions), Italians entered Roman political life immediately after 89 BC on an enormous scale. They were of supreme importance in the history of the late Republic.[204]

Their influx was so enormous that it quickly aroused suspicious reaction and open hostility among the Roman *nobilitas* who were sensitive of the danger that they might be submerged by men from the *municipia*. This is the background for the statements by the patrician C. Manlius Torquatus, reported and refuted by Cicero in his speech *pro Sulla* (62 BC),[205] the objections of Iuventius Laterensis against the knight Plancius from Atina,[206] and the sarcasms of Antony.[207]

The power and exclusiveness of the *nobilitas* crumbled under the assault first of the municipal aristocracies and then of those of lower social origin whose position had been improved by *militia*; this is attested by Cicero, *pro Sulla*, 24, and it is a phenomenon which dominates the Ciceronian age, preparing the way for the coming of Augustan Italy. The figure of the *homo novus parvusque senator*, to use the happy formula of the author of the *Bellum Africum*,[208] became a frequent and familiar one of the post-Sullan age, but, just because they were *novi* and *parvi*, they left scant trace in the tradition and it is more by intuition than by actual proof that we can recognize the phenomenon. The example of the Sullan senate which we have already examined in detail is valid here.

The participation of *municipales* in Roman political life after 89 BC is, then, something that happens of its own accord; it follows necessarily from the pressure of those well-defined interests that had produced the Social War and which can be referred to a general demand for power to take part in political decisions. Powerful personalities like Sulla and Caesar knew how to turn this familiar process to their own advantage: the former believed and expected that it would reinforce the senatorial oligarchy, which he undertook to restore after the Marian interlude, the latter knew how to provide a political climate which favoured those whom Sulla had banished from political life with his measures of reaction and restraint. These people therefore looked on Caesar as the political heir of Marius and as the representative of their political ideals.

VIII
The Romanization of Italy

That the allies should become members of the Roman state had been the wish of those classes which wanted the *civitas* and which had not hesitated to obtain their ends by causing war to break out; to get what they wanted war appeared to them to be essential. This was always the purpose of the struggle in the minds of those who were close to Rome in mood and political outlook. It is folly to pretend, however, that this was a universally held conviction not only outside this upper class, among the mass of the allies for whom acquisition of the citizenship could not bring any substantial or appreciable gain, but also in that very class in which it was widely entertained.

Not everyone could fully appreciate the civic rights of the *civitas* and the possibility of taking part in public affairs at Rome.[209] Some just conceived, demanded and pursued it as the equivalent of 'independence'. These were extremists, played on by varying passions: there were particular geographical areas like Campania, residuary legatee of a powerful tradition of political hegemony, long humiliated and oppressed, or like Samnium, mindful always of having disputed the hegemony with Rome longer than any other people of the peninsula.[210] Making up this group were those like Pontius Telesinus and Papius Mutilus, who thought that by joining the Marian faction they could dominate it and direct all its efforts against Rome's interests. It was only the victory of Sulla which disturbed this foolish Italian dream at a time when, in the context of the *pars*, the Italians had already achieved supremacy.[211] It was a dream which they tried probably to re-enact in Spain, but Sertorius succeeded in controlling them there.

This interpretation of the *civitas* is significant not only because it was accepted by a narrow, albeit powerful, group but also because it was certainly the theme – a sentimental one and therefore easily communicable – which was emphasized to the masses; no one could claim that they should fight for upper class interests which they did not share. The coin types of the Italian rebels make it clear that this was the chief, or perhaps the only, means of propaganda to arouse the masses from their slumbers, and to explain to them the causes behind the struggle. It is in this way that one can interpret the theme of independence which we sometimes find being generalized as the basis of the war.[212]

The Roman victory proved that those who wanted to be 'accepted into the citizenship' were in the right, and it was only with Caesar that those who wanted independence and who had been rendered powerless by the punitive measures of Sulla could also take their place in Roman political life; they were by then convinced – especially after the failure of Sertorius – that the results of the Social War had come to stay. But it could not actually follow from the Roman victory that those principles which were the inheritance of the allied rebels and which found tangible expression in government could be abandoned. For it was desirable, one might even say necessary, to come to terms with the very solid cantonal structure of the individual allied communities. It is well-known how the unity of confederation created by the rebellion of these communities was one which entirely depended on the existence of war with Rome; in the confederacy centrifugal and separatist forces were predominant.[213]

The widespread existence of a jealous (but not outraged) sentiment of local autonomy – of which a characteristic aspect was the return of Capua in 83 BC to the status of an independent community to oblige the Campanian members of the Marian faction – had long been a familiar feature, and must have been a material problem in 91 BC for the group headed by Livius Drusus; for him the supremacy of Rome was not open to even the slightest challenge. It was thought that the problem would be resolved by reconciling the different demands with an oath of fealty or alliance, in which those who owed their citizenship to Drusus recognized in Rome their common mother-land.[214] This formula clearly seems to imply that loyalty to Rome might find its expression in a way which respected local autonomy even if this lacked any properly political significance. It originated certainly with those allied circles disposed to collaborate faithfully with Rome and eager to participate in the political life of the metropolis.

We cannot reconstruct the picture with certainty but this theoretical concept was probably exemplified in the political structure of the rebel confederacy. More significantly, its influence on the structure of the Roman state became more explicit and more profound after 89 BC. As the senatorial class foresaw with some anxiety, the state emerged totally altered by the admission of the allies to the citizenship. From that time dates the birth of the municipal state, in which the citizen is not only a member of his own *municipium* but is also a *civis* of Rome itself.[215] There is a substantial difference between it and the earlier organization of the peninsula, an organization which the new one, of course, presupposes; as far as concerns the basic point of the citizens' ability to take a greater part in politics, the principles of the city-state completely ceased to exist, or rather to have significance.

The importance of the rebels' confederacy lay in this: it demonstrated that the structure of the state, which had been over-enlarged by the extension of citizenship rights, was reconcilable with the maintenance of local autonomy. The new theory, which became basic in juridical thinking in time to come,[216] is formulated by Cicero in a famous passage[217] which, for the warmth of its sentiment, has no equal in the whole of Latin literature[218] and which represents an episode in the history of the polemic, at that time enjoying a heyday, against the *homines novi* or men from the *municipia* in political life, that is, against the results of the Social War.

Cicero's theory of the *communis patria Roma* is in direct descent from the Rome that is the πατρίς of the oath of Drusus. It is another example of the frequency with which the ideas of the conquered triumph over the victor, and all the more significant in this case where the point of view of the defeated party wins the day in a field of such importance as that of the structure of the state.[219]

So the allies who became citizens were Romanized, and their participation in public life highlights it, but they made their contribution too, and that of the highest significance, since the fundamental structure of the state into which they came to be welcomed was transformed according to their own principles.

However, the extremists among the rebel Italians, initially overwhelmed by the mirage of independence and inspired later only by a desire to take their revenge, did not surrender even when the situation in Italy moved decisively towards a compromise solution, one which was still so favourable to their interests. They made a last attempt to achieve their aims by taking part in the war which the most capable of the democratic leaders, Q. Sertorius, conducted in Spain against Sulla's generals. Here their attempt to give an anti-Roman bias to Sertorius' activity failed; by an irony of fate their point of view survives in the historical literature of the oligarchic faction only as something which characterized Sertorius himself.

This is borne out by a re-examination of the Sertorius episode which is too close to the events of the Social War to be considered and explained in isolation. In my view, research must proceed along the lines of finding out above all who were the men taking part in the struggle, leaders and other ranks, and the ideas which guided them. Now in Spain we find the same atmosphere and the same conflict of ideas in deciding important political problems of the time as there had been in Italy with Marius, Cinna and their successors. Our judgement on Sertorius cannot, as we shall see, be different from that which we must make on the part played by the democrats after the Social War.

IX
The problem of Sertorius

In an article which appeared in 1932[220] P. Treves showed clearly the basic absurdity of the different historical views which have appeared on the problem of Sertorius. The dual nature of the ancient tradition, which is a difference of 'tone, not of fact', has not been resolved by modern scholarship. The usual practice has been to abandon the ancient evaluations of Sertorius, products of political prejudice, with on the one side Sallust who saw in Marius 'his' hero, on the other the Livian tradition friendly to Pompey, and replace them with a subjective judgement; as a result, scholars have accepted one or other of the two ancient interpretations and have formulated a new conception which in its turn can produce only condemnation or praise. Hence recent researches have come to revive the notorious interpretations of nineteenth-century historians, centring round the two opposite poles of Mommsen and Ihne, and the eulogy of A. Schulten – whose work has in-spired a decade of Sertorian studies[221] – was at once followed by H. Berve's condemnation of Sertorius.[222]

Treves tried to go 'beyond apologia and beyond condemnation'; it was his object to clarify and to understand the work of Sertorius. It is not perhaps, as important to insist on the essential correctness of Treves' funda-mental thesis – that Sertorius always aimed to return to Rome – which remains true even if in one important particular it is not acceptable,[223] as to emphasize that Treves was well aware that the connexions between Ser-torius' enterprise and contemporary Roman political history must always be tightly drawn. He thought it was all a single picture; to remove this one element of it was to falsify the whole. He realized that this was the way to free himself from the established practice of having to make a judgement along traditional lines.

Treves' approach influenced the later interpretation of W. Schur and V. Ehrenberg. The former's work[224] is not so much an attempt to overcome the traditional dualism as a very important step towards a full appreciation of the interconnexion of Sertorius and the Roman world. In the first place, Schur saw the need to re-examine the source material in detail, showing thereby the high degree of excellence of that tradition which goes back to Sallust's *Historiae* (although the reader gains the impression that Schur has remained, in a certain manner, conditioned or hypnotized by the general lines of Sallust's work, of which the chapter on Sertorius is a basic part, and that therefore his Sertorius is a little too much the Sertorius of Sallust). Secondly, Schur had the merit of emphasizing with singular clarity the fact that Sertorius personified a period of transition in Roman politics, between the time of the Gracchi and that of the dynasts. Something similar was observed by Appian of the Social War with which Sertorius is intimately connected.[225]

Ehrenberg,[226] concentrating on the relationships between Sertorius and his Spanish environment, thought he could detect in his activity an attempt to renew relations between Rome and the provinces on the lines of the solution which he must have seen at work also in Italy, dealing with the problem of the state's structure: I mean the superannuation of the city-state. However, there is truth in a reviewer's point,[227] that this thesis of Ehrenberg's is presented as if it were a firm point, soundly established, on which the reconstruction of the figure of Sertorius (in a 'Roman' sense) can develop, whereas it is really true to say that the point is not a firm one and therefore the reconstruction comes very close to being a *petitio principii*.[228]

The study which follows is intended to fit closely with the approach suggested by Treves and to take his own basic premises a step further; I am convinced by an inquiry into the entourage of Sertorius that his activity must be considered as a continuation of, and a conclusion to, the Social and Civil Wars. This is my general standpoint.

In particular I have forced myself to resist the usual temptation to examine (and in actual fact to consider) some famous episodes of Sertorius' struggle in isolation *per se* for the purposes of drawing general conclusions from them later or of using them as a basis for a judgement of Sertorius, negative or positive according to the solution of the individual problem involved.

The example which seems to me to illustrate this method in the most characteristic way is the pact with Mithridates. As is usually the case in modern research there are two opposing possibilities, corresponding to the two differing accounts in the sources. If Sertorius surrendered the province of Asia to the King of Pontus, as Appian says he did, he was without doubt a traitor; if he did not, as Plutarch maintains, he was not.[229] But the significance of this episode is not brought out only by an accurate examination of the sources, whose excellence, as the facts seem to show, can be maintained by both sides with arguments of equal weight. Leaving aside any moral judgement, the treaty between Mithridates and Sertorius can be understood only by seeing it as a link in the chain of long-standing relationships on the part of Roman and above all Italian politicians with the King of Pontus. So we must emphasize the context in which the idea of a pact originated, its source and the political ideas of those who negotiated and maintained it.

If we are to have the deepest appreciation of Sertorius' purposes in his struggle, it will help us to clarify a point which, though of fundamental interest, has not received the attention of modern scholars, perhaps because it had been glossed over by the ancient sources on whose interpretations moderns depend: this is the relationship between Sertorius and the *Hispanienses* (Romans and Italians living in Spain). Even if the results of this inquiry, given the thin amount of evidence at our disposal, cannot be as exhaustive as one would wish, yet it is not fruitless since the *Hispanienses* were extremely numerous in that period and, what is more important, played a leading role in the social and economic life of the two Spanish provinces.

Our conclusion must be that we should firmly limit the influence which the Spanish context can have had on Sertorius' activity. This influence must essentially be reduced to the 'way' in which Sertorius conducted his struggle, since it is clear that he had to come to terms with the particular circumstances with which his chosen theatre confronted him. It cannot, however, be said that the particular problems of the provinces could ever have changed the character and significance of the struggle. These were always Italian in the fullest sense of the word. What particularly helps to prove this is the origin of those *Hispanienses* among whom Sertorius often found stout partisans.

X

On Roman and Italian emigration to Spain in the second century BC

The provincial organization of Spain dates from 197 BC[230] and the two Spanish provinces ranked third after Sicily and Sardinia. However, the Romanization of the Iberian peninsula had begun earlier, and we can pinpoint the date, 206 BC, the year of the foundation of Italica, the work of Scipio Africanus;[231] the name, deliberately generic, seems to show that the soldiers settled there were not only *cives Romani*. This first foundation was followed by a continuous flow of emigrants from Italy to Spain; we are able to guess at the importance of this only from scattered and scanty information.[232] There were two principal reasons for this phenomenon: the instability of the military situation compelled the Romans to keep considerable forces under arms in Spain, and, as often happens in these cases, the army was followed by a large number of civilians, above all traders.[233]

Furthermore, many soldiers ended up, after long years of service, by settling in the province where they had fought and where they had established friendships or family connexions. The second reason was the exploitation of the mines.[234] It seems probable that for a certain period after the expulsion of the Carthaginians the operations of exploiting the minerals of the Spanish provinces had been directed by the governors and that the mines' revenues were counted in the sums deposited at Rome in the *aerarium* at the time when the governors returned at the end of their period of service.[235] It appears also that it was only towards 179 BC, when the amounts brought back to Rome were diminishing in a way we cannot otherwise explain, that the exploitation of the mines was transferred by the censors, by way of contract, to *societates* of Equites.[236] The working of the mines then assumed much greater proportions than had been the case previously; the operations of extracting minerals at New Carthage alone required c. 40,000 slaves and this was happening about the middle of the second century BC.[237]

It was then that the flow of settlers grew appreciably, inspired by the delusory prospect of being able to acquire riches rapidly,[238] and it continued until the mines were transferred into private hands, probably in the Sullan period.[239] These were the two fundamental reasons for the foundation of a certain number of Romano–Italic communities[240] of hybrid juridical status, and it should be noted that there is no parallel in that period in other provinces. The foundation of Gracchuris in the Ebro valley dates to 179 BC,[241] the upgrading of Carteia to the status of a *colonia Latina* to 171 BC,[242] the latter being populated by sons of Roman soldiers and Spanish women. The settlement of colonists at Corduba dates to 152 BC[243] and natives were admitted as well. To 138 or 137 belongs the foundation of Brutobriga, the work of D. Iunius Brutus Callaicus,[244] the same man who settled some soldiers of Viriathus at Valentia.[245] Finally, to 123 BC date the foundations of Palma and Pollentia in the Balearic Islands, the work of Q. Caecilius Metellus,[246] the most interesting of all for our purposes as the source which mentions the fact says also that the colonists were three thousand Romans coming from Spain.[247] This shows that the Romans of Spain must have been quite numerous if, themselves immigrants, they could supply a new source of migrants.[248]

There are other indications which seem to confirm that this was the situation in the two provinces. For example, only the presence of Roman elements can explain the profound Romanization of the Ebro valley; this had been traversed since the end of the second century BC by a road which, starting from Barcelona, made its way to Ilerda.[249] The presence of *negotiatores* coming from Italy is attested also by numerous numismatic finds, with coins dating back as far as the third century and the most recent of them to the beginning of the first century BC.[250] The antiquity of the first Roman mint in Spain is an additional proof.[251]

The participation of *Hispanienses* (Romans of Spain) in the struggle between Pompey and Caesar provides concrete evidence of their vast numbers by the middle of the first century BC. I shall examine later the evidence of the sources in this respect.[252] Here it is sufficient to emphasize the frequency of the levies of Roman citizens conducted by both sides in the Spanish provinces during those civil wars. Migration to Spain had always had an economic motive as one of its principal incentives, and this explains the presence, attested for one thing by numerous references in the literary sources, of *Hispanienses* possessing the equestrian census; in some measure this can provide an idea of the economic and social distinction which many of the migrants had attained.[253] This economic prosperity is typically reflected in the return of *Hispanienses*, clearly within modest limits, to the motherland to share in political life. There are already some traces of this at the beginning of the first century BC; the most famous case is that of the tribune of 90 BC, Q. Varius Hybrida Sucronensis, whom I have previously mentioned.[254] The process continuously increased in the course of the century until it became of great political importance in the early Imperial period.

We must now try to define those areas of Italy from which this flow of emigrants came, not an easy task if we bear in mind how thin is the evidence, epigraphic and literary, which we can use. Before we see what this evidence can yield, we must first make some observations on the colonization of the Ebro valley and of the district to its north which, as we have seen, was the oldest settlement. Philological research by Menéndez Pidal has pinpointed linguistic phenomena in the region of the Ebro corresponding to others appropriate to the Osco–Umbrian districts of central/southern Italy; the centre of the region would have been represented by the city of Osca (modern Huesca), in Sertorius' time one of the chief towns of the district and of all Spain.[255] This point is extremely important in that it proves that the colonization of northern Spain, which started at the Mediterranean coast and penetrated to the interior along the course of the Ebro – cf. for example Gracchuris – had been fed by elements originating from those regions of Italy which spoke Osco–Umbrian dialects;[256] this is valid even if Menéndez Pidal's theory that derives the name of Osca from the Osci is uncertain and is therefore not a point which can be used to support this thesis.[257]

Confirmation of this view is to be found in the fact that, contemporary with these developments, men from southern Italy – and therefore speaking dialects which were basically Oscan – made up the majority of *negotiatores* in Sicily and the East. Their presence in northern Spain is therefore not an isolated phenomenon, even if the presence in the Spanish interior of populations with a culture more retarded than those of not only the Greek East but also the indigenous kingdoms of North Africa undoubtedly presents a different aspect of the phenomenon; it looks like real colonization. It was the local situation which gave the opportunity to transform commercial relationships into permanent settlement on the spot. This was not only necessary for the direct exploitation of the mineral deposits but also derived weighty support from the presence of standing armies. So it was only in Spain that there were settlements of a size large enough to influence the structure of the country and, as a result, its language.

An examination of the scanty prosopography of pre-Augustan Spain confirms, at least on general lines, what philological inquiry has shown for a limited sector (the Ebro valley in northern Spain). It also proves – I use this word even if the paucity of the material does not justify dogmatism – that, what is more, the migration to Spain had been sustained rather by allies than by *cives Romani*. It has been seen how the most ancient Roman foundation in Spain was Italica; the fact that allies as well as citizens contributed to its formation does not depend only on its name.[258] It is known that this city was the birthplace of the Aelii of the Emperor Hadrian's family, and they had preserved the record of the fact that they came from Hadria.[259] Some names of *Italicenses* are mentioned in the *Bellum Alexandrinum* for 48 BC;[260] despite any possible reservations which depend on the fact that we do not know when these people can have set foot in Spain (this holds for all the later examples), it is none the less significant that, alongside *nomina* of Roman *gentes*, we find a L. Mercello of Etruscan origin and a T. Vasius of Oscan origin.[261] In Carteia, a Latin colony of 171 BC, such *gentilicia* as Raius and Opsilius are attested,[262] at Toletum coins attest C. Viccius, probably Etruscan.[263] Among the Marsi is found the *gentilicium* Turullius, known at New Carthage from an inscription and coins of the Augustan period.[264] Other rare *gentilicia* are found at Valentia; it is not possible to decide whether they refer to soldiers of the Pompeian colony post-73 BC or whether possibly they attest previous Italian settlements. T. Ahius and C. Lucienus bear *gentilicia* attested in Italy in Oscan districts;[265] L. Trinius and L. Coranius show their Etruscan origin by their names.[266] From Spain came Catullus' Egnatius whose name betrays a Samnite origin, and Caesar's Decidius Saxa who was of central Italian origin.[267]

These cases, though of necessity few and far between, are none the less significant; they do not appear to be chance examples, and they can confirm the conclusion reached by Menéndez Pidal. It is certainly typical to find, alongside elements from central/southern Italy, Etruscan names; these, however, occur quite rarely among the *negotiatores* in the East. In any case, it certainly follows that men from the allied zone of Italy shared substantially in the colonization of the Spanish provinces. As I have said, one of the principal factors behind the Romanization of Spain was the presence of a standing army, and therefore it is highly probable that the preponderance of *socii* in the armies of the Spanish provinces in the second century BC made a significant contribution to this end.[268]

XI
Sertorius and the Hispanienses

The wars which Caesar fought in Spain on two occasions, first against the Pompeians Afranius, Petreius and Terentius Varro, and then against Pompey's own sons, are recorded in contemporary works such as the *Bellum Civile* of Caesar himself and the anonymous *Bellum Alexandrinum* and *Bellum Hispaniense*. These eye-witness accounts of the struggle provide us with copious information both on the psychology and the outlook of the *Hispanienses*, no less than on their direct participation in the struggle.[269] Also mentioned are *cohortes colonicae*[270] and we have evidence of levies of knights.[271] In the same way we know of the contributions imposed on Roman citizens.[272]

However, we have no information on the participation of *Hispanienses* in any fighting prior to the events of the second civil war. We know that in 88–87 BC M. Iunius Brutus and other democrats took refuge in Spain to avoid Sulla's reaction against Sulpicius[273] but we are not told whether they found help in Spain with their return which took place a little later. This is, however, said explicitly for the young P. Licinius Crassus; he took refuge in Spain in 85 BC and found assistance there which enabled him to set out again for Africa with 2,500 men.[274] These must have included Romans from Spain alongside the natives.

For the attitude of the *Hispanienses* towards Sertorius there is only a single piece of evidence, that of Plutarch, which refers in any case to the first attempt of Sertorius to establish himself in Spain (83–81 BC): Sertorius armed the young Romans living there.[275] The silence of the sources otherwise is all the more noteworthy as it seems clear that, as was true later with Pompey and Caesar, so in the time of Sertorius the Romans of Spain must have taken part in the struggle. We may plausibly explain the sources' silence by noting that we have no more than fragmentary or second-hand information, but however we explain it we must investigate so far as we can what was the attitude of the *Hispanienses* towards Sertorius and see whether we can properly call it collaboration.

Among Sertorius' lieutenants there was only one Roman of Spain: L. Fabius Hispaniensis. His case is quite interesting. He appears as Q(uaestor) on coins of the Sullan praetor C. Annius who in 81 BC chased Sertorius out of Spain,[276] and since there is no reason to think that he added his *cognomen* to his name during the campaign,[277] we must consider him a Roman citizen who had come from Spain to Rome to engage in a political career. Since Sallust calls him *senator ex proscriptis*,[278] we must suppose that he was one of those who were proscribed following the revolt of M. Aemilius Lepidus and that he therefore followed Perperna to Spain. This example may be unique among Sertorian leaders but it is very interesting since it shows how one section of the upper class *Hispanienses* regarded the activity of Sertorius and what was the support which was given to it.[279]

Some points arising from the composition of Sertorius' army will provide us with more detail here. Plutarch says that Sertorius, after disembarking in Spain from Africa, made for Lusitania with 2,600 men 'whom he called Romans'.[280] Since in the passage these soldiers are contrasted with Mauri who had come with him from Africa and with natives enrolled in Spain, it may properly be argued that we are dealing with Romans or Italians whom he called by a single, generic name. On the other hand, the distinction between 'Roman' soldiers and natives in Sertorius' army is a regular one found also elsewhere.[281] Of course, it is impossible to calculate the proportions of the two groups, and anyway it is difficult to allow that all these soldiers labelled as 'Romans' had followed Sertorius from the start or had joined him later. Parallels suggest that emigration which is politically inspired is always fed by members of the ruling class and such, we may suppose, was the case with that which made its way to the Spain of Sertorius.

It is true that this view would appear to conflict with the evidence of the sources concerning the journey to Spain in 77 BC made by the remnants of Lepidus' army with their leader Perperna. It is not known how many these soldiers numbered; Appian and Plutarch claim they were a sizeable amount.[282] When these forces joined Sertorius some months after their disembarkation, there were, according to Plutarch, fifty-three cohorts.[283] This figure is generally considered by modern scholars to be exaggerated,[284] just like the aggregate figures of Sertorius' army which have been transmitted to us.[285] It would, in fact, be incredible that Perperna had left Sardinia – or Lepidus Italy – with this number of men. Plutarch, however, does not say this but only that this was the size of Perperna's army some months after his landing, and one can well believe that in this interval Lepidus' general had added to his own forces with local levies.[286] In any case, the origin of Perperna's fifty-three cohorts has, I think, been seen by Schulten;[287] they correspond to the twenty thousand infantry and fifteen hundred cavalry at Perperna's disposal at one point during the struggle.[288] To an extent this confirms what is supposed to have been the origin of Perperna's forces; since a man who asserted that he was really a Roman magistrate seems to have preferred to command troops who were not natives,[289] it is probable that the numerical size of his later army has been transferred back to the time when he landed in Spain. Indeed, Perperna had certainly brought with him from Sardinia a useful contribution of manpower, but the soldiers described as 'Roman' in the sources, men whom he seems to have commanded, would have been largely *Hispanienses*, that is, Romans and Italians of Spain.

Since this participation by Roman and Italian elements of Spain was not conscripted – this is shown by the fact that they remained loyal to Sertorius until the end – it is an indicator of the attitude of the *Hispanienses* towards the whole of Sertorius' policy. This attitude requires further definition. Sertorius set up his own capital at Osca, which we have seen was the real centre of a district where the penetration of Oscan elements had been most pronounced. Further, in this district Romanization had been going on for a long time. It is, of course, no accident that Tarraco, one of the centres most frequented by Roman citizens (there was a *conventus* there), was one of the last cities to surrender.[290] The favour shown to Sertorius by localities inhabited by Romans or Italians in the north of Spain has a counterpart, at least to some extent, in the southern areas; these appear, as far as we can tell, rather to be supporters of the Sullan regime, and their governors never fail to control them. For example, Corduba remained loyal to Metellus Pius who wintered there in 77 BC, and earlier in 80 the whole district appears to adopt an attitude of opposition to Sertorius.[291] New Carthage was for a long time in Roman hands.[292] In the neighbourhood of Malaca the outlook of the wealthy class was anti-Sertorian.[293] On the other hand, Valentia was Sertorian and Pompey conquered it only in 75 BC.[294] I am unable to say whether Italica remained in the Romans' hands; a battle took place there in 76 BC between Metellus and Hirtuleius. At Corduba, Carthago and Italica there were *conventus civium Romanorum*.

All this prompts the conclusion that if Sertorius succeeded in obtaining the backing of one section of the *Hispanienses*, it was for preference those whose origin was associated with allied Italy rather than the *cives* who favoured him. How is this attitude to be explained?

'Sertorius avait obtenu l'adhésion des immigrés romains, si nombreux en Espagne. Ces immigrés étaient des Italiens plutôt que des Romains, et Sertorius se présentait sans doute comme un chef Italien, ennemi de Rome.' In these few lines of his *Histoire de Rome*, so rich in ideas and happy inspiration,[295] A. Piganiol has set out the problem and envisaged its solution.

I have tried above to adduce evidence for this interpretation. It emphasizes the fact that substantial sections of the *Hispanienses* were ready to collaborate, and in doing so it proves that Treves' guiding principles on Sertorius were right, particularly his stress on the intimate relationship which prevailed between post-Sullan Roman domestic politics and Sertorius himself. This has to be borne in mind if we are to understand and evaluate the latter's enterprise. At the same time we can see how this interpretation throws light on the motives which inspired Sertorius.

Naturally, if we go more deeply into individual points we can see more precisely the truth of Piganiol's conclusion; we need to make clearer his expression of the problem which is over-schematic. In other words, it will be a matter of seeing to what extent Sertorius was a 'chef Italien' and, as a result, whether he actually was what many think he was, 'un ennemi de

Rome'. We shall have to see how those actions can be interpreted which, within certain limits and from a precise point of view, would appear to make that conclusion legitimate. To be able to make distinctions of this kind we shall have to rely on the point which has been made above[296] concerning the two trends that for a time marked the democratic faction; these trends arose because the assimilation of ex-rebels who had joined the Marians and the traditional nucleus of Roman democrats had not yet taken place and it inevitably needed time to mature.

The conflicts of political ideals which we can detect in Italy in the period immediately after the Social War, barely concealed or else covered by a banner of common political action, existed also in Spain but were not very obvious and are consequently not very clear to us. It is probably with the presence of what one might call anti-Roman currents around Sertorius that oligarchic propaganda made play, and this dominated with its own themes a whole historical tradition so that thereby there emerged the well-known picture of a Sertorius who was the enemy of his own country.

XII
Sertorius' lieutenants

As I have said, only L. Fabius Hispaniensis, who in all probability joined Sertorius along with Perperna, can be regarded as a Sertorian officer of Spanish birth. Of Sertorius' other lieutenants who are mentioned in the sources L. Livius Salinator seems to have been with Sertorius since 81 BC and it may be supposed that he was one of the quaestors who set out with him.[297] The majority joined Sertorius in 77 BC along with Perperna. In addition to Perperna's nephew and three other Romans whose names are unknown to us and whom Perperna had put to death later,[298] we know of L. Cornelius Cinna, son of the famous democratic leader,[299] M. Marius[300] and C. Herennius.[301] These last two (three counting L. Fabius) were senators. In this first group, besides members of famous noble families such as Livius Salinator and Cornelius Cinna, the names of M. Marius and C. Herennius testify to two *gentes* who are well-known in the years either side of the Social War as taking a position favourable to the democrats.[302]

Another group of Sertorius' officers came from the General Staff of Pompeius Strabo's army: C. Tarquitius Priscus,[303] Q. Hirtuleius[304] and L. Insteius.[305] Their presence alongside Sertorius in Spain must be explained against the background of the parley between Cinna and Strabo before Rome in 87 BC. It was certainly on that occasion that some of Strabo's officers and men joined the democratic side.[306] Of those known to us the Insteii were very probably Campanian,[307] and the Hirtuleii, if we bear in mind the evidence of their tribe,[308] were Marsi or Paeligni; one would suppose that they had acquired the citizenship during the Social War.[309] L. Tarquitius was Etruscan.[310] Here one notices an interesting point, that the Etruscans were numerous in Sertorius' entourage. Besides Tarquitius and Perperna[311] there were C. Maecenas[312] and Versius.[313] This phenomenon is to be explained either by the fact that the Etruscan lower classes were pro-Marian,[314] or – and this fits with the general picture I have given – by the participation of Etruscan elements in the revolt of M. Aemilius Lepidus which had its centre in Etruria. However, this point may be part of a general context in which ex-rebels (or at least non-Romans) are found alongside Sertorius and this can explain the goodwill with which Sertorius was welcomed by the *Hispanienses* of Italian origin.[315]

Although they are not actually Sertorian,[316] one must mention here the collaboration between Sertorius and the two emissaries from Mithridates, L. Magius and L. Fannius, officers in the Asiatic army of the democrat C. Flavius Fimbria; after the latter's death in 85 BC they joined Mithridates.[317] L. Magius was probably one of the two sons, who reached the praetorship, of the often-mentioned Minatus Magius of Aeclanum[318] and was certainly related to the famous Capuan family of the Magii whose anti-oligarchic views in the period of the first civil war are well attested.[319] Their move to join Rome's most dangerous enemy, although it can be linked with what was a sort of tradition among Roman political exiles, clearly shows none the less the psychology of the allied aristocracy and their ideals which were still bound up with the anti-Roman and individualistic interests of many ex-rebels who joined the democratic faction. L. Fannius was probably related to M. Fannius who was plebeian aedile and moneyer during the period of the Cinnan supremacy at Rome, perhaps about 82 BC.[320]

Certainly our knowledge of Sertorius' Roman political support is limited if one reflects that he formed a senate of 300 members with Roman exiles, as the tradition says, and perhaps with *Hispanienses*;[321] however, the personalities known to us are sufficient to give us an idea of the composition of the circle. Just as with the popular faction on a larger scale, so there flocked to him men of diverse origins and different outlooks, doubtless bringing with them policies and views of conflicting kinds. Of these we are barely able to do more than catch a glimpse.

On the other hand, Sertorius did not see his field of activity as limited geographically to Spain, and he did not fail to keep up connexions with those Roman anti-oligarchic circles which even the dictatorship of Sulla and the proscriptions could not lay low, and which after 79 BC began once again to assume importance. These connexions to which the sources allude in obscure fashion[322] and which are *per se* enough to put Sertorius' activity in a context of Roman politics, must have made him not only aware that the struggle in which he was engaged had an end beyond itself but also gave him hope, not that he would enjoy merely some sort of constitutional return to Rome, but that he would be able to throw out the restored oligarchic regime with a double force, foreign and domestic. Indeed, Lepidus' movement may have been part of this more general plan, though there is no evidence of any link with Sertorius.

That this was beyond doubt the significance and importance of the connexions maintained by Sertorius with Roman political circles seems to be confirmed by the fact that where we can see with a fair measure of certainty the nature of Sertorius' relationships with Italy we also have the opportunity to confirm the ties between Sertorius and the Italian ex-rebels, ties which seem to have persisted until the end of hostilities in Spain. The support Sertorius enjoyed among the commercial class who especially would have carried to the East with them the reputation of his enterprises[323] finds implicit confirmation in all Cicero's polemic in his so-called *de suppliciis* Verrine oration against Verres' cruelty in Sicily in his treatment of Roman citizens who hailed from Spain and whom he condemned as Sertorian, that is, as enemies.[324]

This evidence shows clearly that there existed widespread exchanges and contacts between Sertorian Spain and southern Italy (from which the majority of the *negotiatores* came); it would be naïve to limit these contacts to the field of commerce. It is not surprising, therefore, to see mentioned in Cicero the *liberti* of a P. Granius,[325] belonging to the family of the well-known traders of Puteoli,[326] whose political outlook in this period is known through the opposition of a Granius to Sulla himself,[327] and also a Herennius,[328] almost certainly the father of the C. Herennius who was Sertorius' lieutenant.[329] These members of the commercial class from southern Italy, by helping and supporting Sertorius' struggle, continued the sort of assistance (especially financial, one would think) with which they had actively encouraged the rebels of the *Bellum Sociale*. In this sense Sertorius' Spanish activity could really appear to be that of a 'chef Italien', to use Piganiol's phrase. But we should remember that these relationships with southern Italy are not the only political contacts Sertorius kept with the mainland; there is reason to believe that they were, so to say, only a sideshow, albeit a characteristic and significant one. Sertorius knew only too well that the political centre was henceforth to be none other than Rome, and that every centrifugal tendency in Italy was merely to be exploited for incidental purposes. Italy could no longer look forward to a successful future of her own.

The Ciceronian evidence shows that there was in Sertorius' entourage a very strong representation of those whose interests were in Italy. What influence they exercised on Sertorian policy we cannot tell except perhaps in one example, the pact with Mithridates. However, that is itself another proof of the necessary connexion between the war of Sertorius and the struggles which accompanied the entry of the *socii* into the citizenship.

We come, then, to this conclusion: Sertorius' political activity cannot be correctly assessed if it is not set against the background of the political life which was taking shape in those very years in the metropolis.

XIII
Characteristics of political life at Rome in the post-Sullan age

Research in recent times has concentrated on defining the limits within which Roman political groups must be interpreted and evaluated, without using those modern reconstructions which cannot apply to ancient politics.[330] All that we need to do here is to remember that if by the term *optimates* we can signify conservative tendencies – and there is some justification for this – we cannot use in a similar way the term which corresponds to and contrasts with it, *populares*. To put it another way, to reduce to a single common description (*populares*) political movements which were quite diverse can only be justified if it be supposed that the term was used in, so to say, a negative sense, that is, if we accept the point of view of the oligarchs. The composition of the ancient political classes was tightly controlled, and the state came to be identified with those groups which held power;[331] so the oligarchs – at least originally – came to treat alike all those whose political ideas or political activity were in any way opposed to those who held power, and to label them with one and the same general description. The historian must try to get behind the recurring terminology and to see on each occasion what is the nature of the movement and the political ideas to which it refers.

These preliminaries are indispensable if we are to appreciate a fact of great importance. Parallel to the change in political method between the end of the second century BC and the beginning of the first – which was in its turn a reflection of the growth of a new range of political problems – came a change from anti-oligarchic, democratic policy which, for simplicity's sake, may be called Gracchan, to another which was dominated by military chiefs and which ended by imposing itself totally on the former; this in turn survived as a sort of outer coating to conceal what was in fact something new underneath. In this process, as I have already said on several occasions,[332] the Social War played a decisive part, for it was responsible for the situation changing; the historian, therefore, can use it as a means of clarifying what actually took place.

The war had this effect: the period which immediately succeeded it – that is, to be more precise, the years from the end of Sulla's dictatorship to Pompey's first consulship (79–70 BC) – should have been marked by the return of normality to Roman public life after the disturbances of the civil wars, but it was in fact a period of transition and therefore, within the limitations imposed by the wretched state of our evidence, one where we can best trace the change to which I have referred. By weighing up the interacting forces at work in Roman politics we may at the same time see how impossible it is to impose an artificial order on their complexity, even when all we want to do is to clarify.

In these years those who fought in the traditional way against the oligarchs limited themselves to measures designed to secure the full restoration of the tribunician power which had suffered a substantial diminution at the hands of Sulla;[333] the object was to acquire thereby the base which they thought was indispensable if those methods of opposition which had been practised in the past were to be adopted again. These attempts occurred in quick succession year by year in the post-Sullan decade, and by coming up again and again seem to show the influence which outmoded methods and political concepts could continue to exercise.

As early as 78 BC the tribunes asked the consuls to take steps to restore the tribunician power but met with a straight refusal;[334] however, one of the consuls, M. Aemilius Lepidus, appreciating the importance of the cause – though this was a matter of propaganda rather than of substance – made himself its champion that year and the next (77 BC).[335] He failed, and therefore in 76 BC we find the tribune Cn. Sicinius raising the question again.[336] So insistent was the demand that the year after, 75 BC, the consul C. Aurelius Cotta took the first step *et legem tulit ut tribunis pl. liceret postea alios magistratus capere;*[337] this restriction had been introduced by Sulla to emasculate the office of tribune. Cotta belonged to the very heart of the Optimate *factio* which thought it useful to stoop to concessions.[338] In 74 the tribune L. Quinctius, *homo maxime popularis,*[339] was deterred by the consul L. Licinius Lucullus from insisting on the usual demand;[340] however, that the power of the tribunes had actually increased is shown by the role played in that year by another tribune,[341] P. Cornelius Cethegus, who, after a dubious change of sides to join Sulla, returned to his original Marian affiliation.[342] In 73 the question was proposed again by C. Licinius Macer who was able to draw on Pompey's support for the full restoration of the tribunician power[343] and who dared to resurrect the complaints of the Etruscans at Sulla's confiscations.[344] In fact, in 71 BC Pompey came forward as the clear supporter of these democratic demands, personified that year by the tribune M. Lollius Palicanus,[345] and in 70 the tribunician power was fully restored by the consular law of Pompey and Crassus.[346]

Although it is right to recognize that re-establishing the tribunician power must have been an important political theme for those opposed to the oligarchs, we cannot follow the example set by some historians of antiquity and be satisfied with an interpretation which explains an extremely complex, new situation in terms of what until then had been the usual procedure in politics. What we can deduce from the repetition of the demand is that pressure to restore the tribunician power had to come from those not tied to the dominant Sullan regime of reaction; in fact, especially after 75 BC, we have evidence, for example in the two cases of Cornelius Cethegus and Licinius Macer,[347] of a revival in politics of those democratic elements which had not in fact disappeared from the scene even after Sulla's measures.[348]

One cannot, of course, say with certainty how far the presence in the governing class during the period 79–70 BC of men alien, or at least not tied, to the policy of reaction can be explained not only by the fact that representatives of the traditional democratic faction had returned but also by the admission of ex-allies who were perhaps of conservative views but who did not totally agree with the Roman oligarchy. However, it seems to me that here we are concerned with one of the most important characteristics of post-Sullan politics. I have in fact shown above[349] how these years saw a continuation of that process of grafting on to the Roman governing class political elements drawn from the ex-*socii*, a process which had begun immediately after 89 BC. We can easily guess – and it is attested by what we know of the ideology of the *novi cives* – that their presence in Rome made political life more complex; at the same time the importance of traditional problems still further diminished, and among these was that which concerned the power of the tribunes.

This is all the more true in that the birth of the privately-raised army during the *Bellum Sociale*[350] plus the employment of military forces in politics, brutally introduced by Sulla in 88 BC,[351] increased the influence of military leaders, already in itself important because of the establishment of a professional army; this influence gradually emerged as a factor of major significance and eventually as the fundamental feature of national life. Despite the measures taken to restore strength to the oligarchic, senatorial regime, Sulla had not been able to abolish his own example[352] and the decade which followed his death was that which saw the establishment of Pompey's power based to a large extent on the army.[353]

This new aspect of the political situation did not escape the attention of Sallust who probably saw in M. Aemilius Lepidus the first politican to have attempted to establish power for himself behind the misleading mask of popularism.[354] Sallust was also the first of the historians who wrote after the death of Sulla to have denied to Pompey that cover of Republicanism with which the tradition drawing its inspiration from Theophanes and reflected in Plutarch's *Life of Pompey* loved to invest him. Sallust showed how Pompey represented nothing more than the military monarch who made every effort to acquire supreme power and who, once he had achieved a position of hegemony in the state, sought the collaboration of the traditional political classes by respecting, more or less sincerely, their prerogatives.[355] On this view the war with Caesar was reduced to a competition for power,[356] as Cicero had seen in a moment of depression[357] (whereas an idealization of

Pompey saw him as playing the role of the defender of traditional liberties). This interpretation of Pompey's personality derived some very significant supporting testimony from his activity in the period before his first consulship. There was his opposition to Sulla when he favoured the election of Lepidus[358] and his opposition to the same Lepidus as soon as the latter's objectives became clear; his behaviour throughout the Sertorius affair, attested in his guiding principles as revealed by his famous letter to the Senate[359] (there is no occasion to doubt the reliability of its theme);[360] his ambition to model himself on Alexander;[361] his espousal of *popularis* movements of which the re-establishment of the tribunician power was a decisive point; and finally the generosity of his treatment of defeated Sertorians.[362] The object of these last enterprises – like the *mandata* of Lepidus in his period – was to obtain a power base under the protection afforded by traditional catchwords dear to the masses. Sallust himself had stigmatized this trading on traditional positions or on powerful catchwords for personal ends: *pauci potentes, quorum in gratiam plerique concesserant, sub honesto patrum aut plebis nomine dominationes affectabant.*[363]

All this leads to two kinds of questions that need to be answered. First, how far can one speak of a 'bifurcation' of *popularis* politics, represented on the one side by military leaders and their supporters among the Equites, and on the other by the successors to the Gracchan tradition and, with certain reservations, to Saturninus and Sulpicius?[364] Did not perhaps the traditional tribunician theme, which seemed to live on only in the strength it drew from its past, become of marginal interest after 79 BC and in any case subject to military leaders' designs? The other question is, if the political situation at Rome after Sulla's death was as we have summed it up, what substantial opportunities could it furnish for the activity of Sertorius? In other words, could it give him a policy with which he could co-operate from Spain? In fact, what were the political forces with which he was in contact and on which he counted?

It is here that one can really appreciate to what extent the struggle between Sertorius and Pompey had been a 'bitter war'.[365] It was a struggle between two ideologies which in effect had the same aims. These aims – and it is not a paradox – were involuntarily achieved by Sertorius, in hostile co-operation with Pompey, in so far as it was the Sertorian affair which gave Pompey an extraordinary military command; this demolished Sulla's constitution and the scene was set for discrediting the oligarchic government.[366] This struggle between Sertorius and Pompey, mutual enemies and enemies of a common enemy, was 'sensed' by Sallust who has personified in the two leaders two conflicting aspects of a single political outlook which was in the process of development: on the one side the old-style politician, on the other the politician of strength and violence. This contrast has been exaggerated by Schur;[367] in any event it has perhaps greater validity as an element of

Sallustian historiography than as a piece of historical reality, for here – as always – one cannot postulate rigid political positions. On the contrary, we should believe that old and new attitudes were blended together: on the Sertorian side new needs were experienced, on the Pompeian the necessity to keep in contact with tradition and the past. Anyway, it is certain that only by remembering what was happening in Roman politics from 79 to 70 BC will we be able to understand the activity of Sertorius, and his innermost motives and aims.

XIV

Sertorius and Rome

It is over the pact with Mithridates and the negotiations which led up to it[368] that we can detect different points of view and different principles behind that tradition which presents the political activity of Sertorius as a uniform whole. We should bear in mind here what we have said about the entry of ex-rebels into the ranks of the Marian democrats; on most occasions these came from extremist circles and were believers in ideals which did not conform to, or were in direct conflict with, the traditional principles of Roman politics. If we remember that, we shall see, as I said above, how the initiative for an alliance with the King of Pontus must have come from those groups of ex-rebels who, to escape the collapse of the revolt, took refuge in the East and offered their support to Mithridates against Sulla.[369] These were joined in 85 BC, at the time when the democratic army of L. Valerius Flaccus and C. Flavius Fimbria was dissolved, by implacable anti-Sullans, and probably ex-rebels, who did not wish to be united with Sulla; among them were L. Fannius and L. Magius, who served as intermediaries for the treaty and whose origins I have already indicated.[370]

The request for aid from Mithridates does not make its first appearance here nor is it a novelty; it is only the continuation of a practice which boasted a good many precedents. The Italian allies had earlier appealed to Mithridates to intervene at a time when they felt their ability to resist was coming to an end, and they had certainly had promises and perhaps financial support even if they did not get the substantial aid for which they had hoped.[371] It is possible that the class of businessmen from southern Italy sought to make use of the intimate relationship which trade had long established with countries of the East, letting it take the concrete form of political and military aid.[372] This also explains how one section of Sertorius' collaborators regarded Mithridates' demands as acceptable *en bloc* since their picture of Mithridates was not of an enemy of the Roman people but of an ally who could, in conjunction with them, administer the knock-out blow to the common enemy whom they both abhorred. It must, therefore, have seemed of minor importance to them, given the animosity for Rome which had accumulated over a long period and which existed also at that actual moment of time, that the *provincia Asia* was to be surrendered.[373]

Naturally, the presence in Sertorius' entourage of people with ideas of this sort, together with the fact that he agreed to an alliance proposed on these lines – even if, as must be said at once, it was accepted by him with other ideas in mind and for other purposes – explains well enough how it has been possible to generalize and to attribute to Sertorius himself and everything he was doing that brand of treachery which clearly an alliance with the King of Pontus would naturally suggest to the Roman mind. But this is a *reductio ad unum* typical of propaganda, the setting for a fable, with Sertorius as a new Hannibal planning to assault Italy from Spain, either by his own inspiration[374] or in response to an invitation to Rome from politicians there with whom he was in contact.[375] Not that we should accept, of course, the opposite interpretation favoured by Sallust, who sees Sertorius as a senti-mental, disillusioned man:[376] μᾶλλον . . . ἐθέλειν ἀσημότατος ἐν Ῥώμῃ πολίτης ἢ φεύγων τὴν ἑαυτοῦ πάντων ὁμοῦ τῶν ἄλλων αὐτοκράτωρ ἀναγορεύεσθαι.[377] It is certain that among the refugees of Spain he – and certainly not he alone – exemplified that point of view which never ceased to look towards Rome: that is to say, he viewed the struggle as one with the object not of overthrowing Rome but of re-establishing there that demo-cratic government which Sulla, and the oligarchy who triumphed with him, had destroyed. This is implicitly recognized even by those sources which are anti-Sertorian in tone (the non-Sallustian tradition) and which speak of the continuity between the civil war in Italy and that against Sertorius,[378] not to mention the Sallustian theme, known to us especially from Plutarch, of the 'Roman character' of Sertorius.[379]

In fact, Sertorius is on precisely the same level as the Marian leaders of the period 87–82 BC and it is by holding firmly to this point that we can under-stand his activity and his purpose. His activity remained on the whole unaltered from his landing in Spain in 82 BC down to his death. The steps he took to ingratiate himself with his Spanish government were measures of marginal effect and their purpose only incidental; without them it would have been difficult if not impossible to support himself.[380]

The fundamental point, however, concerns his relations with Rome. A chance of contact with the metropolis existed only if some fundamental principles were agreed *a priori*, principles which the democrats had never thought of renouncing even in their struggle with the oligarchy which had lasted for many a decade. Sertorius therefore could not, in the case in point, approve a policy of surrendering Asia, or any other province whatsoever: that is, he could not in the struggle substitute for his own ideals, which were those of the genuine Roman democratic tradition, the ends of vendetta or separatism favoured by those extremists who had other ideas in mind and who had enjoyed a very different kind of experience when they united with the Marians. Agreement with these extremists would have meant willingness to conquer but at a cost of excessively serious losses.[381] This Sertorius knew he could not do, if for no other reason than that he would not have been supported by any section of popular opinion at Rome and he would have lost beyond recall the possibility of finding a solid basis for acting in concert with anti-oligarchic groups and, in the specific example of Asia, with the Roman commercial class; the latter's interest in Eastern problems has already been observed, and their ideas on the subject were well-known. They were for resolving the question by a policy of intervention, not of acquiescence.

To return to Piganiol's point, Sertorius could not be 'un ennemi de Rome'. Hence his opposition to the excessive demands of Mithridates, his resistance to the advice of his own senate which was ready to accept the proposals, and his tenacity in keeping faith with traditional principles, at least as far as he could.[382] Perhaps it is this background which explains his sending to Asia as his own representative M. Marius, a Roman senator who had joined him with Perperna. This is to be interpreted as a lack of faith in those who had long been with Mithridates.[383] Sertorius must have attached very great importance to his relations with the democrats in Rome. They were, one might say, the outward visible sign of the link between his struggle in Spain and the wider field of opposition to the Sullan regime. Was there hope at Rome, perhaps, that Sertorius would win a decisive victory over the oligarchic generals? Did Sertorius request, or at least have warning of, the attempt of Aemilius Lepidus? If these questions must remain unanswered, it is none the less only by looking at his connexions with politics at Rome that we can see how his enterprise gradually lost its point.

Above all, with what part of the Roman forces deployed against the oligarchs was he in contact, or rather could he have contact? Certainly with the remnants of the democratic Marian faction which had fled Sulla's proscriptions, and maybe with the representatives of the Italian ex-rebels. But we have seen the position these groups held in the political life of the post-Sullan decade. Among the ex-rebels, those who had loyally accepted the new order were rather inclined to the conservative view; the others, together with the heirs of the Marian faction, had to put up with a system which involved struggle and opposition, a system which no longer had anything concrete to offer them and which was nothing more than a misleading label for a package whose contents were quite different. Political life, and with it a possible resurgence by the *populares*, was now mapped on a different course. Even the conflict between Senate and Equites seems greatly weakened with the establishment of the Sullan Senate, and the *lex Aurelia* of 70 BC on the jury-courts in the *quaestio de repetundis* does not seem to be invested with the same sort of partiality as other laws of that type.

Sertorius, set fast in the outlook and ways appropriate to the democrats down to 82 BC, seems an anachronism in the context of the new situation which had developed and the new problems which presented themselves. It seems that this is the destiny of all those who, in making preparations for their victorious return, have to be out of touch with, and estranged from, the political life of the metropolis. Pompey's arrival in Spain probably seemed to Sertorius like the prosecution of the struggle which he was already conducting with Q. Caecilius Metellus Pius, that is, with Sulla's lieutenants. In his eyes Pompey will always have appeared as Sulla's pupil.[384]

In fact, from that time, the struggle became an end in itself. His contacts with Roman politicians no longer had any real force; the new *popularis* movement, that of the military leaders, chose the very representatives, some sincere, others not, of the old democratic tradition – Lepidus, Sertorius – to build new power on their defeat. It is only indirectly that Sertorius co-operated in the collapse of the Sullan edifice, in so far as he made the Senate invest Pompey with supreme power and thereby demolish with its own hands what Sulla had constructed.[385]

Up to a certain point Sertorius and his followers were aware that they were fighting without purpose, only through sheer inertia. Nothing could be got from Mithridates, nothing could come of the relationships with Roman politicians who either represented only their own selfish interests or were already changing course at the breath of the new breeze. The Spanish element of his entourage began to understand how they were being sucked dry in a cause which had never been theirs. In this atmosphere, while Sertorius' faith wavered, it is easy to understand how the idea could take root that the overthrow of the general might represent for his followers the one way out of a situation which appeared not to offer any other escape, and so bring about in some way their reintegration in Roman political life. This is what in actual fact happened since Pompey, whose interest it was to pose as defender of traditional liberties, generously welcomed the followers of Sertorius[386] and in 70 BC, together with the re-establishment of the tribunician power, supported the *lex Plotia* which granted an amnesty to the Lepidani (and to the Sertorians).[387] It is significant that even the more implacable enemies of the oligarchy and of Rome, Fannius and Magius who supported Mithridates, although declared *hostes* in 70 BC by the Senate,[388] later returned to Rome.[389]

Even these energetic legatees of the Italian cause had learned that Italian independence, as an instrument of power politics, was outmoded, just as there had vanished with the passing of Sertorius the mirage of restoring that democratic state which Sulla had overwhelmed – along with the foolish Italian dream of separatism – at the battle of the Colline Gate.

XV
Conclusion

The fundamental significance of the Social War in the history of the last century of the Roman Republic lies in the fact that those political problems which until then had been Roman (that is, citizen) problems became essentially 'Italian'. This development could not take place without changing the problems themselves and thereby the whole of Roman politics, since the introduction of *novi cives* was not, and could not be, along the same lines of political development which had been followed at Rome in the past.

In fact, the allies had their own individual vision of domestic and foreign political problems. They acquired this by looking at the various questions from a different point of view from that of the Roman political classes. It was clear that account would henceforth have to be taken in Roman politics of their points of view; it would have been more difficult to foresee that in many cases the allies had the capacity to ensure that their views prevailed. This resulted from the fact that the entry of the allies, now *cives*, into the Roman governing class was swift and immediate, and led to a substantial change in the traditional political system which had become stabilized over many centuries. It matters little that respect for political forms seems to have continued, and the historian must not be deceived by the external appearance of Roman politics after 89 BC in terms not very different from those of the preceding period. The pressure of the new citizens, and of the new problems they represented, made itself felt on the old governing class; this was incapable of understanding and therefore of resolving them, and remained only as a relic of the past, one overcome by the new reality. The fact that superficially it survived is explicable only in terms of traditional Roman reluctance to adapt the state's structure; this structure had crystallized in the course of its historical development and the Romans would not accommodate its form to the content, which was in a perpetual process of change and enrichment. The political situation, however, no longer responded to premises that were centuries old and on which it still seemed to rest. So in the first century BC there is the conflict between two political currents which reflected different concepts of political life, although we should not be too schematic and assign them rigidly fixed and established positions.

This is all based on an examination of a fundamental problem, which the Social War certainly is, a problem which consists principally in trying to discover for what reason the allies wanted the Roman citizenship. Apart from the consequences of the Social War I have mentioned above, consequences which it is not easy to believe were not already present in its origin as an underlying cause, I hope I have offered arguments of significant weight intended to show that the need which at that time prompted the request of some of the allies for the *civitas* was actually that of gaining admission to the citizenship in order to participate as of right in Roman political life. Only in this way, strong in the knowledge of their own indispensability in the life of the Empire, could they develop their own political and economic capacity to the full, making their voice heard in the discussion of problems in which they were directly interested.

If this is how we should picture the complex of motives of which I have tried to take account in the course of my study, the theory that keeps on cropping up in the ancient traditions seems fully justified,[390] that of a strict connexion between, or interdependence of, the Social War and the Sullan civil war; the latter was the first occasion on which, according to the account of Diodorus, the *novi cives* took sides on Roman political problems. It was decisive too, since their choice, which in most cases remained fixed for the future as well, sheds a flood of light on the political ideals and convictions of the Italian upper classes. They therefore present themselves to the historian, as much in their total significance as in individual cases, as the personification of those demands to share effectively in the life of the Empire, demands which had led to the Social War itself.

The civil war between Marius and Sulla did not, as far as its basic problems were concerned, finish with the victory of the Sullan forces in Italy. These forces appeared to have completely destroyed both the democratic Marian movement and those Italian rebels who had hoped for the triumph of their own independent point of view by rallying under a traditional Roman political banner. The war continued with Sertorius in Spain. In fact, the 'Italian' themes of the Sertorian struggle seem to me to show that the Spanish setting presented to us by the ancient tradition and emphasized by modern historiography was only fortuitous. It is by seeing the exile and his work in the context of Roman political development in that period, or rather by bringing the one face to face with the other, that we can clarify Sertorius' policy and thereby resolve the grim dilemma posed by the ancient evidence and accepted by a large part of modern scholarship concerning the personality of Sertorius.

At this point we must raise a fundamental question. The demands which typify the movement of the *socii* towards acquisition of the Roman citizenship are demands appropriate to strictly limited upper classes or to clearly defined circles with their own outlook and policies. The entry of such elements into Roman politics altered, as I have said, the life of the state since its basis was changed. It is, however, in a certain sense significant that these new forces at once chose that political movement which of all the traditional Roman views was closest to them. These Roman views thus acquired new life from new forces permanently at work outside Rome.

However, the process of renewal of first-century BC Rome, of which the Social War is the culmination, does not end with the entry of these new forces into Roman politics. All the more significant – because it is impersonal – is the contribution of the 'non-political' classes to whom the *civitas* mattered less and for whom therefore the Social War's significance is to be sought elsewhere. They came in fact to acquire importance in a period in which the strength and significance of closed élites, and of the types of government which they represented, seemed to become less day by day.

I have shown elsewhere how the principal instrument for making the presence of such people felt in Rome's political life was the professional army, which came in the second and first centuries BC to be substituted for the traditional citizen militia.[391] Here it is sufficient to mention that even in this respect the Social War takes on an 'epoch-making' significance – also emphasized by an ancient historian[392] – in that it introduced new revolutionary political methods, largely dominated by military forces.[393]

APPENDIX
Notes on the equestrian class in the Republican period[1]

1. A central point in the evolution of the equestrian class in the Republican period is the moment at which the Equites were distinguished from the rest of the population by a special census qualification. Hill tried to assign this event a chronological context in his article '*Census Equester*', *AJPh* LX 1939, 361 f., where he concluded that the introduction of the equestrian census, for which the first explicit evidence is 67 BC,[2] took place in the Gracchan period. This hypothesis, however, has not found acceptance[3] and I myself have opposed it in a work with which Hill could not, because of the date of publication, have been acquainted.[4] In his book this dating is one of the fundamentals for his whole reconstruction of the historical development of this social group and therefore of the whole of Roman society, since it represents for him the principal proof for the origin of the capitalist class in the last decades of the second century BC.[5] So a re-examination of the question seems legitimate and it is perhaps best to begin – bearing in mind some points made by Stein[6] – with a general definition of a very important point, the significance of the census figures.

These figures, like all those whose purpose it is to subdivide citizens into census categories, have above all a practical purpose, whether they concern military service, tribute or voting. They could not in any way 'create' a social class nor, where one already existed, could they delimit it.[7] No one has ever dreamed of considering the Servian classes as social classes; the only people of whom one could say this are the *proletarii*, those who were outside the classes, although their status was not very different from that of the citizens of the fifth class. The *lex Aurelia* of 70 BC placed *tribuni aerarii* alongside the senators and the knights, but the distinction between them and the Equites, probably entirely a census matter,[8] was so far from being an organic difference that Cicero, *pro Rabirio Postumo* 14, called the two groups *equites* without more ado, and in Schol. Bob. p. 94, 25 Stangl, they are referred to as *eiusdem scilicet ordinis viri*.[9]

Thus it seems very difficult and odd that the significance of the *census equester*, which in my view pre-dates the Hannibalic War, could have changed at a time when, from the Gracchan period onwards, the class of knights was clearly becoming a precise social class.[10] It must always have remained as a sort of formal, external qualification, useful originally for the censors in drawing up a list of those suitable for cavalry service and then to provide a practical indicator of those who could be used for fixed political functions, such as the choice of *iudices*.[11] Even in the Imperial period the equestrian and senatorial censuses represented a means of practical qualification for admission to a given category, without any real effect on the structure of society; they established, that is to say, a political distinction. Among other things Stein[12] makes it quite clear that the distinction between these two orders is no longer economic or social but is political in character.

If, therefore, as I believe, this was how matters stood, the significance of the equestrian census for the Republican period, apart from changes which may have affected it in the course of time, must consist in its recognition that there were a certain number of citizens with a precise economic capacity. To fix the date of introduction of this census figure will therefore be a basic contribution to Roman social history.

Like Hill[13] we shall have to start with the well-known passage of Polybius, VI 20, 8–9. The passage is – at least in its general interpretation – clear and the explanation given by Mommsen[14] is generally accepted: when the cavalry was provided only by the eighteen centuries *equo publico*, the levy of the knights could take place after that of the infantry, but once it became necessary to have recourse as well to those citizens who could provide their own private horse,[15] the levy of those knights had to take place before that of the infantry, in so far as those citizens with the required qualifications could, if not chosen for the cavalry, serve in the infantry. According to Hill, it follows from this that there was not a *census equester*, for if there had been it would not have been necessary to introduce the change in precedence. This conclusion, which is in Hill alone and which seems to follow automatically from his earlier reasoning, has to disregard an extremely interesting phrase in the sentence of Polybius that I have cited. Polybius says: πλουτίνδην αὐτῶν (the knights) γεγενημένης ὑπὸ τοῦ τιμητοῦ τῆς ἐκλογῆς. In his *Middle Class* Hill completely ignores this parenthesis, in *AJPh* p. 360 he calls it extremely vague and says it indicates, as does Livy, V 7, 5, the census of the first class.[16] However, the evidence of Polybius is precise in its reference to the choice operated by the censors on the basis of wealth,[17] and the explanation is very clear if we bear in mind a particular fact to which Hill has not paid attention. The levy described in Polybius is a levy by tribes.[18] As long as the *dilectus* was based on the century, it was necessary and indeed easy for the purpose of enrolling knights to make a selection among the *iuniores* of the first class as a preliminary to enrolling the infantry. Hill's logic therefore fits such a period very well – but it is not the period to which Polybius refers. In fact, when the citizens took to presenting themselves at the levy without distinction of class or century, a procedure to which in fact Polybius alludes in his description, how would it have been possible to operate a preliminary choice if there had not been a list compiled by the censors in which citizens were included on the basis of fixed qualifications? The need for the levy of cavalry to take place before that of the infantry was obviously just as necessary in this situation.

Our first evidence on the levy by tribes dates to 275 BC,[19] and I believe that it was indeed at about that time that the new system was introduced. It seems very probable that the creation of a separate list of citizens capable of cavalry service was strictly connected with the introduction of the *dilectus* by tribes. At all events such a list was already in use in the period of the Second Punic War, as is clear from Livy, XXVII 11, 15, who mentions *qui equo merere deberent*,[20] despite the fact that Hill[21] again disregards the evidence in rather careless fashion. It is also confirmed by that particular point in the constitution of the Latin colonies which I have already mentioned above, *Es. e Soc.* 151 [= 56 above]. The appearance of the term *equites* in 218 BC[22] to indicate a social class defined in economic terms – not by a census but by the grant of land assigned: the difference is not a profound one – superior to others (at Aquileia superior also to *centuriones*: Livy, XL 34, 2) seems to permit the inference that the word is more than a technical term and that we are dealing with more than a military situation affecting the settlers;[23] the word's meaning refers directly to a real social context, here created *ex novo*, and must already have acquired a similar significance in the motherland, which was the model for colonial constitutions.

2. The ancient evidence is in agreement on the fact that the *equites equo publico* were chosen from among those citizens highest in terms of wealth;[24] the usual interpretation is that they came from the *iuniores* of the first Servian class. Did the introduction of the equestrian census, which was devised to facilitate the classification and enrolment of those citizens capable of providing horses at their own expense, have repercussions on the method of composition of the *centuriae equitum*? In other words, was there an extension of the equestrian census to the *equites equo publico* as well? Hill, it seems, does not mention the question, but at one point[25] appears to maintain that this did happen. According to Mommsen, the equestrian census was in force from the time of Camillus, and he maintained that during the Second Punic War the *equites equo publico* already possessed it.[26] He reached this

conclusion from the episode mentioned in Livy, XXVII 11, of the knights *equo publico* who, after Cannae, were compelled as a punishment to serve *equo privato*; for Mommsen this was equivalent to saying that they had the equestrian census. This conclusion, however, does not appear to settle the matter in so far as the measure recorded in Livy has a punitive character and it is more likely that the punishment consisted – over and above the obligation to serve beyond the normal time – actually in making private provision for their cavalry equipment; the only census they enjoyed was that of the first class.

I would be inclined to suppose that the extension of the equestrian census to the centuries *equo publico* was a later measure. We know, both from explicit evidence[27] and from other hints or implications,[28] that the centuries of the *equites equo publico* were composed of senators. Now, if to enter these centuries it had been necessary to enjoy the appropriate census rating, this would in practice have meant that the senator would have had a separate census, a point which, so far as we know, is not attested for the Republican period.[29] Incidentally, there would have occurred the case where senators who enjoyed the census of the first class did not come up to the higher requirement of the *equites equo privato*. About 129 BC a *plebiscitum* removed from the equestrian centuries those senators[30] who along with the members of their families had come to monopolize them.[31]

It is possible that on this occasion, when members of the capitalist class filled the gaps left by senators, the equestrian census was extended to the eighteen centuries as well. In any event, whatever the validity of this theory, it is well-known that, if in the *lex repetundarum* of the *Tabula Bembina* the lacunae at lines 12 and 16 – where the equestrian origin of the jurors must have been indicated – should be supplemented with a census figure,[32] both the knights in the broad sense and those of the eighteen centuries would be included; the case for the latter is proved by the fact that the law contemplates the exclusion of sons and brothers of senators, and these were still at that time the *magna pars* of these centuries.[33]

3. Hill calls the equestrian class 'the middle class'. This reference to the social structure of modern times has long been a commonplace, and for an equally long time there have been warnings about its dangers. If I confine myself here to mentioning the example of Merivale, *A History of the Romans under the Empire*, it is because it provoked in this connexion judicious and precise comments by P. Mérimée[34] to which I shall refer below. Is this identification permissible? It is odd that Hill, over and above his comments on the economic and social position of the knights, supports it with passages from the ancient sources, first of all with Pliny, *NH* XXXIII 2 (8), 34,[35] where he speaks of the *ordo equester* as a *tertium corpus* that had arisen in the state and had taken its place *medium plebei atque patribus*.[36] These passages

from Pliny do not in fact have any connexion with the social structure of the Roman state but refer, along with many others,[37] to that tripartite division which marks the Roman citizenry in the Imperial period,[38] based not on economic and social factors but on political ones. It is well-known – and I have emphasized it above – that the senatorial and equestrian *ordines* during the Principate appear as 'categories' with appropriate functions and characteristics; this followed Augustan measures to give the equestrian order political and administrative functions which were precise and distinct from those of the senatorial class.[39] It is also well-known, on the other hand, that in the economic and social fields the conflict between Equites and Senate which marked the Republican period but which was already weakening in the first century BC[40] eventually disappeared. On the three-runged ladder which consisted not only of the senatorial and equestrian orders but also of the *plebs* or the *populus*, with the latter comprising all who were not members of the privileged orders, the *ordo equester* had the middle position in so far as its *dignitas*[41] was inferior to that of the Senate but far superior to that of all other citizens.[42] Therefore the difference is not one based on economic or social factors, and the 'middle' position of the equestrian class mentioned by the ancient sources has nothing in common with what we think of or understand as 'middle class'.

Let us now see whether this identification cannot have a basis in the actual structure of Roman society. This is what Hill says:[43] 'Their (the Equites') peculiar position, placed as they were between the exclusive senatorial aristocracy which few of them could hope to enter and the mass of the people whom they despised, united them and directed their wealth and very considerable ability mainly towards those commercial and financial activities which are the usual sphere of any Middle Class'.

To be sure, in the second century BC and also in the first although in ever-declining measure, the senatorial class appears as the representative of landed property while the equestrian class represents disposable capital, commerce and finance. This state of affairs is the result *inter alia* of measures of the period of the Hannibalic War which forbade senators to devote themselves to commercial activity.[44] Bearing this in mind one could attempt to justify a comparison with the middle class as we commonly understand it – as is well-known, the concept of middle class cannot be laid down once and for all; its content changes in character according to changes in historical conditions – only at the cost of making a drastic *reductio ad unum*; I am thinking not only of all the diverse activity to which the middle class in all periods of history devotes itself but also of the very composition of the *ordo equester* in the Republic, comprising elements whose origins and social status (from the representative of big business like Atticus to the *publicanus* and *negotiator*) were markedly diverse.

But even outside the economic field this dubious comparison does not hold absolutely, and this was seen clearly by Mérimée.[45] The lack of any active, direct participation in politics proves that the political interest of the equestrian class was limited to a selfish, unilateral conception of their own interests, and as a result shows itself in measures designed to safeguard them. This class never, or only very rarely, manages to make the effort to take a broader view and to incorporate these interests in a political programme which embraces the state as a whole. This leads, as I have already said, to conflict with the Senate in the field of foreign policy and of provincial administration but at the same time we never really find the equestrian class operating on a different basis from that of the Senate whenever it has anything to do with domestic politics and with the concept of the state's structure. All this fits with the traditional, unexpressed but basic distinction of ancient society between *locupletes = boni*, and *egentes = improbi*,[46] a distinction which underlies Cicero's policy of *concordia ordinum*; Cicero, it should be remembered, came from the Equites but had none the less passed beyond their narrow, selfish conception of politics.

Even if much still remains to be said, the themes I have emphasized here seem sufficient for our purpose, which has been to show that the use of the term 'middle class' to indicate the equestrian class can be justified only if accompanied by the warning that it represents in Roman history a conventional expression used to characterize a state of affairs peculiar to a particular period and historical context; we should avoid impossible comparisons with, or reference to, points of time at which that phrase conceals a totally different reality.

In this situation it seems better to accept the term in the significance which it has in the ancient sources, without trying as Hill does to give it an economic or social significance. We should confine its use, that is to say, to giving formal expression to the position of a particular class in the social structure of Roman Republican history.[47]

IV

M. Livius Drusus and Sulla's Reforms*

*To Lily Ross Taylor with gratitude
and deepest respect*

The different interpretations of M. Livius Drusus' tribunate of 91 BC[1] which are preserved in the ancient sources reflect both the complexity of the problems which directly confronted him then and the enthusiasm and serious opposition which his actions inspired. Even though the precise chronology of Drusus' political activity is uncertain,[2] there is no reason to doubt the unity of his political programme. The problem of relations between the senatorial oligarchy and the equestrian class, intensified by the struggle over the composition of the juries in the *quaestiones*, and the problem concerning the grant of the citizenship to the allies are interwoven and interconnected in such a way that, whatever the priority they assumed in the execution of his legislative programme, this does not detract from its essential coherence and unity. Drusus' complex scheme seems to be directed by a precise and shrewd awareness of the historical situation, the political forces at work, and the needs and interests which these forces represented and conveyed. It reveals a political capacity which matched that of Caius Gracchus.

Livius Drusus' solutions for the grave problems I have mentioned were conceived in a political climate which is – to use a modern term – usually and properly called 'reformist'. Substantial changes in the traditional forms of Roman political life he did not even envisage; in fact he wished to strengthen and defend those forms. The policy for which he fought was an extension of the traditional Roman governing class which, by a long historical process known to all of us, had tended more and more to become a closed caste,

131

increasingly out of touch with social reality.[3] In this sense his proposals may be seen as supplementing the Gracchan agrarian reform, for only a careless and superficial judgement would call the latter revolutionary; aimed as it was at reviving the class of small peasant proprietors quite openly for military and imperialistic purposes, and thus restoring that class which was the traditional reservoir of military manpower, it appears rather to have been conservative.

Drusus' judiciary law is known to have had as its object the readmission of senators to the jury courts by means of a sweeping reform of the Senate itself, which was to be doubled in size by the admission of 300 knights chosen from the most influential among them. The jurors were to be drawn from this reformed body.[4] Even if the most conspicuous feature of the proposal was perhaps the institution of a *quaestio* '*si quis ob rem iudicandam pecuniam cepisset*' which covered either the new jurors without distinction or the senators and members of the equestrian class, it seems clear that Livius Drusus' intention was to call the knights to a direct share in governmental responsibility so as to strengthen the power of the oligarchy. The objections of the equestrian class to the law, reported by Cicero in two very important passages of the *pro Cluentio* and the *pro Rabirio Postumo*,[5] show that the knights appreciated this aim no less than its undoubted anti-equestrian purpose (obvious above all in Drusus, the nephew of Rutilius Rufus),[6] and that his proposals did not win them over.

The *rogatio de sociis* had the same aim; it probably represented, if not the basic object of Drusus' programme, certainly its concluding phase.[7] The connexions which the sources record as existing between Drusus and the representatives of the Italian upper classes[8] have been distorted by hostile tradition and interpreted as reflecting a policy of self-interest and treachery harmful to the state; however, they do not go beyond the normal relationships of *amicitia* and *clientela* which bound the Roman and Italian aristocracies together. They make it certain, however, that Drusus and his friends were fully aware of the needs and political ideas of the *principes Italicorum populorum*,[9] those Italian upper classes who drew their wealth from landed property and from their involvement in commercial enterprises in the East. These classes alone had a real interest in the acquisition of the *civitas* and, through it, in participation in the government of the Empire.[10] For all the risk it might entail, and for all the offence it might give to the reactionary traditionalism of a part of the senatorial oligarchy, the granting of the Roman citizenship to the Latins and the Italian *socii* could be seen as following an ancient and famous practice of the Roman government; this policy in its turn meant that new elements would take their place within the customary and defined sphere of Roman politics, elements whose moral, political and economic interests lay in preserving oligarchic government while, as we might say today, broadening its base. By removing the long-standing animosity of the *socii* Rome would acquire new forces that were nearly all decidedly conservative in their outlook. Faced with a chance of gaining this advantage, the more enlightened section of the oligarchy and the majority of the Italian upper classes might justly think that the economic sacrifices imposed upon them by the agrarian and colonial legislation of Drusus were secondary and endurable, indeed that they were but the normal and necessary means of winning the support of the *comitia* which had, after all, to pass the *rogatio de sociis*.[11]

The political forces which supported Drusus were perhaps better endowed with resolution and authority than with numbers. In a Senate which was, as a body, probably uncertain and bewildered, the impassioned words of L. Licinius Crassus managed to maintain support for Livius Drusus until the great orator died, in the early days of September, 91 BC.[12] After that it was easy for the opposition, traditionalist and rigidly conservative as it was and headed by the consul L. Marcius Philippus, to get the upper hand. But it is doubtful, given the state of our evidence, how far the reformist group supported all the proposals of Drusus, or whether some of them were not principally concerned with the *lex iudiciaria* which met the more immediate wishes of the oligarchy. It is not easy, for example, to say if Licinius Crassus himself, who had certainly approved Drusus' agrarian and judiciary laws,[13] also agreed with the *rogatio de sociis*; as consul in 95 BC he had been responsible with his colleague for the *lex Licinia Mucia de civibus redigundis* (though we may assign this law a limited scope).[14] We cannot exclude the possibility that the *rogatio de sociis* may have post-dated Crassus' death.[15] It is also possible that Drusus, at the beginning of his tribunate, had received quite substantial support but that the opposition to his programme gradually grew in articulation and strength as the year passed. This would explain the picture which later senatorial historians drew of Drusus' tribunate. Two phases were distinguished, producing an over-simplification based on partisan distortion: in the first Drusus had the support of the Senate, while the second was marked by his opposition to it and is dominated by demagogic motives and behaviour. In any event it seems likely that Drusus could count on the support of the powerful Metellan faction, and, more generally, on anti-Marian circles;[16] certainly M. Aemilius Scaurus, linked with that group, pressed the tribune to reform the *quaestiones* and the Senate.[17] He was later accused by Servilius Caepio under the *lex Varia* but was acquitted.[18] If we leave aside Licinius Crassus, it is only from the scanty notices concerning those accused under the *lex Varia*, which instituted a *quaestio extraordinaria* in the early months of 90 BC,[19] that we can get an idea, sketchy though it is, of those who had supported Drusus' programme and shared his ideas. As is known, Varius' law, with its *quaestio* composed only of knights, was the instrument for the Optimates' revenge; after the annulment of the Livian legislation on technical grounds, after Drusus' murder before his tribunate was over and after the outbreak of the allies' revolt which succeeded it, the conservative faction, united now in a bizarre and inconsistent alliance with the Equites,[20] was resolved to smash the reformist *nobiles* in a manner which they perhaps hoped would be permanent.

Those accused *ex lege Varia* included C. Aurelius Cotta,[21] the future consul of 75 BC, connected with Licinius Crassus and intimate friend of Drusus;[22] a Mummius who was a descendant of Achaicus;[23] a Calpurnius Bestia, perhaps the consul of 111 BC;[24] M. Antonius, consul of 99 BC,[25] who had shown himself well-disposed towards the allies in his censorship of 97 BC;[26] and Q. Pompeius Rufus, the future consul of 88 BC.[27] One would like to know rather more about L. Memmius, said by the historian Sisenna to have been Drusus' adviser.[28] Certainly the role of Pompeius Rufus and of L. Memmius in Drusus' entourage must have been important if L. Marcius Philippus came forward himself to testify against them.[29] Possibly L. Memmius' son-in-law, C. Scribonius Curio, tribune in 90 BC and therefore a colleague of Varius,[30] had belonged to Drusus' circle, even if it does not seem likely on our evidence that he was put on trial like his father-in-law.[31] It is doubtful whether P. Sulpicius Rufus, the later tribune of 88, was also tried under the *lex Varia*, as a passage in Cicero's *de Oratore* might seem to indicate;[32] certainly, like C. Cotta, he was an intimate of Crassus and of Drusus,[33] and at this time was still connected by very close ties of friendship with Q. Pompeius Rufus.[34]

This short list probably does not so much represent the political forces which supported Drusus, if one excepts the name of Aemilius Scaurus, as denote the men who were especially close to him. There must surely have been many others whose names we do not know. It is probable, however, that L. Cornelius Sulla also belonged to the political group behind Drusus in 91 BC. He is known to have been a great friend of M. Porcius Cato, father of Cato Uticensis,[35] who was tribune in 100 BC[36] and was a brother-in-law of Livius Drusus, since in 97 or 96 BC he had married Drusus' sister (he was her second husband). The political significance of Livia's marriages in the involved history of the *nobilitas* in the first decade of the century has been clearly elucidated by Badian.[37] But beyond this evidence, which is based on prosopographical argument and which not everyone will feel disposed to accept, what is extremely significant is Sulla's policy as consul in 88 BC. The outcome of the armed struggle with the allies had, of course, transformed the political problems that had been debated only three years before. Now that they had acquired the Roman citizenship, the aim of the *novi cives* was to obtain complete equality with the old citizens, especially in the assemblies. Their demand to be enrolled in all the thirty-five tribes becomes a basic issue in the political struggle.

88 BC marks a decisive turning-point. On the one hand, the senatorial oligarchy, strengthened by the victorious conclusion to the war, succeeded in gaining mastery over the Equites; the *lex Plautia iudiciaria*, which must

be dated to 89 BC,[38] changed the composition of the jury-courts in the *quaestiones* to the Senate's advantage.[39] At once it succeeded in getting Varius condemned under his own law.[40] If one accepts a shrewd correction by Pighius of Cicero, *pro Corn.* I fr. 54, adopted by E. W. Gray[41] and reinforced by Badian,[42] the same fate apparently overtook Pomponius, his tribunician colleague of 90 BC. On the other hand, as was in any case to be expected after the grant of the *civitas* to the *socii*, the reformist faction connected with the Metelli seems to have regained control among the *nobilitas*. Such men were the two consuls of 88, Q. Pompeius Rufus, mentioned above, and Sulla, related by marriage to the Metelli (the two consuls were themselves also closely connected by marriage), and such, too, was certainly the tribune P. Sulpicius Rufus.[43] Propaganda hostile to Rufus, perhaps going back to Sulla's *Memoirs*, represents him as an instrument of Marius but there are quite important indications suggesting that Sulpicius Rufus began his tribunate in full agreement with the consuls, and that it was only later that there occurred a radical political change,[44] whose causes escape us, which led him into Marius' camp. To me it does not seem certain that the cause of the breach between Sulpicius and the consuls was the *rogatio de novorum civium suffragiis*.[45] I am inclined rather to believe that the tribune was endeavouring to win over the Equites[46] who were an indispensable element in a reformist policy, as Drusus had already perceived, and who were at that time certainly angered by the admission of senators to the *quaestiones* under the *lex Plautia*; Sulpicius had therefore recognized that certain demands of the Equites had to be complied with,[47] for instance that the command in the war against Mithridates should be entrusted to someone acceptable to them. This was a conclusion the *nobilitas* was quite unable to accept.

The sedition which followed, Sulla's unexpected coup with the help of the army from Campania, the death of Sulpicius and the flight of Marius, paved the way for the reforms of Sulla's consulship. Because they were in part taken up again later by him when he was *dictator reipublicae constituendae*, the account of these reforms is often held – wrongly – to be an anticipation of what was to come and to be untrustworthy.[48] Sulla's position was most ambiguous and uncertain in 88. He could, to be sure, count on the full support of his colleague,[49] and it was in fact together with him that he presented his legislation, but he was beset by general hostility from the *nobiles* who were unable to acquiesce calmly in his brutal *coup d'état*. On the one hand, his reforms followed in the wake of Livian reformism; on the other, he had learned the lesson of Sulpicius' example and distrusted reforms effected through tribunician legislation. Sulla's work was dictated by the need to reinforce the Senate's authority. This explains the measures to limit the power of the tribunes and to ensure that every bill submitted either to the *comitia centuriata* or the tribal assemblies should carry the *auctoritas patrum*. But apparently Sulla also revived the *comitia centuriata* in its older

structure, as it had existed before the reform of the third century BC, a structure which emphasized the privileges of the wealthiest classes.[50] This measure
is extremely important since it gave political power to the upper classes of
the ex-allies. Certainly, Sulla was very much aware of their demands and
sympathetic to their ambitions. We know that during the Social War a
whole legion of Samnites had collaborated with him[51] and it was commanded
by one of the most influential people in the district, Minatus Magius of
Aeclanum. In the tribunician elections for 87 BC, which perhaps fall before
the riots of Sulpicius, a Magius who is commonly held to be the son of
Minatus secured election, probably with Sulla's help.[52]

However, the most significant item is the reform of the Senate which
Sulla proposed.[53] This provided for the admission of three hundred new
members, chosen from those of the highest worth and certainly from the
Equites primarily. Since the source does not tell us that the jurors had to be
taken from this new Senate, and since therefore the *lex Plautia* remained in
force, it seems clear that Sulla's proposals were an exact repetition of Drusus'
plan to associate the Equites with government responsibility. The increased
authority which the Senate acquired gave a special significance to this
extension to the Equites. These reforms of Sulla and Pompeius Rufus probably mark a return to the programme which had been interrupted and compromised by Sulpicius Rufus' change of direction. The earlier legislative
programme entrusted to the tribunate was now handed over to, and carried
through by, the consuls. In this connexion the further item attested by Livy,
Per. LXXVII, that Sulla founded some colonies,[54] has often been rejected by
critical scholars but is intelligible as an attempt by Sulla, following the
precedent of 91 BC, to curry favour with the urban Plebs by a colonial law
that was presumably similar to that of Livius Drusus.

The basic principles of Sulla's policy did not change even after the war in
the East and the civil war. The process of integrating the *novi cives* was now
irreversible and the most that could have been done was an obstruction of
the kind perhaps effected by the *nobilitas* after 79 BC, the blocking of the
appointment of censors down to 70.[55] But Sulla had no intention of acting in
such a way; rather it was in his interest to recognize the situation and to
make use of it, and this all the more since, as has been said, it must have
fitted in with his own ideas.[56] In the letter sent to the Senate towards the end
of 85 BC.[57] Sulla was already declaring that as far as the *novi cives* were concerned he had no complaint to make against them, thereby clearly recognizing
all the measures which had been passed in their interest during his absence,
and which had simply revived Sulpicius' legislation. When he landed in Italy
in 83 he appears to have made arrangements with the individual peoples of
Italy confirming his recognition of the *ius suffragii* granted to them,[58] and he
continued this policy during the war.[59] In the meetings between Sulla and
L. Cornelius Scipio Asiagenus, the consul of 83, *inter Cales et Teanum*, the

two *de auctoritate senatus, de suffragiis populi, de iure civitatis leges inter se et condiciones contulerunt.*[60] It seems certain that they reached an agreement; in any case, the solutions which Sulla devised for these problems in 82–81 BC in his dictatorship *reipublicae constituendae* were a return to the legislation of 88, with allowances made for the different historical situation.[61] The Senate was, indeed, completed and doubled in number by the addition of three hundred Equites, but among them were a large number of Sulla's followers, both old citizens and new.[62] Characteristically the procedure adopted for enlarging the Senate was probably identical with that employed to recruit the juries of the *quaestiones* under the *lex Plautia iudiciaria* of 89.[63] The pre-eminence of the Senate was re-established over the *comitia*, but Sulla made generous use of the latter, where the *novi cives* were bound to be very numerous; it should not be forgotten that the dictatorship of Sulla carried with it censorial powers.[64] The reorganization of the *quaestiones* restored the jury-courts to the new Senate, just as Drusus had proposed. The theory – which goes back to a hostile ancient tradition – of Sulla's anim-osity towards the equestrian class has been shown to be without foundation;[65] one should rather speak of a favourable attitude on Sulla's part towards the Equites.

Sulla showed no great originality and he was a long way from being an extremist. He followed Drusus' example and endeavoured to divert into traditional channels the forces of the *novi cives* whose importance he had come to understand and value. His hope was to re-establish the government of the oligarchy.

It remains to evaluate Sulla's treatment of the traditional political groups at Rome, and for this Cicero's speech *pro Sex. Roscio Amerino* is fundamental; it is the earliest direct evidence we possess for the period of Sulla's dictator-ship. A well-known interpretation of it was given by Carcopino,[66] which placed the trial of Roscius and the speech in 79 BC and saw them as a decisive move against the dictator, made by the *nobilitas* led by the Metelli, which finally compelled Sulla to abdicate. This seems very forced. It is linked also with his theory – which is in my view unacceptable – that Sulla attempted to become king.[67] In fact, most recent scholarship has rightly confirmed the date of the trial as falling in 80 BC, the year of Sulla's second consulship with Metellus Pius.[68] Some passages of the speech probably adumbrate the pos-sibility that Sulla had already laid aside the dictatorship at the end of the previous year, 81 BC.[69]

Furthermore, the theory of E. Badian[70] is, to my mind, one-sided and exaggerated. On his view the case of Sextus Roscius represents a successful attempt by the *nobilitas* to revive with new strength the traditional links of *clientela* with the Italian nobilities. These had been compromised by the emergence of new patterns of power, like that created by the influential freedman Chrysogonus. Badian interprets Cicero's victory as a lasting success which opened Sulla's eyes to the dangers incurred in humbling the *nobilitas* to the advantage of his own devotees.

It is my view, as it is the view of others,[71] that the importance of Roscius' trial has been exaggerated, and that even the political impact of Cicero's speech must be kept within very modest limits. The reality of Cicero's 'opposition' to Sulla is itself questionable. That his journey to Greece was motivated by fear of Sulla is a statement without foundation,[72] and we must wait until after the Ides of March, 44 BC to find any pronouncement by Cicero, and a clearly tendentious one given the political context, about his resistance to Sulla.[73] In 70 BC Sulla's work is mentioned by Cicero with a significant degree of sympathy.[74] Nor can we evade the serious question, already asked by Drumann and Ihne,[75] whether the text of the *pro Roscio*, as it has come down to us, is not a product of later elaboration and has inserted into it additions and modifications. J. Humbert's studies appear to have demonstrated the truth of this suggestion,[76] and we may doubt whether the whole speech can be taken to reflect a single political situation that can be precisely located in the year 80 BC.

The contradictions in the speech seem flagrant. Sulla is several times exculpated from the charge of rascality levied against his satellites,[77] but sarcasm is evident when Cicero compares Sulla with Jupiter[78] and in the play on words when dealing with his *felicitas*.[79] Cicero recognizes Sulla's achievement in restoring the *res publica*,[80] but the cruelty and injustice of the times are mentioned on several occasions in more or less veiled hints,[81] and at some points Cicero's attacks on the proscriptions are extremely open.[82] Even if, as was probably the case, Cicero could have spoken much more freely than he suggests, and even if he has exaggerated the *periculum* arising from the trial (which would come in any event from Chrysogonus and not from Sulla),[83] the most vigorous attacks are almost certainly later additions made at the time of publication of the speech. Taking, however, these points into due consideration – and they must limit the effectiveness the speech had at the time as a piece of polemic – it would still seem that the attitude of the *nobilitas*, as it appears in the text, was not as unanimous as is usually believed. It may well be doubted whether Cicero could, in fact, at the beginning and end of his speech[84] have so bluntly reviled the *nobiles* for their meanness and cowardice, disguised by their pretext that they would not and could not defend Roscius because their arguments were bound to be political and so would have greater consequences than they intended – though it is true, as has been noted, that Cicero's general tone towards the *nobilitas* is rather lukewarm and reserved.[85] Yet despite all this it is clear that there is an identity between Roscius' cause and that of the *nobilitas*,[86] and indeed he affirms clearly that the restoration of the *nobilitas* effected by Sulla's dictatorship will become reality only if resistance is offered to the excessive powers of *homines postremi*, men who had come to the fore in politics by gaining wealth in the massacres and confusion of the civil war.[87] The orator, then, is aware that the cause of the *nobilitas* had not emerged from the civil war and Sulla's restoration in undisputed triumph, and therefore thinks the absence of the *nobiles* from the trial is all the more blameworthy, but he cannot be thought to attribute responsibility for this situation to Sulla; rather, the blame is distinctly assigned to the *nobilitas* itself. § 140 of the speech is decisive, for it suggests that there was a section of the *nobilitas* that defended Chrysogonus and identified their own cause with his.[87a] These plainly cannot be the same *nobiles* who, according to Cicero, kept silent for fear of the freedman's power and the injustice of the times; indeed, his emphasis on the fact that they *equestrem splendorem pati non potuerunt* seems to equate this group rather with the more conservative and reactionary elements of the oligarchy, the men responsible for the failure of Drusus' policies. Nor should it be forgotten that those *nobiles* who profited from the war and the proscriptions had been on Chrysogonus' side, and it may be nearer the truth to suggest that the attacks on illicit gains were intended to strike at these as well, in particular Crassus.[88]

In this complex situation, packed as it is with nuances, what is Sulla's position? A very important passage of the *pro Roscio*, which one would wish were clearer,[89] tells us that the Senate was reluctant to assume (*suscipere*) the initiative for the proscriptions. Plutarch's *Life of Sulla*, which in this section is hostile to the dictator, provides evidence in partial agreement with Cicero; he states that the proscription lists were indeed decided in the Senate, perhaps to put an end to indiscriminate slaughter, but only after a rather lively sitting in which a C. Metellus had played an important part,[90] and then adds that the initiative was Sulla's own.[91] Although we lack any precise chronological clues, it is quite probable that this took place before Sulla's completion and doubling of the Senate.[92] It is typical that we find the Senate in November 82 BC still displaying an independent attitude towards Sulla, and it may be recalled that already in 88 it had been at loggerheads with him as consul;[93] this occurred after his march on Rome and his abandonment by all his officers.[94] Furthermore, recent studies of the period of Cinna agree that there was a certain background of support for him from traditional political groups, and that only quite late in the day was Sulla able to emerge as the defender of legality and the oligarchy.[95]

But the *pro Roscio* also lays emphasis on the policy of *compositio* which some enlightened *nobiles* such as Q. Scaevola had tried to impose.[96] Cicero himself explicitly states that his collaboration with Sulla dated from the time when attempts at mediation and agreement had failed;[97] it was almost, one might say, the choice of a lesser evil. Such a widespread movement, aimed at averting the outbreak of civil war, cannot be ignored, and in my opinion Sulla himself joined it in all sincerity; the truce mentioned above, by which an exchange of ideas and policies took place between the consul Scipio and

Sulla[98] and which resulted in some sort of agreement,[99] broke down, but the responsibility for this falls on the shoulders of Sertorius.[100] In this connexion it is not without significance that Sulla chose L. Valerius Flaccus as his *magister equitum*,[101] who as *interrex* had made him dictator;[102] as *princeps Senatus* after 86 BC he had in 85 or 84 been one of the most convinced advocates of the policy of conciliation and concord.[103]

It is impossible to tell how widely or how sincerely the oligarchy was committed to the dictator's reforms. Sisenna, the pro-Sullan historian, spoke of extensive popular support for the dictatorship[104] and defended Sulla's handiwork even in the decade after 79 BC,[105] while the political pamphleteers could extol the dictator as the new Romulus.[106] M. Aemilius Lepidus, in the speech which Sallust makes him deliver in his *Histories*,[107] acknowledged that with Sulla there were *homines maxumi nominis*.[108] The idea that a dictator was needed to reform the state seems itself to have been discussed in high political circles since the time of the Gracchi.[109]

As has been observed, Sulla's plans were directed to innovation, to secure a renewal and strengthening of older tradition.[110] But not everybody at the time understood;[111] the terrible afflictions of the civil war with its almost inevitable consequences had filled men's minds with horror. Yet Sulla certainly distinguished his own responsibilities from those of the profiteers among his followers. The selfish illegalities perpetrated by Crassus in Bruttium at the time of the proscriptions brought him into disgrace with the dictator.[112] Perhaps for the same reason M. Aemilius Lepidus came into sharp conflict with Sulla.[113] Cicero, therefore, is not wrong to exclude the dictator's participation in the Roscius affair. The *periculum* of the trial, even if exaggerated by Cicero, and the cruelty of the period had their origin in characters like Chrysogonus and their satellites, not in Sulla.

In any event Cicero's speech does not seem to me to give us evidence for, or indications of, hostility either by the *nobilitas* or a section of it towards Sulla. Cicero's polemic is directed against a state of affairs in which the worst elements were reaping profits, counting on others' fear and their own impunity.[114]

To paraphrase some famous lines of the greatest poet in the English language, it may be said that I have come here to praise Sulla, not to bury him nor to rehearse yet again the harshest charges of a cruel tyranny and a fierce despotism, after the fashion of hostile ancient tradition. Yet I would accept that Sulla had some responsibility; it is of a different kind, and was authoritatively set out in Sallust's *Histories*.[115] He was the first to avail himself of the opportunities afforded by the new professional army, and he believed that he could base his own work of enlightened reform above all on the strength and well-tried loyalty of his troops. The example of Livius Drusus must have shown him that to revive the state with no more than the support of traditional political forces was now impossible, uncertain and divided as they were. But history teaches us how wrong is the justification of the man who declares that he has 'uscito dalla legalità soltanto per rientrare nel diritto';[115a] as Sir Ronald Syme has well put it, 'Sulla could not abolish his own example'.[116]

The reservation remains a grave one, yet I believe that one should see in Sulla a man who put into effect the programme of the moderate oligarchs and who, once his task was done, renounced the dictatorship of his own free will. Rather this than the grim restorer of an outmoded reality[117] or the conscious model for future dynasts, wreathed in charismatic haloes and with their course set for monarchical absolutism.[118]

V

The Equestrian Class and Sulla's Senate[*]

The losses suffered by the Roman Senate between 91 and 81 BC were extremely serious, and the number of 200 senators who died, as given by Orosius, V 22, 4, and by Eutropius, V 9, 2, certainly represents the truth. According to Appian, *BC* I 103, 482, the senators who lost their lives because of Sulla, that is to say in the civil war from 83 to 82 and in the proscriptions, numbered ninety. The difference between the number given by Orosius and Eutropius and that of Appian will cover, in addition perhaps to those who died a natural death, those who fell during the Social War or were massacred by the Marians between 86 and 82 BC (App. *BC* I 72, 332 f.: 88, 403 f.).[1] However, one can only make a rough estimate of the number of senators still alive in 81 BC since one must reckon with the *lectio* of 86 BC which must to a large extent have replaced the losses suffered by the Senate down to that year;[2] it may in any case be supposed that it had been reduced to not more than 150 members.[3]

After Sulla the Senate consisted of 600 members.[4] It follows that the dictator had introduced about 450 new senators into the Senate. As is well-known, two different views of the way in which Sulla supplemented the Senate have come down to us. Appian, who is the more detailed, says that in 81 BC Sulla introduced about 300 new members into the Senate, chosen ἐκ τῶν ἀρίστων ἱππέων (I 100, 468), and Livy, *Per.* LXXXIX (*senatum ex equestri ordine supplevit*), agrees with him. However, Sallust, *BC* 37, 6, asserts that there were *gregarii milites* among the Sullan senators, and his evidence seems confirmed by Dion. Hal. V 77, 5, who says that Sulla βουλὴν ἐκ τῶν ἐπιτυχόντων ἀνθρώπων συνέστησε.

Attempts so far made to decide which of the two versions[5] is in error seem to have been unsuccessful. We can, indeed, draw up a list of more or less probable Sullan senators,[6] but the evidence of a hundred such cases will not entitle us to draw general conclusions valid for all who were introduced into the Senate by Sulla, the more so because the list is necessarily almost wholly made up by studying the *cursus* of magistrates in the decade 80–70 BC.[7]

However, a closer examination of the problem allows us, I believe, to reach a satisfactory solution. Sulla's measures for the reorganization of the Roman state in 81 BC (App. I 100, 466–8) were essentially only a revival of the measures which Sulla himself as consul had taken in 88 BC together with his colleague Q. Pompeius Rufus (App. I 59, 266–7) and which had been annulled a little later by the Marians (App. I 73, 339).[8] Now, among the provisions of 88 BC appears the following: κατέλεξαν ἐς τὸ βουλευτήριον, ὀλιγανθρωπότατον δὴ τότε μάλιστα ὂν καὶ παρὰ τοῦτ᾽ εὐκαταφρόνητον, ἀθρόους ἐκ τῶν ἀρίστων ἀνδρῶν τριακοσίους.

The Senate by 88 BC may have suffered losses as a consequence of the Social War and there is a doubt whether the censors of 92 and 89 BC had conducted the *lectio*;[9] for all that, it is wholly incredible that the Senate in 88 was reduced to a state similar to that of 81 BC. It is known, in fact, that in 91 it was almost a full house (App. I 35, 158);[10] hence we feel no little surprise that the number of 300 new senators should not have differed in 88 and 81,[11] when the Senate's situation must have been very different. This is all the more likely because, as I have already said, a conservative calculation makes it probable that Sulla's new senators of 81 were a far higher number. Furthermore, the same number of 300 crops up again in App. I 35, 158, in connexion with the judiciary law of the tribune of 91 BC, M. Livius Drusus, under which knights were to be chosen ἀριστίνδην and introduced into the Senate; the object of increasing the number of senators was not that the number was then too small (Appian's claim that the Senate was reduced to only 300 members διὰ τὰς στάσεις is a notorious error since 300 was the normal number) but that Drusus wanted to hand over the δικαστήρια to a Senate doubled in number.

Furthermore, it should not be forgotten that according to Plutarch's version (*Gracchi* 26, 3), with which to a certain extent Livy, *Per.* LX, is in agreement, the judiciary law of Caius Gracchus would also have envisaged the admission (προσκατέλεξεν) of 300 knights into the Senate and the handing over of τὰς κρίσεις to the new Senate of 600 members.

There must be a suspicion that Sulla in 88, and also in 81, had in mind the problem of the composition of the jury-courts in the *quaestiones perpetuae*, and he in fact handed them over to the new Senate after 81. Therefore Appian's evidence – and also that of the Livian *Periocha* for 81 – alludes to an extraordinary supplementation of the Senate with that end in view. This suspicion seems confirmed by the fact that Appian uses the same word προσκαταλέγειν to indicate the supplementation of the Senate proposed by Drusus (I 35, 158 and 159) as he does for those of Sulla in 88 and 81 BC (I 59, 267 and 100, 468: καταλέγειν at 59, 267); this corresponds to the Latin *adlegere* and points to an increase in the number of Senators over and above what was normal.[12]

From this we can deduce a very probable explanation of the difficulty I have mentioned above of reconciling the number of 300 new senators given by Appian with that far higher number which is required to reach the total of 600 members of the post-Sullan Senate. As Willems already observed, with some hesitation,[13] Sulla must initially have reviewed the normal list of 300 senators, completing it with those magistrates who had ended their term of office after the last *lectio*, that of 86 BC. So far Willems: but the magistrates from 86 to 81 BC would certainly not have been sufficient in number for this purpose. Furthermore, they must have been mainly if not wholly Marians and many would have died on the battlefield or been murdered in the proscriptions or for some reason or other *praeteriti*. The normal supplementation of the Senate, up to 300, was probably carried out in a different way, and here it may be useful to remember the evidence of Sallust: *multi memores Sullanae victoriae, quod ex gregariis militibus alios senatores videbant.* . . . When in 216 BC it was necessary to undertake an extraordinary *lectio* of the Senate which had been greatly reduced by the losses of the Hannibalic War (Livy, XXIII 22, 1–2), the dictator nominated for the task, Q. Fabius Buteo, also entered in the list of senators members *ex iis, qui magistratus ⟨non⟩ cepissent, qui spolia ex hoste fixa domi haberent aut civicam coronam accepissent.*[14] It may easily be supposed that Sulla acted in a similar way[15] and that entry into the Senate was the reward for many of his braver officers, for example L. Fufidius, who according to Orosius (V 21, 3: the MSS. give Fursidius) was *primipilaris*. It goes without saying that many of them certainly came from the lower classes of society; hence we can explain Dionysius' point.

Appian's evidence (and that of the *Periocha*) is, however, a different matter, i.e. the doubling of the Senate's numbers. The Senate, already brought up to strength, was now doubled by the admission of 300 knights. How was this *adlectio* to take place? As far as concerns the plan of 88 BC – of which, as I have said, that of 81 BC was only a renewal – we do not know. We are equally ignorant of the way in which Drusus in 91 would have selected the 300 members of the equestrian class for admission to the Senate, and in fact the requirement τίνες ἀξιώτεροι δοκοῦσιν ἐς τοὺς τριακοσίους καταλεγῆναι (App. I 35, 161) was one of the factors which contributed most to the alienation of the equestrian class from Drusus. According to Plutarch, Caius Gracchus was himself to have power to choose the 300 knights whom his law (in Plutarch's version) admitted to the Senate (*Gracchi* 27, 1).

Now Appian, I 100, 468, after saying that Sulla in 81 introduced 300 knights into the Senate, adds: ταῖς φυλαῖς ἀναδοὺς ψῆφον περὶ ἑκάστου.

It is not clear how the tribes came to be involved, and Appian's evidence has even been doubted,[16] but of course wrongly so. It is usually held that Sulla, simply as a formality, submitted the list of new senators he had prepared to the *comitia tributa* for approval.[17] However, it is probable that Appian's phrase refers to a more complex procedure and so should be interpreted differently. Mommsen in a note in the *Staatsrecht* (III 189, n. 2) was certainly on the right lines in thinking that Appian does not allude to election in the normal *comitia tributa* but that the passage must be related to what we know about the nomination of citizens, made by each tribe and in equal number, to constitute colleges of jurymen. This system is known to us from its use in appointing jurymen for the tribunal of the *Centumviri*. According to Festus (p. 159 Lindsay, *Glossaria*) *cum essent Romae triginta et quinque tribus . . . terni ex singulis tribubus sunt electi ad iudicandum, qui centumviri appellati sunt; et licet quinque amplius quam centum fuerint, tamen, quo facilius nominarentur, centumviri sunt dicti.*[18] Still more important for our purposes is the *lex Plautia iudiciaria* of 89 BC which was based on this principle. Asconius, *in Cornelianam*, I p. 61, 31–6 Stangl, says: *M. Plautius Silvanus tr. pl. Cn. Pompeio Strabone L. Porcio Catone coss., secundo anno belli Italici, cum equester ordo in iudiciis dominaretur, legem tulit adiuvantibus nobilibus; quae lex vim eam habuit quam Cicero significat:*[19] *nam ex ea lege tribus singulae ex suo numero quinos denos suffragio creabant qui eo anno iudicarent. ex eo factum est ut senatores quoque in eo numero essent, et quidam etiam ex ipsa plebe.*[20]

It is very probable that Appian's evidence also refers to a nomination of this kind, and the ἀμφὶ τοὺς τριακοσίους of 100, 468, may indeed show, in conjunction with the passage of Festus which has been cited, that the new senators were not exactly 300, but a few more or a few less. It may be supposed with Mommsen (*SR* III 189, n. 2) that each tribe nominated 8 senators, in which case the total would have been 280; better perhaps is a nomination of 9, making 315 in all. Of course Sulla would have taken the precaution of presenting the names of the candidates previously selected to each tribe; the tribes' only role would have been to vote on these.[21]

If the argument so far is valid, it must follow that the passages of Appian and the Epitomator, *Per.* LXXXIX, on the one side, and of Sallust and Dionysius on the other, are not contradictory but refer to two different aspects of Sulla's treatment of the Senate.

We can now consider the difference which, following the evidence of Appian, we have observed between Sulla's measures of 88 and 81. In the former case the 300 senators were chosen ἐκ τῶν ἀρίστων ἀνδρῶν (59, 267), in the latter ἐκ τῶν ἀρίστων ἱππέων (100, 468). Do the two phrases refer to the same thing? I am aware how dangerous it is to base an argument on Appian's uncertain terminology, but if we bear in mind that Appian's narrative of the Sullan civil war comes more or less directly from Livy,[22]

I think it possible to deduce from these two different pieces of evidence that Sulla introduced some modification in 81 to what he had arranged in 88. In fact it is highly likely that, as was the case with the new juries of the judiciary law of C. Gracchus, so the new senators proposed by Drusus in 91 and by Sulla in 88 and 81, who the sources say were selected from the knights, came from those citizens who possessed a census qualification of a given sum; this sum will have corresponded to the so-called *census equester*.[23] In the measure of 88 Sulla presumably intended to adhere to the provisions of the *lex Plautia* of the previous year,[24] by which jurors could be nominated *etiam ex ipsa plebe* (that is to say, those who were neither senators nor knights),[25] and thus had proposed that in the nomination of the new senators by individual tribes – I put this forward as a hypothesis – men should be selected from citizens who had a rating at least equivalent to that of the first class; choice was not confined to those who were in possession of an equestrian census.

This view presupposes a plan on Sulla's part to strengthen the class-structure of the Roman state, and can perhaps find some sort of parallel in the modifications to the *lex Aurelia* introduced by Pompey's judiciary law of 55 BC.[26] It would be consonant with Sulla's other measure of 88 by which the connexion between tribes and centuries in the *comitia centuriata* was abolished; under that measure the type of organization (the Servian) by which the knights and the first class were sufficient to form a voting majority was restored to that assembly (App. I 59, 266, with some very interesting comments on the need for power to remain in the hands of the propertied classes).[27] After the interruption of the civil wars Sulla revived the legislative proposals of 88 and – to follow Appian – recruited his new senators from a more restricted circle; he returned purely and simply to Drusus' plan, just as he made no attempt to revive the earlier modifications to the *comitia centuriata* which the Marians had abolished along with the other laws of Sulla.

The problem which must now be considered is this: how are we to interpret the equestrian origin claimed for the new senators by Appian and by Livy?[28] Since it is a commonplace in the ancient tradition that Sulla hated the equestrian class and this hatred took the form of savage persecutions,[29] it has indeed been thought that the dictator recruited the 300 new senators from the eighteen centuries of the *equites equo publico* which at that time contained the sons of senatorial families.[30] This explanation relies on nothing more than a schematic identification of the whole equestrian class with the *pars Mariana*, which is surely untenable; in particular this is so when we consider how the equestrian class had increased in size by the admission into it of ex-allies following on the Social War, and how friendly relationships had been established between Sulla and a large number of these *novi cives*.[31] Other evidence, not least the list of probable Sullan senators which I have

mentioned above, offers confirmation that Sulla introduced some representatives of the upper commercial class, and therefore Equites, into the
Senate.[32] Finally, we may reasonably assume that the knight T. Pomponius
Atticus who, on leaving Rome during the Cinnan period to live in Athens,
there met Sulla returning from the East and was on excellent terms with him
(Nepos, *Atticus* 2, 2 and 4, 1–2), was not the only case of this kind; a large
proportion of the 'emigration' to Sulla will have consisted of members of
the wealthier classes.[33]

Some useful distinctions should therefore be made, and we should take the
view that a large part of the equestrian class, those men who were socially
distinguished (the wealthiest), involved in commerce and contracts in the
East, had either been with Sulla from the beginning or had joined him when
he showed that he could repel the invasion of Mithridates. The theory that
the reorganization of the taxes carried out by Sulla in the province of Asia
(Cic. *pro Flacco*, 32; *ad Quint. fr.* I 1, 33; App. *Mithr.* 62, 259–60) led to the
exclusion of the *publicani*[34] seems in fact to have no support in our evidence.

The new Senate now consisted of 600 members; a large number of Sulla's
own officers were admitted as a reward for loyal service during the wars in
the East and against the Marians, and 300 knights elected by the tribes were
also included in it. To this body Sulla re-transferred the task of supplying
the juries in the *quaestiones perpetuae* (Cic. *div. in Caec.* 8; *id.* I *Verr.* 37–40;
49 and *passim*; Vell. II 32, 2; Tac. *Ann.* XI 22, 6).[35]

The inclusion then, of 300 knights in the Senate was an isolated and
exceptional measure, made immediately and unavoidably necessary by the
need to supply an appropriate number of jurors for the *quaestiones*. For the
future the recruitment of the Senate would be conducted in the traditional
manner, by the entry of magistrates at the end of their year of office.

The increase in the Senate's numbers naturally meant that the number of
magistrates had to be enlarged as well to fill the vacancies occurring annually
in the House. Sulla therefore raised the number of quaestors from 8 to 20.
Tacitus (*Ann.* XI 22, 6) says in fact: *post lege Sullae viginti creati supplendo
senatui, cui iudicia tradiderat.* This passage has given rise to two views which
have found wide acceptance but are certainly erroneous. The first states that
the concession of the *ius sententiae dicendae* to *quaestorii* dates from Sulla.
But we must above all be clear that the passage of Tacitus is part of a short
history of the quaestorship; he sets out the successive increases in the
number of quaestors in answer to the state's needs. In this case it is to provide an increased number of senators, which in turn was necessitated by the
transfer of the *iudicia* to them. Not only is there no mention of any grant
of the *ius sententiae dicendae* at the time of this increase, but it seems an
obvious presupposition that the *quaestorii* already possessed the *ius*, and this
moreover can be proved independently.[36]

The second inference which some have wanted to draw from Tacitus is that the increased number of quaestors led to an 'automatic' recruitment of the Senate, and this made it possible for Sulla – who had other reasons for this as well – to abolish the censorship.[37] It is not clear why there should be mention of an 'automatic' recruitment;[38] it was long since established that the curule magistrates, and then the others, had the right to enter the Senate after the year of their magistracy, first acquiring the *ius sententiae dicendae*, and then at the next census being enrolled in the list of senators (unless the censors for some reason wanted to pass them over – *praeterire*). Even if the *quaestorii* had not already possessed the *ius sententiae dicendae*, Sulla's measure would not have involved any innovation; this is all the more true since they did already possess that right. That Sulla suppressed the censorship, either in fact or by law, cannot be supported by any ancient text,[39] and arises only from the observed fact that after Sulla there were no censors until 70 BC.[40]

Five years had passed since the last censorship (86 BC) and Sulla did not proceed to the election of new censors; this does not look like a definite plan to suppress the censorship for all time to come,[41] but seems fully explicable in that Sulla, as *dictator legibus scribundis et rei publicae constituendae* (App. I 99, 462), preferred to carry out the functions himself (as he could do in his position) or to get others to do the job for him. This was so not only with regard to the Senate but also apparently with regard to the letting of contracts (Cic. II *Verr.* 1, 130: 80 BC),[42] *locationes* and auctioning of Asian *vectigalia*; for it seems likely that the indefinite formula of the *S.C. de Asclepiade* of 78 BC (Riccobono, *FIRA*[2] no. 35), line 6 of the Latin text (= line 23 of the Greek) *ma[gistrat]us nostri queiquomque Asiam Euboeam locabunt vectigalve Asiae [Euboeae imponent]*,[43] recognizes that these functions had recently been handled by other magistrates than the censors – i.e. by Sulla (perhaps through his quaestor Lucullus? – Plut. *Lucull.* 4, 1) – and that this was to be reckoned with in the future as well.[44]

Yet the problem of the confirmation of contracts and of tenders must have become important at the quiquennial renewal in 75 BC; a passage of Cicero (II *Verr.* 3, 18) shows that the tithe-contracts on the wine, oil and beans of Sicily were transferred to Rome and the consuls were given the task by a *S.C.*,[45] and we may infer, I think, from this that the consuls took charge of the normal contracts (see also *ibid.* 19: *prudentissimi viri summa auctoritate praediti* (the consuls L. Octavius and C. Aurelius Cotta) *quibus Senatus legum dicendarum in locandis vectigalibus omnem potestatem permiserat populusque Romanus idem iusserat . . .*).

Finally, it is to be noted that the *lex Cornelia de sicariis et veneficiis* repeatedly uses the formula *quive in Senatu sententiam dixit dixerit* (Cic. *pro Cluentio*, 148) and this seems to exclude any intention on Sulla's part to abolish the censorship for the future; in that case all senators entering the House after 81 BC would have remained for ever in the condition of having

only the *ius sententiae dicendae* without being on any official list of senators –
even if in fact such a condition presumably did not amount to a disqualifica-
tion, for example, for the purpose of being selected as a juror.[46] On the other
hand, the revision of the Senate that was annually to be undertaken by a
magistrate charged with allocating the *quaestiones* to the senatorial decuries
must on no account be confused with the powers of the censors in holding
the *lectio*.[47]

If, then, appointment of censors was deferred *per plurimos annos* (ps. Asc.
p. 189, 22 f. Stangl), i.e. in 75 B C, the reason must be sought not in any design
of Sulla's but in the fortuitous interest of the oligarchy which governed
Rome from 80 to 70 BC.[48] Their fear – which cannot be said to be without
foundation – in all probability centred on possible changes in the Roman
electoral body. Indeed, the censors of 70 BC, who were allies of Pompey,[49]
are famous for the severity they showed in purging the Senate (whatever the
truth that this stemmed from their political position,[50] the severity could be
justified by a need to weed out those who were notoriously involved in
scandals of judicial corruption).[51] Yet the most significant feature of their
censorship was certainly the extensive registration of citizens, whose numbers
leapt from 463,000 in 86 BC (Hieron. p. 151 Helm; Eusebius, VII 1)[52] to
910,000 (Livy, *Per.* XCVIII; Phleg. fr. 12, 6 Jacoby, *FgrH*. IIB, p. 1164).
Cicero indeed (I *Verr.* 54) says of that year: *cum haec frequentia totius Italiae
Roma discesserit, quae convenit uno tempore undique comitiorum, ludorum
censendique causa* (see ps. Asc. p. 222, 11 Stangl). It is practically certain that
the censors were a long way from registering all the ex-allies now transformed
into *cives*[53] by the laws *de civitate* of 90 and 89 BC and the Marian measures
of 87 (Gran. Licin. p. 20, 11 Flemisch; App. I 68, 310), which were later
recognized by Sulla (App. I 77, 352).[54] None the less this was a great step
forward, compared with the deliberately slow pace at which the Senate had
until then proceeded in giving effect to those laws.[55]

This tremendous influx of new citizens led to a substantial modification
in the electoral body; probably this was to Pompey's advantage,[56] and
certainly it was to the disadvantage of the oligarchy which Sulla had restored.

The failure, then, to elect censors in 75 BC is part of the traditional
oligarchic policy whereby, in a desperate attempt to defend their privileges,
they sought to contain the numerical preponderance of the *novi cives* which
they feared so much. At first they limited their enrolment to a few tribes[57]
and then, when that barrier was breached, they suspended their registration
in the census, a manoeuvre by which the *novi cives* were prevented from
exercising the vote.

In contrast, Sulla's policy seems much broader in concept. In 81 BC he
had not only admitted to the Senate members of the aristocracies and financial
classes of the Italian cities but had also been ready to give timely recognition
to the rights of ex-allies which had been granted to them with the help of

the Marians and had been opposed by the oligarchy (App. I 77, 352). Nor had he hesitated to manumit and make citizens of ten thousand of his enemies' slaves (App. I 100, 469), a measure indeed difficult to reconcile with oligarchic attitudes on the granting of citizenship (cf. Cic. *pro Arch.* 25; Exup. 5). And so, perhaps, the increase in the number of citizens registered in 70 BC should in part be credited to Sulla.

VI

The 'lex Plotia agraria'*

Only Cicero (ad Att. I 18, 6: January 20th, 60 BC) explicitly mentions the lex Plotia agraria: agraria (lex) autem promulgata est a Flavio sane levis eadem fere quae fuit Plotia.[1] Uncertainty reigns, therefore, among historians concerning its date.

L. Lange, taking over an argument put forward by previous scholars, ascribed the law to the tribune M. Plautius Silvanus (89 BC) and supposed that it regulated the rewards of land given to soldiers of the Social War, both old and new citizens alike.[2] Lange's date was accepted by G. Rotondi,[3] J. Carcopino[4] and W. Schur.[5] However, the observations made long ago by A. W. Zumpt[6] are undoubtedly still fully valid and militate against it; these amounted to the point that, since according to Cicero the lex Plotia was almost the same as the lex Flavia of 60 BC, it also must have contained clauses concerning the well-known possessiones Sullanae and it must therefore certainly be referred to a period after Sulla and possibly to that after the full re-establishment of the tribunician power in 70 BC.

G. Niccolini, therefore, though only by way of hypothesis,[7] ascribed the law to the legislative activity of a tribune Plautius known to us from the rogatio Plautia de reditu Lepidanorum; he belonged either to the college of 70 or to that of 69 BC.[8] We shall find that this suggestion can be entirely substantiated.

In fact, not only the dating of the law but also – and this is what chiefly matters – its purpose is made clearer for us by a passage in Cassius Dio which until now has not been fully exploited. Pompey in his suasio of the lex Iulia agraria of 59 BC[9] inter alia made the following statement (Cass. Dio, XXXVIII 5, 1–2): οὐκ ἐγώ, ἔφη, μόνος, ὦ Κυιρῖται, τὰ γεγραμμένα δοκιμάζω, ἀλλὰ καὶ ἡ ἄλλη βουλὴ πᾶσα, δι' ὧν οὐχ ὅτι τοῖς μετ' ἐμοῦ ἀλλὰ καὶ τοῖς μετὰ τοῦ Μετέλλου συστρατευσαμένοις ποτὲ γῆν δοθῆναι ἐψηφίσατο. τότε μὲν οὖν (οὐ γὰρ ηὐπόρει τὸ δημόσιον) εἰκότως ἡ δόσις αὐτῆς ἀνεβλήθη. ἐν δὲ δὴ τῷ παρόντι (παμπλούσιον γὰρ ὑπ' ἐμοῦ γέγονε) προσήκει καὶ ἐκείνοις τὴν ὑπόσχεσιν καὶ τοῖς ἄλλοις τὴν ἐπικαρπίαν τῶν κοινῶν πόνων ἀποδοθῆναι.

We must clarify to what law Pompey is alluding in this speech, which provided for the settlement of his veterans and those of a Metellus. H. S. Reimar in his valuable edition with commentary of Cassius Dio[10] thought it was the *rogatio Servilia* of 63 BC and identified the Metellus of Dio with Q. Caecilius Metellus Creticus. But the first suggestion is certainly untenable; apart from the very odd fact that Pompey should here refer to a law directed against his interests, as Servilius Rullus' law seems to have been, there is absolutely no mention in Cicero's speeches *de lege agraria* either that the law had the purpose attributed to it in the Dio passage or that it had been approved by the Senate. Finally – and this seems to me a decisive proof – the *rogatio Servilia* did not obtain the approval of the popular assembly since a tribune interposed his veto against it,[11] while the law mentioned in Dio is said to have been approved. Further, in addition to these arguments, an allusion by Pompey to Metellus Creticus is hardly credible; a measure for the soldiers of Pompey and Creticus must be after the return of Pompey from Asia, i.e. 61 BC, but it was actually for the purpose of rewarding his own soldiers that Pompey had the *rogatio Flavia* proposed in 60 BC and this proposal is compared by Cicero to the *lex Plotia*. The latter cannot therefore refer to Pompey's veterans of Asia and must be regarded as preceding his Eastern campaigns, and therefore as coming before 66 BC. This is confirmed by the wretched state of the treasury (οὐ γὰρ ηὐπόρει τὸ δημόσιον) when the law mentioned by Pompey was approved, for this goes well with the period prior to the wars in the East; after these, as Pompey himself adds, the treasury παμπλούσιον . . . γέγονε.[12]

It is best, therefore, to revert to the hypothesis which Ed. Meyer put forward in the form of a question,[13] that Pompey in his speech referred to a measure proposed after the war against Sertorius. The Metellus mentioned by Dio is to be identified with Q. Caecilius Metellus Pius, consul in 80 BC, who returned to Italy from Spain in 71 BC.[14]

Since, therefore, the law which Dio mentions must be placed between 71 and 66 BC it follows without doubt that it must be identified with the *lex Plotia* of Cicero, which has already been very plausibly referred to Plautius, tribune in 70 or 69. In my view, 70 BC would be preferable for the following reasons: (1) in 70 Pompey was consul with Crassus, and a measure for his veterans could have received his full support; (2) in the early months of 70, on the most likely view,[15] there occurred the disbandment of Pompey's army, back from the Spanish campaigns against Sertorius, and we may infer that not long after came the measure to reward them. However, the measure itself could not be put into effect because of lack of funds: ἡ δόσις αὐτῆς (i.e. τῆς γῆς) ἀνεβλήθη. The veterans, as Pompey's speech seems to show, were not rewarded until 59 BC.

VII

Review of A. J. Toynbee, 'Hannibal's Legacy', Oxford 1965[*]

This is a majestic work, outstanding for the wealth of its scholarship, the force of its arguments and the depth of its historical and political thought. Clearly evident are the love and passion of the great historian who has devoted half a century of investigation and reflection to his undertaking and who has finally entrusted his arguments and his findings to a great and enduring monument.

Volume I takes in Rome and Italy before the coming of Hannibal, Volume II concerns itself with the consequences of the Hannibalic War as they affected Rome and Italy. The author is never content to accept the conclusions of previous scholars even when they are generally taken as established and even when he himself ends by agreeing with them; his wish is always to re-study everything patiently and in detail, or at least to set again before the reader all the data surrounding any problem, both the ancient evidence and the modern discussion. As a result, a large number of appendices concern themselves with problems some of which, *prima facie*, are secondary or rather remote from the subject of his research (for example, those on the Etruscans, on the value of the tradition regarding Rome's foreign policy in the decades that immediately followed the burning of the city by the Gauls, or on the Romano–Carthaginian treaties). Other important and complicated problems are treated directly and in full detail in the text: for example, the reliability of Livy's figures for the Roman armies of the period 218–167 BC; the size of Rome's armed forces in the second century BC; and the calculation of comparative Roman and allied fighting strengths. In this respect Toynbee's work is a valuable quarry of original

[*] *RFIC* XCVI 1968, 68–75.

research on detailed points, and it will rightly be used as such; it is not possible here, even in passing, to mention the limitless contributions it offers. Scholars will be aware that they can consult it with profit and, despite inevitable disagreements, with confidence.

Toynbee's basic interpretation of Roman and Italian history of the third and second centuries BC may, I think, be summed up as follows. The political unification of the Italian peninsula which had been substantially achieved by Rome by the eve of the First Punic War had not been accompanied by those reforms of the political, economic and social structure which would have brought Rome and Italy up to the level of Carthage and the Hellenistic states in political and social development. The two major Romano–Carthaginian Wars (the unity of the period of these two wars is a key concept for Toynbee and he is fully justified in emphasizing it) completely shook the Romano–Italian confederacy, and brought in their train those structural changes which, because they were unforeseen and imposed by force of circumstances and so had to be endured by the governing class, were realized only with some difficulty and met every kind of opposition. Out of them developed the revolutionary phase of Rome's history from the Gracchi onwards; this appeared, outwardly at any rate, to find a peaceful outcome in Augustus' compromise, while in reality it undermined the very foundations of the Roman Empire which were thus compromised from the outset.

This interpretation arises out of a comparison between Romano–Italian society of the third century BC and that of the second century which the English historian has patiently reconstructed in all its aspects. He has provided a minute, accurate and fully acceptable picture of the Romano–Italian confederacy of 266 BC in its various constituent parts. In doing so he has singled out those which, in his view, were elements of intrinsic weakness, whether of an environmental, political, social or economic kind. On this assessment it is permissible to express disagreement.

Toynbee blames the Roman governing class for failure to develop the Italian economy when faced with the more 'modern' economies of the Hellenistic kingdoms, and for their inability to adapt the organization of the Roman state, which was always tied to concepts of the city-state and a citizen militia, to the new political demands (I 292–5). It may be objected that these charges are the product of later experience and that they derive mainly from ideas which are peculiar to ourselves. Can one, in fact, talk of a genuine political unification of Italy in 266 BC? And, even if one may do so, can one expect the governing class of an ancient state of the third century BC to produce a planned economy? The Romano–Italian confederacy was a statesmanlike arrangement, designed precisely to safeguard the city-state structure of Rome (and of the other Italian states), and the preoccupation of the Roman governing class both then and later seems to have been not so much to maintain its own supremacy in the existing political system and blindly resist all reforms (I 306 f.) as to see that this system should not collapse owing to excessive territorial expansion. It needed time for the city-state to be transformed into a municipal system. Certainly no Roman of the third century BC could have thought of replacing the citizen militia by a professional army, and the results of the Hannibalic War and of the wars against the Hellenistic monarchies proved the overwhelming superiority of the Roman military system.

This unfavourable assessment of the Roman governing class of the third century BC is also connected with the theory, often maintained and now supported by Toynbee, that the Romans failed to develop democratic forms in political life; this was, he believes, prevented by the conservatism of the aristocratic governing class, which was, however, insecure in its power thanks to the revolutionary movements led by tribunes (I 349). I do not believe that the political struggles in third-century Rome, even granted the lively conflicts between personalities and political principles, give an impression of political instability within the ruling class, nor that that class had closed its mind to new ideas or to the new problems posed by the situation in Italy and the Mediterranean world. The competence with which it was able to face the war with Hannibal is proof of its general efficiency. On the other hand, political struggles were carried on above all on the basis of factions of *nobiles*; although these from time to time embodied various political demands, which might even be popular demands of the moment, one cannot claim that this represented a democratic development, the very preconditions for which were lacking.

Toynbee paints a profoundly dramatic picture of the social consequences of the Hannibalic War for Rome and the allies in the confederacy. Let me say at once that, in my view, this picture is in its essentials correct, even though not all will agree with the author that the consequences are still to be seen in the many serious difficulties that today affect the Mezzogiorno. Although he pays special attention, as we shall see, to changes in the social and economic structure, he also takes account of the political and spiritual aspects of the second century. It is in this period that one can more properly discern the growing rigidity of the Roman governing class and the concentration of power in the hands of the senatorial oligarchy, with consequent loss to other elements of Roman political life; all this was due to the needs imposed by the conduct of the war, and the situation did not subsequently improve. Moreover, it is clear that the Romans began to interfere more and more in their relations with allied communities, and this had a serious effect; evidently the new demands of imperial policy made the contradictions with the city-state pattern more conspicuous. However, if the process of ever greater fusion of Rome with her allies that was started by the Hannibalic War did not immediately produce a corresponding unification of laws among the individual members of the confederacy (II 111), we should reflect that the future advantages of the Roman citizenship would hardly have been apparent at the beginning of the second century BC, and one cannot speak of a demand for it on the part of the allies. I repeat: it is difficult to expect of the Roman governing class a plan to reform and restructure the state, as De Sanctis did, though with fundamental differences, in a famous study ('Dopoguerra antica', *A & R* N.S. I 1920, 3–14 and 73–89; see also 'Rivoluzione e reazione nell'età dei Gracchi', *ibid.* II 1921, 209–37, and Gabba, *RSI* LXXVI 1964, 105 f.), a view which is taken up again by Toynbee; though it is true, as Toynbee well shows, that new ideas and concepts deriving from the Greek world were penetrating deeply into political life no less than into literature, and were giving the Roman oligarchy a new vitality and a new impetus which traditionalist forces proved able to control only in part and then only for a time. Equally, although the spiritual and religious needs of the masses were checked by the conservatism of the governing classes, the ferment was too strong to be completely suppressed.

Toynbee's inquiry into the social and economic consequences of the Hannibalic War and his conclusions therefrom are in my view fully persuasive. He has shown exceptionally clearly the process of 'deracination' of the Roman and Italian peasantry from agriculture which was the result of the war itself, of the extreme harshness of the levies and of the continuous demands for large numbers of soldiers to fight the wars of the second century. There is no doubt that this is the fundamental cause of the collapse of the traditional small peasant farms, much more than the 'scorched earth' strategy which the Romans pursued and the destruction that went with it, for the methods they used were far less scientific than those with which contemporary events have made us familiar. Besides, the phenomenon of urbanization, which took on a new importance during the war itself, must have contributed to the creation of empty wastes in the countryside, although the idea of a major industrialization of the cities in the second century BC seems far too modern and not wholly convincing. Important consequences must also have resulted from the transplantation of able-bodied Italians to the provinces in the second century, for example to Spain, following long periods of residence there because of military service (cf. A. J. N. Wilson, *Emigration from Italy in the Republican Age of Rome*, Manchester 1966: reviewed *RFIC* XCV 1967, 211 f.).

It seems certain that this crisis for traditional agriculture and the small peasant proprietors was accentuated by Roman confiscations of allied territory as a punitive measure at the end of the war. We know, it is true, that in certain particular cases, like the rich and productive *ager Campanus*, the ex-owner became a tenant of the Roman state, but elsewhere, certainly, even supposing that the allied proprietor was merely demoted to the rank of a wage-earner, it is impossible to believe that the traditional system of working the soil was preserved. These conclusions stem from what we are told by Cato, Polybius and Livy, and especially from the description of Italian agrarian conditions provided for us by Appian and Plutarch as a prologue to their accounts of the Gracchi, itself confirmed by the continued existence of a Gracchan 'ideology', for example in Sallust's *Jugurthine War*. These accounts, attesting as they do both the proletarianization of the Italian peasant class and the growth of a latifundist agriculture based on sheep-grazing, arboriculture and large-scale cultivation, as well as on a fairly extensive incidence of slavery, must form the basis of modern reconstructions, as Toynbee is well aware, and cannot be set aside or called in doubt. A recent attempt to do so (M. A. Levi, 'L'Italia dopo Annibale', *Athenaeum* N.S. XLIV 1965, 419 f.) substitutes an explanation of the second century social and economic changes that is excessively modern; according to this account different factors, for instance the imports of products from overseas and the resulting competition that brought about a reduction of agricultural profits, would have led to the collapse of the small proprietors, though they were flourishing at the time and in a phase of over-production. This view, for example, ignores the fact that there was no unified Italian market on account of the difficulties of communications and transport, not to mention other reasons.

In other words, the disappearance of the small peasant proprietor must have been the product of a double set of forces: on the one side decline brought about directly by the war (recruitment of the labour force into the army, ravages, forced sales) and on the other confiscations and exploitation of *ager publicus* by new methods of agriculture, whether on the old *ager publicus* (such as the *trientabula*) or on the new, by those who had liquid capital to invest. Of course this phenomenon stretches over a long period of time. In many cases there may have been a revival after the Hannibalic War of small properties which had been devastated, but the post-Hannibalic colonization schemes, though possibly intended by the Roman governing class to remedy the effects of the war, cannot be said to have played a large part in this work of reconstruction – even without comparing what happened later to Sulla's and Augustus' schemes of colonization. Latin colonization disappeared for various reasons: Toynbee, II 143 f. maintains that the decisive difficulty was not that of finding Roman citizens ready to forfeit their citizenship but the competition for military manpower between Rome and her allies. *Coloniae civium* in peninsular Italy cannot have made any real difference. Gallia Cisalpina is indeed a different story, but the agrarian development of this region and the colonies planted there must in fact have worked to the detriment of agriculture in central and southern Italy, among other things draining off some population from these areas. From Polybius' description it is clear that the Cisalpina was a closed, self-sufficient market in the second century BC.

It was, above all, the new 'capitalist' forms of cultivation used first in the exploitation of *ager publicus* that brought about consequential changes in the patterns of private estates. Medium-sized and large enterprises were favoured at the expense of the smaller ones whose management had become un-economic. The characteristic features of the new 'capitalist' form of agri-culture, where both establishment and development were dependent upon the investment of substantial capital sums, were chiefly the breeding of animals, especially widespread in Apulia and Lucania, and such expensive but profitable forms of arboriculture as vines and olives. In this respect one can speak, as Toynbee does, of a revolutionary change in the Italian landscape and flora beginning in the second century BC. Toynbee (II 157 f. and 268 f.) maintains that the development of capitalist pasturage on a large scale was the result of 'transhumance' [i.e. seasonal migrations of flocks] and that this last could only come into being after the unification of Italy. This could be open to discussion. It will certainly not have arisen because of the presence in second-century Italy of foreign slaves who came from countries where it already existed; it must have been a phenomenon independent of political conditions and so presumably of far greater antiquity. Certainly in the second century BC the existence of slave labour and above all the huge stretches of *ager publicus* in southern Italy must have favoured its develop-ment. On the other hand, arboriculture guaranteed a higher return on capital invested than cereal cultivation and, in order to be economically profitable, needed development over large areas. This decline in traditional cereal cultivation probably meant a drop in the total production of staple foods (wheat, barley), though this presumably presented a serious problem only for Rome where the population was on the increase. The answer was to import supplies of wheat from outside Italy, especially from Sicily, a pro-vince whose agriculture saw a marked development in the post-Hannibalic era. This confirms the conclusion that the various regions of Italy were really self-sufficient as regards staple foods; their economies were as yet restricted and on a small geographical scale. Even in later times the problems of feeding a city like Rome were always to be serious and were overcome by imports from overseas.

The development of this kind of industrialized agriculture was helped by the presence of slave labour. However, in my opinion, one ought not to exaggerate the extent of this in second-century Italy. It seems to me probable that from an economic point of view the use of slaves was comparatively more profitable than the use of free labour. However, the growing pro-letarianization of the rural population and their abandonment of the land were especially due to new methods of cultivation which required less labour.

Confronted with such a profound change in the social and economic structure of Rome and the Italian states, it is not easy to say what the Roman governing class should have done. It would have appreciated – as Ti.

Gracchus did later – the consequences for Rome's military strength, that is to say, the decline in available citizens and allied *adsidui* for the levy. It is to be remembered that in general, partly as a result of the wars in the Hellenistic East, the economy was expanding and that this had led to the growth at Rome and in the cities of Magna Graecia of a wealthy commercial class, ready to seize the new opportunities offered. Interventions by the state to control the economy were unthinkable; in any case, even with the wisdom which comes after the event, we cannot say what exact steps should have been taken at a time when the phenomenon of land settlement schemes in central and southern Italy was coming to an end, not through any wish of the government but because the potential colonists refused to take part. On the other hand, emigration to Cisalpine Gaul and the western provinces was not a planned affair. Indeed, it is very likely that the settlement of Roman citizens and of *socii* outside the traditional limits was not looked on favourably. At some time in the second century BC which cannot be dated with any certainty (between 185 and 180 according to Toynbee, II 554 f.), the Roman government passed a law *de modo agrorum* concerning *ager publicus*, and this was intended to limit, at least on this type of land, the growth of large *latifundia*. It was the only possible measure, but it made no appreciable difference. The political forces behind Ti. Gracchus were clearly well-informed about the situation in Italy, although, as I have said, they considered economic and social factors cold-bloodedly in their relation to a policy of military expansion. And they did not lack courage. However, their idea of reviving a class of small peasants by redistributing allotments of *ager publicus*, to be recovered by a second law *de modo agrorum* that was basically a renewal of the limit laid down fifty years earlier, shows that they had no conception of the main forces at work in the Italian economy (it may be by inference from the Polla *elogium* that Toynbee several times, and especially II 551, thinks that the law of Ti. Gracchus referred only to arable *ager publicus*; this seems to me impossible). The proletarianization of the farmers owning medium-sized estates was without doubt a tragedy in social terms, but from a general, that is cold-blooded, point of view the Italian economy had never been so flourishing (cf. the *laudes Italiae* of the first century BC). The anti-Gracchans were, it is true, dominated by narrow-mindedness, prejudice and egoism, but as happens only too often (by a strange but all too common paradox) they were in a basic sense right. They themselves were not aware of it; in fact, the anti-Gracchan who set up the Polla *elogium* boasted of a policy not basically different from that of the Gracchans. One can truly speak, as scholars have done, of 'the error of the Gracchi'.

None the less, the Gracchi had been able to express the very real needs of a large social group whose ideal was still that of the age in which everyone had his little plot of land and was happy. This explains how the theme of the small peasant driven from his land by his rich and powerful neighbour could, even in subsequent ages, have real political and ideological meaning, until such time as other leaders emerged, more astute and less scrupulous, circulating other propaganda themes which were closer to reality.

Even if one does not share Toynbee's pessimism, one must recognize that the event which marked a new phase and which set in motion the process of change by which political, social and economic affairs were so profoundly transformed was in fact the Hannibalic War. He has succeeded in describing accurately this whole great evolution and has displayed deep perceptiveness in assessing its significance. The two Romano–Carthaginian Wars, especially the second, forced Rome to leave behind the earlier historical phase, that of hegemony in Italy, and to take on the grave and weighty responsibility of supremacy in the Mediterranean world. When the Greek historian of the second century BC [Polybius] set himself to study the causes of Rome's emergence as a power in the fifty years from the outbreak of the Hannibalic War down to Pydna, was he not also in fact inquiring, though in political and military terms, into the consequences of the Roman victory over Hannibal – and therefore into Hannibal's legacy?

VIII

Review of E. Badian, 'Foreign Clientelae', Oxford 1958*

1. The title of this book is rather general for it has to be understood as referring to two substantially different subjects that are treated in the two sections of the work; the author has tried, even with his title, to invest these with a unity that still remains somewhat artificial. 'Foreign Clientalae' serves in the first part to indicate a particular type of relationship between Rome and other states, while later it refers to the *clientelae* which Roman families or individuals succeeded in establishing not only in the provinces but even in foreign states, and employed for political purposes at Rome. It cannot be denied that between these two subjects there exist connexions which B. skilfully brings out, but there is also no doubt that between the two parts of the work a certain hiatus is in evidence. However, I am well aware that these remarks of mine are immaterial to the main point, and that what matters is that B. has produced a work marked by that precision and acumen which are well known to readers of the numerous articles he has published in recent years on Roman Republican history.[1]

2. As I have said, in the first part of his study B. considers the way in which Rome, in her dealings with other states, began by applying in the third century BC certain methods which can be analysed to reveal those dealings as sharing the features of *clientela*-relationships. Several times in the course of this section B. emphasizes that the relations established by Rome with foreign states offer close analogies with private *clientela* (which is sketched briefly in the introduction as though to define the terms of comparison). But to me it is not entirely clear whether he means that the executive organs of the Roman state deliberately applied the principles of *clientela* in their foreign policy, or whether, on the contrary, they came to form such relations by empirically reacting to the various situations that confronted them.[2] B. has an introductory chapter on the organization of Italy before the Hannibalic War, which is necessary among other things in order to show how the Roman attitude came to be modified over the various stages of its expansion in Italy. He has an excellent explanation of the needs which prompted the institution of *civitas sine suffragio* (pp. 16–19), of the consequences of the Latin War of 338, and of the position of the Italian *socii* and the *socii navales*. Especially noteworthy and convincing is his analysis and description of the *foedera*, in which he reacts against rigid and schematic conceptions (pp. 25–8).

Having become deeply involved in the politics of the Mediterranean states through the war against Pyrrhus (p. 22 f.) Rome had come to occupy a position which was new to her and was confronted with new demands and new problems. If the *receptio in fidem* of the Mamertini and the *foedus* concluded with them were only a further step in the traditional policy of protecting small states against powerful neighbours, the consequences of the First Punic War which followed necessitated the application of new methods – naturally enough, because Rome had no wish to see fundamental changes in her own institutions. Hence we find in Sicily the first *civitates liberae*;[3] in my view B. (p. 37 f.) is right to refer this institution to the period immediately subsequent to the First Punic War, against the usual view that it arose only at the beginning of the second century BC.[4] Rome had no *foedus* with these cities, and this should be regarded as a privilege, given that no restriction was placed on their freedom. Rome, however, knew that she had a moral right over them even if no legal ties existed; the *civitas libera* is the *paradeigma* of the client state (p. 42). In Rome's relations with the Illyrian states B. sees a further development of this practice: Rome established a certain number of states in Illyria and these were tied to her, although there were no treaties and they were, formally speaking, free. When Demetrius of Pharos adopted too independent a policy, he had to face a Roman attack; Demetrius is equated with an ungrateful client who has forgotten the *beneficia* of his patron Rome (pp. 46–7). The question of Rome's relations with Saguntum is, of course, studied in depth (p. 48 f.). According to B. Rome had no interests in Spain before 231 BC, and the so-called Ebro treaty of 226 BC must have consisted in a formal assurance not to cross the river; Rome had no treaty with Saguntum, but the Spanish city was in the Roman *fides* from some year between 224 and 221 and, contrary to Polybius' statement, must have entered into that *fides* as a consequence of the appeal for Roman arbitration made by Saguntum at a time of civil discord. Rome's hesitation in 219 shows that the moral obligations resulting from *fides* were not as binding as those from a treaty. Not all these conclusions are certain, and sometimes they seem to be influenced by a wish to see Saguntum (the client) bound to Rome (the patron) as a result of a *beneficium* (the arbitration), and by a wish therefore to bring the case of Saguntum into line with earlier developments. It is possible that Rome had interests in Spain before the Ebro treaty (Mazzarino, *Introd. alle Guerre Puniche*, Catania 1947, 125: 138–9) and it is probable that the Saguntines turned to Rome for arbitration precisely because they already had a standing connexion with her. In any event there is no doubt that in the third century, by abandoning the principle of binding alliances and adopting the more elastic system of the free client state, the Roman government showed concern and hesitation in the face of the obligations which their new position imposed.

We meet this same attitude again, at least initially, in Roman policy towards the Greek world (p. 56 f.). Unfortunately, it is not possible to discuss every point in B.'s treatment, for that would far exceed the limit of a review, all the more so since the author has subjected the tradition to minute analysis; even when his conclusions coincide with the results reached by other scholars we can be certain that he has conducted his own critical re-examination of the material. I shall briefly consider a few points of major significance.

If his conclusions on the Peace of Phoenice are acceptable (p. 60), his theory that the ultimatum to Philip in 201 proved that Rome wanted peace (p. 66 f.) seems more ingenious than convincing; B. maintains that at Rome at this time there was no thought of appearing as champion of the liberty of Greece, and that the ultimatum was contrived to enable Rome to comply with fetial law which recognized only defensive wars. The birth of the idea of 'the freedom of Greece' is put by B. between 200 and 198 BC. He explains it as a clear consequence of earlier Roman policy and is therefore led to minimize both the personal influence of Flamininus and the frequently canvassed connexion with Greek political ideas. His reasoning is, in the main, acceptable even if it may, in my view, be objected that B. here and elsewhere too often assumes as his premiss a poor acquaintance with the Greek world on the part of the Senate. That Roman policy was guided by a healthy empiricism (and cannot be confined or interpreted in terms of a strictly linear development) is clear from the later Roman attitude towards King Antiochus and the Greek cities of Asia (p. 76 f.) and in general from the new policy adopted towards the Hellenistic states down to Pydna. The treaty with the Aetolians shows us for the first time the famous clause on the *maiestas populi Romani* (p. 85); the concept of *libertas* comes to be modified under the influence of Greek thought (p. 87 f.), and with Demetrius, son of Philip V, Rome begins her policy of supporting a 'Roman candidate' for the throne of a foreign state (p. 94). B. examines very acutely the guiding principles of the Roman government in foreign policy but is in turn led to deny, generally speaking, any connexion between this policy and possible conflicts of opinion or factional struggles in domestic politics.[5] He seems in fact to have neglected to consider the political basis of second-century annalistic writing brought out by Gelzer and Bickerman; apart from anything else, the decision of some of these annalists to write in Greek and therefore their desire to address themselves to the Greek world may suggest something concerning the knowledge of that world on the part of the Roman governing class.

The battle of Pydna appears as a turning-point in Rome's foreign policy, as is revealed, for example, by Rome's change of attitude towards Rhodes[6] and the Eastern kings. As B. rightly heads his Chapter IV, there has been progress from 'Protectorate to Domination'. Chapter V, which deals with relations between Rome and the West from 218 to 133 BC (p. 116 f.), even though it appears less original than the earlier chapters, does not lack some excellent comments, for example on the problem of the Third Punic War and Roman policy towards Numidia (p. 133 f.). Chapter VI (p. 141 f.) outlines with clarity the change in Romano–Italian relations after the Hannibalic War, the decline of independence on the part of the *socii*, the growing frequency of Roman interventions and the consequent advantages and disadvantages for the allied communities.

3. The second part of the study ('Internal Politics') is, of course, based on a conception of Roman domestic politics which goes back to the well-known theories of Gelzer and Münzer. B. examines Roman politics from 133 to 70 BC and considers the influence on it of the *clientelae* which important statesmen acquired in Italy, the provinces and the client states. B. studies their origins in some brilliant pages (p. 154 f.) and defines their significance; he is well aware that already in the early second century the allied governing classes (for example in Greece) often kept their position with the support of leading Romans (p. 164 f.) and I believe he is right to emphasize the point that these client connexions were vital factors in holding the Empire together despite its terrible civil wars. Of course, to examine a historical period in the light of one specific problem has the advantage that it illuminates points which are often obscured and presents suggestions which as a rule are not made. On the other hand, there is also the disadvantage of magnifying the importance of the particular problem and making it a key that explains too much. For example, the observation that Ti. Gracchus' hostility towards the Senate was bound up with the need to defend his own *fides* and his own *dignitas vis-à-vis* his Spanish clients is undoubtedly acute, but I do not think one can reduce the causes of his revolutionary activity to these terms (p. 169).[7]

In Chapters VIII, IX and X B. considers what may be called the Italian problem down to the grant of the citizenship to the *socii* and the consequences which flowed from it, a topic which is extremely controversial and which the author succeeds at many points in clarifying. Essentially he sets out to show

how the traditional policy of *clientela* did not succeed in solving the allied problem and how, once the *socii* had obtained the citizenship by force of arms, the oligarchy sought to direct the new flood into traditional channels. He also shows how *clientela*-relationships had been profoundly changed by the intervention in politics of professional armies (a new form of *clientela*), bound by strict ties to ambitious generals who thus prepared the way for the growth of their personal power (for example Pompey), and how this stream of events eventually debouched into the Principate (cf. the researches of von Premerstein).

The reviewer, grateful as he is for the care and courtesy with which B. always mentions his work, has not always been convinced by B.'s account; some doubts may perhaps be mentioned here. There has been endless discussion whether the *lex agraria* of Ti. Gracchus concerned only Roman citizens or whether it extended also to the allies; as is well known, the latter suggestion comes from Appian. B. takes the view that the law envisaged allocation only for *cives*. As I have said elsewhere (*Appiano e la storia delle guerre civili*, 43, n. 1), I do not know whether this problem is capable of solution with the evidence which we have, but I do not believe that the texts summoned in support confirm B.'s thesis. Above all, it tends to be forgotten that the passages of Appian, *BC* I 9, 35 f. and 11, 43 f., come from Ti. Gracchus' speeches, preserved probably by Cornelius Nepos, and that the same must hold for Plutarch, *Gracchi* 9, 4–6 (= *ORF*³ 13), although the passage is in conflict with Appian.[8] The fragment in Cicero's *de Republica* III 41 appears as follows in the third edition of Ziegler (1955): **Asia Ti. Gracchus, perseveravit in civibus, sociorum nominisque Latini iura neclexit ac foedera.* I must admit that without the preceding context I do not understand very well what Cicero means precisely by *perseveravit in civibus*: the word *Asia* with which the fragment opens allows of various hypotheses. But with the best will in the world I cannot see how it can be deduced from the second half of the phrase (violation of treaties) that the *socii* and the Latins were excluded from the allotments. The most one can do is to refer the fragment – and also *de Rep.* I 31 – to the recovery by the state of *ager publicus* in allied hands (see my Commentary,[2] *Appiani Bell. Civ. lib. I*, on I 19, 78: p. 59 – referred to hereafter as *Comm.*). I share M. A. Levi's view (*RFIC* 1929, 237) that in the *lex agraria* of 111 BC, at lines 3 and 15, there is a reference to viritane allocations to citizens, but one may raise objections to the conclusions B. draws from line 29, of which J. Göhler (*Rom und Italien*, Breslau 1939, 182 f.) has provided the correct interpretation.[9] I should also add that in general B.'s ideas on Appian do not seem to me to be correct.[10] The connexion of the Eudemus episode with the Asiatic *clientelae* of the Sempronii Gracchi (p. 174 and 183 f.) is stimulating, and B.'s observations on Pennus' law (p. 177) and the quaestorship of C. Gracchus in Sardinia (p. 180 f.) are convincing. But again I cannot agree with B.'s reconstruction (p. 186 f.) of C. Gracchus' attempts to launch the *rogatio de sociis*, since it is based on a chronology of the events of 123–121 BC which in my view is mistaken. B. also deals with the problem in Appendix A, pp. 300–1. It seems to me that the real mistake is to have abandoned Appian as a guide (his account, although 'very compressed', does offer a sequence of events which is clear and intelligible) and in having adopted Plutarch instead; the latter's chapter 26, as Fraccaro has shown ('Ricerche su C. Graccho', *Athenaeum* N.S. III 1925, 87 f. = *Opuscula*, II 27 f.), is subject to very serious confusion in that, for example, it records the principal laws twice. The *rogatio de sociis*, in fact, appears in Plutarch divided into three different measures (26, 2; 29, 3; 30, 5) which must be explained rather by a reference to Appian, I 23, 99 (see *Comm.* 79 and B. himself, pp. 299–300): Appian is aware of only one measure. B., however, has compounded Plutarch's confusion with a new misunderstanding. He maintains, on the basis of Plutarch 33, 3 that C. Gracchus brought the *rogatio de sociis* before the *comitia* after his return (placed by B. in about April, 122) from his visit to Africa to set up the colony of Junonia, and that the *rogatio* was defeated by the intervention of the consul Fannius in expelling from Rome the *socii* who had flocked there *en masse*. In this account by Plutarch there is no mention of a veto interposed by Livius Drusus against the Gracchan *rogatio*, but this is stated by Appian, I 23, 101, and cannot have been invented by him. B. supposes that Gracchus had originally proposed the *rogatio* in the period December 123–January 122 (p. 186 and p. 301) and that Livius Drusus had then given advance notice of the veto.[11] This idea is very odd; in particular I do not understand why Drusus did not interpose his veto later in May 122. Furthermore, it is not clear why Gracchus, having given up the attempt to *promulgare* the bill in December–January because of the threat of a veto, should promulgate it later in May 122; did he know that Drusus would not again propose a veto? In short I do not see (and B. himself, p. 187, cannot explain it) why C. Gracchus should set out for Carthage precisely in January 122, leaving the question of the *socii* half-finished. B., it may be added, maintains that it was precisely during Caius' absence that Drusus put forward his plan which aimed at detaching some of the allies from the Gracchans; Caius must have been out of his mind to revive his proposed *rogatio de sociis* in such a situation in May 122.[12] In fact, as Fraccaro has already observed, Plutarch's evidence can be used provided we follow the chronological order of Appian, I 23, 98 f. The bill on the allies, introduced at the beginning of 122 and attacked by Fannius both at public meetings and by means of the expulsion of non-citizens (Appian, I 23, 100: *Comm.* 80), failed because of Drusus' veto (Appian, I 23, 99–100). Drusus brought forward his plan and detached from Caius both the *plebs Romana* and some of the allies (Appian, I 23, 101). As a result Gracchus failed in his attempt to be re-elected a third time to the tribunate (July 122: Appian, I 24, 102 *init.*).

Caius and Flaccus took themselves off to Africa to found the colony at Carthage, dividing and allocating more allotments than prescribed in an attempt to win back the favour of the Roman Plebs and the allies (August–September: seventy days according to Plutarch, 32, 3); when they returned they enrolled colonists from all Italy (winter 122–121). The arrival of the colonists at Junonia must have taken place in the spring of 121. There is no doubt that this reconstruction, based on Appian, is the only one that is logical and coherent. Of course, if we reject B.'s chronology it follows that it is difficult to accept his interpretation of the anti-Gracchan activity of Drusus (p. 189 f.).

His reconstruction of the period of Marius' pre-eminence seems to me sound, barring some points of detail which I would not wish to labour here. The relations between Marius and the Metelli are carefully examined, the significance of Saturninus' agrarian law is properly brought out, the allies' participation in the events of 100 BC is shown in its proper light (p. 207) and so too is Marius' attitude in that year and the following decade. I am also in agreement with him on the significance of the *lex Licinia Mucia* of 95 BC (p. 213).

However, I cannot accept B.'s version of the activity of the tribune Livius Drusus in 91 BC because of his interpretation of the well-known passage in Appian, I 36, 163. Although I am aware that on this point Appian must have abbreviated a good deal, I still believe that with δοκιμασία he refers to the vote on the *rogatio de sociis* (see *Comm.* 123). In my view the passage in Appian concerning the coming of the Etruscans and the Umbrians to Rome ἐς ἀναίρεσιν Δρούσου is strictly connected with what follows in 36, 164, where it is said that Drusus, who was aware of their intentions, was murdered. Drusus' death is subsequent to the repeal of his laws, which in its turn is subsequent to the death of Licinius Crassus (seven days after the Ides of September), but prior to the end of Drusus' tribunate: *in magistratu occisus est (Inscr. Ital.* XIII 3, 74). The episode of the coming of the Etruscans and Umbrians to Rome is therefore to be placed towards the end of Drusus' life, and since the agrarian and judiciary laws had already been approved some time before, δοκιμασία must refer to the voting on the *rogatio de sociis* which probably never became law, either because of Drusus' death or because it was withdrawn after the repeal of his previous legislation. B. does not accept this explanation because it would involve him in conceding that the Etruscans and Umbrians were principally opposed to the bill on the *socii*, and he is forced to attribute to δοκιμασία the significance of 'senatorial inquiry' (into the validity of Drusus' laws) which is contrary to Appian's usage (I 10, 42 and 29, 132; IV 27, 127) and which is not supported by any instance in any other ancient writer.[13]

That the Etruscan–Umbrian opposition centred on the *rogatio de sociis* is clear from the fact that they take no part later in the revolt and that their belated intervention was of little importance, brief and localized.[14] If later on they accept the citizenship (Appian, I 49, 212–13: this is the passage which shows that Appian considered Etruscans and Umbrians to be among the 'Ιταλιῶται), the explanation must lie in the change in the general situation brought about by the war and also in the fact that the *civitas* was now being offered without any strings attached, as had not been the case in the time of Drusus, whose agrarian law met universal opposition from the Italians. Of course, in my view, both the Etruscans/Umbrians who were opposed to the *rogatio de sociis* and the allies who were favourable to Drusus belonged to the upper classes (see *Comm.* on I 21, 86: p. 67); it was the upper classes which could have an interest in the *civitas*, and it was the wealthy who, like their Roman counterparts, feared the agrarian laws. All the more so because the allied states were in a situation analogous to that of Rome where, as is universally admitted, peasant proprietors had been disappearing. We are not entitled to believe that small peasant proprietors were preserved just in Etruria![15] The attitudes of the lower classes escape us. In rebel Italy I believe that they were won over to the cause of independence (see *Athenaeum* N.S. XXXII 1954, 54 = *Es. e Soc.* 210 [= 75 above];[16] as far as concerns Etruria and Umbria one cannot say, although it is possible to think that the attempts at insurrection that were quickly put down had been instigated precisely by them. Certainly it was they who subsequently supported Marius here in the civil war.

The consequences of the Social and Civil wars are carefully examined by B., and his assessment seems acceptable. He shows an acute understanding of the significance of the extended *civitas* for the *clientela*-dominated political life of the oligarchy, and his observations on Sulla's activity and on the new situation which was created by the intervention of professional armies – a new form of *clientela* – are convincing. I think he is right in his picture of Cinna's regime (pp. 240–1).

The last chapter (which is also the one nearest in spirit to the title of the book) deals with *clientelae* outside Italy, a problem which is connected with the growth and consolidation of Pompey's power and which was to reveal its true importance in the years after 70 BC; it is sufficient to reflect on the much-discussed Pompeian 'escape' to the East in 49 BC. B. also has some excellent observations on the assumption of a Roman name by provincials who took the citizenship (p. 253 f.), and establishes some very useful criteria of judgement and definition. He notes that the power granted to military commanders to award the citizenship began with the Social War; the similar actions of Marius were illegal (p. 260). In an appendix on the point he lists the known cases of *viritim* grants of the citizenship, and sets out (p. 310 f.) the results of his researches on the nomenclature of Narbonensis, Spain and Africa, comparing the names there with those of the governors of the respective provinces.[17] His conclusions are of the highest interest. The importance of these *clientelae* outside Italy is illuminated by an examination of Pompey's career down to the consulship of 70 BC, possibly the most brilliant and most convincing part of the whole book.[18] It leaves us with the wish and the hope that he will show us in a new volume what was the role of *clientela* in the civil wars which followed and in the rise of the Principate.

Notes

Notes to I

* *Athenaeum* N.S. XXVII 1949, 173–209. Cf. R. E. Smith, *Service in the Post-Marian Roman Army*, Manchester 1958, 1–10; T. F. Carney, *A Biography of C. Marius* (*PACA* Suppl. I), 1961, 25–8; J. Harmand, *L'armée et le soldat à Rome de 107 à 50 avant notre ère*, Paris 1967, 11–20, and 'Le Prolétariat dans la légion de Marius à la veille du second Bellum Civile', in *Problèmes de la guerre à Rome*, Paris–The Hague 1969, 61–73. M. J. V. Bell, 'Tactical Reform in the Roman Republican Army', *Historia* XIV 1965, 404–22, is very important for the military aspects of Marius' 'reform'.

1. Livy, I 43, 8: Dion. Hal. IV 18: Gell. XVI 10, 10–11. The exclusion of those without property from military service occurs commonly in many ancient states: see H. Liers, *Das Kriegswesen der Alten*, Breslau 1895, 10 f.

2. The conversion of ten asses to the drachma, in the Greek writers who mention these figures, applies to the sextantal as which is the tenth part of the silver denarius: see De Sanctis, *Storia dei Romani*, II 198. For H. Mattingly, 'The Property Qualifications of the Roman Classes', *JRS* XXVII 1937, 104–6, the 'Servian' scale was an invention of the Sullan period and its figures were reckoned in sesterces.

3. Livy, XXIV 11, 7–9.

4. H. Mattingly and E. S. G. Robinson, 'The Date of the Roman Denarius', *PBA* XVIII 1933.

5. *Art. cit.*, *JRS* XXVII 1937, 103.

6. E. Cavaignac, 'Le problème de l'organisation centuriale', *RH* CXCVI 1946, 35, thinks the figures of the *S.C.* go back to Coelius Antipater who substituted for the simple indication of classes I, II, III and IV the census figures of his own age. See also Cavaignac, *RIDA* II 1949, 173–88.

7. Livy, XL 51, 9: cf. A. Piganiol, *AHS* 1933, 113 f.; E. Cavaignac, *art. cit.* 34.

8. Milne, *CR* L 1936, 215–17: id. *JRS* XXVIII 1938, 73: *ibid.* XXXIV 1944, 49 f: *ibid.* XXXVI 1946, 99 f. Cf. A. Stazio, 'Bigati e argentum oscense', *Numismatica* Jan.–June 1947, 11 f., and L. Breglia, 'La monetazione di Capua e il problema del denario', *ibid.* Jan.–June 1948, 11 f.; R. Thomsen, *Early Roman Coinage*, I–III 1958–62.

9. Livy, I 43, 8. The figure of 12½ minae (=12,500 asses) found in Dion. Hal. IV 17–18 is thought to be due to a wish to make it fit with the other figures: see Mommsen, *SR* III 250, n. 1. However, cf. Botsford, *Roman Assemblies*, New York 1909, 88.

10. Polyb. VI 19, 2: (the citizens perform military service) πλὴν τῶν ὑπὸ τὰς τετρακοσίας δραχμὰς τετιμημένων. The usual view, on the basis of the equation (already mentioned) of one drachma with ten (sextantal) asses, is that the 400 drachmas in Polybius are equal to 4,000 asses, but Mattingly, *art. cit. JRS* XXVII 1937, 101 f., maintains that Polybius means the Aeginetan drachma equal to 12½ asses. The 400 drachmas mentioned in the passage would then be equal to 5,000 asses, and the 10,000 drachmas of Polyb. VI 23, 15 would correspond to 125,000 asses. The figure (4,000 or 5,000 asses) is of little importance in itself: what matters is its relationship to the 11,000 asses of Livy. However, in this article I take the 400 drachmas of Polybius as equivalent to 4,000 asses, following the traditional interpretation.

11. Cf. *Es. e Soc.* 9 n. 23 [= 4, n. 23 below].

12. Cic. *de Rep.* II 40: *qui* (Servius Tullius) *cum locupletis assiduos appellasset ab asse dando, eos, qui aut non plus mille quingentos aeris aut omnino nihil in suum censum praeter caput attulissent, proletarios nominavit* (cf. Nonius, p. 228 Lindsay). Gell. XVI 10, 10: *qui in plebe, inquit* (Iulius Paulus), *Romana tenuissimi pauperrimique erant neque amplius quam mille quingentum aeris in census deferebant, 'proletarii' appellati sunt, qui vero nullo aut perquam parvo aere censebantur, 'capite censi' vocabantur; extremus autem census capite censorum aeris fuit trecentis septuaginta quinque.* On Gellius' source in this passage see the edition of Hosius, Leipzig 1903, I, pp. LI–LII.

13. *SR* III 230. A distinction between a minimum for military service and a minimum for purposes of *tributum* is made also by A. Rosenberg, *Untersuchungen zur röm. Zenturienverfassung*, Berlin 1911, 41.

14. The figure of 4,000 asses is almost universally regarded as a reduction from the original 11,000.

15. *SR* III 237, followed, for example, by Bonfante, *Storia del diritto romano*, 1934, I 99.

16. Gellius in fact adds (§ 11) *neque proletarii neque capite censi milites . . . scribebantur*; cf. Fraccaro, '*Tribules* ed *Aerarii*', *Athenaeum* N.S. XI 1933, 153, n. 2 = *Opuscula*, II 152, n. 11.

17. De Sanctis, *op. cit.* II 210, thinks, however, that originally this was the case.

18. The fiscal purpose of the 'Servian' organization in which Beloch, *RG* 283, believed is not in fact tenable: see Fraccaro, 'Ancora sull' età dell'ordinamento centuriato', *Athenaeum* N.S. XII 1934, 60 = *Opuscula*, II 296 (military purpose) and G. Gianelli, 'Origini e sviluppi dell'ordinamento centuriato', *A & R* ser. III, III 1935, 237 (electoral and political purpose). The military character of the organization is also maintained by H. Last, 'The Servian Reforms', *JRS* XXXV 1945, 34.

19. Guiraud, 'L'impôt sur le capital à Rome', in *Études économiques sur l'antiquité*, Paris 1905, 192.

20. With the exception of the passage of Gellius: see *Es. e Soc.* 9, n. 23 [= 4, n. 23 below].

21. As is clear from the reconstructions of Mommsen, *SR* III 297–8, and Botsford, *op. cit.* 89. *Pace* the latter, p. 89, n. 5, there is no parallel between this classification and the categories of citizens rated at over 100,000 asses, mentioned in the *S.C.* of 214 BC (Livy, XXIV 11, 7–9), because the subdivision of citizens rated below 4,000 asses was considered official and regular while the categories indicated in the *S.C.* over 100,000 asses were temporary only, and were fixed for the purposes of an extraordinary allocation of military obligations. For the same reason it is impossible that, at the time of the first reduction to 4,000 asses, a sixth class was formed for military purposes with various subdivisions, as was suggested by Lipsius, *De*

militia romana, I 2 (= III, p. 21, Vesalia 1675) and Poeschelius, *Polybii de militia romana libellus*, Nuremburg 1731, 21–3, and was at first accepted by Mommsen, *Röm. Tribus*, Altona 1844, 116 (see *RG* I[8] 819).

22. Such citizens for Mommsen are *adsidui* and serve at their own expense, although they do not possess the minimum census qualification for military service (4,000 asses); according to Botsford, they pay *tributum* but do not perform military service even though they belong to the fifth class. Madvig's solution of the difficulty (*Verfassung und Verwaltung des röm. Staates*, I 1881, 112, n. 2) – that 1,500 asses was not the census maximum of the *proletarii* but the minimum – is impossible, not only because it has to posit an error common to Cicero and Gellius, but also because it does not explain the position of the citizens with census rating below 1,500 asses.

23. Gellius (passage cited *Es. e Soc.* 6 n. 12 [= 3, n. 12]) distinguishes the *capitecensi* from the *proletarii* and mentions the figure of 375 asses as that which separated the two categories. It is highly likely that the figure of 375 asses is only an invention to justify a distinction between *prol.* and *cap. censi* which we know did not exist (cf. De Sanctis, *op. cit.* II 197, n. 5. Rosenberg, *op. cit.* 41 f., did not believe in the figure of 375 asses but held that the distinction between *prol.* and *cap. censi* was a real one). This figure cannot even represent a distinguishing limit for military purposes as applied to the *proletarii*, as Mommsen, *SR* III 238, n. 2, seems to have believed; it is clear on inspection that such a category distinction does not exist even in Gellius: in XVI 10, 11 he says *neque proletarii neque capite censi milites, nisi in tumultu maximo, scribebantur*, i.e. in times of *tumultus* even the so-called *capite censi* were enrolled, and it is only later that he modifies this original statement when (§ 13) he limits enrolment in time of *tumultus* to *proletarii*. The first statement is certainly the more correct. Finally, 375 asses cannot represent a later third reduction of the census minimum (from 1,500 to 375 asses), given the short interval of time which elapsed between the second reduction (period of the Gracchi) and the total abandonment of the census as a basis for enrolment (107 BC). It is difficult to believe that the reduction was subsequent to 107 BC, bearing in mind that these reductions were for a military purpose.

24. Mommsen, *SR* III 272 and n. 4. A similar situation arose in Athens (of uncertain date) with the reduction from 200 to 150 drachmas as the dividing-line between zeugitae and thetes: (Dem.) *contra Macar.* 54: Beloch, *Gr. Gesch.*[2] I 1, 303, n. 2: Glotz, *La cité grecque*, 1928, 402. Cf. however Busolt-Swoboda, *Gr. Staatskunde*, II[3] 837 and 880.

25. Mommsen, *SR* III 273, n. 1; Rosenberg, *op. cit.* 42.

26. Madvig, *op. cit.* I 122. Many scholars have not taken this into account.

27. Lange, *Röm. Alterth.* I[3] 499–500; Bouché-Leclercq, *Manuel des institutions romaines*, 1931, 269 (cf. earlier E. Herzog, 'Die Bürgerzahlen in röm. Census', in *Comment. in hon. Th. Mommseni*, 1877, 137); Soltau, *Altröm. Volksversammlungen*, 1880, 348. Mommsen is vague on this point: *RG* I[8] 819; *SR* III 273. It should be noted that the connexion between the reduction of the census minimum for military service and the introduction of pay on which many scholars rely does not exist.

28. Gell. XVI 10, 11–13. If one follows the reading of Schweighäuser in Polyb. VI 19, 3, the citizens with a census qualification below 400 drachmas would have served in a crisis καὶ πεζῇ for 20 campaigns. But it is clear that for καὶ πεζῇ one should read οἱ πεζοί. See Marquardt, *De l'organisation militaire chez les Romains*, 80, n. 6. The first enrolment of *proletarii* in time of *tumultus* dates from 281–280 BC and is mentioned frequently: Ennius, *Ann.* 183–5 Vahlen (= Gell. XVI 10, 1); Cass. Hem. fr. 21 Peter (= Nonius, p. 94 Lindsay); Oros. IV 1, 3; Aug. *De civ. dei*, III 17; cf. the extensive commentary of Vahlen, *Ennianae poësis reliquiae*,[2] 1903, CLXXV–VI.

29. Livy, XXII 11, 8; XXII 59, 12; see Th. Steinwender, *Die röm. Bürgerschaft in ihrem Verhältniss zum Heere*, Danzig 1888, Progr., 7–9.
30. Köchly–Rüstow, *Gr. Kriegsschriftsteller*, II 1, 1855, 52, n. 133; Delbrück, *Geschichte d. Kriegskunst*, I³, 1920, 287. Cf. however Marquardt, *op. cit.* 41, n. 2: Madvig, *op. cit.* II 1882, 485. The view of Fr. Fröhlich, *Die Bedeutung des zweiten punischen Krieges für die Entwicklung der röm. Heerwesens*, Leipzig 1884, 377 f., accepted also by Kroymayer-Veith, *Heerwesen u. Kriegführung der Griechen und Römer*, 1928, 309, that essentially it is only a change of name (from *rorarii* to *velites*) which is in question here seems at variance with the fulness of the passage.
31. Livy, XXVI 4, 4; Val. Max. II 3, 3; Front. *Strat.* IV 7, 29 dwell chiefly on the tactical use of *velites* in conjunction with the cavalry. Ed. Meyer, 'Das röm. Manipularheer' (*APAW* 1923, no. 3), now in *Kleine Schriften*, II², Halle 1924, 260–1, maintains that the passage on the *velites* is worthless. On the question of the sources see A. Klotz, *Livius und seine Vorgänger*, II 1941, 172–3.
32. A. Piganiol, *La conquête romaine*, 1927, 198; E. Cavaignac, *art. cit. RH* CXCVI 1946, 34.
33. Livy, XXIV 11, 7.
34. Livy, XXII 11, 8.
35. As had already happened after Cannae: Livy, XXII 57, 7.
36. In fact, as also J. H. Thiel, *Studies on the history of Roman sea-power*, Amsterdam 1946, 12 and n. 28, partly admits, when the sources refer to Roman citizens enrolled for naval purposes, it is nearly always a question of *libertini*. Even Cato, fr. 180 Malc.³ (= Fest. p. 266, 27 Lindsay), cited by Mommsen, *SR* III 297, n. 2, in support of the passage in Polybius, refers to *libertini*: see Livy, XLII 27, 3. In general the whole chapter of Polybius, VI 19, deals with arrangements made during the Second Punic War.
37. According to Herzog, *mem. cit.* 138, the reduction to 4,000 asses took place between 208 and 203 BC, as the increase in the number of citizens at the census of 203 BC testifies. Apart from the question of the true significance of the census figures on which Herzog relies, it is not possible that the Romans decided to take such a step only when the greatest peril had passed and the need for soldiers had diminished. It is understandable that the reduction of the census minimum (in my view 214–212 BC) did not leave any trace in the figures of the period (e.g. in 208 BC) because it would have gone only some way to making good the very heavy losses which the figures reveal. The date of 214 BC for the lowering of the census minimum for 4,000 asses is also accepted by P. A. Brunt, *Italian Manpower, 225 BC–AD 14*, Oxford 1971, 402–3, though for different reasons.
38. See Fraccaro, 'La riforma dell'ordinamento centuriato', in *Studi Bonfante*, I, Milan 1930, 109–12 = *Opuscula*, II 176–80.
39. De Sanctis, *op. cit.* II 197, n. 5; Fraccaro, '*Accensi*', *Athenaeum* N.S. V 1927, 137 = *Opuscula*, II 317–18. The view of Cavaignac, *Population et Capital*, 1923, 88 f., that the figure was reckoned in semilibral asses and therefore belongs to a period prior to that of the 400 drachmas of Polybius, is improbable.
40. Soltau, *op. cit.* 348, refers the reduction to 1,500 asses to Marius or a censor of his time.
41. Cf. Kornemann, *Philologus* LXXXVI 1931, 173.
42. De Sanctis, *op. cit.* III 1, 205 f.; Ciaceri, *RAL* XXVII 1918, 241. Walbank, 'Polybius on the Roman Constitution', *CQ* XXXVII 1943, 87–8, thought, however, that Polybius changed his mind on the Roman constitution (hence the second edition of Book VI) under the influence of the conquest of Corinth and Greece (146 BC). Walbank has subsequently adopted a view which treats Book VI as a unity and sees

its publication date with the first five books about 150 BC: *A Historical Commentary on Polybius*, I, Oxford 1957, 635–6.

43. Plut. *C. Gracc.* 5, 1: ὁ δὲ στρατιωτικὸς (νόμος) ἐσθῆτά τε κελεύων δημοσίᾳ χορηγεῖσθαι καὶ μηδὲν εἰς τοῦτο τῆς μισθοφορᾶς ὑφαιρεῖσθαι τῶν στρατευομένων καὶ νεώτερον ἐτῶν ἑπτακαίδεκα μὴ καταλέγεσθαι στρατιώτην (cf. Diod. XXXIV–V 25, 1, and the interpretations of Bloch-Carcopino, *Histoire Romaine*, II 1, 245 and n. 1, and of H. Last, *CAH* IX 62, n. 1). The law would have contained a clause limiting the period of military service if a proposal to this effect which is attributed by some sources (Plut. *Ti. Gracc.* 16, 1; Cass. Dio, fr. 83, 7 Boiss.) to Tiberius Gracchus is really to be referred to his brother, as Fraccaro, *Studi sull'età dei Gracchi*, I 1914, 154 f. and J. Carcopino, *Autour des Gracques*, 1928, 40–4, maintain. See, however, E. v. Stern, *Hermes* LVI 1921, 276–7 and Täger, *Tiberius Gracchus*, 1928, 89. The fragment of a speech (57 Malc.) reported by Carisius, p. 270, 12 Barwick, has nothing to do with the law of Caius Gracchus: see Fraccaro, *Studi storici per l'antichità classica*, VI 1913, 117.

44. Cass. Dio, fr. 83, 7 Boiss: ὅτι ὁ Γράκχος τοῖς στρατευομένοις ἐκ τοῦ ὁμίλου νόμους τινὰς ἐπικουροῦντας ἔγραφε (on the legislator see preceding note); Diod. XXXIV–V 25, 1: τοῖς δὲ στρατιώταις διὰ τῶν νόμων. Bloch-Carcopino, *loc. cit.*, refers to three separate plebiscites. NB the passage of Asc. *in Corn.* p. 54, 25 f. Stangl where it is said that the consul Iunius Silanus (109 BC) *plures leges, quae per eos annos ab iis qui gratificabantur populo latae erant, quibus militiae stipendia minuebantur, abrogavit.*

45. *CAH* IX 62–3.

46. Cass. Dio, *loc. cit.*, says in fact that the law applied τοῖς στρατευομένοις ἐκ τοῦ ὁμίλου.

47. Very probably the reduction of the census minimum to 1,500 asses was closely connected with the retariffing of the as (16 asses = 1 denarius) which took place between 133 and 123 BC: see E. A. Sydenham and Mattingly, 'The Retariffing of the Denarius at Sixteen Asses', *NC* XIV 1934, 81–91. It would be especially significant if the passage in Plin. *NH* XXXIII 13, 45 which follows on that dealing with the retariffing of the as (*in militari tamen stipendio semper denarius pro decem assibus datus est*) were connected with the clause of the law of Caius Gracchus.

48. See Gabba, 'Ancora sulle cifre dei censimenti', *Athenaeum* NS. XXX 1952, 161–73 = *Es. e Soc.* 521 f.

49. See Mommsen, *SR* II³ 375.

50. It is clearly out of the question that such a formula was valid only on the two occasions (Livy, III 3, 9: *Per.* LIX) for which it is attested with slight variations (Mommsen, *SR* II³ 365, n. 3). In that case one would have to suppose that the census figures do not have, generally speaking, a constant significance but that they can represent different groups of citizens at different times; this, despite the generous freedom of action which the censors enjoyed in compiling their lists, seems incredible.

51. Mommsen, *SR* III 236; 256, n. 4.

52. It is not likely that the expression *civ. capita*, with the additional clause concerning *orbi* and *orbae*, means all adult males, and it is no accident that Beloch, for whom the census figures indicate all adult males (*Die Bevölkerung der griechisch-römischen Welt*, Leipzig 1886, 314) contradicts himself later (*ibid.* 375) when he curiously understands by the term *civium capita* all the *capita libera* (see the criticism of Kornemann, *Jahrb. für nat. Oecon. und Stat.* 1897, 293). Naturally this second view of Beloch's is even more impossible than the first since there can be no purpose in a list of all *capita libera* with the sole exception of *orbi* and *orbae*.

53. Livy, I 44, 2 = Polyb. II 24, 16 (δυνάμενοι ὅπλα βαστάζειν). I call it a 'part-formula' because the expression *civium capita praeter orbos orbasque* was apparently a simplified version of a more complex formula which may perhaps have been the

following: *capita civium Romanorum tot. eorum qui arma ferre possunt tot. orbi orbaeque tot* (see Mommsen, *SR* II³ 411, n. 1).

54. Cf. J. Göhler, *Rom und Italien*, Breslau 1939, 140. *Inter alia*, if the formula alluded to physical requirement, one would have to suppose that those who were unable to bear arms *per aetatem* would have been excluded from this list of citizens. This is the case when the phrase *arma ferre posse* is used of barbarian peoples (see e.g. the passages of Caesar collected by H. Meusel, *Lexicon Caesarianum*, I 1887, col. 305) but it is not possible that at Rome in the late third century (225 BC is the context of the passage of Polybius cited in the previous note) the *seniores* were not included among the *civium capita*.

55. Naturally enough, at least from a theoretical point of view, bearing in mind the successive reductions of the census minimum.

56. See Mommsen, *SR* II³ 405–7.

57. The term *capite census* (like *duicensus*, Beloch, *op. cit.* 316) refers only to registration with the censors, before whom the *proletarii* also appeared (Mommsen, *SR* II³ 366); they were thus enrolled in tribes and could vote in the *comitia*. The assertion of Caspari, *Klio* XIII 1913, 197, that it is a term of the Imperial period does not take into account Sall. *BJ* 86, 2 and Cic. *de Rep.* II 40.

58. The statement of Beloch, *Klio* III 1903, 478, that the *capite censi* must have been included in a list compiled on the occasion of the *tumultus Gallicus* of 225 BC does not hold, since in 225 BC there was no tumultuary levy; it was entirely a question of making a list of eligibles to which the *proletarii* are irrelevant.

59. Indeed, the *tumultuarius dilectus*, until this time uniquely employed in the ancient institution of the *tumultus*, came in the second century to be the means by which legions on occasions were formed without going through the delays which attended the traditional *dilectus* (Livy, XXXI 2, 5–6; XXXII 26, 12; XL 26, 6; XLI 5, 4; XLIII 11, 11). It is also possible that the Romans had recourse to levies of this kind as a purely voluntary method of enrolment: we should note the poor standing accredited to the *tumultuarii* (Livy, XLIII 11, 11).

60. Hence the earlier conclusions of E. Herzog, *mem. cit.* 124 f., can be accepted. The objections which Beloch, *op. cit.* 318, lodged against them do not appear decisive. Beloch's assertion that 'even less can we understand how the expression *censa sunt civium capita tot* could exclude the *capite censi*', conflicts with what has been said above, *Es. e Soc.* 20 n. 57 [= 8, n. 57 above]. His point that 'if the freedmen, as far as military service was concerned, were actually equated with the *capite censi*, they ought, in a list devoted to citizens fit for military service, to have been treated as the *capite censi* were' (and, therefore, excluded from it, though we know that from a certain period some were classified with the first two classes and therefore included in a list of *civium capita*: Herzog, *mem. cit.* 139) does not take account of the fact that the *libertini* were clearly classified with the first two classes for purposes of *tributum*, but not military service (see, however, Mommsen, *SR* III 449).

61. To summarize, it is dateable to 133–123 BC by the following three arguments: (1) it is before 107 and after 133 (or 146) BC; (2) it is before 123 BC, the year of Caius Gracchus' military law; (3) the census returns of 125 BC are a consequence of it.

62. Concerning the various views put forward to explain the census returns of 125 BC, we may refer to the careful summary of Fraccaro, 'Assegnazioni agrarie e censimenti romani', in *Scritti in onore di C. Ferrini*, I 1947, 262 f. = *Opuscula*, II 87 f., although I do not accept his conclusions.

63. Cf. A Bernardi, 'Incremento demografico di Roma e colonizzazione latina', *NRS* XXX 1946, 272 f. (esp. 277–9: 287–9). Cf. Polyb. I 64, 1–2 and the speech of Metellus in H. Malcovati, *ORF*³, p. 107.

64. Cic. *de Off.* II 73.

65. As appears from Dion. Hal. IV 18, 2 (= VII 59, 6): τοὺς δὲ λοιποὺς πολίτας, οἳ τίμησιν εἶχον ἐλάττονα δώδεκα καὶ ἡμίσους μνῶν, πλείους τὸν ἀριθμὸν ὄντας τῶν προτέρων, ἅπαντας εἰς ἕνα συντάξας λόχον κ.τ.λ. This statement should be compared, but not confused, with the information that the centuries of the lower classes comprised more citizens than the first class in its entirety, as Cic. *de Rep.* II 40, also says. I cannot accept the reconstruction of L. Homo, *Les institutions politiques romaines : de la cité à l'état*, 1927, 153 f.

66. This entitles us to reject the view of Fraccaro, *Athenaeum* N.S. IX 1931, 292, n. 1 = *Opuscula*, II 54, n. 1, that, if in 131 BC there were 300,000 *adsidui*, there would have been no justification for the concern of the Gracchi. Fraccaro wishes to use this point as an argument against the theory of Herzog on the census figures.

67. Polyb. VI 23, 15: οἱ δὲ ὑπὲρ τὰς μυρίας τιμώμενοι δραχμάς, ἀντὶ τοῦ καρδιοφύλακος σὺν τοῖς ἄλλοις ἀλυσιδωτοὺς περιτίθενται θώρακας. This has to be considered as a relic of the distinguishing armour of the different census classes, which had still survived in the legions, perhaps down to the Hannibalic War (Domaszewski, *RE* s.v. 'bewaffnung', col. 377; Fraccaro, *art. cit. Athenaeum* N.S. XII 1934, 60 = *Opuscula*, II 296). Giannelli, *art. cit. A & R* Ser. III, III 1935, 237, n. 18, thought it to be an old distinction 'which was a survival from the period in which all the heavy infantry was provided by one class', but this seems highly unlikely. In fact it is after the Second Punic War that the threefold division of the legion came to be based solely on the criterion of age without taking any account, as before, of armour.

68. If in 171 BC Livy (XLII 52, 11) makes Perseus say: *arma illos* (the Romans) *habere ea quae sibi quisque paraverit pauper miles, Macedonas prompta ex regio apparatu*, he is only alluding to the general difference between the citizen militia of a timocracy and the army of an absolute monarchy (Liers, *op. cit.* 37): no conclusions for the Roman army of the second century BC can be drawn from this.

69. The verb προσδέομαι refers only to ὅπλου, as is shown by the position of ἄν; on the other hand the two genitives τοῦ . . . σίτου καὶ τῆς ἐσθῆτος are only prolepses of πάντων τούτων. The Latin translation of the Didot edition, *Polybii Reliquiae*, 1880, 362, is correct: *Romanis vero sive frumentum sive vestis tribuatur, aut etiam si quibus armis denuo opus habuerint, horum omnium certa praetia quaestor de stipendio deducit.* The prefix προς (= *denuo* in the Latin translation) must be understood as 'in addition' and refers to the clothing and the food. The interpretation of Clerici, *Economia e finanza dei Romani*, I, Bologna 1943, 446 f. is to be rejected.

70. Probably the state originally bought the arms from private manufacturers (Livy, XXII 57, 11): the first armouries and arsenals in state hands are attested only in 100 BC (Cic. *pro Rab. perd. reo. 20*).

71. Cf. Tac. *Ann.* I 17, 6 (AD 14). The deductions abolished by C. Gracchus were perhaps restored in 109 BC (see Asc. *in Corn.* p. 54, 25 f. Stangl).

72. Concerning the rewards offered to the soldiers of the Hannibalic War, we know that to begin with the *S.C.* of 201 BC ordered that Scipio's African army should receive allotments on the parts of Samnite and Apulian land which had been confiscated (Livy, XXXI 4, 1–3) and that in the following years the provision was extended to include soldiers from Spain, Sardinia and Sicily (Livy, XXXI 49, 5–6; XXXII 1, 6), i.e. the measures affected only all soldiers who had fought outside Italy, and who naturally had not secured discharge (*milites qui per multos annos stipendia fecissent* as Livy says). However, in the second century the settlement of soldiers in Spain is attested, a phenomenon which was to occur later in the Imperial period on a large scale. From 206 to 123 BC we know of foundations of the cities of Italica (App. *Iber.* 38, 153), Gracchuris (Livy, *Per.* XLI; Fest. p. 86, 5 Lindsay); Carteia (Livy, XLIII 3); Corduba (Strabo, III 2, 1); Palma and Pollentia (Strabo, III 5, 1). On all these problems see *Es. e Soc.* 105 f. [= 40 f. below]. On the

political and military consequences of the Spanish War see Ed. Meyer, 'Untersuchungen zur Geschichte der Gracchenzeit', *Kleine Schriften*, I² 401 and n. 1; A. Schulten, *Numantia*, I 1914, 270–80.

73. Livy, XXVIII 46, 1; App. *Lib.* 8, 30 f.

74. Livy, XXXI 24, 2 (XXXII 3, 3); XXXII 9, 1; XXXVII 4, 3; XLII 32, 6. Fröhlich, *op. cit.* 33 f.

75. Although the militia was adapted to the new situation arising out of the growth of Roman territory there was no corresponding development of the state organization beyond the city-state structure (Ed, Meyer, 'Das röm. Manipularheer', *Kleine Schriften*, II² 226): hence the conflict between the army and the political system which was a characteristic of the civil wars of the first century BC. Cf. L. Topa, 'La relazione tra la forma di governo e l'organizzazione militare romana dai Gracchi ad Augusto', *Ephem. Dacoromana* IX 1940, 119 f.

76. Delbrück, *op. cit.* I³ 445. It also appears from Cato, fr. 152 Malc.³ (= Nonius, p. 93 Lindsay): *expedito pauperem plebeium atque proletarium*, that the burden of service fell principally on the poor. The fragment belongs to the speech *de tribunis militum* of 171 BC. Less probable is the explanation of the fragment given by B. Janzer, *Hist. Untersuchungen zu den Redenfragmenten des M. Porcius Cato*, Würzburg 1937, 62.

77. App. *Iber.* 84, 365. On this passage see De Sanctis, *Storia dei Romani*, IV 3, 259–62; A. E. Astin, *Scipio Aemilianus*, Oxford 1967, 136: J. Hellegouarc'h, *Problèmes de la guerre à Rome*, Paris–The Hague 1969, 159–60.

78. *Op. cit.* I³ 453. Cf. also the account of H. Last, *CAH* IX 133–4.

79. Cf. *Es. e Soc.* 13 n. 36 [= 6, n. 36 above].

80. I omit, of course, any treatment of Marius' purely military innovations which do not concern the political historian. The accounts of this period all deal more or less adequately with Marius' reforms. The only work to my knowledge totally devoted to the subject is that of W. Votsch, *C. Marius als Reformator des röm. Heerwesens*, 1886 (in *Sammlung gemeinverständlicher wissenschaftlicher Vorträge*, Virchow and Holtzendorff, N. F. 1st Series, Heft 6). For further reference cf. the works on Marius, esp. A. Passerini, 'C. Mario come uomo politico', *Athenaeum* N.S. XII 1934, 32–3, and Weynand, *RE Suppl.* VI s.v. 'Marius', col. 1420–2. Worth consulting are the military histories of Marquardt, *op. cit.* 141 f.; Delbrück, *op. cit.* I³ 442 f.: Parker, *The Roman Legions*, Oxford 1928, 21 f.: Kromayer-Veith, *op. cit.* 376 f. Finally, see L. Topa, *art. cit. Ephem. Dacoromana* IX 1940, 149 f. and *id.* 'Considerazioni politiche sulla riforma militare di Mario', *Atti del V Congresso di Studi Romani*, II 513 f. (Topa's thesis is, however, unacceptable).

81. *BJ* 86, 2.

82. Plut. *Mar.* 9, 1; Flor. I 36, 13; Exup. 2. Cf. Val. Max. II 3, 1; Lyd. *de mag.* I 48.

83. XVI 10, 14.

84. *Decl.* III 5: *quanta cura robora militum legeris, imperator* (Marius), *ut hostibus prope humanas vires excedentibus* (the Cimbri and Teutones) *opponeres parem dilectum, vel ex eo manifestum est quod cum scires non ex censu esse virtutem, praeterita facultatium contemplatione vires animosque tantum spectasti. quid prodest? en quanta dilectui tuo fit invidia? diceris adversus Cimbros puerum probasse. sed neque te militaris aetas fefellit cuius certissima mensura est posse fortiter facere.* Cf. Mommsen, *SR* III 298.

85. Kromayer-Veith, *op. cit.* 378 and n. 3.

86. Measures to increase the number of eligible citizens are recorded for 105 BC by Gran. Lic. p. 14 Flemisch.

87. Sall. *BJ* 86, 3.

88. Asc. *in Corn.* p. 54, 25 Stangl.

89. Sall. *BJ* 38, 6; 43, 4; 84, 2.

90. *BJ* 38, 6; 39, 2; 43, 4; 84, 2; 93, 2; 95, 1; 100, 2; 105, 2.

91. *BJ* 86, 3.
92. The explanation of Val. Max. II 3, 1, that the *capite censi* had been enrolled by Marius *novitatis suae conscientia* (cf. Flor. I 36, 13: the common source is Livy) is called puerile by Passerini, *art. cit. Athenaeum* N.S. XII 1934, 32–3.
93. Sall. *BJ* 84, 3; 85, 3. Cf. Exup. 2: as will be seen later, the volunteers came principally from the rural Plebs.
94. Cf. P. Zancan, 'Prolegomeni alla Giugurtina', *AIV* CII 1942–3, 655–6. The statement of Val. Max. (cf. *Es. e Soc.* 33, n. 92 [= 14, n. 92 above]) also falls into this category.
95. *BJ* 86, 2. NB Plut. *Mar.* 9 uses almost the same words to report the matter: ἀναγορευθεὶς (Marius) δὲ λαμπρῶς, εὐθὺς ἐστρατολόγει παρὰ τὸν νόμον καὶ τὴν συνήθειαν πολὺν τὸν ἄπορον καὶ δοῦλον καταγράφων κ.τ.λ. Reference to the principle of volunteering is all that is lacking. Concerning the alleged enrolment of slaves see Passerini, *art. cit.* 32.
96. This is the meaning of Sallust's phrase *neque ex classibus* (= Plut. παρὰ τὸν νόμον).
97. Cf. Votsch, *op. cit.* 24; Mommsen, *SR* III 298.
98. Liebenam, *RE* s.v. 'dilectus', col. 611; Kromayer-Veith, *op. cit.* 380–1.
99. Sall. *BJ* 84, 2.
100. For example, those contingents which Sulla took with him to Africa: Sall. *BJ* 95, 1.
101. Some scholars have wanted to construe (erroneously) the veteran problem in the time of Saturninus (103–100 BC) as an Italian problem, and so have misunderstood the question discussed here. J. Göhler, *op. cit.* 197 (see also Passerini, *art. cit.* 32) took the phrase *capite censi* in Sall. *BJ* 86, 2 more broadly to include also the Italian allies, although it is clear that only Roman citizens are intended (Gelzer, *Gnomon* XVII 1941, 152 = *Kleine Schriften*, II, Wiesbaden 1963, 94). Certainly we do not know the social background of the allied soldiers furnished *ex formula* although it is extremely probable that, as with the Romans, the lowest social classes were in the majority. This, however, does nothing to favour any imagined Italian content in the Marian *dilectus* of 107 BC.
102. Sall. *BJ* 84, 8; 85, 3.
103. Sall. *BJ* 73, 6.
104. For 103 see *auct. de vir. ill.* 73, 1; for 100 Plut. *Mar.* 29, 2; App. *BC* I 29, 130; *auct. de vir. ill.* 73, 5.
105. Cic. *pro Sest.* 37; Livy, *Per.* LXIX; Plut. *Mar.* 28, 7; App. *BC* I 29, 132.
106. App. *BC* I 29, 132: Saturninus asked for help from τοῖς οὖσιν ἀνὰ τοὺς ἀγρούς, οἷς δὴ καὶ μάλιστα ἐθάρρουν ὑπεστρατευμένοις Μαρίῳ (cf. also I 30, 134; 136; 31, 139; 32, 143). Appian 29, 132, adds: πλεονεκτούντων δ' ἐν τῷ νόμῳ τῶν Ἰταλιωτῶν ὁ δῆμος ἐδυσχέραινε. The term Ἰταλιῶται which crops up on other occasions in Appian, especially in his account of the Gracchan tribunates, is not easy to interpret. The traditional view – followed by Göhler, *op. cit.* 76 f., and by Samonati, 'L. Appuleio Saturnino e i federati', *BMIR* VIII 1937, 30 – sees the reference as one to Italian *socii*, but this has been abandoned by Gelzer, *Gnomon*, V 1929, 298–9 = *Kleine Schriften*, II 75–6, and by Kontchalovsky, *RH* CLIII 1926, 176; they understand by it 'Roman citizens of the countryside'. Without discussing the question fully it seems to me that, in the specific case of the sedition of Saturninus, the former interpretation is impossible (cf. H. Last, *JRS* XXX 1940, 82) since it results in a total misinterpretation of the events of 100 BC, when the allied question had only a minor importance. Samonati, *art. cit.* 34, also comes to this conclusion. My view on the problem is further treated in *Appiano e la Storia delle guerre civili*, Florence 1956, 76–8 and in my Commentary² on Appian (*Appiani Bell. Civ. Lib.* I, Florence 1967, 105). See also *Es. e Soc.* 200 f. [= 72 f. below].

107. Sall. *BJ* 86, 4. See E. Badian, *Foreign Clientelae, 264–70 BC*, Oxford 1958, 197, n. 5; F. Hand, *Tursellinus*, I, Amsterdam 1969, 252–6; Krebs-Schmalz, *Antibarbarus d. Lat. Sprache*, I⁸, 1962, 140.

108. Sall. *BJ* 84, 4.

109. Topa, *art. cit. Atti V Congr. Studi rom.* II 513–14: 'the Marian levy was based on men who wanted to enrol, men who were waiting for the moment'. Cf. *id. Ephem. Dacoromana* IX 1940, 150–2.

110. See *Es. e Soc.* 113 f. [= 43 f. below]; P. A. Brunt, 'The Army and the Land in the Roman Revolution', *JRS* LII 1962, 69–86.

111. The assertion of Plut. *Mar.* 9, 2 is typical: οὐ μὴν ταῦτά γε (the enrolment of *capite censi*) μάλιστα διέβαλλε τὸν Μάριον, ἀλλ' οἱ λόγοι θρασεῖς ὄντες ὑπεροψίᾳ καὶ ὕβρει τοὺς πρώτους ἐλύπουν κ.τ.λ.

112. Topa, *art. cit. Ephem. Dacoromana* IX 1940, 150–1.

113. That such a theory stands in Val. Max. can be evidence for its prior mention in Livy: see *Es. e Soc.* 33 n. 92 [= 14, n. 92 above]. Similarly connected are Plut. *Mar.* 9, 1 (τῶν πρόσθεν ἡγεμόνων οὐ προσδεχομένων τοὺς τοιούτους – the *capite censi* – ἀλλ' ὥσπερ ἄλλο τι τῶν καλῶν τὰ ὅπλα μετὰ τιμῆς τοῖς ἀξίοις νεμόντων, ἐνέχυρον τὴν οὐσίαν ἑκάστου τιθέναι δοκοῦντος) and Gell. XVI 10, 11 (*sed quoniam res pecuniaque familiaris obsidis vicem pignerisque esse apud rem publicam videbatur amorisque in patriam fides quaedam in ea firmamentumque erat, neque proletarii neque capite censi milites nisi in tumultu maximo scribebantur, quia familia pecuniaque his aut tenuis aut nulla esset*). NB. Exup. 2, though it is not clear how its pure anti-Marian sentiment (*hos* – the *capite censi* – *igitur Marius quibus non fuerit res publica committenda duxit ad bellum*) can be reconciled with that author's generally agreed dependence on Sallust, or, more specifically, how the passage can derive from the *BJ* (cf. Maurenbrecher, *Sall. hist. reliquiae*, I, p. 13; Schanz-Hosius, *Röm. Litteratur*, IV 2, 1920, 82; Wissowa, *RE* s.v. 'Exuperantius'). In Sall. *BJ* 86, 3 there is a theme which seems similar at first sight: *homini potentiam quaerenti egentissimus quisque opportunissimus, quoi neque sua cara, quippe quae nulla sunt, et omnia cum praetio honesta videntur*, but it is clear that the author is thinking of, and is concerned with, only the political aspect of the phenomenon, and not with any doctrinaire formulation. See also Dion. Hal. IV 19, 3–4, and *Athenaeum* N.S. XXXIX 1961, 107–9.

114. As Last, *CAH* IX 133, describes it. It is striking that the theoretical statement of the timocratic foundations on which the Roman citizen militia rested appears in its axiomatic form only on this occasion. It is not irrelevant to mention here that the same concept – i.e. that private property guaranteed the loyalty of citizens to their country and their involvement in the affairs of the state – is also basic to the arguments of Ti. Gracchus in 133 BC in proposing the resumption of *ager publicus* and its distribution to the *proletarii* (see Appian, I 11, 44–6, with my Commentary). The Catonian ideal of the citizen-soldier, as put over by Ti. Gracchus, has clearly a conservative origin, but we should remember that the tone of Gracchus' arguments was very different when he addressed the Plebs (Pl. *Ti. Gracc.* 9, 4) rather than the upper classes.

115. Liers, *op. cit.* 10–11 and n. 1.

116. Cf. Cary, *CAH* IX 491 f.; Yavetz, *Historia* XII 1963, 485–99.

117. Plut. *Caes.* 5, 2–3. That Catiline also claimed in some sense to be linked with Marius is suggested by the fact that the standard he used for his own army was the eagle which Marius had had in the Cimbric War (Sall. *BC* 59, 3).

118. G. De Sanctis, *Problemi di storia antica*, 1932, 212–13. De Sanctis, *ibid.* 215, maintains that the conduct of the Numidian War by Metellus was limited by his dependence on an army still recruited on the class-system, and by a wish to conserve the

resources of the Roman middle class, a consideration which did not hamper Marius. But in view of the actual composition of the Roman army, especially after 125 BC, the different methods of warfare are probably to be explained by the different characters of the two generals. To justify his own earlier conduct towards Metellus – which was far from noble – Marius had to try to finish the war in the quickest way possible. NB however (cf. K. v. Fritz, 'Sallust and the attitude of the Roman nobility . . .', *TAPhA* LXXIV 1943, 158–9), the speed of Marius' campaign in Numidia has been deliberately exaggerated by Sallust who, by confining within relatively few chapters the activity of Marius, in comparison with Metellus, wants to make the former appear superior to the latter.

119. M. A. Levi, *La costituzione romana dai Gracchi a Giulio Cesare*, 1928, 54. For a more precise interpretation of M. Livius Drusus, tr. pl. 91, see *Es. e Soc.* 383 f. [= 131 f. below].

Notes to II

* *Athenaeum* N.S. XXIX 1951, 171–272. See P. J. Cuff, *JRS* XLIV 1954, 132–3; R. E. Smith, *Service in the Post-Marian Roman Army*, Manchester 1958; W. Schmitthenner, 'Politik und Armee in der späten röm. Republik', *HZ* CXC 1960, 1–17; P. A. Brunt, 'The Army and the Land in the Roman Revolution', *JRS* LII 1962, 69–86; L. Polverini, 'L'aspetto sociale del passaggio dalla repubblica al principato', *Aevum* XXXVIII 1964, 448–57; J. Harmand, *L'armée et le soldat à Rome de 107 à 50 avant notre ère*, Paris 1967; M. Rambaud, 'Légion et armée romaines', *REL* XLV 1967, 112–46; H. Botermann, *Die Soldaten und die röm. Politik in der Zeit von Caesars Tod bis zur Begründung des Zweiten Triumvirats*, Munich 1968; *Problèmes de la Guerre à Rome*, Paris–The Hague 1969 (articles by J. Harmand, 61 f.; P. Jal, 75 f.; C. Nicolet, 117 f.).

1. Fustel de Coulanges, *La cité antique*,²² 1912, 381 f. For Rome: Livy, I 43 and Dion. Hal. IV 19 and 21 (particularly penetrating). For reasons of clarity I give a brief summary of the conclusions reached in my earlier work, *Es. e Soc.* 1 f. [= 1 f. above].

2. G. Veith, in Kromayer-Veith, *Heerwesen und Kriegführung der Griechen und Römer*, 1928, 329. Cf. C. Gatti, 'Riflessioni sull'istituzione dello *stipendium* per i legionari romani', *Acme* XXIII 1970, 131–5.

3. For the fourth century: Fest. p. 406, 30 Lindsay; cf. De Sanctis, *Storia dei Romani*, II 149.

4. Ennius, *Ann.* 183–5 Vahlen; Cass. Hem. fr. 21 Peter; Oros. IV 1, 3; Aug. *de civ. dei*, III 17; cf. *Es. e Soc.* 11, n. 28 [= 5, n. 28 above].

5. In the period of the Hannibalic War the divisions of the legion were, and had been for some time, based on age and no longer on distinctions of armour: cf. H. Delbrück, *Geschichte des Kriegskunst*, I³, 1920, 445.

6. De Sanctis, *op. cit.* II 207.

7. Polyb. VI 23, 15: cf. *Es. e Soc.* 23, n. 67 [= 9, n. 67 above]. The *velites*, moreover, always came from the poorest of the population (πενιχρότατοι: Polyb. VI 21, 7); they were abolished by Marius (see A. Schulten, *Hermes* LXIII 1928, 240). On the change from century to tribe as the basis of enrolment see Appendix I.

8. Dion. Hal. IV 19; the text is cited at length in Appdx. I.

9. Cf. Fraccaro, 'La riforma dell'ordinamento centuriato', *Studi Bonfante*, I 1930, 121 = *Opuscula*, II 189.

10. Fustel de Coulanges, 'Les institutions militaires de la république romaine', *Revue des deux mondes* XC 1870, 296 f.

11. Fraccaro, *mem. cit.* 118 f. = *Opuscula,* II 185 f.
12. In my view G. Tibiletti, *Athenaeum* N.S. XXVII 1949, 223 f. has, with the aid of the *Tabula Hebana,* given a definitive exposition of the organization of the reformed *comitia centuriata.*
13. See *Es. e Soc.* 22–5 [= 9–10 above].
14. *De Rep.* II 39; cf. Livy, XXXIV 31, 17. On the 'exclusive' tendency of governing classes see the acute observations of E. Betti, *Il Filangieri* XXXVIII 1914, 170–1.
15. *Es. e Soc.* 11 [= 5 above].
16. *Es. e Soc.* 17 f. [= 7 f. above].
17. Dion. Hal. IV 18 (= VII 59): cf. *Es. e Soc.* 22, n. 65 [= 9, n. 65 above].
18. 214–212 BC: *Es. e Soc.* 12 [= 5 above].
19. Polyb. VI 19, 2.
20. *Es. e Soc.* 13 f. [= 6 f. above].
21. Tibiletti, *Athenaeum* N.S. XXVII 1949, 37 f.
22. Ed. Meyer, 'Das röm. Manipularheer' (*APAW* 1923, no. 3), now in *Kleine Schriften* II², Halle 1924, 226. The political organization of Roman Italy which had developed over many centuries by continually adapting itself to changes in situation and context and which reached completion in the second century BC, cannot be considered, *pace* A. Bernardi, 'Dallo stato-città allo stato municipale in Roma antica', *Paideia* I 1946, 213 f., as an absorption of the city-state in a municipal system. On the contrary, the Roman system adopted the standard principle of allowing various communities, subject to Rome in different forms, a certain independence in their internal administration; in the different approaches it adopted it aimed, in my view, at stabilizing a state of affairs that was to the fullest possible degree consistent with a firm intention to maintain the city-state structure of the metropolis. This succeeded to such an extent that, when the political organization of Italy was complete, the city-state structure – as Bernardi himself has to admit – was not in fact supplanted but exposed its own impotence to deal with the new situation. Furthermore, the concept of the city-state remains, even in time to come, the essential overriding factor – and not only in the view of the oligarchs.
23. On all this see *Es. e Soc.* 25 f. [= 10 f. above].
24. App. *Iber.* 78, 334 (140 BC). The measure apparently had no general validity: cf. H. Last, *CAH* IX 135. See Plut. *Ti. Gracc.* 16, 1 and Cass. Dio, fr. 83, 7 Boiss. on which cf. Fraccaro, *Studi sull'età dei Gracchi,* I 1914, 154 f. and J. Carcopino, *Autour des Gracques,* 1928, 40–4. In general for the consequences of the Spanish Wars see A. Schulten, *Numantia,* I 1914, 270 f. Cf. also E. Betti, *Il Filangieri* XXXVIII 1914, 161–208.
25. E. Kornemann, in Vogt-Kornemann, *Röm. Geschichte* (= *Einl. in d. Alt.*³, III 2), 1933, 65.
26. Plut. *Ti. Gracc.* 9, 5.
27. Cf. *Es. e Soc.* 15 f. [= 6 f. above]. Note Cato, fr. 152 Malc.³ (171 BC).
28. App. *Iber.* 84, 365.
29. In general see *Es. e Soc.* 30 f. [= 13 f. above] for this conclusion.
30. Sall. *BJ* 73, 6.
31. App. *BC* I 29, 132: οἷς (i.e. τοῖς οὖσιν ἀνὰ τοὺς ἀγροὺς) δὴ καὶ μάλιστ' ἐθάρρουν ὑπεστρατευμένοις Μαρίῳ. Cf. the discussion of this and other passages, *Es. e Soc.* 38, n. 106 [= 16, n. 106 above]: see my Commentary² (*Appiani Bell. Civ. lib.* I, Florence 1967) *ad loc.* (All subsequent citations of Appian refer to books of his *BC*.)
32. Various sources tell us (see *Es. e Soc.* 38, n. 105 [= 16, n. 105 above] for the evidence) that the followers of Saturninus were principally Marius' veterans. Hence the equation Marius' veterans = rural Plebs is certain. This seems to refute the

assertion of L. R. Taylor, *Party Politics in the Age of Caesar*, Berkeley–Los Angeles 1949, 54 and 202 (n. 23), that Marius' reform resulted in the entry into the army of citizens from the urban tribes (while hitherto, according to Mommsen, *SR* III 451 and 784, military service seems to have required membership of a rural tribe). In Taylor's view these citizens of the urban tribes would have become members of the rural tribes and, what is more, of these tribes' propertied class, via land distributions. But in the first place the statement of Mommsen, at least in so far as the examples which he adduces show, seems to concern only the Imperial period, and secondly, to the extent that arguments *ex silentio* can be valid, Polybius' description of the Roman levy (VI 19–20) does not display knowledge of the exclusion of any tribe. In fact, citizens of the urban tribes must have been in the Roman army before Marius' time and of course it is not impossible that also after Marius they performed military service (e.g. during the Social War even the *libertini* served, and it is well-known that they were confined to the urban tribes: cf. Marquardt, *De l'Organiza-tion militaire chez les Romains*, 144–5). Taylor's principal assertion, however, is in error, given the fact that the post-Marian army came chiefly from the countryside, and this is further confirmed by the well-known passage of Sall. *BJ* 84, 3 (*neque plebi militia volenti putabatur*), where the context shows that the reference is to the urban Plebs. Very probably Sallust had in mind the attitude of the urban Plebs of his day. As for the entry of ex-soldiers into the propertied classes of the rural tribes, this is equally valid – or, in fact, is more valid – if the reference is to a decadent rural Plebs. However, as we shall see later, the purpose of the military colonies was often of a purely fortuitous nature.

33. Cf. Plut. *Ti. Gracc.* 9, 5; App. I 7, 29; Sall. *BJ* 41, 7; *id. Hist.* I 11 Maur.; (Sall.) *ad Caes.* II 5, 4; Cic. *de leg. agr.* III 14; Horace, *Od.* II 18, 23 f. Evidence for the expulsion of the small proprietors for the first century AD is collected by E. Lepore, *Pompeiana. Raccolta di Studi per il 2° Centenario degli Scavi di Pompei*, Naples 1950, 9 and n. 3 (extract). The same theme appears in the well-known fragment of Vegoia, in *Gromatici Veteres*, I 350, 18 f. Lachmann. L. Zancan, *A & R* ser. III 7, 1939, 203 f. esp. 213, rightly says that even if it is difficult to find in the fragment a specific reference, as L. Piotrowicz, *Klio* XXIII 1930, 334–8, wished to do, it does fit with all that we know of the Etruscan farming classes in the age of Sulla. Cf. J. Heurgon, 'The Date of Vegoia's Prophecy', *JRS* XLIX 1959, 41–5; W. V. Harris, *Rome in Etruria and Umbria*, Oxford 1971, 31–40. We shall examine later the extent to which the provision of rewards for veterans has influenced the overall development of this theme. In general, for observations on the conditions of the Italian agrarian class in the first century BC, see M. Rostovtzeff, *The Social and Economic History of the Roman Empire*,[2] ed. Fraser, Oxford 1956, 35 and n. 32.

34. Cf. also F. B. Marsh, *Modern Problems in the Ancient World*, University of Texas Press, Austin 1943, unfortunately not known to me except from M. Cary, *JRS* XXXV 1945, 148. Cicero, *Phil.* X 22, for example, calls the centurions *rustici atque agrestes*. The consequence was that the social status of the soldiers was low: R. Syme, *The Roman Revolution*, Oxford 1939, 457; cf. Tac. *Ann.* IV 4, 4 (AD 23): *nam voluntarium militem deesse, ac si suppeditet, non eadem virtute ac modestia agere, quia plerumque inopes ac vagi sponte militiam sumant*. Such a state of affairs should certainly not be a novelty or confined to that period. We should therefore reject the contrary view of M. Rostovtzeff, *op. cit.* 41. In general see Brunt, *JRS* LII 1962, 69–86; peasant proprietors among the soldiers are firmly established, for example, by App. *Mithr.* 90, 411–12 (cited by P. J. Cuff, *JRS* XLIV 1954, 132) and above all by Cass. Dio, XLVIII 8, 5 and 9, 3 (see my Comm. on Appian, *BC* V, Florence 1970, pp. XXXIII and LXVI–LXVII), but the general picture painted here must hold.

In general, for a treatment of the problems of military institutions in the early

Principate, see A. Momigliano in *Augustus. Studi in occasione del Bimillenario Augusteo*, Rome 1938, 195 f., esp. 197, 202–3, 205, 208. On Caes. *BC* I 34, 2; 56, 3; and Cass. Dio, XLI 11, cf. Rostovtzeff, *op. cit.* 30–1. The reservations advanced by Haywood, *AJPh* LIV 1933, 150 f., who sees in the case of Domitius a purely Etruscan phenomenon, do not deprive the evidence of weight and significance.

35. Evidence in Liebenam, *RE*, s.v. 'dilectus', col. 609 f. and Fiebiger, *ibid.* s.v. 'conquisitores'.

36. (Sall.) *ad Caes.* I 8, 6; *Bell. Alex.* 56, 4.

37. Dig. XLIX 16, 4, 10 (Arrius Menander): *sed mutato statu militiae recessum a capitis poena est, quia plerumque voluntario milite numeri supplentur.*

38. The view of L. Topa, *Ephem. Dacoromana* IX 1940, 149 f. and *id. Atti del V Congresso di Studi Romani*, II 513 f. Cf. *Es. e Soc.* 40 f. [= 17 above], (changing the original text in *Athenaeum* N.S. XXVII 1949, 205 f.).

39. This phenomenon is by its nature so universal (it usually follows on a policy of conquest or, more generally, on the formation of professional armies) that it is interesting to refer to what B. Constant wrote (*De l'esprit de conquête*, Chapters VI and VII) 'on the influence of *l'esprit militaire* on a people's domestic structure', in connexion with the army of Napoleon, the more so as some of the points mentioned show explicitly how a Frenchman involved in politics drew on examples which the history of ancient Rome could provide.

40. Caesar, who could quell a military revolt by referring to his soldiers as *Quirites*, is a famous example: Suet. *Caes.* 70; App. II 92–4; Cass. Dio, XLII 52–5. However, it must be borne in mind that there is no question of a substantial difference of out-look between soldiers and civilians, as A. Momigliano, *JRS* XXX 1940, 79, has rightly pointed out; the distinction is between a citizen's life as a soldier and his political activity, i.e. strictly a distinction between army life and Roman society. This supports what I shall have to say on the conflict between the countryside and the city of Rome.

41. Livy, XXXI 14, 2 (cf. XXXII 3, 3); XXXII 9, 1; XXXVII 4, 3; XLII 32, 6. Cf. Fr. Fröhlich, *Die Bedeutung des zweiten punischen Krieges für die Entwicklung des röm. Heerwesens*, Leipzig 1884, 33 f.

42. App. *Iber.* 84, 365–6.

43. A.v. Premerstein, *RE* s.v. 'clientes', col. 37. Cf. *id. Vom Werden und Wesen des Prinzipats*, *ABAW* N.F. XV 1937, 109.

44. Fustel de Coulanges, *Hist. des Institutions polit. de l'anc. France. Les origines du système féodal*, 1890, 223. On the passage of Appian see also A. Passerini, *Le coorti pretorie*, Rome 1939, 5 f.

45. What I have said above proves that this phenomenon does not originate with the reform of Marius (Taylor, *op. cit.* 47) but precedes it. In the same way the army was proletarian in character prior to the time of Marius.

46. Premerstein, *Vom Werden*, 23 f.

47. Cf. R. Heinze, '*Fides*', *Hermes* LXIV 1929, 151–2 (the article is reprinted in *Vom Geist des Römertums*, 1938, 25–58).

48. An acute observation by Premerstein, *Vom Werden*, 26–7.

49. Premerstein, *Vom Werden*, 44 and 73, distinguishes two oaths, the regular military oath and the oath to the general. For the significance of this interpretation see Momigliano, *art. cit.* in *Augustus*, 197 and n. 1. Cf. also Taylor, *op. cit.* 199 (n. 72). K. Zakrzewski, *Eos* XXXII 1929, 71 f., has demonstrated the significance for ancient states in general, and for Rome in particular, of more or less self-contained groups, bound to a political or military leader by an all-embracing oath. On the oath of Drusus in 91 BC (Diod. XXXVII 11) cf. Taylor, *op. cit.* 46 and 198 (n. 67).

50. We should not, of course, misinterpret as political ideologies any taking of sides

which was dictated by particular regional affiliations; this latter is explained by *clientela* ties, e.g. the Picenes and Pompey, on which cf. M. Gelzer, 'Cn. Pompeius Strabo und der Aufstieg seines Sohnes Magnus', *APAW* 1941, no. 14, 1 f. = *Kleine Schriften*, II, Wiesbaden 1963, 106–38); *id. Pompeius*, Munich 1949, 37; L. R. Taylor, *op. cit.* 45. The defection of Labienus, a Picene and certainly a *cliens* of Pompey, at the beginning of the Civil War is in all probability to be accounted for in this way: cf. R. Syme, *JRS* XXVIII 1938, 113–25 (in my view no basis for the doubts in Daly, *CW* XLIII 1950, 107); contrast the statement of the Caesarian centurion in *Bell. Afric.* 45, 2–3.

Concerning the Picenes (and the Umbrians: cf. the Camertes and Marius – see later – and the T. Matrinius of Cic. *pro Balb.* 48: Münzer, *RE* s.v. no. 3 and Schulze, *Zur Geschichte lateinischer Eigennamen*, 1904, 192; M. Annius Appius from Iguvium: Cic. *pro Balb.* 46; in general E. Badian, *Foreign Clientelae 264–70 BC*, Oxford 1958, 260; also Cic. *pro Mur.* 42; *ad Att.* VIII 12b, 2; App. III 93, 384; 94, 386), it should be noted that there is ample evidence for their service in the Roman armies. This service seems to go beyond the ties of *clientela* and, *pace* Gelzer, *Pompeius*, 37, to be part and parcel of a local tradition of true mercenary service. Picene soldiers were probably present in the Marian army; at least this seems to be the implication of the mention of Q. Labienus, the uncle of the future Caesarian legate and fierce supporter of Appuleius Saturninus in 100 BC. The latter, in fact, invoked the aid of the *ager Picenus universus* in his revolution (Cic. *pro Rab. perd. reo*, 22; cf. Passerini, *Athenaeum* N.S. XII 1934, 294, n. 3): this evidence, combined with what I have said above (*Es. e Soc.* nn. 31 and 32 [= 24, nn. 31 and 32 above]) on the support of Marius' veterans for Saturninus, encourages the belief that Labienus addressed himself to the Picene veterans of Marius. Picene officers are attested in the *consilium* at Asculum in such numbers that it has been held that the soldiers coming from Picenum formed a legion of their own at that time (Dessau, *ILS* 8888; Carcopino, *Hist. rom.* II 381, n. 155). NB the origin of a Pompeian *clientela* in Picenum is to be dated after the Social War, just as his Picene *latifundia* probably are (Plut. *Pomp.* 6, 1): this is the view – and it is the correct one – of E. Pais, *Dalle guerre puniche a Cesare Augusto* (II), 679 f. (on the basis of Dessau, *ILS* 6629, he envisages the possibility that the *gens Pompeia* was not really Picene in origin: cf. also Cichorius, *Römische Studien*, Leipzig 1922, 185 f.). In any case see Gelzer, *Abh. cit.* 6; 8 and n. 3; 15. Cf. also for 49 BC Cic. *ad Att.* VIII 12b, 2. In this picture we can fit the anti-Pompeian attitude of other Picenes (in general cf. Syme, *PBSR* XIV 1938, 20 f.) including the well-known Marian and Cinnan family of the Herennii (Münzer, *RE* s.v. nos. 6, 7, 9: Syme, *RR* 92: cf. on the Ventidii Plut. *Pomp.* 6, 5, and also the case of L. Minucius Basilus: Syme, *JRS* XXVIII 1938, 124, n. 74). Also in the early Empire the Picenes provided soldiers and officers, and some of the latter reached the consulship: Syme, *RR* 362 and n. 2. Cf. the important passage of Tacitus, *Ann.* IV 5, 5 (AD 23) on the praetorian cohorts: *Etruria ferme Umbriaque delectae aut vetere Latio et coloniis antiquitus Romanis*, confirmed by the evidence of inscriptions (A. Passerini, *Le coorti pretorie*, 146 f. and 159). This important demonstration of the use of Picenes and Umbrians as a source of professional soldiers in the true sense of the word provides further substance for the view that the army was just not interested in politics. This is also shown by the ever-growing numbers of non-Italians in the legions (see, for example, Carcopino, *Hist. rom.* II 381, n. 155, and in general Liebenam, *RE* s.v. 'dilectus', col. 612 f.): their outlook can only have been that described in a typical episode by Diod. XXXVII 17.

51. Taylor, *op. cit.* 47.

52. H. Drexler, 'Parerga Caesariana' *Hermes* LXX 1935, 225 f. has explained this

extremely clearly by his analysis of *Bell. Hisp.* 17. If the defeated Pompeian soldier presents himself as a *civis Romanus* and refers to *patriae luctuosam perniciem*, that is relevant only to the object he has in mind, viz. to move the compassion of the victor. In fact, political considerations, in so far as they are seen as questions of national concern, remain completely alien: there is no emphasis on the problem of the freedom of the *respublica* or on the position of Caesar *vis-à-vis* that problem. The Pompeian realizes that he is no more than a conquered enemy in the eyes of Caesar, and his position is a veritable *deditio*. The principle, however, which underlies the Pompeian's speech is this: *utinam quidem dii immortales fecissent, ut tuus potius miles quam Cn. Pompeii factus essem et hanc virtutis constantiam in tua victoria, non in illius calamitate praestarem* (the criticism by O. Seel, 'Hirtius. Untersuchungen über die Pseudocaesarischen Bella und den Balbusbrief', *Klio, Beiheft* XXXV, Leipzig 1935, 108–9, does not, in my view, undermine the basis of Drexler's interpretation; cf. also p. 62 f.). See my article in *Legio VII Gemina*: Catedra de San Isidoro, Instituto Leones de Estudios Romano-Visigoticos, Leon 1970, 133 f. (= *Es. e Soc.* 473 f.). It is typical, for example, that in Caes. *BC* III 91, 2 the centurion Crastinus makes the *dignitas Caesaris* take precedence over the freedom of the Roman people; the latter theme is clearly of lesser importance.

53. Cic. *Phil.* X 12. See also the assertions of Cassius in App. IV 93, 390 and 98, 410; cf. V 17, 68. The remark of Crassus that no one can truly be called rich who cannot equip an army at his own expense is well-known (see the evidence collected by A. Garzetti, *Athenaeum* N.S. XIX 1941, 10 and notes). It shows that using the means of military revolution to establish one's position had become a fundamental part of the outlook of a Roman politician from the time of the Social War; this had seen the origin of the illegal private army (Vell. II 16, 2 and 29, 1). Appian, whose source aimed to show how the history of the first century BC prepared the way for the origin of monarchy (see E. Kornemann, *Klio* XVII 1921, 33 f.) emphasizes the change introduced by the Social War in Rome's domestic politics: cf. I 2, 7 (on which see also Premerstein, *Vom Werden*, 26): 34, 151; 55, 240; 60, 269. Cf. also Cass. Dio, LII 1, 1.

54. *Contra*, Seel, *op. cit.* 108: but see below, *Es. e Soc.* 89 [= 35 below].

55. Drexler, *art. cit.* 226 and n. 1 f. Caesar's maxim (cf. Caes. in Gell. V 13, 6: *neque clientes sine summa infamia deseri possunt*) is famous.

56. Cf. e.g. Sulla's statement in Sall. *Hist.* I 50 Maur. On the *beneficia* which, together with *gratia* and *fides*, dominated relations between general and soldier, see also V. Pöschl, *Grundwerte röm. Staatsgesinnung in den Geschichtswerken des Sallust*, Berlin 1940, 95.

57. See L. R. Taylor, *op. cit.* 47–8. For the veterans of Marius we should bear in mind Diod. XXXVIII–XXXIX 12.

58. This comes out clearly in a chapter of Appian (V 17). It is interesting to note here, in contrast with what emerges from *Bell. Hisp.* 17, that it is no longer the particular soldier who is in question (i.e. an individual instance of *clientela*) so much as the whole army; it enjoys a quite different importance as far as its dependence on a general is concerned. I give the whole passage: αἴτιον (τῆς δυσαρχίας) δ'ἦν, ὅτι καὶ οἱ στρατηγοὶ ἀχειροτόνητοι ἦσαν οἱ πλείους, ὡς ἐν ἐμφυλίοις, καὶ οἱ στρατοὶ αὐτῶν οὐ τοῖς πατρίοις ἔθεσιν ἐκ καταλόγου συνήγοντο, οὐδ'ἐπὶ χρείᾳ τῆς πατρίδος, οὐδὲ τῷ δημοσίῳ στρατευόμενοι μᾶλλον, ἢ τοῖς συνάγουσιν αὐτοὺς μόνοις, οὐδὲ τούτοις ὑπὸ ἀνάγκῃ νόμων, ἀλλ' ὑποσχέσεσιν ἰδίαις, οὐδὲ ἐπὶ πολεμίους κοινούς, ἀλλὰ ἰδίους ἐχθρούς, οὐδὲ ἐπὶ ξένους, ἀλλὰ πολίτας καὶ ὁμοτίμους. τάδε γὰρ πάντα αὐτοῖς τὸν στρατιωτικὸν φόβον ἐξέλυεν, οὔτε στρατεύεσθαι νομίζουσι μᾶλλον, ἢ βοηθεῖν οἰκείᾳ χάριτι καὶ γνώμῃ, καὶ τοὺς ἄρχοντας ἡγουμένοις ὑπὸ ἀνάγκης αὐτῶν ἐς τὰ ἴδια ἐπιδεῖσθαι. τό τε αὐτομολεῖν, πάλαι 'Ρωμαίοις ἀδιάλλακτον ὄν, τότε καὶ δωρεῶν ἠξιοῦτο. καὶ ἔπρασσον αὐτὸ οἵ τε στρατοὶ κατὰ πλῆθος,

καὶ τῶν ἐπιφανῶν ἀνδρῶν ἔνιοι, νομίζοντες οὐκ αὐτομολίαν εἶναι τὴν ἐς τὰ ὅμοια μεταβολήν. ὅμοια γὰρ δὴ πάντα ἦν, καὶ οὐδὲ ἕτερα αὐτῶν ἐς ἔχθραν κοινὴν ʽΡωμαίοις ἀπεκέκριτο· ἤ τε τῶν στρατηγῶν ὑπόκρισις μία, ὡς ἁπάντων ἐς τὰ συμφέροντα τῇ πατρίδι βοηθούντων εὐχερεστέρους ἐποίει πρὸς τὴν μεταβολήν, ὡς πανταχοῦ τῇ πατρίδι βοηθοῦντας. ἃ καὶ οἱ στρατηγοὶ συνιέντες ἔφερον, ὡς οὐ νόμῳ μᾶλλον αὐτῶν ἄρχοντες, ἢ ταῖς δωρεαῖς. οὕτω μὲν ἐς στάσεις τότε πάντα, καὶ ἐς δυσαρχίαν τοῖς στασιάρχοις τὰ στρατόπεδα ἐτέτραπτο. In this connexion note the well-known judgement of Cornelius Nepos, *Eum.* 8, 2: *namque illa phalanx Alexandri Magni . . . , inveterata cum gloria tunc etiam licentia, non parere se ducibus, sed imperare postulabat, ut nunc veterani faciunt nostri. itaque periculum est ne faciant quod illi fecerunt, sua intemperantia nimiaque licentia ut omnia perdant neque minus eos, cum quibus steterint, quam adversus quos fecerint.* See Syme, *RR* 250, for the historical context of the latter passage; cf. my Comm. on Appian, *BC* V p. XXIII f.

59. L. R. Taylor, *op. cit.* 57 f.

60. Principal evidence in Taylor, *op. cit.* 205 (n. 47): 69 and 210 (n. 106).

61. The contribution of the Latins and the *socii* to the Roman military machine, whether one considers the numbers employed or the fact that Roman and allied formations developed a greater similarity of structure culminating with the adoption by Rome of the cohort (H. M. D. Parker, *The Roman Legions*, Oxford 1928, 27 f.: cf. also 23), had in the course of the second century BC become such that the Italians could no longer be considered to be purely auxiliary (in general see A. Afzelius, 'Die röm. Kriegsmacht', *Acta Jutlandica* XVI 2, 1944, 66 f.). For example, the remarks of Scipio Aemilianus on the contribution of the Latin and Italian allies which he was in a good position to appreciate and evaluate, and which drove him to take a stand in their favour against the Gracchi (App. I 19, 79), are well-known. I have shown elsewhere, *Es. e Soc.* 33 [= 14 above], how the fact that allied forces are frequently mentioned in the wars of the last decade of the second century BC cannot be explained simply as a generalization on the Roman habit of sparing their own forces (in Numidia cf. Sall. *BJ* 38, 6; 39, 2; 43, 4; 77, 4; 84, 2; 93, 2; 95, 1; 100, 2; 105, 2; App. *Num.* fr. 3; against the Teutones cf. Plut. *Mar.* 19, and the evidence on the Camertes recorded below; see also *Es. e Soc.* 64, n. 50 [= 27, n. 50 above]. The contribution of the allies was properly evaluated by the generals who employed them, and this is clear not only from the fact that Scipio Aemilianus became their champion; indeed, it is at the end of the second century BC that cases of grants of the citizenship to Latin or allied soldiers by Roman military leaders begin to multiply (Mommsen, *SR* III 135 f.), *pari passu* with the recognition of the Latins' right to the Roman citizenship in cases where they had held magistracies in their native towns or had conducted successful prosecutions for extortion against Roman magistrates; cf. A. Bernardi, 'Ius Ariminensium', *Studia Ghisleriana* I no. 9, Pavia 1948, 257 and n. 63. In this context grants of the citizenship are, as it were, the visible, solid demonstration of a brotherhood in arms and a unity of outlook realized within the framework of army service. The well-known example is that of Marius who rewarded *in ipsa acie* some cohorts of Camertes (Cic. *pro Balbo*, 46–7; Val. Max. V 2, 8; Plut. *Mar.* 28, 3) and there is a corollary in the power granted to Marius by the agrarian and colonial law of Saturninus in 100 BC to create three Roman citizens in each colony, as long as the colonists were ex-soldiers, although this measure goes back to an old tradition (see Gabba, *Athenaeum* N.S. XXIX 1951, 17 and n. 2). For examples of grants of the citizenship by Sulla, Pompey, Caesar and other generals see the evidence in Mommsen, *loc. cit.* nn. 4–5; in his view such a privilege was not part of the ordinary powers of a general but had to be granted by a special law (on Marius see also the points made by Samonati, *BMIR* VIII 1937, 27 f.). In general see Badian, *FC* 252 f.

62. For the Principate conceived as a triumph of Italy over Rome see the fine pages of Syme, *RR* 453 f.

63. On the date see the bibliography in my article in *Aufstieg und Niedergang d. röm. Welt*, I 1, Berlin 1972, 771, n. 35, and 805, n. 251.

64. Fraccaro, *Athenaeum* N.S. VII 1919, 73 f., esp. 89 f. = *Opuscula*, II 191–206. Cf. also *Atti del Congresso Intern. di Diritto Romano*, I 1934, 195 f., esp. 205 f. = *Opuscula*, I 103–14. The objections of Ernst Meyer, *Röm. Staat und Staatsgedanke*, Zurich 1948, 268, n. 1 are rightly rejected by A. Bernardi, *RSI* LXII 1950, 289 and by G. Tibiletti, *Athenaeum* N.S. XXVIII 1950, 216, n. 1.

    On the problem of the allies cf. J. Vogt, *RG* I, *Die röm. Republik*, 1932, 206 f. The persistent opposition of the Senate in the second century BC to the creation of new provinces is in the same tradition.

65. Concerning the colony of Capua founded in 83 BC I have tried in Appendix II to bring out the position of Campanian members of the Marian and Cinnan faction.

66. A professional army on a permanent basis is not, however, in every case the same as a mercenary army, and the two should not be confused: cf. Münzer, *DLZ* XLVIII 1927, col. 2111.

67. As is well-known, Pompey disbanded his army on arrival at Brundisium. On the impression this act left on his contemporaries, in contrast to the fears that attended his coming, cf. A. Garzetti, *Athenaeum* N.S. XXII–XXIII 1944–5, 1 f. Generally this episode is considered the fundamental motif in Pompey's political life; on the contrary opinion of Gelzer, *Pompeius*, 124, see the proper observations of G. Tibiletti, *Athenaeum* N.S. XXVIII 1950, 173. It is important to remember that the fears which arose over Pompey's attitude were probably coloured by memories of the threatening letter which we find in Sall. *Hist.* II 98 Maur. (on which cf. W. Schur, *Sallust als Historiker*, Stuttgart 1932, 266 f.). On the attitudes of the dynasts note the observations of Cass. Dio, LII 13, 2 (on the Metellus here mentioned – Pius – cf. J. A. Crook, *CR* LXII 1948, 59 and A. R. Burn, *ibid.* LXIII 1949, 52; see also Sall. *Hist.* IV, 49 Maur.).

    On a more general level we should note the fact that from 70 to 49 BC. Pompey's army constituted one of the fundamental factors in Roman politics: cf. Taylor, *op. cit.* 48. As proof of this cf. the highly important remark of Pompey (to be taken closely with what I have said, *Es. e Soc.* 67, n. 53 [= 27, n. 53 above]) mentioned in Cic. *ad Att.* II 16, 2 (59 BC): *oppressos vos tenebo exercitu Caesaris*, where *exercitus* should not be understood either as a collection of partisans (so, for example, C. H. Oldfather, *CJ* XXV 4, 1930, 299 f.) or, more specifically, as colonists established in Campania by the *lex Iulia* of 59 BC (so Gelzer, *Hermes* LXIII 1928, 116 and *id. Caesar der Politiker und Staatsmann*[3], 1941, 94) but in fact as Caesar's army in Cisalpine Gaul (R. Syme, *JRS* XXXIV 1944, 98: Chr. Meier, *Historia* X 1961, 79 f.: for the relationship between Pompey and Caesar at that time see Taylor, *TAPhA* LXXIII 1942, 1 f.).

68. For the identity of *boni* and *locupletes* see W. Kroll, *Die Kultur der Ciceronischen Zeit*, I 1933, 72 f. Cf. Cic. *de Rep.* II 39; 40.

69. Gell. XVI 10, 11; cf. Val. Max. II 3; Plut. *Mar.* 9, 1; Exup. 2; see *Es. e Soc.* 42, n. 113 [= 18, n. 113 above]. The basic concept behind this attitude is, of course, that put forward by Panaetius, 'that the concrete principle for a common goal and for the foundation of a balanced State is care for the protection of private wealth, for private property': M. Pohlenz, *Antikes Führertum* (*Neue Wege zur Antike*, II 3) 1934, 115 f. However, the non-involvement of the army in politics appears to be conceived by the oligarchs as a lack of interest in civic affairs and a lack of patriotism. Sallust approaches the matter from a different political point of view but

against the same background of private property as an essential feature in a citizen's outlook, and brings out sharply the political consequences of the enrolment of the *proletarii* (*BJ* 86, 3): *homini potentiam quaerenti egentissimus quisque opportunissimus, quoi neque sua cara, quippe quae nulla sunt, et omnia cum pretio honesta videntur.*

Everything I have said about the army's lack of involvement in politics is opposed to Syme's view, *RR* 353 f., that the army was an element of party politics, and helps to prove the correctness of Momigliano's observation in *JRS* XXX 1940, 79 = *Secondo contributo alla storia degli studi classici e del mondo antico*, Rome 1960, 407–16. My work owes a great deal, here as well as elsewhere, to the ideas set out in this important review.

70. Set out *Es. e Soc.* 42 f. [= 18 above]: principally the fact that it was approved by the Equites, and the military objects of the levy.

71. Cf. *Es. e Soc.* 47 f. [= 20 f. above]. For this reason the exclusion of the proletarian class from military service was common in ancient states: H. Liers, *Das Kriegswesen der Alten*, Breslau 1895, 10 f.

72. (Xen.) Ἀθ. πολ. I, 2; Arist. Ἀθ. πολ. 27, 1; *id. Pol.* V 1304a; cf. G. De Sanctis, *RFIC* LII 1924, 294 f.; H. Frisch, *The Constitution of the Athenians* (*C & M* Diss. II) 1942, 187 f. See also Liers, *op. cit.* 11 and n. 1.

73. It is well-known that even Cicero's political position does not move beyond this conception of the state's structure: cf. J. Vogt, *Ciceros Glaube an Rom* (*Würzburger Studien zur Altertumswissenschaft*, VI), Stuttgart 1935, 56 f.

74. M. A. Levi, 'Classe dominante e ceto di governo', *Acme* I 1948, 87 f.

75. (Sall.) *ad Caes.* II 8, 1: *sed magistratibus creandis haud mihi quidem apsurde placet lex, quam C. Gracchus in tribunatu promulgaverat, ut ex confusis quinque classibus sorte centuriae vocarentur.* Levi's hypothesis (*La costituzione romana dai Gracchi a Giulio Cesare*, 1928, 18–19; 67; 188–90) which is accepted by J. Carcopino, *Hist. rom.* II 244–5, is, of course, arbitrary: cf. A. Momigliano, *SDHI* IV 1938, 518, n. 4 = *Quarto contributo alla storia degli studi classici e del mondo antico*, Rome 1969, 372, n. 19. For the theories of C. Nicolet see *Athenaeum* N.S. XXXVIII 1960, 213, n. 108. Cf. Cic. *pro Mur.* 47: *confusionem suffragiorum flagitasti* (Servius Sulpicius Rufus), *perrogationem* (Mommsen: *praerogationem* codd.) *legis Maniliae, aequationem gratiae, dignitatis, suffragiorum. graviter homines honesti atque in suis vicinitatibus et municipiis gratiosi tulerunt a tali viro esse pugnatum, ut omnes et dignitatis et gratiae gradus tollerentur* (63 BC). For various interpretations of this passage see, for example, A. W. Zumpt, pp. XXXI–IV of the preface to his edition (Berlin 1859): comments *ad loc.* by Koch (1928²), p. 37, and Freese (1930), pp. 91–2: Münzer, *RE* s.v. 'Manilius', no. 10, col. 1134; G. Carlson, *Eine Denkschrift an Caesar über den Staat*, Lund 1936, 91 f. We must, I think, distinguish the *confusio suffragiorum*, which certainly refers to a proposal of the C. Gracchus type, from the *perrogatio legis Maniliae*; this was a renewal of Manilius' law of 67 on the *libertini*. Both measures would have resulted in an *aequatio gratiae dignitatis suffragiorum*.

In my view it is certain that a strict connexion existed between the oligarchs' views on the army as a social danger and as an institution which helped to promote the *proletarii*, and the proposals set out above for reform against the interests of the wealthy classes.

76. Cic. *de Off.* II 78: as we have seen (cf. *Es. e Soc.* 74 n. 69 [= 30, n. 69 above]), the oligarchs' objections to C. Marius were based on the same fundamental principles.

77. Cf. especially M. Pohlenz, *Antikes Führertum, op. cit.* 115 f. and *id. Die Stoa*, Göttingen 1948, 205 f. See also R. Scalais, *LEC* III 1934, 545–6.

78. Fears aroused by Caesar's *lex agraria* of 46 BC find an echo in the famous group of letters in Cicero, *ad Fam.* XIII 4; 5; 7; 8, and in Cicero himself in *ad Fam.* IX 17.

79. Pohlenz, *Führertum*, 116.

80. I do not know to what extent this theme can have influenced the common interpretation of the Gracchan agrarian movement given by historians down to the time of Niebuhr; in any event, for the influence the Ciceronian passage has had on some of the more recent Gracchan historiography, cf. L. Zancan, *AAT* LXVII 1932, 71 f.; *contra*, G. Cardinali, *Historia* VII 1933, 517 f., esp. 522, and G. Tibiletti, *Athenaeum* N.S. XXVI 1948, 176 f.

81. *Führertum*, 119 f.

82. We shall see below how the Caesarian pamphleteer speaks of the 'Romulean' identity of countryman and soldier, perhaps to weaken this impression by a reference to a past Golden Age.

83. Cic. *de Off.* II 73.

84. It is not certain to what extent this interpretation was fostered by the theme of Marius as the outstanding example of the fickleness of fortune (cf. his death immediately after his coveted seventh consulship): what is clear is that the theme is democratic, not oligarchic in origin as E. Norden, *RhM* XLVIII 1893, 540 f. claimed, tracing it back to Posidonius. It occurs already in *Rhet. ad Her.* IV 54, 68; cf. subsequently Plut. *Mar.* 45, 8 = C. Piso, in Peter, *HRF* 374; and also Fir. Mat. I 7, 25–38 (a relic of democratic historiography: A. Passerini, *Athenaeum* N.S. X 1932, 180 and Boll, *RE* s.v. 'Firmicus', col. 2369). Other evidence showing how that theme had become a commonplace is to be found in Ed. Müller, *Philologus* LXII 1903, 82 f. (see also Sall. *Hist.* I 24 Maur.: Gran. Licin. p. 17, 1 Flemisch). NB the Ciceronian *Marius* is to be dated to the years of Cinna's supremacy (87–86 BC) as P. Ferrarino, *RhM* LXXXVIII 1939, 147 f., has exhaustively demonstrated: cf. also C. Marchesi, *Storia della lett. latina*, I[8] 1950, 268. The orthodox view that puts it after Cicero's exile is still to be found in E. Malcovati, 'Cicerone e la poesia', *AFLC* XIII 1943, 228, n. 4, and 266.

    Marius as a political figure has been illuminated by A. Passerini, *Athenaeum* N.S. XII 1934, 10 f.; see also his comprehensive study *Caio Mario (Res Romanae)*, Rome 1941. In my article in *Aufstieg und Niedergang*, I 764–805, I discuss the different assessments of Marius which have appeared in the last twenty years.

85. On Caesar and the Marians cf. L. R. Taylor, *CP* XXXVI 1941, 113 f; *id. TAPhA* LXXIII 1942, 1 f; *id. Party Politics* etc. 122. On the recurrence of *popularis* families in the factions of Marius and Caesar see Syme, *RR* 90, n. 7; 91, n. 1. On Caesar in particular see Plut. *Caes.* 5–6. The attraction of Marius' name is evidenced by Sall. *BC* 59, 3 and App. III 2, 3 (Herophilus). It is worth recalling, however, that Sallust saw his democratic ideal personified in Sertorius rather than in Marius: see V. Paladini, *Sallustio*, 1948, 12: cf. 53 and n. 102. The democratic view of Marius was certainly helped by the fact that the other great *popularis* leader, Cinna, had scarcely represented *popularis* tendencies: Taylor, *Party Politics*, 194 (n. 67).

86. The pro-Marian explanation occurs in ps. Quintil. *Declam.* III 5, on which cf. *Es. e Soc.* 43 and 30 f. [= 18 and 13 f. above]: *cum scires* (Marius) *non ex censu esse virtutem, praeterita facultatium contemplatione, vires animosque tantum spectasti.*

87. On a more general level this is the case with Sallust, for example. However, for Ed. Meyer, *Caesars Monarchie und das Prinzipat des Pompeius*[3], 1922, 389 f., Sallust seems to be still tied to the concept of the city-state. This turns on what has been said above: opposition to this concept did not spring from theoretical principles but originated with practical political problems. There is an echo of attitudes of this kind in the views of (Sallust) on the *comitia* (*ad Caes.* II 8, 1–2), on the colonial problem (*ibid.* II 5, 8) and on the influence of wealth (*ibid.* II 7, 3 and 10; I 7, 3, not to be interpreted as anti-capitalist in theme – so Syme, *RR* 52, n. 3 – but as written from a moral and political point of view). The same thing appears on other occasions; for example, the whole purpose of the Gracchan reforms was essentially

conservative (see S. Katz, *CJ* XXXVIII 2, 1942, 65 f.): they aimed, as has been pointed out elsewhere, at the revival of a class of small landed proprietors; the programme belonged to a city-state setting. However, Caius Gracchus is the man who deliberately shattered the external appearances of the city-state with transmarine colonies.

88. On this cf. the observations of Zakrzewski, *Eos* XXXII 1929, 71 f. On the well-known passages of Sall. *BC* 37–9 and *id. BJ* 41–2 see V. Pöschl, *op. cit.* 72.

89. W. Ensslin, 'Die Demokratie und Rom', *Philologus* LXXXII 1927, 313 f., esp. 324 f.

90. Ensslin, *art. cit.* 327: on Cinna see Taylor, *op. cit.* 194 (n. 67); in general see *Es. e Soc.* 67, n. 53 [= 27, n. 53 above]. For a fresh evaluation of the Cinnan regime E. Badian, 'Waiting for Sulla', now in *Studies in Greek and Roman History*, Oxford 1964, 206–34, is fundamental.

91. See Rostovtzeff, p. 26.

92. See Rostovtzeff, pp. 24–5.

93. J. N. Madvig, *Verfassung und Verwaltung des röm. Staates*, II 1882, 505 and 510; R. Syme, *JRS* XXVII 1937, 128–9: S. J. De Laet, *AC* IX 1940, 13–23 and, more generally, C. Nicolet, 'Armée et société à Rome sous la République', in *Problèmes de la guerre à Rome*, Paris–The Hague 1969, 141–56.

94. Val. Max. IV 7, 5: cf. Münzer, *RE* s.v. no. 88.

95. Oros. V 21, 3; cf. Münzer, *RE* s.v. no. 4; C. Nicolet, *REL* XLV 1967, 297–304; T. P. Wiseman, *New Men in the Roman Senate, 139 BC–14 AD*, Oxford 1971, 232.

96. Caes. *BC* III 104, 2. According to Münzer, *RE* s.v. no. 9, Septimius would have been *trib. mil.* also in 67, but the passages which he assembles do not support this; on the contrary, in Plut. *Pomp.* 78, 1, Septimius is called ταξίαρχος for which the proper translation is *centurio*, not *trib. mil.* (cf. the passages in Liddell-Scott-Jones, s.v.). All these three examples are mentioned by Kübler, *RE* s.v. 'equites romani', col. 292, and I do not understand why Syme, *JRS* XXVII 1937, 128, n. 14, thought only the case of Fufidius was valid. Furthermore, the case of Horace, military tribune without ever having possessed equestrian status – and certainly not even the census qualification required to attain it, *pace* L. R. Taylor, *AJPh* XLVI 1925, 161–70 – seems to provide fresh confirmation of the existence of weakening criteria governing access to officer status: on the question see C. Marchesi, *Storia della lett. latina, op. cit.* 467, n. 3. It is true that V. Ussani, *RFIC* XLII 1914, 41–4, maintains that the existence of Horace's military tribunate is wrongly derived from *Sat.* I 6, 45–8, but see, most recently, W. Wili, *Horaz*, Basle 1948, 28.

97. See Syme, *JRS* XXVII 1937, 128 and *id. PBSR* XIV 1938, 13, n. 57.

98. NB the well-known passages of Sall. *BC* 11, 5, and Plut. *Sulla*, 12, 12; for a particular aspect of the problem see Fiebiger, *RE* s.v. 'donativum', col. 1543. It is worth noting that the attractions of high pay induced citizens of equestrian rank to enter on a legionary centurion's career (see A. Passerini in De Ruggiero, *Diz. Epigr.* s.v. 'legio', 596 and 599).

99. See Appendix III.

100. On Caesar's Senate see R. Syme, 'Caesar, The Senate and Italy', *PBSR* XIV 1938, 1 f.; *id.* 'Who was Decidius Saxa?', *JRS* XXVII 1937, 122 f.; *id. RR* Chap. VI. But see Münzer, *RE* s.v. 'Fuficius', no. 5, who in my view is correct in seeing Caesarian senators in all three names recorded in Cic. *ad Att.* XIV 10, 2; *contra*, Syme, *JRS art. cit.* 128, and *id. PBSR art. cit.* 13 and nn. 59 and 60.

101. Cic. *Phil.* I 20; cf. Syme, *JRS* XXVII 1937, 129 and *id. PBSR* XIV 1938, 13 and n. 57. Whatever one's reservations on the authenticity of the evidence of Maecenas' *oratio* to Augustus, the advice given in Cassius Dio, LII 25, 6, concerning the

introduction of 'other ranks' to the Senate is significant (cf. Marquardt, *Organis. mil.* 77, n. 1. and M. Hammond, *TAPhA* LXIII 1932, 95).

102. Tac. *Ann.* III 75, 1: cf. M. Gelzer, *Die Nobilität der röm. Republik*, 1912, 3, n. 2 [= trans. Seager, 5, n. 14] with the reservations of H. Hill, *CQ* XXVI 1932, 170.

103. Syme, *JRS* XXVIII 1938, 124, n. 80; Münzer, *RE* s.v. no. 3. NB the observations of Münzer, *RE* s.v. no. 4; Wiseman, *op. cit.* 250.

104. Suet. *Vesp.* 1, 2; cf. Syme, *RR* 354.

105. Seel, *Klio, Beiheft* XXXV, *cit.* 108.

106. There are already characteristic hints at the end of the second century BC; cf. G. Veith, in Kromayer-Veith, *op. cit.* 314 f., esp. 316 ('militarization' of the tribunes). Cf. also 398 f.

107. Cf. e.g. L. Valerius Flaccus and C. Pomptinus in Sall. *BC* 45, 2; M. Petreius, *ibid.* 59, 6; Q. Marcius Crispus in Cic. *in Pis.* 54; C. Volusenus Quadratus, on whom see Syme, *RR* 70. The P. Considius of Caes. *BG* I 21, 4 (cf. Münzer, *RE* s.v. no. 5) who had served with Sulla and with Crassus against Spartacus is probably a centurion. The professionalism of the officer class is later specifically attested for the category of *legati*: cf. T. Rice Holmes, *Caesar's Conquest of Gaul²*, 1911, 563; G. Veith, in Kromayer-Veith, *op. cit.* 398; R. E. Smith, *Service in the Post-Marian Roman Army*, 62 f.

108. App. I 57, 253: cf. *Es. e Soc.* 67 [= 27 above]. The quaestor is identified by Badian, 'Waiting for Sulla', *Studies*, 220, with L. Licinius Lucullus.

109. He thought of Pompey, his patron, not the Republic: cf. *Es. e Soc.* 64, n. 50 [= 27, n. 50 above].

110. V 17, cited *Es. e Soc.* 68, n. 58 [= 28, n. 58 above].

111. Set out above, *Es. e Soc.* 66 [= 27 above].

112. Seel, *loc. cit.*: in Caes. *BC* I 74, 4, it also seems clear that soldiers, centurions and tribunes shared the same sentiments. In general, on the views of the non-political Italian class in the *Rechtsfrage* between Caesar and the Senate, cf. the excellent observations of Syme, *PBSR* XIV 1938, 18.

113. Carcopino, *Hist. rom.* II 381, n. 155; N. Criniti, *L'Epigrafe di Asculum di Gn. Pompeo Strabone*, Milan 1970.

114. On the connexion between Marius and the lower classes of Etruria cf. Piotrowicz, *Klio* XXIII 1930, 337–8; Syme, *RR* 93; see *Es. e Soc.* 578, n. 15 [= 169, n. 15 below] and also *Aufstieg und Niedergang*, I 789. The following examples come to mind; C. Norbanus (Etruscan according to Syme, *RR* 200, n. 2; see rather Münzer, *RE* s.v. no. 5; S. Panciera, *Epigraphica* XXII 1960, 13–19); Carrinas, Etruscan or Umbrian (Syme, *RR* 90, n. 4; Münzer, *RE* s.v. no. 1); Burrienus, Etruscan or Picene (cf. Syme, *JRS* XXVIII 1938, 123, n. 70); C. Tarquitius (Cichorius, *Röm. Studien*, 167, and Pais, *Dalle guerre puniche*, I 194). On Perperna cf. Gelzer, *Die Nobilität*, 41, n. 5 [= Seager, 51, n. 457]; Münzer, *RE* s.v. coll. 892–3, and *id. Röm. Adelsparteien und Adelsfamilien*, 1920, 95 f. Cf. also the examples collected by Syme, *RR* 362, n. 2 (3 Picenes).

115. Cf. Syme, *PBSR* XIV 1938, 14, n. 71.

116. In this sense cf. the point made by Cicero, *pro Mur.* 22, that at Rome the soldier was more highly esteemed than the jurist.

117. See O. Seeck, *Geschichte des Untergangs der antiken Welt*, I⁴ 1921, 234–68, reproduced from the first edition with the title 'Das römische Heer', in *Deutsche Rundschau* XXI 1894, 48–65.

118. Cf. Cic. *pro Sulla*, 24, and Sherwin-White, *The Roman Citizenship*, Oxford 1939, 179; see the general theme of Syme's article in *PBSR* XIV 1938, 5 f., 21, 30. It is in this context that we must set the phenomenon described below in Appdx. III (the Sullan Senate). See also *Es. e Soc.* 407 f. [= 142 f. below].

119. Gelzer, *Nobilität*, 11 [= Seager, 14 f.]. Seneca, *ad Lucil.* V 6 (47), 10, is very revealing for the power of military service to elevate men in politics in the first half of the last century BC, although of course it refers to members of the municipal upper classes: *Mariana clade multos splendidissime natos, senatorium per militiam auspicantes gradum, fortuna depressit, alium ex illis pastorem, alium custodem casae fecit.* I am aware that some scholars prefer the conjecture of Lipsius, *Variana* (*L. Annaei Senecae . . . Opera . . . a I. Lipsio emendata³*, Antwerp 1632, 462, nn. 27 and 29; cf. the edition of the Letters to Lucilius of F. Préhac (*Les Belles Lettres*) II 1947, 19; C. Marchesi, *Seneca³*, 1944, 243 and *id. Storia d. lett. latina*, II⁷ 1949, 116, n. 3), but the learned arguments advanced by Axelson, *Neue Senecasstudien*, Lund–Leipzig 1939, 177–8, do not convince me that this reading is preferable to the original text. *Mariana clade* must clearly be understood not as 'through defeat in the struggle against Marius' but as 'in the defeat of Marius' or, better, 'of the Marians', thanks of course to Sulla in the Civil War. The fierce attacks on the Marians, legally or illegally, during the dictatorship of Sulla are too well-known for me to have to give here an extensive description of the situation. But perhaps I may be allowed to advance a hypothesis: the propaganda directed against the Caesarian Ventidius is famous, and the hostile tradition loves to emphasize that he plied the trade of muleteer in his youth (Gell. XV 4, and cf. Cic. in Plin. *NH* VII 42 (43), 135; Planc. in Cic. *ad Fam.* X 18, 3, and Cass. Dio, XLIII 51, 4. The identification of him with the muleteer Sabinus of Virgil, *Catal.* X, should be ruled out: A. Rostagni, *RFIC* LVIII 1930, 409 and n. 3; Münzer, *RE* s.v. 'Sabinus', no. 2, col. 1593: see Gundel, *RE* s.v. 'Ventidius', no. 5; Syme, *Latomus* XVII 1958, 73–80). The passage of Gellius which discusses the matter in some detail is not free of exaggeration: Ventidius is called a Picene, of humble origin, brought to Rome before Strabo's chariot during his triumph for the capture of Asculum. We know, however, that the Ventidii were a very important family at Auximum and Syme is right to reject the contrary evidence of Gellius (*RR* 71, n. 3 and 92, n. 3: cf. 359). In my opinion, one can go further and doubt the connexion of Ventidius with Strabo's triumph; in fact the Ventidii were still very powerful after 90 BC if it really was the case that in 83 BC Pompey had to deal with them (Plut. *Pomp.* 6, 5); they were therefore of the Marian persuasion. For a P. Ventidius leader of the rebels in the *Bellum Sociale* see, however, App. I 47, 204 and the *app. crit.* of Mendelssohn-Viereck's edition.

If the evidence – which is certainly authentic – of powerful Ventidii appears to conflict with what we are told about a Ventidius obliged early in life to take up a humble profession, one may nevertheless surmise that the decadence of the family is traceable to their Marian affiliations and therefore to Sulla. Hence the evidence about Ventidius in the triumph of Strabo would be propaganda, if it is not the product of some confusion with the son Magnus who, as we have seen, was certainly in conflict with the Ventidii. Since it seems impossible to doubt the wretched early condition of Ventidius or the evidence on his occupation as muleteer, it could be said that the general statement of Seneca, referring to the period of the first Civil War, finds in this example of Ventidius (often mentioned in Imperial times) a specific illustration.

120. This fundamental limitation has been emphasized by A. Momigliano, *JRS* XXX 1940, 78, apropos the *Roman Revolution* of R. Syme. Cf. my own observations in this context concerning the Sullan Senate (Appdx. III) and, with regard to the Caesarian Senate, R. Syme himself, *PBSR* XIV 1938, 30.

121. Syme, *RR* 359 f.

122. Syme, *RR* 360 f., 456 f. Cf. O. Cuntz, *JŒAI* XXV 1929, 70–80, and for army problems in the Augustan period see Momigliano, *art. cit.* in *Augustus*, 208 f.

123. Cf. *Es. e Soc.* 87, n. 104 [= 34, n. 104 above].
124. Cf. M. A. Levi, *art. cit. Acme* I 1948, 92.
125. On Roman agrarian and colonial politics of the second century BC cf. the excellent account of G. Tibiletti, 'Ricerche di storia agraria romana', *Athenaeum* N.S. XXVIII 1950, 185 f., esp. 206 f.
126. Cf. Livy, III 1, 7, and Tibiletti, *mem. cit.* 211.
127. Vell. I 15, 5: *de Dertona ambigitur*; cf. Tibiletti, *Athenaeum* N.S. XXVI 1948, 198, n. 2, and P. Fraccaro, *ibid.* N.S. XXVIII 1950, 163; *id.* 'La colonia romana di Dertona (Tortona) e la sua centuriazione', *Opuscula*, III 123–50.
128. Vell. *ibid.*: cf. also *Es. e Soc.* 106, n. 154 [= 41, n. 154 below]. Narbo, however, was founded in the aftermath of C. Gracchus' overseas colonization scheme: cf. O. Hirschfeld, *Kleine Schriften*, Berlin 1913, 30, and C. Jullian, *Hist. de la Gaule*, III 128, n. 7.
129. Vell. *ibid.*; cf. P. Fraccaro, *Annali dei Lavori Pubblici* LXXIX 1941, 719 f. = *Opuscula*, III 93–121.
130. On this list see E. T. Salmon, *JRS* XXVI 1936, 48, n. 8: *id. Roman Colonization under the Republic*, London 1969.
131. I 15, 5.
132. I 14, 1.
133. Burmann corrected: *ex ipsarum . . . nomine*, and the correction was accepted by, for example, W. Weber, *Princeps*, I 252.
134. So Hyg. *de limit. const.* in *Gromatici Veteres*, p. 176, 8 f. Lachmann.
135. Of course the opposition to the Gracchan proposals is quite a different thing.
136. Cf. the *lex Plotia agraria* of 70 or 69 BC: see *Es. e Soc.* 443 f. [= 151 f. below].
137. The most characteristic illustration of this new situation (already emphasized by Rudorff, *Grom. Instit.* in *Die Schriften d. röm. Feldmesser*, II 1852, 333 f.) is the identity of the founders themselves. During the first century BC they are no longer magistrates elected by the people but private citizens who act as the direct agents of a revolutionary leader or his officers. The only exceptions are the *XXviri* of the *lex Iulia* of 59 BC (see, however, *Es. e Soc.* 115 [= 44 below], and Meyer, *Caesars Monarchie*[3], 1922, 65 f.) and the *VIIviri* of Antony in 44 BC (for one of these cf. Syme, *JRS* XXVII 1937, 135 f.). For Sulla we know the founder of Pompeii, P. Sulla, relative of the dictator (Cic. *pro Sulla* 62), and perhaps that of Praeneste, M. Terentius Varro Lucullus (cf. *CIL* I² 742 = *ILLRP* 369a, and *CIL* I² 846, interpreted by Münzer, *RE* s.v. 'Licinius' no. 109, col. 416). For the allocations of Caesar 46–44 BC we have the names supplied by Cic. *ad Fam.* XIII 4; 5; 7; 8; *id. ad Att.* XVI 16a, 5, and Suet. *Tib.* 4; cf. Fraccaro, *Athenaeum* N.S. XXVIII 1950, 141–2. For the Triumviral period cf. e.g. *CIL* VI 1460 = XIV 2264. In general cf. De Ruggiero, *Diz. Epigr.* s.v. 'colonia', 431 f.; E. Kornemann, *RE* s.v. 'coloniae', col. 570.
138. E. Pais, *Dalle guerre puniche*, II 649 f. gives a list of the localities with the names Faventia, Fidentia, Florentia, Pollentia, Potentia, Valentia, adding that these names, which bear witness to the citizens' interest in their state's greatness, were no longer in general use after the second century BC. It is not certain whether the Sullan colony of Arretium had the title Fidentia; it seems clear, however, that the Arretini Fidentiores of *CIL* XI 6675 are the Sullan colonists (see below, Appdx. IV). On Scolacium Minervium, Tarentum Neptunia, Carthago Iunonia, Narbo Martius, Herculia Telesia and Veneria Abellinum cf. the observations of Beloch, *RG* 494. For Italica in Spain see *Es. e Soc.* 105 n. 153 [= 40, n. 153 below]. It is true that in the Caesarian and Augustan periods colonies and *municipia* with augural names are found in Italy and the provinces (Pietas, Laus, Virtus, Felicitas etc.: a list in A. Degrassi, *AIV* CII 1942–3, 670–1 = *Scritti vari di antichità*, II, Rome 1962, 915–6), but the added reference to the *gens Iulia* shows how this was directed not, as before,

to the prosperity of the Roman people but to that of the founder. The prototype for this usage seems to have been Laus Pompeia founded by Pompeius Strabo (89 BC: *CIL* V p. 696; cf. also his Alba Pompeia). On the significance of the epithet Concordia for Beneventum cf. *CIL* IX p. 137 and E. Jullien, *Hist. de L. Munatius Plancus*, Paris 1892, 140; for Carthago cf. R. Cagnat, *Rev. Épigr.* N.S. I 1913, 6 f. (with list of other cases) and H. Dessau, *Hermes* XLIX 1914, 510.

139. Assmann, *De coloniis oppidisque romanis quibus imperatoria nomina vel cognomina imposita sunt*, Lägensalzae 1905, 2–3, says that this became general usage for the first time in Julius Caesar's settlements. Already in the second century BC some generals had given their own names to new foundations: cf. the numerous *fora* in Italy followed by a genitive. Outside Italy cf. Gracchuris, on which see *Es. e Soc.* 106, n. 153 [= 40, n. 153 below].

140. See *Es. e Soc.* 101, n. 143 [= 39, n. 143 below].

141. Cf. *Es. e Soc.* 25 f. [= 10 f. above].

142. E.g. Livy, II 10, 12 (Horatius Cocles); Val. Max. IV 3, 4 (Coriolanus); Dion. Hal. X 25 (Cincinnatus); Val. Max. IV 3, 5 (M'. Curius). Examples from the Greek world are collected by P. Guiraud, *La Propriété Foncière en Grèce* . . . , 1898, 235. Although in my view there is no connexion with the Roman world, it is worth mentioning the measures on the veterans' behalf in the Hellenistic period, on which see in general M. Rostovtzeff, *The Social and Economic History of the Hellenistic World*, 1941, I 148 f. (and III 1346, nn. 22 and 23).

143. In fact some allocations to Roman soldiers prior to that period are mentioned, but the evidence is not very good. Cf. Diod. XIX 101, 3 (313 BC): μετ' ὀλίγον δ' ἐμβαλὼν (Κόιντος Φάβιος αὐτοκράτωρ) εἰς τὴν τῶν πολεμίων χώραν, Κελίαν καὶ τὴν Νωλανῶν ἀκρόπολιν ἐξεπολιόρκησε, καὶ λαφύρων μὲν πλῆθος ἀπέδοτο, τοῖς δε στρατιώταις πολλὴν τῆς χώρας κατεκληρούχησεν. For the difficulties arising from the topography and the allusion to the dictator Fabius cf. Mommsen, *CIL* IX pp. 359 and 444; G. De Sanctis, *Storia dei Romani*, III 325, n. 2, and Beloch, *RG* 408; according to E. T. Salmon, *Phoenix* VII 1953, 99, it might be Saticula. The Livian tradition for that year does not mention the matter: Niese (*Hermes* XXIII 1888, 418 and 419 with n. 1: see also *HZ* N.F. XXIII 1888, 504, n. 3) suggested that Livy would have thought a division of land by a dictator in conflict with public law. Perhaps Diod. alludes to a case similar to that mentioned in Livy, XXX 24, 4: cf. also *Es. e Soc.* 102, n. 146 [= 39, n. 146 below]. The fact that in the passage the colonists were dubbed 'soldiers' can be explained by the fact that they would by preference have been chosen from the soldiers who had fought in that theatre of war, following a precedent which seems to have been common in viritane allotments, at least according to Mommsen, *SR* II³ 636 and n. 2; see De Ruggiero, in *Diz. Epigr.* s.v. 'adsignatio', 107. But there is no support for this theory in Front. *Strat.* IV 3, 12 which deals with the Sabine allocations of M'. Curius Dentatus and mentions *consummati milites*. Despite A. Klotz, *SBAW* V 1942, 40–1 (but see earlier G. B. Niebuhr, *Hist. rom.* tr. De Golbery, III 219, n. 356, and IV 165, n. 250, who used the passage of Front. for the general theory that in every period military service would have been the legal basis for distributions of land), it is clear that Front. has projected back into the third century BC the standard usage of his own day (end of the first century AD) which he, both as a brave general and an experienced land-surveyor, knew full well. In fact, the rest of the tradition (Val. Max. IV 3, 5; Plin. *NH* XVIII 3 (4), 18; Colum. I *praef.* 14; *auct. de vir. ill.* 33, 5; Plut. *Apophth. Curi,* 1 (on which see T. Frank, *Klio* XI 1911, 370–1) and *id. Crass.* 2, 10 (see Gabba, *Athenaeum* N.S. XXIX 1951, 18)) does not mention the point found in Frontinus.

It is hardly necessary to make the point that the verses of Juvenal, XIV 161–4: *mox etiam fractis aetate, ac punica passis | proelia vel Pyrrhum immanem gladiosque molossos | tandem pro multis vix iugera bina dabantur | vulneribus* are the product of a moralist's yearning for the past and have no claim to historical validity (cf. P. Bonfante, *Scritti giurid. vari*, II 1918, 9 f. and also E. Lepore, *RSI* LX 1948, 196 and n. 6; 197 and n. 1).

144. Livy, XXXI 4, 1–3; 49, 5; XXXII 1, 6; cf. Cato, fr. 230 Malc.[3] (Gelzer, *Die Nobilität*, 15 [= Seager, 20]).

145. This is clear from Livy, XXXII 1, 6, who says the beneficiaries were the *milites qui per multos annos stipendia fecissent*. On soldiers' leave in Italy cf. De Sanctis, *op. cit.* III 2, 256, n. 109; 289, n. 147.

146. There is a close connexion with the tour of inspection made by the dictator P. Sulpicius: Livy, XXX 24, 4 (App. *Hann.* 61, 252, is in error); if we wish to find a valid criterion for delimiting the zones of the allocations, we may consider which districts in Apulia and Samnium had defected to Hannibal. In Apulia: Salapia, Aecae, Arpi, Herdonea; in Samnium (Irpini): Compsa, Marmorae and Melas; (Caudini): Compulteria, Trebula Balliensis, Telesia. Also Fagifulae. We should perhaps exclude Tarentum (Livy, XLIV 16, 7). For Aeclanum cf. *CIL* I[2] 643–5, and Pais, *Storia della colonizzazione di Roma antica*, I, 1923, 156. For the *ager Taurasinus* cf. Livy, XL 38 (180 BC). The fact that in the great colonial activity of 194 BC (see Tibiletti, *Athenaeum* N.S. XXVIII 1950, 196 f.) no colony, except Sipontum, was founded in these localities confirms (NB Pais, *Storia interna di Roma*, Turin 1931, 111) that the allocations mentioned above had taken place there.

A. Bernardi, 'I *cives sine suffragio*', *Athenaeum* N.S. XVI 1938, 274, asserts that the five prefectures on the borders of Samnium and Campania (Atina: Cic. *pro Planc.* 19; Casinum: *CIL* X 5193–4; Aufidena: *CIL* IX 2802; Venafrum and Allifae: Fest. p. 262, 14 Lindsay) originated with the allocations to Scipio's veterans. This is impossible. I have already mentioned how the allocations were connected with the punitive confiscations imposed on the cities which had defected to Hannibal. None of the five communities mentioned was of that kind and none was conquered by Hannibal. There is no mention in the sources of Atina and Aufidena during the Second Punic War (for Venafrum cf. B. L. Hallward, *CAH* VIII 80); the territory of Allifae is mentioned only incidentally (Livy, XXII 18, 5 and XXVI 9, 2); Casinum clearly remained faithful to the Romans (cf. De Sanctis, *op. cit.* III 2, 124 and 336). Hence the prefectures date to the period of the Roman conquest: Atina and Venafrum to 290 BC (Livy, X 39; De Sanctis, *op. cit.* II 364, n. 1); Aufidena to 298 BC (Livy, X 12, 9); Allifae to 310 (Livy, IX 38, 2; Hülsen, *RE* s.v.; De Sanctis, *op. cit.* II 330); Casinum to 313 (De Sanctis, *op. cit.* II 325, n. 1). On the other hand, according to Mommsen, *SR* III 575, n. 1, Venafrum and Allifae would have been included in the *pars Samnitium* which had the *civitas sine suffragio* in 348 BC (Vell. I 14, 3). However, these are prefectures with *civ. s.s.*, not *optimo iure* as Bernardi, *art. cit.* 274–5, argues, and it is odd that E. Manni, *Per la storia dei municipi . . .* , 1947, 149, who says that they are prefectures with *civitas sine suffragio*, should then accept the hypothesis of Bernardi (but cannot say when they received full rights: *loc. cit.*, n. 3). How could the reward to the veterans have consisted in depriving them of full citizenship?

147. J. Kromayer, 'Die wirtsch. Entwicklung Italiens', *NJA* XXIII–XXIV 1914, 150. My own calculations (favouring the lower of the two figures) give an average of ten years' service, i.e. 20 *iugera* each.

148. E. De Ruggiero, in *Diz. Epigr.* s.v. 'colonia', 430. The veterans of Sardinia and Sicily seem to have been accommodated by the urban praetor (acting perhaps in concert with the *Xviri*) of 200 BC, C. Sergius Plautus, whose *imperium* was prorogued (Livy, XXXII 1, 6: cf. Mommsen, *SR* II[3] 627, n. 3).

149. Livy, XXVIII 11, 8; cf. *id.* XXXIX 3, 5.
150. Cf. e.g. *Es. e Soc.* 55 f. [= 24 f. above] and 27 and nn. 73–4 [= 11 and nn. 73–4 above].
151. E. Bormann, *CIL* XI p. 940, believed that the colony of Pisaurum of 184 BC must be the subject of some passages of the Gromatici, esp. p. 157 f. Lachmann, where there is a mention of veterans settled in such localities as Pisaurum and Potentia, which should therefore be considered military colonies; on the problem see Tibiletti, *Athenaeum* N.S. XXVIII 1950, 201 and n. 4. But Bormann's view cannot be confirmed by Plaut. *Amph.* 193 (*praeda atque agro adoriaque adfecit popularis suos*) especially if it were certain that the comedy is to be dated to 188 BC (W. B. Sedgwick, *AJPh* LXX 1949, 379 and 382) and that the play contains references to M. Fulvius Nobilior, conqueror of Aetolia (H. Janne, *RBPh* XII 1933, 515 f.; L. Halkin, *AC* XVII 1948, 297 f.; L. Hermann, *ibid.* 317 f. The view which sees the play as a parody of Ennius seems highly likely; vv. 304–5 would then allude to the grant of citizenship to the Rudian poet. NB on the other hand some prefer a date around 201 BC: cf. A. Ernout, *Plaute, Comédies* (*Les Belles Lettres*), I 4–7.
152. See *Es. e Soc.* 54 f. [= 23 f. above].
153. Cf. Q. Caecilius Metellus, cos. 123 BC, and the cities of Palma and Pollentia (Strabo, III 5, 1); Abbott, *CP* X 1915, 371 f., made this interesting observation. Probably, however, the two cities were not colonies; cf. Hübner, *CIL* II p. 494 and 496; M. Gwyn Morgan, *CSCA* II 1969, 217–31. Frank's view, *Economic Survey of Ancient Rome*, I 1933, 220, that they were Latin colonies and consisted of veterans (see also A. Degrassi, *MAL* ser. VIII, II 6, 1949, 312 f. = *Scritti vari di antichità*, I, Rome 1962, 137) can be accepted (though only for the latter point), in so far as the Roman colonists, who came from Spain according to Strabo, were perhaps ex-soldiers with their families.

In chronological order the Spanish foundations are: Italica (206 BC), the work of Scipio (App. *Iber.* 38, 153); besides Roman and allied soldiers (hence the name) there were also perhaps native colonists, some of whom were made Roman citizens (*CIL* II 1104 and 5375). In the second century BC it was a *vicus* of notable importance if Mummius gave it part of the booty of Achaea (*CIL* II 1119 = I² 630: cf. Mommsen, *RG* II⁵ 1869, 4 and 48, n. 1). Gracchuris was founded in 179 BC by Ti. Sempronius Gracchus and represented the Romanization of a pre-existing city (Livy, *Per.* XLI; Fest. p. 86, 5 Lindsay; cf. App. *Iber.* 43, 179). In Plin. *NH* III 3 (4), 24, it is an *oppidum latinum vetus*, on the coins a *municipium* (Hübner, *Mon.ling. iber.* no. 65); cf. *CIL* II 2857, and Mommsen's commentary; for Iliturgis cf. Degrassi, 'Epigraphica III', *MAL* ser. VIII, XIII 1, 1967, 34–8. That Calagurris Nasica was founded by Cornelius Scipio Nasica, praetor 194 BC, is the view of Pais, *Hist. rom.* I 547, but he is in error; the conquest dates to 186 BC. It is possible that the name derives from the patronage of this Nasica in 171 BC. Carteia was founded in 171 BC as a *colonia latina* (Livy, XLIII 3; see Hübner, *RE* s.v.). Corduba (152 BC) was settled by Roman citizens, certainly some ex-soldiers, through the consul C. Claudius Marcellus in a *vicus aut conciliabolum civium romanorum cum peregrinis selectis consociatum* (so Hübner, in *CIL* II p. 506, relying on Strabo, III 2, 1); for Brutobriga, *c.* 137 BC, see *Fontes Hispaniae Antiquae* IV p. 140; Palma and Pollentia I have already discussed (for Valentia see *Es. e Soc.* 114, n. 172 [= 43, n. 172 below]). In general see A. J. N. Wilson, *Emigration from Italy in the Republican Age of Rome*, Manchester 1966, 22 f. and 29 f.
154. On the importance of Spain in the history of the first century BC see the review of A. Momigliano, *JRS* XXX 1940, 78. See also 'Aspetti della lotta di Sesto Pompeo in Spagna', in *Legio VII Gemina*, Leon 1970, 133–55 = *Es. e Soc.* 473 f.

The colony of Narbo Martius (118–115 BC) is mentioned by Velleius in his list

(I 15, 5), hence a non-military colony. The popular faction wanted its foundation, and they included the young (later famous) orator Licinius Crassus who on that occasion delivered an oration supporting it and who was a member of the commission charged with its settlement (Cic. *Brutus*, 160; *id. de Orat.* II 223; *id. pro Cluentio*, 140; cf. C. Jullian, *Hist. de la Gaula*, III 125, n. 7). On the problem see Badian, *Roman Imperialism in the late Republic²*, Oxford 1968, 98, n. 32. On the chronology of the foundation and the colony's significance see bibliography and discussion in *Aufstieg und Niedergang*, I, 771 and 805, n. 251. H. Mattingly, relying on some Republican *denarii*, held that Cn. Domitius Ahenobarbus was a member of the same commission (see *JRS* XII 1922, 230–2). Using this interpretation Carcopino, *Hist. rom.* II 279 f., followed by W. Schur, *Das Zeitalter des Marius und Sulla (Klio, Beiheft* XLVI), Leipzig 1942, 50, n. 3, invoked the well-known Louvre relief (reproduced in, for example, *Antike Denkmäler*, III 1, Plate 12), which pictures a scene of censorial *lustratio* and which a long-established tradition connected with the Domitii, and put forward the view that it is not a *lustratio* which is represented but the enrolment of colonists for Narbo. The presence of soldiers and civilians in the scene encourages one to believe that the settlers included soldiers; Narbo would therefore be a military colony. But C. Anti, *AIV* LXXXIV 1924–5, 473 f., had already shown that the connexion of the relief with the Domitii was based on an inadequate hypothesis which has been given the force of fact only by the passage of time; the scene reproduced in the relief is in fact the operation of the *census* and must be referred to a censor of the first century BC, whoever he may have been (this hypothesis of Anti's is accepted by P. Ducati, *L'arte in Roma* ... 1938, 92 f.: cf. also A. Piganiol, *MEFR* LI 1934, 28 f.). The hypothesis that Narbo was a military colony therefore fails and one must return to the evidence of the literary tradition. This speaks of a conflict between Senate and *populares* apropos the foundation, and rightly places it in the aftermath of the Gracchan tradition of overseas colonization. Cf. F. Castagnoli, *Arti Figurative* I 1945, 81 f.; F. Coarelli, *DArch* III 1968, 302 f.

155. *Auct de vir. ill.* 73, 1; *Inscr. Ital.* XIII 3, 7; on the question see Gabba, *Athenaeum* N.S. XXIX 1951, 15 f. For evidence of the African colonization of Marius see a new inscription discovered at Thiburnica and published with an acute commentary by P. Quoniam, *CRAI* 1950, 332–6. Cf. L. Teutsch, *Das Städtewesen in Nordafrika*, Berlin, 1962, 9 f.; Wilson, *Emigration from Italy*, 45–6; J. Gascou, *MEFR* LXXXI 1969, 555 f., who emphasizes the difficulty of distinguishing the settlements which arose under the law of 103 from those of the Gaetuli to whom Marius granted land and citizenship (*Bell. Afric.* 56); see Brunt, *Italian Manpower, 225 BC–AD 14*, Oxford 1971, 577 f.

156. Cf. *Es. e Soc.* 44 [= 18 above].

157. The two *Xviri* known to us belong to the *gens Iulia*: *Inscr. Ital.* XIII 3, 6 and 7. One, C. Iulius Caesar, the dictator's father, was Marius' brother-in-law; Marius had married his sister. The other, C. Iulius Caesar Strabo, cousin of the Caesar just mentioned, seems to have belonged to the oligarchic faction, judging by the death he later met. For the attitude of the Iulii in the *seditio* of 100 BC cf. Cic. *pro Rab. perd. reo*, 21.

Perhaps I may append some further details on the career of the *Xvir* C. Iulius Caesar Strabo. In the *elogium Inscr. Ital.* XIII 3, 6 = *CIL* I² 27, a quaestorship is recorded (*Corpus* I² omits Q by an oversight). The most recent editor, Degrassi, leaves the year of this magistracy uncertain. I think, however, that it can be fixed with sufficient reliability if we remember that towards the end of the second century BC, in all probability 103 BC – cf. J. Klein, *Die Verwaltungsbeamten von Sicilien und Sardinien*, 1878, 236 and 286; (Drumann)-Groebe, *GR* III 123, n. 6; IV 326, n. 5.

Pais, *St. d Sardegna e d. Corsica*, I 92, put it 'in the Sullan period, shortly before 92 BC'(?) – Caesar Strabo defended the interests of the Sardinians in a trial *de repetundis* against T. Albucius; the latter had plundered them in his praetorship in 105 or 104; (Drumann)-Groebe, *loc. cit.*; Klebs, *RE* s.v. 'Albucius', no. 2; Diehl, *ibid.* s.v. 'Iulius', no. 135, col. 429; T. R. S. Broughton, *The Magistrates of the Roman Republic*, I 560. Cicero says (*div. in Caec.* 63); *Iulius hoc secum auctoritatis ad accusandum afferebat quod ut hoc tempore nos ab Siculis sic tunc ille ab Sardis rogatus ad causam accesserat*. Since we know that Cicero was engaged by the Sicilians as patron against Verres because of the happy memories of his quaestorship at Lilybaeum, it seems possible to deduce from the passage I have cited that Caesar Strabo had been quaestor in Sardinia (and this must obviously have been about 104–103 BC) and that he was later engaged by the Sardinians as patron. On the trial and its implications see E. S. Gruen, *Roman Politics and the Criminal Courts, 149–78 BC*, Cambridge (Mass.) 1968, 171–2.

158. *Lex agr. epig.* lines 85, 87–8. Cf. W. Barthel, 'Röm. Limitation in der Provinz Afrika', *BJ* CXX 1911, 39–116, and more specifically T. Frank, *AJPh* XLVII 1926, 55 f. Cf. also Sherwin-White, *op. cit.* 172.

159. It is not possible to assess accurately the purpose of the proposal of L. Marcius Philippus in 104 BC, mentioned in Cic. *de Off.* II, 73. The context (see *Es. e. Soc.* 77 f. [= 30 f. above]) seems to rule out the view of H. Last, *CAH* IX 164, that the object was to provide for the veterans of Africa who had gone on to fight in Gaul. Cf. however the observations of De Ruggiero, *Enc. Giur. Ital.* s.v. 'agrariae leges', 827.

160. See *Es. e Soc.* 56 [= 24 above].

161. Of course, the tradition does not specify whether it is a question of a *lex satura* or two separate laws. App. I 29, 130, mentions a law which divided land in Gaul (on the problem whether the reference here is to Transalpine or Transpadane Gaul cf. Fr. W. Robinson, *Marius, Saturninus und Glaucia*, 1912, 67, for the former view; *contra*, for example, Fraccaro, *Ann. Lav. Pubbl.* LXXIX 1941, 721 = *Opuscula*, III 98 f. On the problem see 'Note Appianee', *Athenaeum* N.S. XXXIII 1955, 225 f. = *Es. e Soc.* 546 f.). *Auct. de vir. ill.* 73, 5, refers to a law on the founding of colonies in Sicily, Achaea and Macedonia (here, however, it is no longer a question, as it was in the first law, of viritane allotments: Cic. *pro Balbo*, 48), and the other sources which are not specific use a singular or a plural without discrimination (Fraccaro, *art. cit.* 720 and 738, nn. 20–4 = *Opuscula*, III 97, nn. 20–4). The former view (*lex satura*) seems preferable since the *lex Caecilia Didia* of 98 BC which forbade *rogationes per saturam* ought to have been passed in response to the Appuleian legislation of 100 BC (Robinson, *op. cit.* 71). For the clause on the *aurum Tolosanum* in *auct. de vir. ill. loc. cit.*, cf. M. Segre, *Historia* III 1929, 624, n. 98: *contra*, De Ruggiero, *art. cit.* 834–5. However, Appian clearly says that the allotments were on *ager publicus*.

162. For Spain, cf. *Es. e Soc.* 105, n. 153 [= 40, n. 153 above]. Especially interesting is the evidence of Strabo, III 5, 1. For Africa cf. Sherwin-White, p. 172 f. Cf. in general for the period which follows Rostovtzeff, *SEHRE* 35.

163. See *Es. e Soc.* 71 f. [= 28 f. above].

164. Passerini, *Athenaeum* N.S. XII 1934, 127; other soldiers would certainly have benefited from the measures, e.g. those of Catulus' army, on whose feelings towards Marius cf. Plut. *Mar.* 27, 10.

165. Passerini, *art. cit.* 294 f. and 379. Reservations expressed by G. De Sanctis, *RFIC* LXIII 1935, 127.

166. Passerini, *Athenaeum* N.S. XVII 1939, 68 f.

167. I am now convinced that the view (which I tried to maintain in *Athenaeum* N.S.

XXIX 1951, 12 f.) that Saturninus' laws of 100 BC were abrogated is incorrect, and I willingly acknowledge the validity of the objections levied by Badian and other scholars. It is a common view that the *lex Titia agraria* of 99 BC aimed at a revival of the proposals of Saturninus (De Ruggiero, *art. cit.* 839; Rotondi, *Leges publicae populi Romani*, Milan 1912, 333; Robinson, *op. cit.* 73; Carcopino, *Hist. rom.* II 374); it was annulled.

168. See *Es. e Soc.* 67, n. 53 [= 27, n. 53 above].

169. That part of Pais' article which concerns Pompey (*AAN* N.S. VIII 1924, 330 f.) contributes nothing to this question.

170. Cic. *ad Att.* I 18, 6; Cass. Dio, XXXVIII 5, 1–2; cf. *Es. e Soc.* 443 f. [= 151 f. below], to be supplemented with Plut. *Lucull.* 34, 4, as R. E. Smith, *CQ* N.S. VII 1957, 82–5 pointed out. According to Carcopino, *Sylla, ou la monarchie manquée*, Paris 1931, 169 (relying on Plut. *Pomp.* 14, 4) Sulla would either have rewarded the Pompeian soldiers of the civil wars quite inadequately or would have completely ignored them.

171. Cf. *Es. e Soc.* 98 [= 39 above].

172. Some had already obtained a settlement at Nicopolis: Cass. Dio, XXXVI 50, 3; cf. Oros. VI 4, and Rice Holmes, *The Roman Republic and the Founder of the Empire*, Oxford 1923, I 434. Also the settlements of veterans in Spain at Valentia after the capture of the city in 73 BC (Sall. *Hist.* II 54M.; Plut. *Pomp.* 18, 5) derive their origin from Pompey (cf. *CIL* II 3733–7; 3739; 3741, where *Valentini veterani et veteres* are recorded, the latter being soldiers of Viriathus settled there in 138 BC by D. Iunius Brutus (Livy, *Per.* LV): cf. Hübner, *CIL* II p. 500 f.; *contra*, C. H. V. Sutherland, *The Romans in Spain, 217 BC–AD 117*, London 1939, 79 and 233, n. 12, and A. Schulten, *RE* s.v. 'Valentia', col. 2148 (see, however, A. N. Sherwin-White, *JRS* XXX 1940, 120). Possibly also at Corduba in 55 BC (Strabo, III 2, 1, and Hübner, *RE* s.v.). Metellinum, founded by Metellus Pius during the war against Sertorius, is a *castrum* rather than a *col. civ. Rom.*: Schulten, *RE* s.v.

173. Cic. *ad Att.* I 19, 4: cf. I 18, 6, and II 1, 6; Cass. Dio, XXXVII 50.

174. Cass. Dio, XXXVII 49, 3; Plut. *Pomp.* 44, 3.

175. See *Es. e Soc.* 73, n. 67 [= 29, n. 67 above].

176. Cic. *ad Att.* I 19, 4.

177. Cass. Dio, XXXVII 50.

178. That it is a question of two laws, one dealing with *ager publicus* in Italy apart from Campanian land (Cass. Dio, XXXVIII 1, 3), the other with the *ager Campanus et Stellatis* (Suet. *Caes.* 20; Vell. II 44) is the view of Zumpt, *Commentationes epigraphicae*, I, Berlin 1850, 288; Meyer, *Caesars Monarchie³*, 63, n. 1, and Rice Holmes *op. cit.* 476–9, with which I agree. Cf. L. R. Taylor, *Studies Johnson*, Princeton 1961, 68–78.

179. Mommsen, 'Die italischen Bürgercolonien von Sulla bis Vespasian', *Hermes* XVIII 1883, 169 = *GS* V 210.

180. W. Ensslin, 'Die Ackergesetzgebung u.s.w.', *NJA* LIII–LIV 1924, 23.

181. Cic. *ad Fam.* XIII 4, 2; cf. Cass. Dio, XXXVIII 1.

182. Plut. *Pomp.* 48, 1; *id. Caes.* 14, 5; Cass. Dio, XXXVIII 5, 1; App. II 4, 36. Indeed, Cass. Dio, XXXVIII 1, 3, when dealing with the first law speaks of 'citizens' but the presence of Pompey on the agrarian commission (on which see Meyer, *op. cit.* 65 and n. 3) is significant and still more so is the intervention of Pompeian soldiers at the voting. In the law on the *ager Campanus* there is a clause that the colonists had to have at least three sons (discussion in M. A. Levi, *A & R* N.S. III 1922, 521 f.) but it is clear from Caes. *BC* I 14, 4 that it refers to Pompeian veterans. Cic. *Phil.* II 100 refers to the allotments of 46 BC.

183. It is not easy to say where the *lex Iulia* on *ager publicus* (the Campanian land

excepted) operated, given the confusion with the legislation of 46 and with the Triumviral measures taken in Caesar's name (Mommsen, *art. cit.* 183 = *GS* V 224). Meyer, *op. cit.* 64, n. 2, inclines to the view that the evidence of the *Libri col.* dates to 59; this view can be accepted only in the cases where *Vviri* are mentioned, i.e. for Praeneste p. 236, 14, and Venafrum, p. 239, 7L. Colonists were also settled perhaps at Tarentum, since in my view the evidence of Serv. *ad Georg.* IV 127 = III 1, p. 239, 30 Thilo is to be referred to the allotments that resulted from this law; this passage is perhaps made more precise in Ps. Prob. III 2, p. 385, 20 Hagen: *Tarentinorum agros veteranis divisit* (Pompeius) etc.; see Rudolph, *Stadt und Staat im römischen Italien*, 1935, 125 and 161, n. 2. The mention of a pirate settlement at Tarentum – which is referred to in the passages I have cited – is usually believed (see P. Wuilleumier, 'Tarente' (*Bull. Éc. franç. d'Athènes et de Rome* CXLVIII) 1939, 167; M. Gelzer, *Pompeius*, 1949, 84; but NB the 'perhaps' of T. R. S. Broughton, in T. Frank, *ESAR* IV 523 and the tone of scepticism in H. E. Ormerod, *Piracy in the Ancient World*, 1924, 241, and in *CAH* IX 375). It must, however, have originated from a misunderstanding of Virgil by Suetonius (but see another explanation in Servius which he prefers; for various modern views see L. Hermann, *REL* IX 1931, 281 f. and Wuilleumier, *ibid.* X 1932, 48 f.), and this misunderstanding was probably connected with some Caesarian propaganda themes against Pompey; there are traces of this in Lucan, I 346, which however refers only to Pompeiopolis: Comm. Bern. *ad loc.* p. 27, 19 Usener. All the tradition on the Pirates War in fact makes no reference to this. On the possibility that pirates were settled at Cyrene see J. Reynolds, *JRS* LII 1962, 97–103. Under the law on the *ager Campanus* a colony was founded at Capua (Cass. Dio, XXXVIII 7; *Grom. Veter.* p. 231, 19 Lachmann; see Cic. *ad Att.* II 19, 3; *id. post red. in sen.* 29; *id. pro Sest.* 19; *id. in Pis.* 11). Contrary to the orthodox view (Mommsen, *art. cit.* 168–9 = *GS* V 210; Abbott, *CPh* X 1915, 377) I prefer a date of 46 BC for the colonies of Calatia and Casilinum.

184. I have thought it necessary to spend a little time over the rewards proposed for the veterans in the second century BC since they are fundamental for the explanation of the origins of the phenomenon; I have also dealt in detail with those in favour of Pompey's veterans since they lend themselves to some interesting observations. However, to throw into relief the political and social factors, I think it is proper to refer, for what is really the antiquarian topic of the other allocations to the veterans of the first century BC, to the specific papers listed below and to those which will be cited from time to time as the need arises. In general, in addition to the broad treatment of A. W. Zumpt, *De coloniis Romanorum militaribus*, in *Comment. Epigr.* I 319 f., which is still fundamental for a complete discussion of the phenomenon and for the collection of the material, see the magisterial article of Mommsen, *Hermes* XVIII 1883, 161 f. = *GS* V 202 f.; those of Pais, 'Le colonie militari dedotte in Italia dai Triumviri e da Augusto', *Museo Ital. di Ant. Classica* I 1884, 33 f.; *id.* 'Serie cronologica delle colonie romane e latine', *MAL* VI I, 1925, 362 f. Also *id.* *Storia della colonizzazione*, *cit.* I 1923, *passim*; E. De Ruggiero, in *Encic. Giur. Ital.* I 2, 1, s.v. 'agrariae leges', 365 f. and in *Diz. Epigr.* s.v. 'colonia' (reproduced in part in *Le Colonie dei Romani*, Spoleto 1904); E. Kornemann, *RE* s.v. 'coloniae', col. 524 f. Also the historical studies of the period: e.g. for Caesar's colonies in 46–44 BC Ed. Meyer, *Caesars Monarchie*[3], 483 f. For the question of the colonies in Pliny see R. Thomsen, *The Italic Regions* (*C & M Dissertations* IV) 1947, 41 f. For provincial colonies cf. Kornemann, *art. cit.*, and e.g. H. Matkowski, *Eos* XXXIV 1932–3, 438 f. (Augustan period) and A. H. M. Jones, *The Cities of the Eastern Roman Provinces*, Oxford 1937, *passim* (see Index, s.v. 'Roman Colonies').

185. Cf. the list in Appdx. IV. In a review of the *Imagines* of Degrassi published in *GIF* XIX 1966, 183–6, E. V. Marmorale has offered a new interpretation of *CIL* I² 1815 = *ILLRP* 146 (from Alba Fucens). His view is that it is a dedication by African soldiers of Metellus Numidicus (*Caecilianis* being an archaic nominative in -*is*) to whom land had been assigned by the Senate after the Numidian triumph of Metellus. This hypothesis, which has not been mentioned by Degrassi although he cites the review elsewhere (*Acta of the Fifth Int. Congress of Greek and Latin Epigraphy*, Cambridge 1967, Oxford 1971, 164), is favourably mentioned *inter al.* by J. Reynolds, *JRS* LXI 1971, 140. I think that the view of Marmorale is not acceptable, but he deserves our gratitude for suggesting another and more probable solution. This is that the soldiers in question are those of Metellus Pius; he had fled to Africa during the domination of Cinna and had enrolled there an army which probably consisted (Plut. *Crass.* 6, 2) of his father's clients (for the Caecilii in Africa see Badian, *Foreign Clientelae*, 309, 312; for Pius' initiative 266–7). These troops took part with him in the civil war and it is only logical to suppose that they were rewarded with allotments of land, in the same way as other Sullan troops. NB Alba Fucens makes a dedication to Sulla (*CIL* I² 724 = *ILLRP* 355) and this city, besieged by the Italians during the Social War (Livy, *Per.* LXXII) and remaining loyal to Rome (as, it seems, one should deduce from *Rhet. ad Herenn.* II 28, 45), had been severely damaged. It was probably revived with these grants of land. The *mag(ister)* of the inscription will perhaps have been that of a *pagus* into which (cf. Pompeii) the soldier-settlers will have been regrouped. Less probable, I think, is a connexion of the inscription with the allotments proposed by the *lex Plotia* (see *Es. e Soc.* 443 f. [= 151 f. below]) for the soldiers of Metellus returning from the war against Sertorius.

186. Strabo, V 4, 11: see E. Pais, 'La persistenza delle stirpi sannite', *AAN* N.S. VI 1918, 452 f.

187. Cf. the *ager Hirpinus* (rather than *fundus: totum enim possidet*) of Valgus, father-in-law of Servilius Rullus, in Cic. *de leg. agr.* III 8; see also I 14; II 69. Cf. H. Dessau, *Hermes* XVIII 1883, 620 f. On the name Valgus cf. Pais, *Coloniẓ.* I 156; *CIL* IX 1140 (*Aeclanum*) = *ILLRP* 523, and *CIL* X 844 (*Pompeii*) = *ILLRP* 646; *CIL* X 852 = *ILLRP* 645; 5282 (Casinum) = *ILLRP* 565 (see also 598); cf. *Es. e Soc.* 121, n. 195 [= 45, n. 195 below].

188. I rely on the excellent 'Orientamenti per la storia sociale di Pompei' of E. Lepore, in *Pompeiana. Raccolta di Studi per il secondo centenario degli Scavi di Pompei*, Naples 1950 (I cite from the extract), where modern contributions to the problem are accurately and profitably assessed.

189. Lepore, pp. 6–7.

190. Lepore, pp. 4–5; 11–12.

191. Lepore, p. 8, n. 3.

192. Lepore, pp. 7–9. This question could be clarified if we knew the numbers of colonists stationed at Pompeii. However, any calculation must be conjectural. Lepore, p. 7 and n. 2, has accepted the interpretation of Carcopino, *Sylla*, 213, n. 4, who corrected the Livian evidence (*Per.* LXXXIX) of *XLVII legiones* to $\overline{XLVII}$ *legionarios*, referring to Campania alone, out of a total of 120,000 soldiers which we know from App. I 104, 489; he supposed that there was a settlement at Pompeii of 4,000–5,000 veterans. But the correction and interpretation of Carcopino are certainly arbitrary and it is better to accept the view of Pais, Serie cronologica . . . *MAL* VI 1, 1925, 352, who, relying on App. I 100, 470, reads *XXIII legiones* in Livy as well.

193. As, however, Lepore, p. 9, seems to believe.

194. Lepore, p. 5 and n. 1.

195. Cic. *de leg. agr.* II 78. See Cic. *in Cat.* I 8, and also *id. de leg. agr.* III 14: *fundos quos in agro Casinati optimos fructuosissimosque continuavit* (Valgus), etc.

196. The association of Sulla's name with some small places in Latium which we find in the Gromatici must be interpreted on the lines set out in Beloch, *RG* 163 and Rudolph, *Stadt und Staat*, 42 (see 23, n. 1), 90, 96. Cf. also Forum Cornelii in Cisalpine Gaul on which note the observations of Carcopino, *Hist. rom.* 476, n. 143, and of E. Andreoli, *Historia* II 1928, 334 f. We cannot, of course, exclude the scattering of nuclei of veterans in the new *municipia*.

197. As was the case at Volaterrae and Arretium: Cic. *ad Att.* I 19, 4; *id. pro Mur.* 49; *ad Fam.* XIII 4 and 5. For a general treatment of Sullan colonization in Etruria which is valuable if not wholly acceptable see W. V. Harris, *Rome in Etruria and Umbria, op. cit.* 251 f.

198. On the colonists at Fiesole cf. Gran. Lic. p. 34 Flemisch; Cic. *in Cat.* III 14; Sall. *BC* 24, 2; 27, 1; 30, 3; 59, 3. On Arezzo see also Sall. *BC* 36, 1.

199. On the *homines percussi Sullani temporis calamitate* (Cic. *pro. Mur.* 49) see Gran. Lic. p. 34 Flemisch; Sall. *Hist.* I 65 Maur.; App. I 107, 501; Exup. 8 (all with reference to the attempted revolution of 78 BC) and Sall. *BC* 28, 4.

200. As can be deduced from the famous passage of Cic. *in Cat.* II 20, and from Sall. *BC* 16, 4.

201. On the large estates of Domitius Ahenobarbus see T. Frank, *ESAR* I 364.

202. See *Es. e Soc.* 120, n. 192, [= 45, n. 192 above].

203. On the treatment meted out by Sulla to the Italian cities cf. App. I 96, 445–8 and my Commentary², 257 f. and also my article in *SCO* XIX–XX 1970–1, 461 f. = *Es. e Soc.* 361 f. On the questions concerning confiscation see the account of E. De Ruggiero, in *Enc. Guir. Ital.* I 2, 1, s.v. 'agrariae leges', 853 f.

204. Without justifying the claims of E. Ciaceri, *Cicerone e i suoi tempi*, I 1926, 35. The assertions of Aemilius Lepidus in Sall. *Hist.* I 55, 23 Maur. (leaving aside any question of the speech's authenticity which is denied by C. Lanzani, *Roma* XII 1934, 435–42, and maintained (rightly) by E. Bolaffi, *Rivista Indo–Greca–Italica di filologia* XX 1936, 61–6 and by Carcopino, *Sylla²*, 1942, 274: cf. A. La Penna, *Sallustio e la rivoluzione romana*, Milan 1968, 258 f.) are certainly dominated by propaganda: cf. Cic. *de leg. agr.* II 71.

205. Enough to mention here Cic. *de leg. agr.* II 68; 69; 70; 98; III 12; *ad. Att.* I 19, 4; *ad Fam.* XIII 4, 2; 8, 2 (*assignationes et venditiones*).

206. Some of Sulla's colonies survived for some time: see below. For evidence in 45 BC cf. Cic. *ad Fam.* XIII 8, 9. The mention in the *Gromatici* of a *lex Cornelia*, p. 169, 1 Lachmann, and of *limites Sullani*, p. 165, 10–17, may be important here.

207. Carcopino, *Sylla*, 62; *id. Hist. rom.* 475–6. *Contra* (and rightly) E. Heitland, *Agricola*, 1921, 176, and T. Frank, *An Economic History of Rome²*, 1927, 172–3, and id. *ESAR* I 303.

208. The conditions described by Varro refer to the period 67–54 BC: cf. Heitland, *op. cit.* 178–9, and Frank, *ESAR* I 367. See also R. Scalais, *Mél. Thomas*, 1930, 618 f. The dramatic date of Book III of the *de re rust.* seems to be 50 BC: Badian, *Athenaeum* N.S. XLVIII 1970, 4–6.

209. On this view cf. H. V. Canter, 'Praise of Italy in Classical Authors', *CJ* XXXIII 8, 1938, 457 f., esp. 459, 462 and 466; *ibid.* XXXIV 7, 1939, 396 f. On Varro as a source here see also F. Christ, 'Die röm. Weltherrschaft in der antiken Dichtung,' 1938 (*Tübinger Beiträge zur Altertumswissenschaft*, XXXI) 144 f.

210. As Beloch, *RG* 512, maintains.

211. *CIL* IX 5074 = I² 1903a = Dessau, *ILS* 5671 = *ILLRP* 617; *CIL* IX 5075 = I² 1904 = *ILS* 6562 = *ILLRP* 618.

212. Its citizens are separately classified as *Veteres* (*CIL* XI 1849 = *ILS* 6608), *Fidentiores*

(*CIL* XI 6675, 1: these would be the Sullan colonists) and *Iulienses* (Augustan colonists). For a different view see Bormann, in *CIL* XI p. 372. But cf. Mommsen, *CIL* X p. 89, n. 2.

213. *Clusini Veteres et Novi* in Pliny, *NH.* III 5 (8), 52.

214. *Nolani veteres* are mentioned in *CIL* X 1273 = *ILS* 6344; see, however, Mommsen in *CIL* X p. 142.

215. Here in fact the Sullan colonists did not come within the city walls but were distributed in *castella* (Gran. Lic. p. 34 Flemisch). Faesulae remained a *municipium* while the colonists formed a colony: see the excellent explanation of A. Degrassi, *MAL Ser.* VIII, II 6, 1949, 292, who covers the question of the double community at 285 f., 292 = *Scritti vari di antichità*, I 104 f. See also the narrower view of H. Rudolph, *Stadt und Staat*, 92, n. 2, and 93 (but Paestum is not a Sullan colony: Degrassi, *art. cit.* 325 = *Scritti vari*, I 153).

216. *pro Sulla*, 21.

217. In any case the *pagus Felix*, going back certainly to Sulla, of *CIL* X 814, 853, 924, 1042, 1074, provides food for thought: see Nissen, *Pomp. Studien*, 1877, 881, and Sogliano, *NS* 1898, 499, and 1899, 237. See also *Es. e Soc.* 120 [= 44 f. above].

218. As happened at Faesulae and at Clusium, where it is irrelevant that the community born of the fusion of the old *municipium* and the Sullan colony preferred a colonial constitution: cf. Degrassi, *art. cit.* 292–3 = *Scritti vari*, I 112–4. Life in such towns must have been even more idyllic if one accepts the conclusions of Rudolph for Pompeii, *op. cit.* 93, n. 1 (immediate fusion of the two elements, with the older predominating as evidenced by the *IIIIviri* of the municipium who became *II viri* of the *colonia*) and for *Nola*, 93, n. 4. (apropos *CIL* X 1236 = *ILS* 5392). But against this are the observations of Degrassi, *art. cit.* 287–8 = *Scritti vari*, I 107–8, and they point to a different interpretation of the epigraphic evidence. On the case of Pompeii see my review of Sartori, *Athenaeum* N.S. XXXII 1954, 285 f. = *Es. e Soc.* 600 f.

The interesting observations of F. Hampl, 'Zur röm. Kolonisation in der Zeit der ausgehenden Republik und des früheren Principats', *RhM* N.F. LIX 1952, 52–78, and the study of the Sicilian senators mentioned by Cicero in II *Verr.* 2, 120–5 (*Athenaeum* N.S. XXXVII 1959, 304–20) have subsequently led me to modify substantially the theory I have set out above. I prefer to think now that in many Sullan colonies, and not only at Pompeii, double communities were not created (the case of Interamnia Praetuttianorum is perhaps an exception: see A. La Regina, *Enc. Arte Antica*, VII 712–3) but that new colonists and *veteres* citizens lived together and shared in the administration of their town on an unequal basis. In other words, the separate categories of citizens which I have cited above and which are attested as existing together in some Sullan colonies would not indicate civic bodies that were administratively autonomous. I have preferred to leave my old view in the text as a proof of the complexity of the problem.

219. Sall. *Hist.* I 65; 77, 14 Maur.; Livy, *Per.* LXXXIX; Gran. Lic. p. 32 Flemisch. The view of Lange, *RA* III² 161, that Nola and Volaterrae were inspired to rebel because they did not wish to receive Sullan colonists does not appear to have any basis in fact.

220. Cic. *pro Caec.* 18; 97.

221. For the *ademptio civitatis* see Cic. *de domo*, 79; Sall. *Hist.* I 65 Maur. (see also I 77, 14) and ps. Asc. p. 189 Stangl; for the results J. Beloch, *Bevölkerung*, 352. For the remarks of Cic. *pro Caec.* 97, see V. Arangio-Ruiz, *Storia del diritto romano⁶*, 1950, 137.

222. II 9, 28. For another limiting factor when considering the bias of the tradition on

Sulla's activity see *Es. e Soc.* 119, n. 186 [= 44, n. 186 above]. On the passage of Florus see *SCO* XIX-XX 1970–1, 461 f. = *Es. e Soc.* 361 f.

223. There must, of course, have been exceptions, as for example at Praeneste.

224. A passage of Front. *de Contr.* p. 52, 21 L. might make one believe that, on the contrary, the Augustan allotments at Fanum placed the *incolae* in an inferior position politically: cf. Pais, *Colonizzazione*, XVIII. On the passage see U. Laffi, *Adtributio e Contributio*, Pisa 1966, 198–202.

225. Cf. *Es. e Soc.* 60 [= 25 above].

226. *Op. cit.* 54 and 202 (n. 23). Cf. what has been said above, *Es. e Soc.* 56, n. 32 [= 24, n. 32 above]. For the rest, the connexion between Sullan colonists and Catilinarians (too well-known to need more than a reference here to the passages cited in *Es. e Soc.* 122, n. 200 [= 45, n. 200 above]) shows that often the colonists returned to their original status.

227. Cf. above, *Es. e Soc.* 94 [= 37 above].

228. Cic. *de leg. agr.* II 78. As Ciaceri, *op. cit.* I 35, also believes, it is a question of a renewal, pure and simple, of the analogous provision of Ti. Gracchus, but of course with a totally different purpose. *Contra*, Carcopino, *Hist. rom.* 475. That the *lex frumentaria* of Sulla had as its object the protection of the new colonists is the view of A. Passerini, *Athenaeum* N.S. X 1932, 181, which I am unable to accept.

On the inalienability (limited, however, to twenty years) of the Caesarian allotments cf. Appian, II 140–1, 581 f. (speech by Brutus) and III 2, 5.

229. App. I 96, 448. Of interest are the remarks of Cic. *de leg. agr.* II 75 on the dangers presented by colonists dispersed at strategic points in the peninsula, since it is very probable that the orator has the Sullan colonies in mind.

230. It is, of course, consistent with his well-known interpretation of Sulla's political activity that Carcopino, *Sylla*, 63, should say that the veterans were so settled as to keep an eye on the property of the aristocracy.

231. The well-known verses which Lucan places in the mouth of Caesar, for example at the crossing of the Rubicon (I 343–4): *quae sedes erit emeritis? quae rura dabuntur / quae noster veteranus aret? quae moenia fessis?* and on the eve of a battle (VII 257–8): *haec eadem (dies) est hodie quae pignora, quaeque penates / reddat, et emerito faciat vos Marte colonos* reflect admirably the situation of the second half of the first century BC. Contrast the well-known episode reported in Caes. *BC* I 17, 4.

232. All part and parcel of the state of mind described above, *Es. e Soc.* 68 [= 28 above].

233. Syme, *RR* 207 f.

234. More limited interests dictated the Julian legislation of 59 BC: see *Es. e Soc.* 115 [= 44 above]. Those allotments were not to last; they were swept away in the civil war which followed. Cf. Pompey's enlistments at Capua: Caes. *BC* I 14, 4 and Suet. *Caes.* 81, 1.

235. The theme mentioned here is in that political pamphlet which M. Pohlenz, 'Eine politische Tendenzschrift aus Caesars Zeit', *Hermes* LIX 1924, 184, has reconstructed from the early chapters of Book II of Dion. Hal. (I call attention to II 28). A. v. Premerstein, *Vom Werden und Wesen*, 9 f., followed by E. Kornemann, *Klio* XXXI 1938, 80 f. and also by W. Seston, *PP* V 1950, 180, has, however, referred the pamphlet to the period of Augustus. But this is rejected by L. Wickert, *Klio* XXX 1937, 253, n. 1; *ibid.* XXXII 1939, 332; *id. NJAB* IV 1941, 16 and n. 7. In fact, for the point which is at issue here, it is difficult to maintain a senatorial origin (which v. Premerstein regards as the general tenor of the pamphlet) for such a justification of the principle of rewards for veterans.

I have also changed my view on this point [since publication of my article] and I think I have set out [elsewhere] arguments which can demonstrate an origin for the Romulean pamphlet in the propaganda and period of Sulla: see *Athenaeum* N.S.

XXXVIII 1960, 175–225. But the controversy is far from over. G. Ferrara, 'Commenti al dopoguerra aziaco (III)', *Cultura* VIII 1970, 22–39, returns to a date in the Augustan period, and J. P. V. D. Balsdon, 'Dionysius on Romulus: A Political Pamphlet?', *JRS* LXI 1971, 18–27, denies that Dion. Hal.'s chapters are a political pamphlet and emphasizes Dionysius' own work in co-ordinating various sources.

Another theme of Caesarian propaganda seems to be that which aimed at shielding Caesar from the reputation which weighed heavily on Sulla. The sources, in fact, say that the dictator settled his soldiers on *ager publicus* or on land belonging to him, land which was consecrated or had been purchased: App. II 94, 395; Cass. Dio, XLII 54, 1; XLIII 47, 4; Suet. *Caes.* 38. However, it is certain that land was confiscated, as is clear, for example, from the drift of Brutus' speech in App. II 139–41 and from the fact that a *S.C.* had to guarantee the allotments assigned to the veterans: App. II 133, 557 and 135, 565. Cf. further Cic. *ad Fam.* IX 17; XIII 4; 5; 7; 8. For Africa see *Bell. Afric.* 57, 1 and Cass. Dio, XLIII 14, 1.

236. As conceived by Wickert, for example, *art. cit.* (preceding note).

237. *ad Caes.* II 5, 8.

238. In this sense see the fine pages of Syme, *RR* 449 f.

239. In general see the article of Mommsen cited above, *Es. e Soc.* 117, n. 184 [= 44, n. 184 above], at p. 169 = *GS* V 211 f. Cf. also Syme, *RR* 196 f.; 207 f.; 233 f. and my article on the Triumviral colonies of Antony (*PP* VIII 1953, 101 f. = *Es. e Soc.* 459 f.) and my Comm. on Appian, *BC* V, pp. LIX–LXVIII.

240. *c.* 170,000: the number of legions is not certain (App. V 5, 21; 6, 25; 22, 87).

241. App. IV 3, 10 f., reduced later to 16.

242. I should perhaps point out that there is no basis of fact in the assertion of M. A. Levi, *Ottaviano capoparte*, Florence 1933, II 11 f., relying on the supposed identity of the γεωργοί of App. V 43, 182 with tenants (*ibid.* p. 12, n. 1), that the cities belonged to the category of those which had become *dediticiae* after the Social War. The treatment reserved for the cities which had opposed Rome in the *Bellum Sociale* was agreed by Sulla on his return to Italy in 83 BC in full recognition of their right to Roman citizenship (Livy, *Per.* LXXXVI, to be interpreted as Levi, *Costituzione*, 163, and Carcopino, *Hist. rom.* II 474 suggest) and of course – as Zumpt, *op. cit.* 242, saw long ago – with restitution of the land which had been confiscated. Naturally those towns which sided later with the Marians were exceptions and it is only to their cases that the view of E. De Ruggiero, *art. cit. Enc. Giur. Ital.* 853–4, can apply.

243. Though they are involved: Levi, *Ottaviano*, II 16, n. 1.

244. Cass. Dio, XLVIII 9, 4; I cannot, however, accept the view of Syme, *RR* 208, who speaks of this opposition as the last struggle of Italy against Rome.

245. Cf. e.g. Virgil, *Ecl.* I and IX, and *id. Dirae*, on which see T. Frank, *Vergil*, 1922, 122 f.; Propertius, IV 1, 127–30, on which see U. Ciotti, *BCAR* LXXI 1943–5, app. 14, 53 f.; Horace, *Epist.* II 2, 49–52. See App. V 12, 49.

246. See *Es. e Soc.* 120–1 [= 45 above].

247. See in this connexion the detailed observations of Sherwin-White, *op. cit.* 172 f. Interesting also is the connexion between the evidence of Suet. *Caes.* 42 and the *colonia Genetiva Urbanorum* founded by Caesar at Urso: see Kornemann, *art. cit.* col. 527. See also my article 'The Perusine War and Triumviral Italy', *HSPh* LXXV 1971, 139–43.

248. On Antony's colonies in Italy see in general Mommsen, *art. cit.* 188 = *GS* V 229. Cass. Dio, LI 4, 6 is basic evidence: see Syme, *RR* 304. On Cass. Dio, XLIX 14, 5, see Mommsen in *CIL* X p. 368, and Levi, *op. cit.* II 86. See also *PP* VIII 1953 101 f. = *Es. e Soc.* 459 f.

249. Collected in Syme, *RR* 352.

250. See U. Wilcken, 'Zu *Impensae* des *Res Gestae divi Augusti*', *SDAW* 1931, 779 f. The principle of buying land on which to settle colonists had been opposed by Cic. *de leg. agr.* II 73. On the evidence of *auct. de vir. ill.* 73, 5, see *Es. e Soc.* 110, n. 161 [= 42, n. 161 above].

251. *Res Gestae* 17 (III 35); Cass. Dio, LV 25, 2; cf. the admirable remarks of H. Last, *CAH* IX 137.

252. Syme, *RR* 352 f.; 450 f. It is in this changed atmosphere that the idyllic version of Ovid, *Amor.* II 9, 19, is to be placed and explained (*fessus in acceptos miles deducitur agros*), where it is clear how things have changed since the Triumviral period when *rudis infestis miles radiabat in armis* (Prop. IV 1, 27). The outcome of Augustan colonization is expressed as follows by Augustus himself in *Res Gestae* 28 (V 36–8): *Italia autem XXVIII colonias quae vivo me celeberrimae et frequentissimae fuerunt, meis auspiciis deductas habet.* The famous passage of Tacitus, *Ann.* XIV 27, 3, on the decline of military colonies reflects a later state of affairs when, as Tacitus himself says, military colonies in Italy came to lack any political or social purpose.

253. T. Frank, *ESAR* I 322.

254. Rostovtzeff, *SEHRE* 33: doubts and contradictions in Salvioli, *Il capitalismo antico*, 1929, 156 f.

255. Rostovtzeff, p. 33.

256. The only ones which affect the problem. On the Augustan measures of 14 BC (acquisition of provincial land) see Kornemann, *art. cit.* col. 506, and also T. R. S. Broughton, *TAPhA* LXVI 1935, 18 f.

257. See *Es. e Soc.* 120 [= 45 above].

258. Cic. *in Cat.* II 20: *Hi* (Sulla's colonists) *dum aedificant tamquam beati*, etc.

259. Cic. *ad Att.* II 16, 1; cf. Rullus' proposal (Cic. *de leg. agr.* II 78 and 79). See also the promises of Domitius Ahenobarbus in Caes. *BC* I 17, 4: 4 *iugera* of Etruscan land (i.e. if the correction *quaterna* of Glareanus, which is generally accepted for the XL of the MSS., is agreed: however, P. Fabre, *César, La Guerre Civile* (*Les Belles Lettres*), 1936, reads *quina dena*: cf. A. Klotz, *PhW* LVII 1937, col. 896).

260. *Lib. Col.* p. 214, 14 Lachmann = p. 18, 14 and 20, 1 Pais. These figures seem to be confirmed, for example, by the size of the plots at Concordia: see L. Bosio, *AIV* CXXIV 1965–6, 249 f. In general see my Commentary on Appian, *BC* V, p. LXVII.

261. Sic. Flacc. p. 156, 10 Lachmann; Hyg. *de lim constit.* p. 176, 13 Lachmann; see Caes. *loc. cit.* It may be said in passing that this reflects not only varying grades of reward but also the need, already present in an earlier age (G. Tibiletti, *Athenaeum* N.S. XXVIII 1950, 222 f.), that the governing class – in this case the centurions and *tribuni militum* who became magistrates of the new colony – should be distinguished by a higher census qualification.

262. See for Aquileia, 181 BC, Livy, XL 34, 2 and for Luna, 177 BC, Livy, XLI 13, 5.

263. Cass. Dio, LV 23, 1: 20,000 sesterces to the praetorians, 12,000 to the other soldiers; see Liebenam, *RE* s.v. 'exercitus', col. 1674.

264. Mommsen, 'Die ital. Bodentheilung u.s.w.', *Hermes* XIX 1884, 398 = *GS* V 128; Frank, *op. cit.* I 365.

265. Probably the opposite: according to E. G. Hardy, 'Augustus and his legionaries', *CQ* XIV 1920, 187 f., esp. 190 f., the 120,000 veterans mentioned in *Res Gestae*, 15 (III 19) (29 BC) were those demobilized in 30 BC, on which see *Res Gestae* 16 (III, 22); Hyg. *de lim. const.* p. 177 Lachmann and Cass. Dio, LI 4. Such settlements concern Italy. Since the measures of 14 BC (*Res Gestae*, 16 (III, 23)) concern the provinces (see *Es. e Soc.* 137 n. 256 [= 50, n. 256 above] and Hardy, p. 191) we must believe that the 600 million sesterces spent by Augustus *pro Italicis praediis* (*Res Gestae* 16 (III 24)) refer to the measures of 30 BC (Hardy, p. 192). In that case each of the 120,000 veterans had on an average land worth 5,000 sesterces, i.e. *c.* 5

iugera. In general see W. Weber, *Princeps,* I 247, n. 672. For Augustus' allocations see now P. A. Brunt, *Italian Manpower,* 332–42.

266. Cic. *Phil.* II 101.

267. *RR* 450, n. 4.

268. *CIL* XI 600, on which see E. Pais, *Studi Bonfante,* I 175 f.; G. Susini, *Atti e Mem. Deput. St. Patria Prov. Romagna* N.S. V 1953–4, 1–3 (extract).

269. *Op. cit.* 33, n. 31.

270. The whole problem results, of course, from our limited knowledge of the distribution of land in Italy in the first century BC. NB the reconstruction of J. Ruelens, *LEC* XII 1943, 28–32, is based above all on a very uncertain premiss, for the significance of the famous remark of the tribune L. Marcius Philippus in 104 BC *non esse in civitate duo milia hominum qui rem haberent* (Cic. *de Off.* II 73) is not very clear. Carcopino, *Hist. rom.* II 303, n. 163, thought that it referred only to Rome and not to all Italy (see also Salvioli, *op. cit.* 31). Some useful remarks on landed property in that period are, however, to be found in R. Scalais, *Mél. Thomas,* 618 f.

271. As is clear, for example, from Hor. *Sat.* I 6, 72–3, referring to pre-Caesarian times. The commentary of Kiessling-Heinze,[5] 1921, *ad loc.,* explains it by saying that Venusia was a Sullan military colony and that the centurions Horace mentions were veterans who had been settled there and who adopted an attitude of condescension towards the small peasant proprietors of the region (as at Pompeii, it may be added). But it is not necessarily the case that Venusia was a Sullan colony, and App. I 100, 470, cited by K.-H. is irrelevant. Hence Horace's evidence must be understood as a generalization for a situation which was common at that time. See also *CIL* I[2] 791 = *ILLRP* 502; *CIL* X 1271 = *ILLRP* 1630 (from Nola).

272. Cass. Dio, XLIX 14, 3; App. V 128, 531 (see my Commentary on Appian, *BC* V, pp. 212–13): cf. Kübler, *RE* s.v. 'decurio', col. 2325, and Syme, *RR* 243. See the examples in *CIL* IX 1604 = *ILS* 6491 (cf. *CIL* IX 1603 = *ILS* 2235 and comm. there); *CIL* X 4723 and also *CIL* V 2501 = *ILS* 2243 (Ateste). Cf. *CIL* X 5713 = *ILLRP* 498a.

273. It is in fact now that we meet colonies which have in their name the legion to which the colonized soldiers used to belong: Kornemann, *art. cit.* coll. 527–8 and 564–5; Sherwin-White, *op. cit.* 173, n. 4. Cf. App. II 120, 507. Cf. also the Caesarian colonies in Gallia Narbonensis on which J. Kromayer, *Hermes* XXXI 1896, 1–19, is fundamental. That Sulla introduced this system is stated (without any basis) by A. v. Premerstein, *Vom Werden und Wesen,* 24.

274. Cic. *Phil.* II 102; Tac. *Ann.* XIV 27; Hyg. *de lim. constit.* p. 176, 9 f. Lachmann. The inscription *ILLRP* 592 probably refers to a Triumviral colony founded at Firmum Apulum: S. Panciera, *Epigraphica* XXIV 1962, pub. 1963, 79 f.; see also the commentary of Degrassi.

275. *CIL* XI 4183a, 4184, 4187, 4189–94; Bormann, *ibid.* p. 611; Interamna Nahartium is not an Augustan colony; see, however, Pais, *Coloniz.* I 188.

Some other examples: *CIL* XI 4746; see 4650 = *ILS* 2230 (Tuder col. Iulia); *CIL* X 4876 = *ILS* 2227 (Venafrum col. Iulia Augusta: Pais, *op. cit.* 248, and Ritterling, *RE* s.v. 'legio', col. 1483); *CIL* IX 2353 = *ILS* 6513 (Allifae, Triumvirate colony: see Hülsen, *RE* s.v. col. 1586). Important also are *CIL* XI 1217 (Placentia, Triumvirate colony?: Bormann, *ibid.* p. 242; Hanslik, *RE* s.v. col. 1905); *CIL* XI 7495 (Falerii, not apparently an Augustan colony; see, however, Pais, *op. cit.* 171); *CIL* XIV 3906 = *ILS* 6544 (Amiternum); *CIL* IX 2648 = *ILS* 2228; *CIL* IX 2645 and 2674 (Aesernia); *CIL* VIII 14697 = *ILS* 2249 (Thuburnica). For *Ann. Épig.* 1937, no. 64, from Luceria, see Degrassi, *Scritti vari,* I 79–82. For *CIL* IX 1005, F. Coarelli, *DArch* I 1967, 46–71, is most important.

276. This is the view of Sherwin-White, *op. cit.* 178–9, which may be valid in certain

cases (cf. e.g. *CIL* V 50 = *ILS* 2229 and the commentary of A. Degrassi, *AIV* CII 1942–3, 664 f., 676 = *Scritti vari*, II 913 f., 921; *CIL* X 5713 = *ILS* 2226; see Ritterling, *RE* s.v. 'legio', col. 1564), especially with reference to the *lex Iulia mun.* line 89, but it should not be used to support generalizations which would go against what has been said *Es. e Soc.* 58 f. [= 24 f. above].

277. See *Es. e Soc.* 64, n. 50 [= 27, n. 50 above].

278. See *Es. e Soc.* 92 f. [= 36 f. above]. Service in the army made this possible even for those with inferior qualifications.

279. Suet. *Aug.* 46. v. Premerstein, *Vom Werden u. Wesen*, 103, n. 5, is right to observe that the privilege must apply to the magistrates of the Augustan colonies. Cf. also Syme, *RR* 364. According to J. Lesquier, 'L'armée romaine d'Égypte', *Mem. de l'Instit.fr. d'Arch. Or.* XLI 1918, 336, a clause of this kind would have been included in the edict *de veteranis* of the Triumvir Octavian (*Caesaris Aug. Opera*[3], ed. Malcovati, 55–6 = Riccobono, *Leges*[2], 316); at line 13 he would prefer to read, instead of (*ce*)*nseri*, (*ce*)*nsere*. See, however, for a different view P. Roussel, *Syria* XV 1934, 35, relying on the *epistula ad Rhosenses*, lines 25–6.

280. This conclusion, of course, rules out agreement with Syme's interpretation (*RR*) of the crisis which hit the Roman Republic in the first century BC although, as is clear from my notes, I have a lasting and enormous debt to his work. Syme's view can in fact be briefly summed up in one of his own phrases (p. 16): 'With the Gracchi all the consequences of Empire – social, economic and political – broke loose in the Roman State, inaugurating a century of revolution. The traditional contests of the noble families were complicated, but not abolished, by the strife of parties largely based on economic interest, of classes even, and of military leaders'. From the review of Syme by A. Momigliano, *JRS* XXX 1940, 75 f., esp. 77–80 = *Secondo contributo alla storia degli studi classici*, 407–16, I take this passage which pinpoints with exceptional acuteness the limitations of Syme's interpretation (p. 77): 'Two leading ideas not clearly distinguished presented themselves to the writer (Syme): the Revolution as a new oligarchy; the Revolution as the end of a *Roman* oligarchy. The latter was the right one, but the former prevailed.'

Notes to Appendix I

1. 20, 2: the *tribuni militum* κληροῦσι τὰς φυλὰς κατὰ μίαν καὶ προσκαλοῦνται τὴν ἀεὶ λαχοῦσαν. See Cato *apud* Fest. p. 268, 1 Lindsay: *Primanus tribunus apud Catonem* ⟨*est, qui primae legioni tributum scribebat . . .* ⟩, to be interpreted, of course, with Mommsen, *SR* III 194, n. 2. On the passage of Polybius see F. W. Walbank, *A Historical Commentary on Polybius*, I, Oxford 1957, 697–701.

2. Mommsen, *SR* III 279, n. 4; E. Herzog, *Geschichte und System der röm. Staatsverfassung*, I 1884, 1026; A. Bouché-Leclerq, *Manuel des Institutions romaines*, 1931, 271, n. 2.

3. Sall. *BJ* 86, 2; Livy, XXXIV 31, 17. The census minimum required for service in the legions in the time of Polybius was 4,000 asses (Polyb. VI 19, 2).

4. See the principal evidence cited in Liebenam, *RE* s.v. 'dilectus', col. 596.

5. G. Giannelli, *A & R* ser. III 3, 1935, 236–7; *La Repubblica romana*, 1944, 144–5, on which see Fraccaro, *Athenaeum* N.S. XVI 1938, 317–8.

6. Fraccaro, *Athenaeum* N.S. XII 1934, 60 = *Opuscula*, II 296–7; H. Last, *JRS* XXXV 1945, 34 and 47.

7. G. De Sanctis, *Storia dei Romani*, II 204 f.

8. See Fraccaro, *art. cit.* 1934, 60 f. = *Opuscula*, II 296–7. *Contra*, Mommsen, *SR* III 268, n. 1. V. Arangio-Ruiz, *Storia . . . romano*[6], 36 has put forward some arguments

against this theory, but they are based on arithmetical computations and can be rejected simply by referring to Fraccaro, *art. cit.* 1934, 62 f. = *Opuscula*, II 297–300, whose conclusions are accepted also by Giannelli, *art. cit.* 234.

9. L. Lange, *RA* I³ 525, and also Mommsen, *Die röm. Tribus*, Altona 1844, 132: *contra*, W. Rein, *Zeitschr. für die Alterthumswissenschaft* 1846, no. 128, col. 1021. It is curious that references still continue to be made to this work on the point under discussion even after the diffidence which Mommsen expressed in *SR* III 268, n. 2. Cf. also H. Delbrück, *Gesch. des Kriegskunst*, I³ 270.

10. J. Beloch, *RG* 270 f. See now Ernst Meyer, *Röm. Staat und Staatsgedanke*, 54.

11. I 43, 13, on which, however, see Mommsen, *SR* III 268, n. 2.

12. See also Arangio-Ruiz, *op. cit.* 36.

13. The relationship between the centuriate and the tribal organization is, on the contrary, that illustrated by Last, *art. cit.*

14. On the derivation from Calpurnius of all Dionysius' narrative dealing with the regal period see Cichorius, *RE* s.v. 'Calpurnius', no. 96, col. 1395. At IV 15, Fabius Pictor, Vennonius and Cato are, however, also mentioned. Scholars have noted the coincidence between Dion. Hal. IV 14, 1–2, and the well-known *Pap. Oxyrhyn.* XVIII no. 2088, which at line 13 says:]*exque pagis milites conquirebantur et tributum*[. The papyrus gives an excerpt of a Latin historian whom A. Piganiol, *Scritti in onore di B. Nogara*, Città del Vaticano 1937, 376, thought to be possibly Aelius Tubero. On the basis of what has been said about Dion. Hal. IV 14, Calpurnius cannot be ruled out: see Piganiol, p. 379, n. 2. As I have tried to show in *Athenaeum* N.S. XXXIX 1961, 98–121, Dion. Hal. has worked up material from different sources in the chapters of Book IV which deal with the reign of Servius Tullius. For example, the arguments in chapters 19–21 on the Servian centuriate organization (including the passage which interests us here) echo the influence of the post-Sullan annalists (pp. 107–9). But this does not conflict with the view that the material itself goes back to a fully trustworthy antiquarian source. See also P. A. Brunt, *Italian Manpower*, 625–34 (controversial).

15. It is well to keep in mind that the evidence on the holding of the levy on the Campus Martius (Varro, *de re rust.* III 2, 4; Livy, III 69, 6; Cass. Dio, XXX–XXXV fr. 109, 5 Boiss.; see the important note *ad loc.* of Valesius, in Reimar's edition, I, Hamburg 1750, p. 54, § 188) – in the time of Polybius it took place on the Capitol: VI 19, 6; Livy, XXVI 31, 11 – is not so much a testimony to the use of a levy by centuries (Bouché-Leclerq, *op. cit.* 271, n. 2) as a reference to a custom later than Polybius. See Marquardt, *Organis. milit.* 81, n. 4 and the proper observations of Veith in Kromayer-Veith, *Heerwesen und Kriegführung*, 304.

16. On which see in general Mommsen, *SR* I³ 152, n. 2; *id. Strafrecht*, 44, n. 1.

17. This last point is rejected by Mommsen, *Röm. Tribus*, 133, but is, however, confirmed by comparison with App. *Iber.* 49, 209.

18. In Daremberg-Saglio, *Dict. d. Antiq.* s.v. 'dilectus', 214.

19. *Ibid.* p. 213 and n. 22.

20. E. Bolisani, *Varrone Menippeo*, Padua 1936, 111.

21. *Op. cit.* 82 f.; see Bouché-Leclerq, *op. cit.* 273, n. 4.

22. Livy, IV 46, 1 says: *dilectum haberi non ex toto passim populo placuit: decem tribus sorte ductae sunt.* It is worth remarking that the antiquity of the event deprives the evidence of credibility. Also, the episode (the war against Labici) is connected with numerous members of the *gens Servilia*; this has led some to suspect that the story has been contaminated by falsifications and that these are the work of the Servilii who were especially powerful in the last years of the Second Punic War and immediately after it (W. Soltau, *Die Anfänge der röm. Geschichtsschreibung*, Leipzig 1909, 144; Münzer, *RE* s.v. 'Servilius', no. 37, col. 1775. See also M. L. Patterson,

TAPhA LXXIII 1942, 337 f.). Cf. the observations of B. G. Niebuhr, *RG* (Fr. trans. De Golbery, IV 1835, 165, n. 250) and of E. Pais, *Storia di Roma*[3], III 70, n. 1.

23. Mommsen, *SR* III 271: De Sanctis, *op. cit.* II 207; III 1, 337; Arangio-Ruiz, *op. cit.* 84, who admitted the possibility (only as an hypothesis) that originally the centuries had been levy-districts.

24. Polyb. VI 20, 8–9: ὅταν δ' ἐκλέξωσι τὸ προκείμενον πλῆθος (τῶν πεζῶν). . . . μετὰ ταῦτα τοὺς ἱππεῖς τὸ μὲν παλαιὸν ὑστέρους εἰώθεσαν δοκιμάζειν ἐπὶ τοῖς τετρακισχιλίοις διακοσίοις, νῦν δὲ προτέρους, πλουτίνδην αὐτῶν γεγενημένης ὑπὸ τοῦ τιμητοῦ τῆς ἐκλογῆς. See Mommsen, *SR* III 258 and 479–80; Cagnat in Daremberg-Saglio, *Dict. d. Antiq.* s.v. 'Equites', 774 f.; and now see also J. Wiesner, *Klio* XXXVI 1943, 56; C. Nicolet, *L'ordre équestre à l'époque républicaine*, I, Paris 1966, 47 f.

25. This is how πλουτίνδην αὐτῶν γεγενημένης ὑπὸ τοῦ τιμητοῦ τῆς ἐκλογῆς in Polybius must be understood: see Herzog, *op. cit.* I 1046 and n. 1.

26. Mommsen, *SR* III 258 and 259, n. 1.

27. See Mommsen, *SR* III 478, n. 2.

28. Ernst Meyer, *op. cit.* 85 f.; 436, n. 91.

29. On all this cf. G. Tibiletti, *Athenaeum* N.S. XXVIII 1950, 222 f.

30. Asc. *in Pis.* p. 12 Stangl.

Notes to Appendix II

1. Cic. *de leg. agr.* II 89; 92; 98.
2. II 92.
3. Münzer, *RE* s.v. 'Iunius', no. 52; Drumann-Groebe, *Gesch. Roms*, IV 18; *contra*, A. W. Zumpt, *Comment. Epigr.* I 245.
4. Cic. *pro Quinctio*, 65; 69; some uncertainty in Last, *CAH* IX 271.
5. Münzer, *loc. cit.*; see also M. A. Levi, *A & R* N.S. III 1922, 249.
6. J. Carcopino, *Hist. rom.* II 434.
7. As, however, Beloch, *Campanien*[2], Breslau 1890, 305, asserts. See F. Castagnoli, *BCAR* LXXII 1951, append. 15, 51. Colonists would become local tenants, as later they did with Caesar (Levi, *art. cit.* 251).
8. A. N. Sherwin-White, *Roman Citizenship*, 83.
9. G. Bloch, *La république romaine*, 1913, 307. On the *rogatio* of Rullus see Gabba, *Mélanges Piganiol*, Paris 1966, 769–75 = *Es. e Soc.* 449 f.
10. II 87–98; see I 18–22.
11. The only scholar I know to have accepted, without discussion, the statement of Cicero is C. Lanzani, *Mario e Silla*, Catania 1915, 390 f. On Capua in the period between the Hannibalic and the Social Wars see J. Heurgon, *MEFR* LVI 1939, 5–27 and M. W. Frederiksen, *PBSR* XXVII 1959, 80 f.
12. M. Pohlenz, *Die Stoa*, Göttingen 1948, I 205.
13. See J. Carcopino, *BAGB* XXII Jan. 1929, 15, n. 11.
14. Recorded in App. I 60, 271, and Cic. *Brut.* 168; the latter evidence escaped the notice of Pais, *AAN* N.S. IV 1916, 67–72, hence his failure to consider Rubrius.

This attempt of mine to show Marian connexions in Campania met with hostile criticism from E. Badian, 'Caepio and Norbanus', *Historia* VI 1957, 344–6; his article has been re-published, with corrections, in *Studies in Greek and Roman History* (59–62 contain the appendix dedicated to my study). To sum up, Badian recognizes the two Insteii and the two Fimbriae as of Campanian origin, is unable to deny the possibility of Campanian extraction for the two Granii and the two Magii, and cannot accept the other cases. See, however, T. P. Wiseman, *New Men in the Roman Senate, 139 BC–14 AD*, 234 (Ti. Gutta); 256–7 (Q. Rubrius Varro, perhaps connected with Casinum).

15. See Münzer, *RE* s.v. 'Granius', no. 4.
16. Münzer, *RE* s.v. 'Granius', no. 1, and R. Syme, *RR* 90, n. 7; 91, n. 1.
17. Münzer, *RE* s.v. 'Rubrius', no. 24.
18. Münzer, *RE* s.v. 'Rubrius', no. 2; that these Rubrii are Campanian can, I think, be deduced from the presence of other Rubrii at Capua in that period: *CIL* I² 679 = X 3780 = *ILS* 3341 = *ILLRP* 716; see Münzer, *RE* s.v. 'Rubrius', no. 14; *CIL* I² 686 = X 3783 = *ILS* 6303 = *ILLRP* 722.
19. Münzer, *RE* s.v. no. 9; his Campanian origin – the name is Etruscan: Schulze, *Zur Geschichte lateinischer Eigennamen*, 1904, 187 – can perhaps be deduced from the presence of Cn. Laetorius, *magister pagi*, in Capua in 94 BC: *CIL* I² 682 = X 3772 = *ILS* 6302 = *ILLRP* 719; Münzer, *RE* s.v. no. 6. A C. Laetorius C. f. Vel. appears in the *consilium* of Asculum in 90 BC: cf. Münzer, *RE* s.v. no. 4.
20. Münzer, *RE* s.v. no. 10. I do not know whether the attested support of Campanians for C. Gracchus (e.g. Blossius and, probably, Rubrius and Laetorius whom I have mentioned) entitles us to suppose that he conceived a purpose similar to that of Brutus for the colony at Capua which he appears to have planned (Plut. *C. Gracc.* 8, 3; *auct. de vir. ill.* 65, 3; see Greenidge, *Hist. of Rome*, 225).
21. On the Iunii in the Marian period see Münzer, *RE*, s.v. no. 1, col. 961. Cf. especially L. Iunius Brutus Damasippus, praetor 82 BC; Münzer, *RE* s.v. no. 58.
22. See Münzer, *RE* s.v. col. 438.
23. G. Niccolini, *Fasti dei tribuni della plebe*, Milan 1934, 232 f.; see Münzer, *RE* s.v. nos. 8 and 10.
24. Münzer, *RE* s.v. no. 6. Cf. the participation of Blossius in the revolt of Aristonicus: Dudley, *art. cit. JRS* XXXI 1941, 98–9.
25. App. I 90, 416; see Münzer, *RE* s.v.
26. Münzer, *RE* s.v. 'Insteius', nos. 1 and 2; see C. Cichorius, *Röm. Studien*, 167. C. Tarquitius L. f. Fal. is generally held to be Etruscan, despite the tribe: see Pais, *Dalle guerre puniche*, I 194; Cichorius, *op. cit.* 167.
27. Cf. Münzer, *RE* s.v. 'Helvius', no. 15. I do not know whether one may use the presence at Cales in the Imperial period of a Flavius Fimbria (*CIL* X 4649 = *ILS* 6299; see 5922 in Anagnia) to attest Campanian origins for the well-known Flavii Fimbriae, democrats in the Marian period (see Syme, *op. cit.* 94, n. 2). Likewise, it is unknown whether L. Flavius Fimbria, *cos. suff.* in AD 71 (*PIR* II¹, 1897, 68, no. 182 = *PIR*² F 269; see F 188; Münzer, *RE* s.v. 'Flavius', no. 89) is to be connected with the Flavii of Cales and with the Republican democrats of the same name.
28. Cic. *de leg. agr.* II 94.
29. On the structure of agriculture in Etruria, Umbria and Picenum, where a system of *latifundia* and tenants prevailed, and in Apulia, Samnium and Latium (dominated by pasturage) cf. M. Rostovtzeff, *SEHRE* 30. On Campanian conditions, on the other hand, where enterprises were administered on a capitalistic and industrialized basis, see *ibid.* p. 30. On the importance of all this for the Social War see A. Bernardi, *NRS* XXVIII–XXIX 1944–5, 67–8; *contra*, J. Carcopino, *BAGB cit.* 21 and 22 with n. 1.
30. See R. Syme, *JRS* XXXIV 1944, 93 f. Cossutii are attested at Puteoli: see Ch. Dubois, 'Pouzzoles antique' (*Bibl. Éc. franç. d'Athènes et de Rome* XCVIII), 1907, 47 (though he emphasizes the rarity of the name in Campania).
31. Dubois, *op. cit.* 71 f.; T. Frank, *ESAR* I 375–6; Rostovtzeff, p. 17, n. 12.
32. Marius' relations with the businessmen in the provinces confirm this conclusion; though we have only scanty references, they are not the less suggestive for that. Pliny *NH* XXXVI 15 (24), 116: *unde M. Scaurus pater, totiens princeps civitatis et*

Mariani sodalicii rapinarum provincialium sinus? (on which see A. Passerini, *Athenaeum* N.S. XII 1934, 280. For the correction *Magiani* see Fraccaro, *RAL* V 20, 1911, 187 = *Opuscula*, II 139–40, and Pais, *Dalle guerre puniche*, I 114) and, above all, the dedication to Marius, on the occasion of his visit to the East, in the agora at Delos (*CIL* III 7241: see Passerini, *Athenaeum* N.S. XVII 1939, 69–73), by 'the Italians who were in Alexandria'; the inscription, however (*ILLRP* 343) has to be supplemented for the name of the beneficiary. It is useless to emphasize Marius' unbroken relationship with the class of Equites from which he came: see the observations of G. De Sanctis, *RFIC* LXIII 1935, 12, and for a particular case *id. Problemi di Storia antica*, 1932, 212–3. On the problem see *Es. e Soc.* 219 f. [= 78 f. below].

33. An example of exaggeration would be the polemic directed against the title of *praetores* assumed by the two magistrates of the colony, Sex. Saltius and L. Considius (or Consius, the reading of Mommsen, *CIL* X p. 368, following the *cod. Erfurtensis*); cf. Sherwin-White, *op. cit.* 83.

34. Cf. Val. Max. IX 3, 8 and Plut. *Sulla*, 37, 3, on the disagreements of Sulla with the Granii of Puteoli, on which see Dubois, *op. cit.* 27 f. That Puteoli had favoured Sulla's cause is asserted without any basis in fact by Pais, *AAN* XXI 1900–1, 150. On the democratic tendencies of Naples see Pais, *op. cit.* 148. For Pompeii see Cic. *pro Sulla*, 21. Appropriately enough (and highly significantly) the one colony founded by Sulla *ex novo* was established at Urbana, on the borders of the *ager Campanus* (but outside it: Mommsen, *CIL* X p. 460: cf. p. 368. See also M. A. Levi, *AAT* LVII 1921–2, 604 f.), not far from Capua (Pliny, *NH* XIV 6 (8), 62; see *CIL* X 4697, Cales: to that colony refers the evidence of *Lib. col.* p. 231, 19 Lachmann; cf. p. 232, 8). This example is doubly interesting, in so far as it shows a clear intention to keep a neighbouring eye on a district which was notoriously recalcitrant (for a comparable case, at least in part – Aleria and Mariana in Corsica – see *Athenaeum* N.S. XXIX 1951, 20) without going so far as to settle veterans on the *ager Campanus* proper (in this sense Cic. *de leg. agr.* II 81); this is a pointer to be considered in conjunction with others mentioned elsewhere that Sullan colonization worked in a way which was less disastrous than the tradition indicates.

Notes to Appendix III

1. The problems concerning the Sullan senate are dealt with elsewhere, *Es. e Soc.* 407 f. [= 142 f. below]. I shall not, therefore, repeat here the more recent bibliography on the problem; I confine myself to the observation that C. Nicolet, *L'ordre équestre à l'époque républicaine*, I Paris 1966, 581 f., has provided a list of Sullan senators who are relevant to the problem of the Equites, and that T. P. Wiseman, *New Men in the Roman Senate, 139 BC–14 AD*, provides at 209 f. a list of senators who were *homines novi*: when the case arises I refer to these two works in my own list.

2. H. Hill, 'Sulla's New Senators in 81 BC', *CQ* XXVI 1932, 170 and nn. 5–12.

3. *Art. cit.* 173.

4. Hill, p. 173, n. 1, adduces as examples the cases of L. Cornelius Sisenna and D. Iunius Brutus, who in fact do not appear to be relevant to his argument; as Hill acknowledges at p. 175, we do not know their career prior to 81 BC, but this should not lead us to believe that they entered on it only after 81 BC. If L. Cornelius Sisenna, praetor in 78, is – as I too think he should be – counted among the Sullan senators, D. Iunius Brutus, cos. 77, must certainly be excluded since it is impossible that he was not in the Senate before 81 BC.

5. See P. Willems, *Le Sénat de la république romaine*, I² 232 f.

6. Hence men like P. Cornelius Lentulus Sura are also to be excluded (Willems, *op. cit.* I² 419; *RE* s.v. no. 240; Hill, p. 174). A. Manlius (*RE* s.v. no. 13 = 76, col. 1195; Hill, p. 175, n. 5) and C. (or L.) Valerius Triarius (Willems, p. 455, n. 5; Hill, p. 175, n. 5) were quaestors actually in 81.
7. See P. Fraccaro, 'I *decem stipendia* e le *leges annales* repubblicane', in *Per il XIV Centenario . . . Giustiniano*, Pavia 1934, 493 f., esp. 494, 500, 503 = *Opuscula*, II 207 f. See also J. Carcopino, *Mélanges Bidez*, I 65.
8. And Hill himself emphasizes it, p. 174.
9. Hill, p. 174, n. 3.
10. *RE* s.v. 'Licinius', no. 104.
11. Hill, pp. 174–5: members of senatorial families.
12. In passing it should be stated categorically that the man present at the trial of Roscius as defence counsel for the accused was not this M. Metellus (Hill, p. 174; *RE* s.v. 'Caecilius', no. 78) but a Q. Metellus, as some of the MSS. say and as Carcopino, *Sylla*, 165–6, has shown; in any case, this episode can lend no support to Hill's assumption.
13. Hill, p. 175, n. 5.
14. *RE* s.v. no. 55.
15. P. 173 and n. 2.
16. Cic. I *Verr.* 30; Schol. Gron. p. 337, 28 Stangl.
17. Willems, *op. cit.* I² 504 f.; *RE* s.v. no. 15.
18. Hill, p. 176.
19. Cic. *Brut.* 179.
20. App. IV 25, 162; Syme, *PBSR* XIV 1938, 23, n. 116, held that he was a Sullan senator of 88 BC; however, on App. I 59, 267, see E. G. Hardy, *JRS* VI 1916, 59–61. But see Syme, *RR* 88 and n. 2.
21. *PBSR* XIV 1938, 1 f., esp. 22; *id. JRS* XXVII 1937, 127; *id. RR* 78 f.
22. See Oros. V 22, 4; Eutr. V 9, 2.
23. Mommsen, *SR* III 847; M. Gelzer, *Caesar . . . Staatsmann*³, 38, holds that the post-Sullan senate comprised only 450 members; *contra* (rightly) R. Syme, *JRS* XXXIV 1944, 102 (as he says *inter alia*, the number of sixty-four senators expelled in 70 BC presupposes a far higher total).
24. As Appian says, I 100, 468. On the method see Mommsen, *SR* III 189, n. 2; E. G. Hardy, *JRS* VI 1916, 59 f. and Hill, p. 177.
25. On all this see the extensive discussion in Willems, I² 404 f.
26. We cannot, however, accept the hypothesis of Hill on the eighteen centuries. Syme, *PBSR* XIV 1938, 22, denied any such possibility long ago.
27. Carcopino, *Sylla*, 65, n. 2, anticipated by Herzog, *Geschichte und System*, I 513.
28. W. Schur, *Das Zeitalter cit.* 194 f.
29. See, for example, nos. 3, 7, 14, 30, 45, 61, 65, 80, 82, 83, 85, 89, 94, 95, 97, 98, 102.
30. *Op. cit.* I² 411 f.
31. Hill, p. 171.
32. See Syme, *RR* 66.
33. See L. R. Taylor, *TAPhA* LXXIII 1942, 12, n. 23.
34. *Sylla*, 65; *id. Hist. rom.* II 455; see A. Passerini, *Athenaeum* N.S. X 1932, 181.

Notes to III

* *Athenaeum* N.S. XXXII 1954, 41–114: 293–345. The first part of this work, devoted to the origins of the Social War, has not in general met with a great deal of support: both J. P. V. D. Balsdon, *Gnomon* XXVI 1954, 343–4, and A. N. Sherwin-White,

JRS XLV 1955, 168–70, have emphatically denied that there is any good evidence for the commercial class playing an important part in Italian upper-class determination to obtain the Roman citizenship by force. The principal exception in my favour has been E. T. Salmon, 'The Cause of the Social War', *Phoenix* XVI 1962, 107–19. Those who criticize my views subscribe, on a more general level, to an interpretation of Roman history from the mid-second century BC to Sulla which denies, or minimizes as far as possible, any connexion between Roman expansionism and 'economic' prime causes; this school also claims that one cannot explain the political conflict between the Senate and the equestrian class in the Gracchan and post-Gracchan period in terms of economic interests and trading differences. The principal exponents of this view are E. Badian, first in *Foreign Clientelae, 264–70 BC*, Oxford 1958, and then especially in *Roman Imperialism in the Late Republic²*, Oxford 1968, and P. A. Brunt, 'The Equites in the late Republic', Deuxième Conférence Int. d'Histoire Économique, 1962, I, Paris 1965, 117–49, and *id. Italian Manpower, 225 BC–AD 14*, Oxford 1971, *passim*. This school has favoured reconstructions of Roman politics of the second and first centuries BC that make far too much of factional struggles to the exclusion of everything else so that they fail to encompass the major political themes; it reacts, probably not without reason, against interpretations which sometimes are cast in excessively modern terms and against a conception of the conflict between Senate and Knights which is too schematic. However, in its own turn – at least in my view – it goes too far; I have tried in my article in *Aufstieg und Niedergang der römischen Welt*, I, Berlin–New York 1972, (esp. 772 f.) to establish some points on the economic and commercial factors at work in Roman imperialism from the mid-second century BC. However, to return to the problem of the causes of the Social War, I would urge two points. First, in trying to develop a point of Hatzfeld's and to connect the extremely urgent demand of the allies to acquire the Roman citizenship with the fact that they had recently become aware of their real position and rights, and that they had had this experience thanks to the Italian commercial class, it was not my purpose in fact to narrow down to this single topic (however important it may be) the causes of the war; these were complex and varied from people to people, and represented the reasons why the Italian allies at a certain moment of time counted it absolutely necessary to unleash a war to obtain the Roman citizenship. Secondly, it was my object to call attention to the profound change in ideals, interests, attitudes and demands which overtook the Italian allies between the Gracchan period and 91 BC. I tried to explain how and why the allies first demanded a share in government and in the enjoyment of the Empire and, as a means to reach that end, demanded the Roman citizenship so that they could directly intervene in Roman politics. In this broad context I tried to evaluate the commercial experience overseas of large sections of the Italian upper classes. It is clear that the demand for the citizenship was particular to the upper classes, the *principes Italicorum populorum*; it is generally admitted nowadays that the Italian commercial class was, in its native districts, wholly at one with the governing class, given that the wealth it acquired in trade was normally invested in land (*Aufstieg und Niedergang*, I 786 f.). There is no doubt that the Cimbric War must have accelerated a unanimity of sentiment between Romans and Italians; this had been growing in the course of the second century BC and was accompanied by a certain levelling of political and juridical institutions (emphasized afresh by P. A. Brunt, 'Italian Aims at the time of the Social War', *JRS* LV 1965, 90–109; he agrees with me in recognizing that the demands of the allies were politically inspired but does not accept the reasons I have proposed). However, I repeat my suggestion that a large part must have been played in the final stages of this process and above all in the change which took place in the allies' attitude after the Gracchi – and the Gracchi themselves were largely responsible – by the extraordinary development of Italian commercial expansion in the provinces. The following is a list of abbreviations used in the course of this paper:

Broughton, I and II = T. R. S. Broughton, *The Magistrates of the Roman Republic*, I (509 BC–100 BC) 1951; II (99 BC–31 BC) 1952.

Carcopino[3] = G. Bloch–J. Carcopino, *Des Gracques à Sulla[3]*, 1952 (*Histoire Romaine*, II, I in G. Glotz, *Histoire générale*).

FHA, III–VI = *Fontes Hispaniae Antiquae*, III 1935; IV 1937; V 1940; VI 1952.

Grueber, I–III = H. A. Grueber, *Coins of the Roman Republic in the British Museum*, I–III, London 1910.

Hatzfeld, *Trafiquants* = J. Hatzfeld, *Les Trafiquants Italiens dans l'Orient Hellénique* (*Bibl. Éc. franç. d'Athènes et de Rome* CXV) Paris 1919.

Hill, *Middle Class* = H. Hill, *The Roman Middle Class in the Republican Period*, Oxford 1952.

Magie, I and II = D. Magie, *Roman Rule in Asia Minor to the end of the Third Century after Christ*, I–II, Princeton 1950.

Rostovtzeff = M. Rostovtzeff, *The Social and Economic History of the Roman Empire[2]*, ed. Fraser, I–II 1957.

Schulze, LE = W. Schulze, *Zur Geschichte lateinischer Eigennamen*, *Abhand. k. Gesellschaft der Wiss. ʒu Göttingen, Phil.-hist. Klasse*, N.F. V 2, 1904.

Syme = R. Syme, *The Roman Revolution*, Oxford 1939.

App. is used to indicate Appian's *De bellis civilibus*. I cite this work in accordance with the division into chapters and paragraphs used in the Teubner second edition of L. Mendelssohn revised by P. Viereck, 1905.

1. The ancient evidence and modern views are set out by A. Bernardi, 'La Guerra Sociale e la lotta dei partiti in Roma', *NRS* XXVIII–XXIX 1944–5, 62, n. 1; cf. 62–79.

2. The fact that there were exceptions (emphasized by Bernardi, *art. cit.* 60–1) cannot undermine the general validity of this statement.

3. Cic. *de Off.* II 75: *tantum Italicum bellum propter iudiciorum metum excitatum* (Bernardi, *art. cit.* 79 f.). On the general drift of this part of the *de Officiis* see *Es. e Soc.* 77 f. [= 30 f. above].

4. This is the theme of the article by A. Bernardi cited above.

5. See below, Chap. V. The reply by the Senatorial class is given in Plin. *NH* XXV 5 (21), 52: *Drusum . . . cui . . . optimates vero bellum Marsicum imputavere*. In Diod. XXXVII 2, 1–2, it is said that αἰτίαν . . . πρώτην. . . . τοῦ πολέμου was the corruption of Roman manners which had led to division within the citizen body (the theme is well-known and is to be traced to the Scipionic circle). But note that the connexion between the Social War and Roman domestic politics which comes later does not seem to originate with the oligarchs, in so far as the Senate is presented in Diodorus as the body which would have promised the Italians the citizenship in exchange for their aid. Even here, however, there is an echo of the theme emphasized in Cicero.

6. Val. Max. IX 5, 1: *M. Fulvius Flaccus consul, M. Plautii Hypsaei collega, cum perniciosissimas rei publicae leges introduceret de civitate danda et de provocatione ad populum eorum, qui civitatem mutare noluissent* etc. Cf. J. Göhler, *Rom und Italien* (*Breslauer Historische Forschungen*, XIII), 1939, 132–5.

7. *Lex repet.* § 78 and the Tarentine fragment published by R. Bartoccini, *Epigraphica* IX 1947, 3 f., esp. 22 (see also A. Piganiol, *CRAI* 1951, 59). In general see Göhler,

p. 159; A. Bernardi, 'Ius Ariminensium', *Studia Ghisleriana* I 9 (Pavia 1948), 257; G. Vitucci, in De Ruggiero, *Diz. Epig.* s.v. 'Latium', 442. It is probable that the *lex Servilia Glauciae* (100 BC) restricted this privilege to Latins alone (Cic. *pro Balbo*, 54).

8. Cf. H. Last, *CAH* IX 46 f.

9. App. I 34, 152: Flavius Flaccus ἠρέθιζε τοὺς Ἰταλιώτας ἐπιθυμεῖν τῆς Ῥωμαίων πολιτείας ὡς κοινωνοὺς τῆς ἡγεμονίας ἀντὶ ὑπηκόων ἐσομένους.

10. Last, *loc. cit.*; see also Ch. Wirszubski, *Libertas as a Political Idea at Rome*, Cambridge 1950, 68 f.

11. *Prima facie* there is a difficulty here in the fact that the Latin colony of Fregellae revolted after the defeat of Flaccus' proposal (Plut. *C. Gracc.* 3, 1; *auct. de vir. ill.* 65, 2 mentions Asculum as well as Fregellae, but there is certainly confusion here with the famous episode post-91 BC: see however L. Pareti, *Storia di Roma e del mondo romano*, III 351); it could prove that there was an interest in acquiring the Roman citizenship which went beyond the context of agrarian issues that cropped up from time to time. It is not easy to explain this event, but it does look like nothing more than an isolated phenomenon. Carcopino's explanation, 'Les lois agraires des Gracques et la guerre sociale', *BAGB* XXII Jan. 1929, 12 (see Carcopino[3], 247) is acceptable in general even by those who do not adopt the celebrated French historian's views on the censuses of that period (cf. Fraccaro, in *Scritti in onore di C. Ferrini pubblicati in occasione della sua beatificazione*, I 1947, 262 f. = *Opuscula*, II 87 f.). The special feature of the situation at Fregellae arises from Livy's evidence for 177 BC of the immigration to that town of 4,000 families from the Paeligni and Samnite populations; they came hoping to acquire the benefits connected with the *ius Latii* (Livy, XLI 8, 8; G. Tibiletti, *Athenaeum* N.S. XXVIII 1950, 204 and notes). It is possible that these groups of immigrants, who certainly grew in number between 177 and 125 BC, had seen their expectations disappointed of having their position regularized and had organized the revolt. In fact the attitude of the wealthy people of Latin origin there seems to stem from the so-called treachery of Q. Numitorius Pullus (Cic. *de Fin.* V 62 and *Phil.* III 17).

12. Cic. *pro Balbo*, 21; cf. E. Ciaceri, *Storia della Magna Graecia*, III, Milan 1932, 214.

13. Ciaceri, p. 20 (Naples); Cic. *pro Balbo*, 50 (Heraclea).

14. App. I 34, 152 (quoted *Es. e Soc.* 198, n. 9 [= 71, n. 9 above]. See also I 35, 155: τούτου γὰρ δὴ μάλιστα ἐπεθύμουν ὡς ἑνὶ τῷδε αὐτίκα ἡγεμόνες ἀντὶ ὑπηκόων ἐσόμενοι.

15. *Contra*, A. N. Sherwin-White, *The Roman Citizenship*, Oxford 1939, 126 and 129. For Just. XXXVIII 4, 13, see 'Italia e Roma nella 'Storia' di Velleio Patercolo', *CS* I 1962, 7 = *Es. e Soc.* 357.

16. Οἱ Ἰταλιῶται. . . . περὶ τῷ νόμῳ τῆς ἀποικίας ἐδεδοίκεσαν.

17. See D. Kontchalovsky, *RH* CLIII 1926, 177–8; Göhler, *op. cit.* 81.

18. *Art. cit.* 86, n. 3. See, however, Thomsen, 'Das Jahr 91 v. Chr. und seine Voraussetzungen', *C & M* V 1942, 17.

19. Flor, II 5, 6: *exstat vox ipsius* (i.e. Drusus') *nihil se ad largitionem ulli reliquisse, nisi si quis aut caenum dividere vellet aut caelum.* Cf. *auct. de vir. ill.* 66, 5.

20. App. I 36, 163, says: Τυῤῥηνοί τε καὶ Ὀμβρικοὶ ταὐτὰ δειμαίνοντες τοῖς Ἰταλιώταις καί, ὡς ἐδόκει, πρὸς τῶν ὑπάτων ἐς τὴν πόλιν ἐπαχθέντες ἔργῳ μὲν ἐς ἀναίρεσιν Δρούσου, λόγῳ δ' ἐς κατηγορίαν, τοῦ νόμου φανερῶς κατεβόων καὶ τὴν τῆς δοκιμασίας ἡμέραν ἀνέμενον. Cf. Bernardi, *art. cit.* 95 and notes 1 and 3.

21. Carcopino[3], pp. 365–6.

22. Carcopino, *BAGB art. cit.* 3 f.; Carcopino[3], 377 f.

23. Carcopino, *BAGB art. cit.* 16.

24. Cf. E. Pais, *Storia della colonizzazione di Roma antica*, I 1923, 20, 22, 28.

25. Cf. also L. Piotrowicz, *Klio* XXIII 1930, 334 f.

26. See also J. Haug, 'Der römische Bundesgenossenkrieg 91–88 v. Chr. bei Titus Livius', *Würzburger Jahrbücher für die Altertumswissenschaft* II 1947, 132, n. 1.

27. See also C. Lanzani, *RFIC* XL 1912, 279. See my Commentary[2] on Appian, *BC* I, Florence 1967, p. 121 f.

28. Haug, *art. cit.* 132.

29. Carcopino[3], p. 368, n. 52; cf. G. Rotondi, *Leges publicae populi Romani*, Milan 1912, 336. The reference is not to the agrarian law or the judiciary law as J. L. Strachan-Davidson, *Appian, Civil Wars: Book I*, Oxford 1902, *ad. loc.* p. 41, seems to believe. For my refutation of Badian's explanation (*FC* 219, followed by Brunt, *JRS* LV 1965, 94 and by E. J. Weinrib, *Historia* XIX 1970, 442) that Appian is referring to the senatorial inquiry into the validity of Drusus' law see *RFIC* N.S. XXXVII 1959, 196 and *Aufstieg und Niedergang*, I 787–9.

30. Cf. L. Lange, *Röm. Alterth.* III[2] 102.

31. Diod. XXXVII 10, 3: ὅτι ὁ Δροῦσος, τῆς συγκλήτου τοὺς νόμους αὐτοῦ ἀκυρούσης, ἔφη ἑαυτὸν ἐξουσίαν ἔχοντα πᾶσαν τῶν νόμων δυνάμενόν τε ἑαυτὸν κωλῦσαι δόγματα γράφειν, τοῦτο μὲν ἑκουσίως μὴ ποιήσειν, καλῶς εἰδότα τοὺς ἐξαμαρτήσαντας ταχὺ τευξομένους τῆς προσηκούσης δίκης κ.τ.λ. Cf. Last, *CAH* IX 183 and Carcopino[3], p. 371.

32. Carcopino[3], p. 365.

33. Cf. the remarks of the consul L. Marcius Philippus in Cic. *de Orat.* III 1, 2.

34. So Bernardi, *art. cit.* 90 f.

35. App. I 36, 163 (cited above) is explicit and leaves no doubt.

36. This difference of attitude to the problem is the only opposition that appears in App. I 36, 163, between the majority of the Ἰταλιῶται on the one hand and the Etruscans and Umbrians on the other. Appian, as is clear from the text, knows very well that the Etruscans and Umbrians are also Ἰταλιῶται (cf. the Commentary of Strachan-Davidson, 38); Kontchalovsky, *art. cit.* 178 and H. White, *Appian's Roman History*, III 73, n. 1 (Loeb Classical Library ed.) are in error. Thomsen, *art. cit.* 39 f. makes a shrewd appraisal of two strands of different political attitudes found among the Italians. He concludes that, since socially and economically the allies were certainly in a similar position to that of Roman citizens, the two views must be the outcome of different attitudes of different social classes: the proletariat favoured the comprehensive scheme of reform put forward by Drusus, the capitalists were opposed since the acquisition of the *ius civitatis* would have provided poor compensation for the economic loss which the agrarian law would have inflicted. In my view this theory (already advanced in part by Mommsen) is absolutely to be rejected; Thomsen does not take into account the particular local origins of the opposition to Drusus and above all does not consider the attitude of the upper classes in those districts which rebelled (see following chapter). For the Umbrians see also G. Devoto, *Gli antichi Italici*[2], 1951, 335. Of course, what I have said here shows that I do not accept the fundamental claim that the agrarian and citizenship questions in 91 BC were inter-connected, except as a matter of chance of the times. I have dealt with the problem of the Etruscans' and Umbrians' opposition to Drusus in *Aufstieg und Niedergang*, I 788–9.

37. Cf. C. Cichorius, *Röm. Studien*, Leipzig 1922, 116 f. The *lex Saufeia* of *CIL* I[2] *Elogia* XXX = *Inscr. Ital.* XIII 3, 74, was also repealed or shelved.

38. Similar reasoning in L. Pareti, III 531.

39. On these facts, for which cf. Livy, *Per.* LXXIV and Oros. V 18, 17, see Piotrowicz, *art. cit.*; Gabba, *Aufstieg und Niedergang*, I 789; W. V. Harris, *Rome in Etruria and Umbria*, Oxford 1971, 202 f.

40. See Bernardi, *art. cit.* 81 f.

41. See the evidence and discussion in Bernardi, *art. cit.* 92 and notes. Since my particular interest is in trying to clarify the allies' attitude on the citizenship question, I

have purposely refrained from going into detail on the more general problem of Drusus' tribunate and of his guiding principles, a problem which goes back in the last analysis to the different interpretations in the sources of Drusus' activity (Last, *CAH* IX 178; Thomsen, *art. cit.* 14 f.). Even here, as we shall see later in the case of Sertorius, the difference lies not in the facts but in the colouring with which for political reasons the facts themselves are presented. If I have emphasized many times the high quality of Appian's account, this is the result not so much of the fact that I regard it *per se* as more credible but that it seems to me less influenced by immediate political considerations than is the case with the Livian tradition or the Ciceronian evidence (the treatment of Drusus' tribunate in the Livian tradition and in Cicero depends to a great extent on the authors' political sympathies: this is particularly well brought out, of course, by J. Haug, 'Der röm. Bundesgenossenkrieg', *art. cit.* 106; 113; 120 *et passim*, and this detailed piece of research makes any further analysis of the historical tradition on the Social War unprofitable). Of course, I am fully aware that the different standpoint of Appian's account of Drusus' tribunate is partly due to the fact that Book I occupies the position it does in the general scheme of Appian's work (in this sense R. Thomsen, 'Das Jahr 91 v. Chr.', *art. cit.* 14 f.). However, this fact – which involves an undeniable risk that particular historical events have been distorted – has enabled us to get from Appian's source a clear picture of the perspective and the problems which alone can explain the origin of the Roman Revolution. We must, I think, prefer Appian's account for the following reason (and it is equally valid for the period after the Social War), that the citizenship question which he emphasizes was really the most important theme of Drusus' tribunate and indeed the most important factor in contemporary politics. As a result, in my view, there can be no question of placing any reliance on what has become a basic feature in contemporary accounts (Carcopino, Last, Thomsen, Bernardi), namely that in 91 BC the agrarian and citizenship questions were interconnected. This means that we must reject the connexion (at least as seen by Bernardi: cause and effect) between internal politics – composition of the courts in the *quaestio de repetundis* – and the allies' demand for the citizenship, although this is the impression given by all the sources except Appian. I have dealt with the significance of Appian's account of Drusus' tribunate in *Appiano e la Storia delle Guerre Civili*, Florence 1956, 13 f.

How can one explain, if there was no deeply-felt demand to participate in Roman public life, the fact that the *principes Italicorum* sought with every means at their disposal to infiltrate into the Roman citizenship and that, as a result of the *lex Licinia Mucia* of 95 BC (cf. Rotondi, *Leges* 335; Carcopino³, 358), their minds *ita alienati . . . sunt . . . ut ea vel maxima causa belli Italici quod post triennium exortum est fuerit* (Asc. *in Corn.* p. 54, 17–18 Stangl)? I cannot see how this law, and the situation which it aimed at remedying, can have any connexion with the agrarian question.

On the contrary, I have shown elsewhere ('Politica e Cultura in Roma agli inizi del I secolo a.C.', *Athenaeum* N.S. XXXI 1953, 259 f. = *Es. e Soc.* 175 f.) that the first decade of the century, generally considered to be nothing more than a period of reaction and of political inactivity, was on the contrary sharply and profoundly disturbed by the allied question. The *lex Licinia Mucia* was nothing more than the consequence of the illegal entry of upper class Italians into the Roman citizenship, which had developed over the years and which the law sought to oppose. The phenomenon had already found a champion in the Marian *popularis* tradition, with the principal exponent C. Norbanus. The causes naturally went beyond those deriving from the circumstances of the Gracchan period; in fact, we are able to follow the repercussions, or at least the general lines of development, which this political situation had in the cultural sphere, symbolizing the importance and very existence of the allied problem as it was most widely manifested. Indeed, a cultural movement came into existence in which the allies were well represented, and its nature seems to have been that of opposition to philo-Hellenic tendencies as they were personified by the oligarchs.

42. Cf. e.g. the attitude of the *principes Italicorum populorum* in Asc. *in Corn.* p. 54, 17–18 Stangl [cited in the previous note]. For them to obtain the *ius civitatis* in 125 BC would have meant they were placed in a position of parity with the Roman *cives* in that it had a connexion with the enjoyment of personal liberty under the guarantee given by Roman laws. However, the alternative that, as we have seen, Flaccus' proposal offered shows that the upper classes, who ought mainly (or perhaps exclusively) to have resented their oppression by Roman authority, either did not consistently consider the *ius civitatis* the best means of guaranteeing the rights of personal *libertas* or – better still – did not consider it opportune to renounce their own traditional forms of self-government in order to obtain these rights with the *civitas*. In this connexion we may note that of the two basic themes comprised in the concept of *libertas* – form of government: rights that went with the *civitas* – it is not true that the former clearly predominated at Rome (so Wirzsubski, *Libertas* 66), since the numismatic evidence cited by A. Momigliano, *JRS* XLI 1951, 147, contains allusions to *provocatio* (cf. Grueber, I 151, no. 1023 and n. 1; 153, no. 1032 and n. 1 = E. A. Sydenham, *The Coinage of the Roman Republic*, 1952, no. 502; see note). The *Libertas* which appears on coins subsequent to the *Bellum Italicum* is difficult to interpret (Grueber, I 399–403, nos. 3274–3311), although perhaps the most probable explanation is a political allusion (Momigliano, *loc. cit.*). These points lead to a better understanding of what the Italian rebels would have meant by *civitas* and *libertas*. As will be clearer subsequently, the demands which arose after the Gracchi demonstrate the allies' need to participate directly in the life of the Roman state (and *civitas* for the allies in 91 BC means in fact participation in government: Wirzsubski, *Libertas*, 67–9), but they did not moderate their demand that as far as possible the traditional structure of the individual cities should be left intact (see the points made by E. Lepore, *RSI* LXIII 1951, 564 and also the example of Capua examined *Es. e Soc.* 151 f. [= 56 f. above]).

43. *Études sur l'histoire romaine*[3], Paris 1869, 74; cf. 84; 88, n. 4.

44. App. I, 38, 173.

45. On this cf. Chapter VIII.

46. In general it has been emphasized that many rebel leaders (a list is to be found in Haug, *art. cit.* 241 f.: see also my Comm.[2] on Appian, I, pp. 132–3) belonged to families already known from the period of the fourth century BC wars: cf. G. De Sanctis, *Per la scienza dell' antichità*, 1909, 207 f. I append some brief comments on some of the more noteworthy personalities.

Herius Asinius of the Marrucini (cf. Klebs, *RE* s.v. 'Asinius', no. 5) was the grandfather of C. Asinius Pollio (Groebe, *ibid.* no. 25; J. André, *La vie et l'œuvre d'Asinius Pollion*, 1949, 9); his social status is well-known. On the family of the Cluentii from Larinum – a Lucius was a leader of the rebels: Münzer, *RE* s.v. 'Cluentii', no. 1 – cf. Cic. *pro Cluentio* 156. Marius Egnatius the Samnite was descended from the well-known Gellius Egnatius, leader of the confederates at Sentinum (Münzer, *RE*, s.v. nos. 9 and 10); as Hatzfeld, *Trafiquants*, 244, n. 1, emphasizes, his *gentilicium* is that of an important family of traders on Delos and of bankers in Asia. On the Egnatii in the post-Sullan period see later. The status of T. Herennius, Picene (cf. Münzer, *RE* s.v. no. 15) is perhaps deducible from the position of the many Herennii of the post-Sullan period (Syme, p. 92). Minius Ieius (Münzer, *RE* s.v. 'Iegius') is mentioned on a coin which refers to the pact with Mithridates (on this see A. Pagani, *RIN* IV, Series 4, 1944–7, 9 f. and Sydenham, *op. cit.* no. 643; the coin is considered to be of dubious authenticity by E. Bernareggi, *RIN* V 14, 1966, 61–4. See, however, E. T. Salmon, *Samnium and the Samnites*, Cambridge 1967, 369, n. 2), and very probably he belongs to the commercial class. In the case of C. Papius Mutilus, of an old Samnite family (Münzer, *RE* s.v. no. 12), his relationship to Papius Brutulus of the fourth-century wars is attested (De Sanctis, *loc. cit.*). The social status of the Ventidii – a P. Ventidius seems to have controlled forces in the *Bellum Sociale*: App. I 47, 204; cf. the *app. crit.* of the edition of Mendelssohn-Viereck – has been clarified by Syme, p. 71, n. 3 and 92; see also *Es. e Soc.* 93, n. 119 [= 37, n. 119 above]. On Q Poppaedius Silo see Plut. *Cato minor*, 2: ἀνὴρ πολεμικὸς καὶ μέγιστον ἔχων ἀξίωμα. For Vettius Scato the Marsian cf. Syme, p. 91: it is clear that the poverty of his descendants in the Ciceronian period (Syme, *loc. cit.* n. 5) was the result of his discomfiture.

47. Mommsen, *RG* II⁵ 1869, 230; cf. G. De Sanctis, *Bollettino di Filol. Classica* VIII 1901–2, 277.

48. *BAGB* art. cit. 21–2.

49. Cf. Livy, XXXIX 3, 4–6 (187 BC); XLI 8, 6–12 (177 BC): Paelignian and Samnite families at Fregellae. In general see the points made by Bernardi, *art. cit.* 69 and by G. Tibiletti, *Athenaeum* N.S. XXVIII 1950, 203.

50. See below, Chap. X.

51. On this see E. Lepore, 'Orientamenti per la storia sociale di Pompei', in *Pompeiana. Raccolta di studi per il secondo centenario degli scavi di Pompei*, Naples 1950, 9 (extract).

52. T. Frank, 'On the Emigration of Romans to Sicily', *AJPh* LVI 1935, 61 f.

53. M. Dubois, *Pouzzoles antique* (*Bibl. Éc. franç. d'Athènes et de Rome* XCVIII), Paris 1907, 47; J. Hatzfeld, 'Les Italiens résidant à Delos', *BCH* XXXVI 1912, 10–218; *id. Trafiquants*. Cf. also W. A. Laidlaw, *A History of Delos*, Oxford 1933, 201 f. See A. Donati, 'I Romani in Egeo. I documenti dell'età repubblicana', *Epigraphica* XXVII 1965 (pub. 1966), 3–59; A. J. N. Wilson, *Emigration from Italy in the Republican Age of Rome*, Manchester 1966, 85; P. A. Brunt, *Italian Manpower*, 209 f.

54. The commercial activity of many *gentes* who produced oil in Campania and Apulia and sold it directly to Delos (e.g. the *gens Plotia*) is well-known; cf. Hatzfeld, *Trafiquants*, 212 f., esp. 214; Rostovtzeff, II 547, n. 15; J. Heurgon, *MEFR* LVI 1939, 17, n. On the large-scale participation by the landed aristocracy at Pompeii in the most diverse commercial and industrial forms of activity see Lepore, *art. cit.* 4 with notes, and 6. For Naples see Lepore, *PP* VII 1952, 313 f. These close contacts between the class of landed proprietors and that of the *negotiatores* seem to show that Mommsen's second assertion is also in error, viz. that the latifundists sided with Rome. This theory generalizes from the Etruscan and Umbrian phenomenon, but this is too localized to admit of parallels in rebel Italy (except, as we shall see, some cases here and there). Mommsen's view has been taken up to a certain extent by R. Gardner, *CAH* IX, 186, who holds that the ties which existed between the Roman government and the upper classes in Italy may explain the loyalty of certain isolated communities in the heart of rebel cantons. He cites the example of Pinna which refused to make common cause with the Vestini, the case of Minatus Magius of Aeclanum, and the upper classes of Apulia who resisted Vidacilius. It is certain that there were individual cases such as those of the Greek cities I have cited and which are cited also by Gardner, but they are isolated and therefore may not be used as a paradigm. In any case the example of Pinna is not clear; cf. Diod. XXXVII 20, 1–4, and Val. Max. V 4, 7; K. Scherling, *RE* s.v. 'Pinna', col. 1711. All the more should we beware of generalizing from instances in

which men adopted individual attitudes, e.g. Minatus Magius (Vell. II 16, 2; Münzer, *RE* s.v. 'Magius', no. 8); he remained loyal to the Romans. We know that his sons reached the praetorship in the period of Cinna and exhibited democratic tendencies (Münzer, *ibid.* nos. 6 and 10; cf. no. 19; see *Es. e Soc.* 155 [= 58 above]. See also I. Lana, *Velleio Patercolo*, 1952, 58 f.). With Magius cf. P. Sittius (Cic. *pro Sulla*, 58; Münzer, *RE* s.v. no. 2: cf. coll. 408–9); he too remained loyal to Rome in the *Bellum Italicum*. It is impossible to tell whether the Sullan Valgus (see below, and *Es. e Soc.* 119, n. 187 [= 44, n. 187 above]; cf. also H. Dessau, *Hermes* XVIII 1883, 620 f.) was pro-Roman on this occasion. Statius the Samnite (App. IV 25, 102), in the Senate from 86 BC, is an ex-rebel, later a Marian, who escaped the Sullan proscriptions: *Es. e Soc.* 162 [= 61 above]. In any event ties of hospitality and kinship (on which see Münzer, *Römische Adelsparteien und Adelsfamilien*, 1920, 50–1) did not bind a man; this is amply demonstrated by Cic. *Phil.* XII 27, which also militates against the view that the upper classes were pro-Roman. The passage of App. I 42, 190, cannot in fact be used to prove it for Apulia: Οὐιδακιλίῳ δ' ἐν' Ἰαπυγίᾳ προσετίθεντο Κανύσιοι καὶ Οὐενούσιοι καὶ ἕτεραι πόλεις πολλαί. τινὰς δὲ καὶ ἀπειθούσας ἐξεπολιόρκει, καὶ τῶν ἐν αὐταῖς Ῥωμαίων τοὺς μὲν ἐπιφανεῖς ἔκτεινε, τοὺς δὲ δημότας καὶ δούλους ἐστράτευε. Appian is referring here to *cives Romani*, and the different ways they were treated certainly mean it was a political measure to distinguish responsibility for the war and to make it fall on the shoulders of the stubborn Roman governing class (Sisenna, fr. 6 Peter alludes to the flight of Romans from Apulia: see Peter's commentary). A parallel is attested in 90 BC with C. Papius at the capture of Nola: two thousand Romans living there were forcibly enrolled, but their leaders were murdered (App. I 42, 185: cf. Sisenna, fr. 62 Peter and Livy, *Per.* LXXIII where through an error Nola is called a *colonia*). It is notable the rebel commanders, except in one or two cases (cf. above), did not bear the names of those families known to belong to the commercial class, and therefore it would seem rather that they belonged to the class of landowners. We may suppose that command in the war was entrusted to those who had long family traditions (see the recurrence of names of the period of the Samnite Wars) and who were the most professional and the most experienced: here it should be noted that Poppaedius Silo was called ἀνὴρ πολεμικός (Plut. *Cato Minor* 2) and that the Lucanian Cleppius, one of the last to abandon the struggle (Diod. XXXVII 2, 11) was ἀνὴρ στρατηγικὸς καὶ ἐπ' ἀνδρείᾳ περιβόητος (he had taken part in the slave wars in Sicily: Diod. XXXVI 8, 1; Münzer, *RE* Suppl. III, col. 253).

55. For Pompeii (although not all the points and generalizations he makes are acceptable) cf. Rostovtzeff, I 22: for Capua see Heurgon, *art. cit.* 17 and note, and for an instructive comparison with Rome p. 27. See M. W. Frederiksen, 'Republican Capua: A Social and Economic History', *PBSR* XXVII 1959, 80–130. We should, however, bear in mind the great building programmes which followed the Social War and which were intended either to remedy the huge destruction that had taken place or to cope with the phenomenon of urbanization which followed of necessity on municipalization. I intend to deal with this problem in an appropriate study. Other inscriptions of *magistri* referring to the construction of the theatre at the end of the second century BC are published by A. De Franciscis, *Epigraphica* XII 1950, 124 f. (= *Ann. Épig.* 1952, nos. 54–5). All the inscriptions of *magistri* of Capua are published with commentary by Degrassi, *ILLRP* vol. II Florence 1963, nos. 705–23b (p. 135 f.). On the reconstruction of the walls at Aeclanum in the Sullan period see *CIL* I² 1722 = *ILS* 5318 = *ILLRP* 523. It was carried out at the expense of one of the sons of Minatus Magius (Münzer, *RE* s.v. no. 19) and of C. Quinctius Valgius (cf. Dessau, *Hermes* XVIII 1883, 620 f.). While the latter may have become rich during the Sullan proscriptions, the former came from a family

which enjoyed wealth and influence at the time of the *Bellum Italicum*. I do not know whether it is possible to establish the approximate dating of *CIL* I² 1747 = *ILS* 5328 = *ILLRP* 675, referred to the post-Sullan period by L. Quilici, 'Studi di urbanistica antica', *Quaderni dell' Istituto di Topografia antica* (Univ. of Rome) II 1966, 85–106, relative to the building works at Telesia (see Münzer, *RE* s.v. 'Mummius', no. 8). On the initiative in building taken by the rebels at Corfinium see Diod. XXXVII 2, 4. It is certainly not a pure accident that this phenomenon is better attested in Campania than elsewhere.

56. I refer to the Granii of Puteoli whose business contacts with the East are attested by a singular abundance of evidence (Hatzfeld, *Trafiquants*, 392). Members of this family held the highest offices in the Sullan period also, even though they were of the Marian persuasion (Val. Max. IX 3, 8; Plut. *Sulla*, 37, 5; see *Es. e Soc.* 155 and 158 [= 58 and 59 above]). For the Cluvii cf. Hatzfeld, *Trafiquants*, 251. On the Messii, recorded in the East in the mid-second century BC and in administrative positions at Capua at the end of the same century, see Münzer, *RE* s.v. col. 1242; cf. also no. 2, col. 1243.

57. Rostovtzeff, I 22; cf. also W. Schur, 'Homo novus', *BJ* 1929, 66, and *Das Zeitalter des Marius und Sulla* (*Klio*, *Beiheft* XLVI) 1942, 193 f.

58. Cf. Chap. VII.

59. Hatzfeld, *Trafiquants*, 242 f.

60. Hatzfeld, *Trafiquants*, 244.

61. This centralizing tendency of the Roman government in the course of the second century BC is demonstrated by A. H. McDonald, 'Rome and the Italian Confederation (200–186 BC)', *JRS* XXXIV 1944, 11 f. The favourable attitude to Rome of the Italian upper classes in this period (McDonald, 14, 22, 33 *et passim*) perhaps weakens after the Gracchan reforms but is in any event the *sine qua non* of demands for complete equality within the Roman citizenship which the same social classes exhibited at the end of the second century BC and the beginning of the first. The demands of the Italian upper classes were certainly influenced to an important degree by consideration of the superior position of those who governed the Latin colonies and who largely enjoyed the *civitas*; they in fact kept their cities out of the revolt of 91 BC. Cf. G. Tibiletti, *RIL* LXXXVI 1953, 54, 58, 59 *et passim*. For a penetrating analysis see Badian, *FC* 141 f. and 168 f.

62. Cf. M. Gelzer, 'Nasicas Widerspruch gegen die Zerstörung Karthagos', *Philologus* LXXXVI 1931, 261 f. (= *Kleine Schriften*, II, Wiesbaden 1963, 39 f.).

63. On all the aspects of the question see H. Werner, *Der Untergang Roms* (*Forschungen zur Kirchen- und Geistesgeschichte*, LX), 1939, Chaps. V and VI.

64. See H. Strasburger, *Concordia ordinum*, Leipzig 1931, 4 f. and also W. Kroll, *Die Kultur der Ciceronischen Zeit*, I 1933, 72 f.

65. Strasburger, *Concordia ordinum*, 13 f.

66. Varro, *de vita populi Romani*, fr. 114 Riposati = Nonius, p. 728, 20–3 Lindsay; cf. Flor. II 5, 3. All the other ancient evidence is in Hill, *Middle Class*, 109, n. 6.

67. Similar remarks, in a way, in Last, *CAH* IX 77. These points make it difficult to accept the sort of history of the late Republic which sees a Senate–Equites struggle as its dominant theme; the attitude of the capitalists is an important element in it but it can only be explained against the more general background of contemporary social change. It cannot be seen in isolation or divorced from the reality of which it is a part. The support given by the equestrian class to the Cinnan regime – it is enough to cite Asc. p. 69, 20 Stangl: *equester ordo pro Cinnanis partibus contra Syllam steterat*: for the *equester splendor* in this period see Cic. *pro Rosc. Am.* 140 – must not be interpreted as if the government of the popular faction had been directed or even just shaped by the capitalist class or its elements; it is only another

example of an attitude, though a more binding one, adopted in favour of political groups which were framing a policy closer to their own interests. In general one should proceed with caution in evaluating the collusion between Equites and *populares*. These problems are tackled with different preconceptions, for example, by Chr. Meier, *Res Publica Amissa. Eine Studie zur Verfassung und Geschichte der späten römischen Republik*, Wiesbaden 1966 (on which see P. A. Brunt, *JRS* LVIII 1968, 229–32) and by E. S. Gruen, *Roman Politics and the Criminal Courts, 149–78 BC*, Cambridge (Mass.) 1968. Badian, *FC* 154 f. and C. Nicolet, *L'ordre équestre à l'époque républicaine (312–43 BC)*, I, Paris 1966, are, as always, fundamental.

68. Evidence in Hill, *Middle Class*, 92 f.

69. The two opposing views are reflected at opposite extremes by T. Frank, *Roman Imperialism*, 1914, 243 f., who has come out against Roman economic interests in the East before the Gracchan period (see also *An Economic History of Rome²*, New York 1962, 115) and by Rostovtzeff, 22, who maintains that these interests existed and with them an interference in political decisions. One can also consult C. Barbagallo, *NRS* V 1921, 657 f. See introductory note, *Es. e Soc.* 193 [= 70, n. * above].

70. Cf. on this point the discussion of the evidence in Hill, *Middle Class*, 96 f. We must make one point clear: if it was economic motives which influenced these and other political measures in the East, it is certain that in the end the pressure came from the class of *negotiatores* (cf. Heitland, *Roman Republic*, Cambridge 1909, II 156, cited in Hill, *Middle Class*, 97, n. 4); their origin was not Roman but Italian. This leads to the premiss that the *negotiatores* of southern Italy, especially those from Campania, were somehow able to make their voice heard in the Senate and found spokesmen there to represent their interests (on Cato's interest in commerce, originating perhaps from his close contacts with Campanian circles, see H. H. Scullard, *Roman Politics 220–150 BC*, Oxford 1951, 11, n. 4); on the problem of the economic interests of the Senatorial class in politics already attested for the third century BC see F. Cassola, *I gruppi politici Romani nel III sec. a. C.*, Trieste 1962: I offer some reservations in *CS* II 1963, 206–10. For example, it is known that in 177 BC the immunity from *portoria* at the port of Ambracia was granted to Roman citizens and *socii nominis Latini* (Livy, XXXVIII 44, 4). Hill's view (*Middle Class*, 98) on the relationship at Delos in 166 BC between *negotiatores* and the Roman governing class is valid, if at all, only for a later period (cf. e.g. Carcopino³, 87 and n. 48). Concerning the Italians on Delos before 166 BC cf. G. Colin, *Rome et la Grèce de 200 à 146 a. J. Chr. (Bibl. Éc. franç. d'Athènes et de Rome* XCIV) Paris 1905, 265; J. Hatzfeld, *BCH* XXXVI 1912, 102 and *Trafiquants*, 28). Of special interest are Hatzfeld's observations (*Trafiquants*, 247 f.) where he answers in the negative the question whether the freedmen, predominant in Italian communities in the East, operated as representatives of the great Roman capitalists (no new argument for the opposite conclusion in J. Day, *An Economic History of Athens under Roman Domination*, 1942, 63).

It is well-known that a strict distinction must be observed between the *negotiatores* of Italian origin and the Roman equestrian class (so Hill, *Middle Class*, 77 and 89); the latter, which devoted its attentions principally to contracts and to provision of supplies, i.e. to commercial and economic undertakings of enormous range, was chiefly occupied in this period (the middle of the second century BC) with the economic exploitation of the Western provinces (for Spain see below, Chap. X). Polyb. XXXIV 10, 13 = Strabo, IV 6, 12 (see Pais, *Dalle Guerre Puniche a Cesare Augusto*, II 620) records Ἰταλιῶται in Noricum in this period. Large-scale intervention by the Roman equestrian class in Asia is connected with the establishment of direct rule in that part of the world. That the Senate of the second century BC

looked on this 'Western' concentration of economic activity with a friendly eye and sought to encourage it is asserted by M. Besnier, *RA* ser. V 10, 1919, 45.
71. Cf. Hill, *Middle Class*, 99: also R. Feger, 'Cicero und die Zerstörung Korinths', *Hermes* LXXX 1952, 436–56, esp. 440 f. On the attitude of the Roman governing class on these occasions see Scullard, *op. cit.* 214 f.; 228 f.; 236 f.
72. See below, Chap. X.
73. Livy, XLV 18, 3–4: *metalli quoque Macedonici, quod ingens vectigal erat, locationes praediorumque rusticorum tolli placebat; nam neque sine publicano exerceri posse et, ubi pubicanus esset, ibi aut ius publicum vanum aut libertatem sociis nullam esse.* See Rostovtzeff, *Social and Economic History of the Hellenistic World*, II 737 and 758; III 1471, n. 39; Hill, *Middle Class*, 59 and 90. *Contra*, M. Cary, *Mélanges Glotz*, I 142. This decision is perhaps confirmed by other protectionist measures taken by the Senate in this period (second half of the second century BC) whatever may have been the motive on the occasion concerned – in every case it seems to have been unfavourable to the capitalist class: for example, measures concerning the mines in Italy and especially the gold mines in Cisalpine Gaul (evidence and discussion in Besnier, *art. cit.*; Pais, *Dalle Guerre Puniche*, II 595, who thinks in terms of the period 140–100 BC), and concerning viticulture in Gallia Narbonensis (see L. Bellini, *MAL* ser. VIII 1, 1948, 387 f., who suggests a date of 123–118 BC). On this last problem which is tied up with the interpretation of Cic. *de Rep.* III 16, see the different solutions offered by A. Aymard, *Études d'histoire ancienne*, Paris 1967, 585–600; Wilson, *Emigration from Italy*, 67–8; Badian, *Roman Imperialism*[2], 19–20.
74. See W. Ferguson, *JRS* XI 1921, 86 f.
75. Senatorial intervention through Aquilius took the form of the usual commission of ten *legati* (Strabo, XIV 1, 38). On the whole question see Magie, I 153 f.: II 1042 f.
76. Carcopino[3], 242, n. 117. It is true that the moving force behind the trial was the *princeps Senatus*, P. Cornelius Lentulus: Cic. *div. in Caec.* 69; cf. App. I 22, 92.
77. Magie, I, 164; II, 1054 f. Note, however, A. Passerini's reservations on the orthodox view (*Athenaeum* N.S. XV 1937, 279 f.). The so-called *S.C. de agro Pergameno* (the inscriptions of Smyrna studied by Passerini have provided very important corollaries for the original fragments known by the name of the *S.C.* of Adramyttium; now in R. K. Sherk, *Roman Documents from the Greek East*, Baltimore 1969, 63–73), which must be dated to 129 BC (Passerini, 261: the doubts of Magie, II 1055 f. have been shown to be without foundation: cf. Broughton, I, 497 (n. 1 of p. 496) and also E. W. Gray, *JRS* XLII 1952, 125), may perhaps attest the political importance which the capitalist class by now possessed. In fact, the *consilium* which assists the magistrate is composed of more than senators (Passerini, p. 263 f.) and I would draw an inference from the fact that some of the persons there mentioned who remain unidentified carry names of *gentes* known in the East among the *negotiatores*. They are (the numbers are those in Passerini's list): 13 Γέσσιος: Hatzfeld, *Trafiquants*, Index s.v.; 24 Σείλιος: *ibidem*; 48 Λόλλιος: *ibidem* and the comm. of Passerini; 39 Λαβέριος: *ibidem*; 29 Νεμετώριος: Hatzfeld, *BCH* XXXVI 1912, 56. May one perhaps assume that the non-senatorial members of the *consilium* included those of the commercial class who were experts in Eastern affairs? (Broughton, II 487, considers all the members of the *consilium* to be senators. However, in reply to a question of mine on the subject – I would like to repeat here my thanks to him for his kindness – he has (31.5.1953) hedged the view he previously expressed. He admits now the possibility that not all the members of the *consilium* were senators; he prefers to believe, however, that the non-senators were rather 'leading young men' (something similar in Passerini, *comm.* on nos. 12, 18, 51). He still holds that the case of C. Numitorius mentioned in the inscription is very important. Although this *gentilicium* is found, as has been said, on Delos at this time, Numitorius is

certainly to be identified with the moneyer of the same name dated by Sydenham, *op. cit.* p. lx and 54, no. 466, to the period 133–126 BC (Grueber, I 141, no. 971, dates to 124–103). In 129 BC Numitorius would have been at the beginning, or nearly at the beginning, of his senatorial career (see, however, Münzer, *RE* s.v. no. 2, where a connexion with the *negotiatores* of Delos is envisaged). Broughton also emphasizes the difficulty that names of businessmen are found preceding politically influential senators in the list. However, this observation applies also to Broughton's own view). See Sherk, pp. 72–3.

78. Admitted also by Frank, *Roman Imperialism*, 251; but see 243 f., esp. 249.
79. *Es. e Soc.* 155 [= 58 above].
80. See Fraccaro, *Athenaeum* N.S. III 1925, 88–9 and 96–7 = *Opuscula*, II 27–8 and 32–4.
81. See *Es. e Soc.* 105, n. 153 [= 40, n. 153 above]; see also Chap. X below, and M. Gwyn Morgan, *California Public. Class. Antiquity*, II 1969, 217–31.
82. Evidence and discussion *Es. e Soc.* 106 [= 41 above]; on the date of the colony of Narbo see most recently B. Levick, *CQ* XXI 1971, 170–9: other bibliography and discussion of the significance of the colony in *Aufstieg und Niedergang*, I, 771–2. For the *ara* of Domitius Ahenobarbus cf. F. Castagnoli, *Arti Figurative* I 1945, 81 f. On Roman politics in southern Gaul cf. C. H. Benedict, 'The Romans in Southern Gaul', *AJPh* LXIII 1942, 38 f. (esp. 50) and also *A History of Narbo*, 1942.
83. Frank, *Roman Imperialism*, 267.
84. Cf. Vell. II 11, 2: *hic* (Marius) *per publicanos aliosque in Africa negotiantes criminatus Metelli lentitudinem*. On the episode see Passerini, *Athenaeum* N.S. XII 1934, 23 f. Cf. De Sanctis, *Problemi di Storia antica*, 1932, 212 f. See also Sall. *BJ* 64, 5; 65, 4. On Italians in Africa cf. in general S. Gsell, *Histoire ancienne de l'Afrique du Nord*, V 192; VII 71; Hill, *Middle Class*, 120. Further discussion in *Aufstieg und Niedergang*, I 776–7.
85. In the last few years evidence of Marius' African colonization under Saturninus' *lex agraria* of 103 BC (discussion of the literary and epigraphic evidence in *Athenaeum* N.S. XXIX 1951, 15 f.) has increased considerably: the latest inscription is one published by P. Quoniam, *CRAI* 1950, 332 = *Ann. Épig.* 1951, no. 81. This evidence suggests that the colonization was important for more than the development of Romanization in Africa (cf. A. Merlin–L. Poinssot, *Les Inscriptions d'Uchi Maius* (*Notes et Documents* II) 1908, 17 f. and above all T. R. S. Broughton, *The Romanization of Africa Proconsularis*, 1929, 32 f.). The fact that colonization took place in the most fertile part of the kingdom of Numidia (Sall. *BJ* 46, 5 and 87: the district was pinpointed by Frank, *AJPh* XLVII 1926, 55 f., esp. 60) seems to indicate a precise, overall plan, which it is not easy to believe was different from that envisaged by Rostovtzeff, p. 21, i.e. it was in the interest of the Roman latifundists, who were producers of oil and wine and whose collaboration with the *negotiatores* is well-known, to limit the production of these two commodities as far as Africa was concerned. What better means to obtain this end than to parcel out areas of industrialized agriculture into many small lots with an economy strictly based on that of the single family? It is not always easy to distinguish the settlements going back to the colonization of 103 BC from those granted to the Gaetuli among whom Marius had distributed also the Roman citizenship on a large scale: for this last problem see J. Gascon, *MEFR* LXXXI 1969, 555 f.; on Marius' African colonization in general see L. Teutsch, *Das Städtewesen in Nordafrika*, Berlin 1962, 9 f.
86. On the question of the *leges de repetundis* see G. Tibiletti, 'Le leggi *de iudiciis repetundarum* fino alla Guerra Sociale', *Athenaeum* N.S. XXXI 1953, 5 f.
87. See *Es. e Soc.* 108 [= 41 above]. Add B. R. Motzo, *SS* I 2, 1935, 10 f.

88. Not everyone agrees, however, that Caepio was tried under the law of *maiestas*: see e.g. J. Lengle, *Hermes* LXVI 1931, 306; *contra*, *Athenaeum* N.S. XXIX 1951, 22, n. 4. On the view which refers the trial of Caepio to 95 BC cf. Gabba, *Athenaeum* N.S. XXXI 1953, 264, n. 4. = *Es. e Soc.* 182; Gruen, *Roman Politics and the Criminal Courts*, 164–5.

89. Gabba, *Athenaeum* N.S. XXIX 1951, 22, n. 4.

I accept the date of 100 BC for the *lex Servilia Glauciae* (so Passerini, *Athenaeum* N.S. XII 1934, 132 f.; for a different interpretation Gruen, *Roman Politics and the Criminal Courts*, 166–7, thinking of 104 or 103). This date raises, however, the problem of the year to which we must assign the trials *de repetundis* involving C. Memmius and C. Flavius Fimbria. They are mentioned in Cic. *pro Font.* 24 and 26; *Brutus*, 168; and in Val. Max. VIII 5, 2. In these trials M. Aemilius Scaurus was an unheeded witness for the prosecution. Cicero says explicitly that the juries were comprised of Roman knights on both occasions (*pro Font.* 26) and this demonstrates (accepting the premiss put forward above that the *lex Servilia Caepionis* remained in force from 106 to 100 BC) that the two trials did not take place during this period. However, it is generally held that the two trials are intimately connected and that they took place after 104 BC, the year in which C. Flavius Fimbria was consul and C. Memmius was praetor (see Broughton, I 558, 559, n. 4 on 562, 564 and n. 9 on 566 (is C. Memmius the Μέμμιος ὁ ἀνθύπατος of *IG* V 1, 1432?), anticipated by Robinson, *Marius, Saturninus und Glaucia*, 1912, 33; Münzer, *RE* s.v. 'Memmius', no. 5, col. 606; 'Flavius', no. 87, col. 2599; see also Hill, *Middle Class*, 124). Passerini, taking into account the difficulty which these trials pose for the dating of Glaucia's law to 100, argued that the evidence was not such as to permit a firm date for the trials (*art. cit.* 133, n. 4).

There seem to be two solutions, if my premisses hold: either (and this is less probable) the Equites here are that part of the jurors who, in accordance with one of the two versions of Caepio's law, shared the judicial power in the courts with the senators and whose view prevailed in these trials (on the question see, together with the evidence of the sources, Hill, *Middle Class*, 122 and n. 1: this version of the *lex Servilia C.* seems, however, less secure than that which sees the senators completely in control of the courts), or one should follow the course suggested by Niccolini, *Fasti dei tribuni della plebe*, 197. That is to say, one should reject any connexion between the two trials, which actually are placed side by side in Cicero only because of the presence, common to both, of Aemilius Scaurus as witness for the prosecution. Of the two trials, the one against Fimbria, launched by M. Gratidius (Cic. *Brutus*, 168), would have been later than his praetorship which cannot in any event be later than 107 BC (Broughton, I 551 and n. 4 on 552) and therefore was prior to Caepio's reform. That involving Memmius would have been after Glaucia's law – passed in the first months of 100 BC – but prior to the consular elections of the same year, which were held in December, when Memmius was killed. See Gruen, *Roman Politics and the Criminal Courts*, 174–6.

Of even greater interest than the chronology is the question of the plaintiffs and defendants in these trials, since it provides a warning against generalizing from individual episodes; such generalizations may certainly be seductive but they often bear little relation to reality. Hill, *Middle Class*, 124, speaks of anti-senatorial bias in the trial of Fimbria. He belonged to the Marian faction, as is clear not only from his joint consulship with Marius in 104 BC but also from the fact that he was a *homo novus*, often mentioned by Cicero, and from the well-known political attitude of the son of the same name. But all that we know of the man who attacked him, M. Gratidius, leads us to the same conclusions. His son was the famous Marian M. Marius Gratidianus (Cic. *Brutus*, 168), his father the Gratidius who in 88 BC was

Marius' legate in accordance with the *rogatio Sulpicia* (Münzer, *RE* s.v. 'Gratidius', no. 1): one could not imagine tighter ties with Marius. I am not sure whether one should not speak here of struggles between financiers, particularly because Scaurus, whose enmity for Fimbria is emphasized by Cic. *pro Font.* 24, and 26, had far-ranging commercial connexions. Moreover, it seems odd that the attack should have its origin in the Senate since it should have been evident *a priori* that it would not have been able to be pushed home against the wishes of an equestrian jury who would of course have been sympathetic to defendants of the same or similar outlook. The same holds for C. Memmius, whose sympathies were very probably with the class of financiers (Last, *CAH* IX 171) and whose activity as tribune had been wholly anti-Senatorial (see Hill, *Middle Class*, 118 f.). Nor is the contrary proved by the fact that at the end of Saturninus' activity in 100 BC we find both Fimbria and Memmius opposed to the demagogue (Cic. *pro Rab. perd. reo*, 21: Passerini, *Athenaeum* 1934 *art. cit.* 281, n. 3), since it is well-known that the equestrian order – and the less radical elements of the popular faction, above all Marius – were alienated by Saturninus when he showed signs of going beyond the proper limits and of wanting to inaugurate a policy of violence which clearly could not command the support of the classes of law and order.

90. In 103 according to Carcopino³, pp. 353 and 422.
91. Diod. XXXVI 15 speaks explicitly of corruption of senators to serve the interests of the king of Pontus. This is a traditional theme in discrediting the Eastern policy of the Senate. I do not believe, therefore, that one should accept the scepticism of Passerini, *Athenaeum* 1934 *art. cit.* 117.
92. Hatzfeld, *Trafiquants*, 31 f. and earlier (for Delos) in *BCH* XXXVI 1912, 114–15 and *ibid.* XLV 1921, 471 f.
93. Rostovtzeff, p. 8; Hill, *Middle Class*, p. 125.
94. Now in *Suppl. Epigraph. Graecum*, III 378.
95. *Athenaeum* 1934 *art. cit.* 134–9 and 'Epigrafia Mariana', *ibid.* N.S. XVII 1939, 62–4.
96. 'Sur la loi du monument de Paul-Émile', *Mélanges Glotz*, I 117 f. and also Carcopino³, p. 353 f.
97. This is the date generally accepted for the law: Gabba, *Athenaeum* N.S. XXIX 1951, 23 f. See G. Tibiletti, in De Ruggiero, *Diz. Epig.*, s.v. 'lex', 718–19; F. T. Hinrichs, 'Die lateinischen Tafeln von Bantia und die *lex de Piratis*', *Hermes* XCVIII 1970, 471–502.
98. This is clear from the dedication made at Delos by 'the Italians who were in Alexandria': *CIL* III 7241 = *ILLRP* 343 (the name of Marius is supplied: see Degrassi's commentary); see Passerini, *Athenaeum* 1939 *art. cit.* 69 f. and also W. Otto-H. Bengtston, 'Zur Geschichte des Niedergangs des Ptolemäerreiches', *ABAW* N.F. XVII 1938, 101 f. For the relations between Marius and the *negotiatores* see also *Es. e Soc.* 157, n. 32 [= 59, n. 32 above]: cf. also Barbagallo, *NRS* V 1921, 661.
99. Cf. *Gnomon* XXIV 1952, 289. The dating to 92–91 BC is supported by Broughton, *MRR* II 22, and by Badian, *Studies in Greek and Roman History*, Oxford 1964, 87 and 101 (n. 105). On the Asian tour the best assessment is in T. J. Luce, 'Marius and the Mithridatic Command', *Historia* XIX 1970, 162–8.
100. Cf. Carcopino³, p. 423. The situation in Asia is set out in ample detail in Magie, I 204 f.
101. Hill, *Middle Class*, 130.
102. *Es. e Soc.* 157, n. 32 [= 59, n. 32 above].
103. On M. Aemilius Scaurus the splendid pages of Carcopino³, p. 280 f. should be consulted.
104. Carcopino³, p. 426. M'. Aquilius had been Marius' colleague in the consulship of

101 BC. The steps he took were affected by his anti-Senatorial outlook: this can be shown by the fact that he had with him Manlius Maltinus (Just. XXXVIII 3, 4; 3, 8 and 4, 4: in App. *Mithr.* 19 Μαγκῖνος) who is the same Manlius Mancinus as the supporter of Marius in 107 BC (Sall. *BJ* 73, 7 and Gell. VII 11, 2). Münzer, *RE* s.v. 'Manlius', no. 59, maintained that the proper form of the *cognomen* was Malt(h)inus, comparing *CIL* IX 5073, and inclined to the view (*ibid.* no. 61, col. 1190, 52) that also in Sallust the true reading is Maltinus. See on the question Broughton, II 35 and n. 19 on p. 39; Badian, *Studies*, 167, n. 112; *contra*, Luce, *Historia* XIX 1970, 188–9; Gabba, *Aufstieg und Niedergang*, I 794.

105. App. *Mithr.* 11, 36–7: ἐγκειμένων δὲ τῶν πρέσβεων, ὁ Νικομήδης, πολλὰ μὲν ὑπὲρ τῆς ἐπικουρίας τοῖς στρατηγοῖς καὶ τοῖς πρέσβεσιν ὡμολογηκὼς χρήματα δώσειν, καὶ ἔτι ὄφλων, πολλὰ δ᾽ ἄλλα παρὰ τῶν ἑπομένων ᾽Ρωμαίων δεδανεισμένος, καὶ ὀχλούμενος, ἄκων ἐσέβαλε ἐς τὴν Μιθριδάτου γῆν. Attempts to deny the presence of equestrian interests are to be found in Brunt, 'The Equites in the late Republic', *art. cit.* 132, and Badian, *Roman Imperialism²*, 56–9; see Luce, *Historia* XIX 1970, 186–7.

106. On the massacre of the *negotiatores* – App. *Mithr.* 22, 85; 23, 91 distinguishes between '*Ρωμαῖοι* and '*Ιταλοί* – cf. Magie, I 216 f.; II 1103. Brunt, *Italian Manpower*, 224–7, seeks to limit the number of these murdered.

107. Hatzfeld, *BCH* 1912, 119 f. and 127.

108. Cf. T. Frank, 'On Some Financial legislation of the Sullan Period', *AJPh* LIV 1933, 54 f. A different account of economic and monetary problems of the Sullan age in Z. Yavetz, *Recherches sur les structures sociales dans l'antiquité classique*, Caen 1969, Paris 1970, 133–157: see also M. M. Crawford, *PCPhS* N.S. XIV 1968, 1 f.

109. The basic passage is Plut. *Sulla*, 8, 2 and 3.

110. Hatzfeld, *Trafiquants*, 3–4, collected the ancient evidence which clearly shows the distinction between, on the one hand, Roman *publicani* and the *societates* which they controlled, and, on the other, the *negotiatores* involved in business (cf. for example Cic. *de imp. Cn. Pomp.* 17–18; *pro Flacco*, 38; Caes. *BC* III 32, 6). Of course, this difference disappeared when common interests and identity of outlook developed.

111. If in the passage of App. *Mithr.* 11, 36–7 which I have cited the term '*Ρωμαῖοι* must be understood in the sense commonly attributed to it in the Hellenized East, one could conclude that, in the matter of Nicomedes, Roman magistrates and legates worked along the same lines as Italian businessmen. Of course one cannot deny the possibility of local conflicts between *publicani* and *negotiatores*, like that – and it would not have been unique – mentioned in Cic. *ad Att.* II 16, 4 (cf. S. J. De Laet, *Portorium*, 1949, 109 f. and also 58–9) concerning a *portorium circumvectionis*. These cases cannot in any way lessen the overall truth and importance of our conclusion.

112. Interesting points are raised by the well-known passage of Sall. *BJ* 26, 1: *ea postquam Cirtae audita sunt, Italici, quorum virtute moenia defensabantur, confisi deditione facta propter magnitudinem populi Romani inviolatos sese fore* etc. By *Italici* Sallust means Roman and allied businessmen (*togati* in 21, 2; cf. 26, 3 and 41, 1): this was the comprehensive term used to indicate Roman and allied businessmen in documents translated into Latin (Hatzfeld, *Trafiquants*, 243). What is more significant is that the latter considered themselves to be just as much protected by the *magnitudo populi Romani*, even if most of them did not enjoy Roman legal status. That this was a normal and common state of affairs is shown not only by the natural way in which Sallust mentions the matter, but also (on a much larger scale) by all Cicero's polemical Verrine *de suppliciis*. We know, thanks to the observations of T. Frank, *AJPh* LVI 1935, 61–4 – cf. also J. Carcopino, *RIDA* IV 1950 (= *Mélanges De Visscher*, III), 229 f. – that many of those whom Verres sent to their deaths without trial were not *cives*, probably because after 89 BC they had not registered as such.

However, when Cicero lays the blame at Verres' door for this, it cannot be said that he does it only for the specific purpose which interests him; he also does it because among the businessmen a distinction between *cives* and *socii* was not under the law any longer possible after 89 BC and had never in practice existed. In fact, when Cicero says (II *Verr.* 5, 167: *homines tenues, obscuro loco nati, navigant, adeunt ad ea loca quae numquam ante viderunt, ubi neque noti esse iis quo venerunt neque semper cum cognitoribus esse possunt. hac una tamen fiducia civitatis non modo apud nostros magistratus . . . neque apud cives solum Romanos . . . fore se tutos arbitrabantur, sed quocumque venerint, hanc sibi rem praesidio sperant futuram*), he clearly refers to the *negotiatores* and not only pinpoints a particular fact at the time but also deals with a state of affairs which had been going on for some time: i.e. all were looked on as 'Ρωμαῖοι. It is clear that in Numidia or in Bithynia the *magnitudo populi Romani* or the *fiducia civitatis* had the same effect (though there is a nuance which we can detect and whose historical significance we can explain).

113. Sall. *BJ* 26 (Cirta); cf. also 47 and 66 (Vaga). See G. De Sanctis, *Problemi di storia antica*, Bari 1932, 197.

114. *Es. e Soc.* 151 [= 56 above].

115. Münzer, *RE* s.v. 'Pedius', col. 38. See also Otto-Bengtson, *op. cit.* 102 and n. 4, and Syme, *JRS* XXXIV 1944, 93.

116. I mention also the case of Magius, interested in the Roman *sodalicia* for stripping the provinces (Cic. *de Orat.* II 265); he was probably *praefectus sociorum* under L. Piso Caesoninus before 107 BC (Münzer, *RE* s.v. 'Magius', no. 1) and was certainly related to the well-known family of Capua and Aeclanum. The connexion suggested by Fraccaro, 'Scauriana', *RAL* V 20, 1911, 187 = *Opuscula*, II 139 with Plin. *NH* XXXVI 15 (24), 116 (where *Mariani* has to be corrected to *Magiani*) serves no purpose. See *Es. e Soc.* 157 n. 32 [= 59, n. 32 above]: see also *Aufstieg und Niedergang*, I 773.

117. It is important to note that rebel leaders such as Papius Mutilus, Lamponius and Pontius Telesinus sided with the Marians.

118. On the question of Drusus' Senate see Hill, *Middle Class*, 133 f. Appian's version (I 35, 157–8; *auct de vir. ill.* 66, 4) on the admission of 300 Equites to the Senate seems preferable, especially when we take into account the later Sullan measures. See 'Osservazioni sulla legge giudiziaria di M. Livio Druso (91 a. C.)', *PP* XI 1956, 367 f. = *Es. e Soc.* 375 f.

119. Fraccaro, *op. cit.* 193 = *Opuscula*, II 144. All the problems raised by the *lex Varia* are illuminated by the fundamental inquiry of E. Badian, 'Quaestiones Variae', *Historia* XVIII 1969, 447–91.

120. So App. I 37, 165–6: καὶ οἱ ἱππεῖς ἐπίβασιν ἐς συκοφαντίαν τῶν ἐχθρῶν τὸ πολίτευμα αὐτοῦ τιθέμενοι, Κόιντον Οὐάριον δήμαρχον ἔπεισαν εἰσηγήσασθαι κρίσεις εἶναι κατὰ τῶν τοῖς Ἰταλιώταις ἐπὶ τὰ κοινὰ φανερῶς ἢ κρύφα βοηθούντων, ἐλπίσαντες τοὺς δυνατοὺς ἅπαντας αὐτίκα εἰς ἔγκλημα ἐπίφθονον ὑπάξεσθαι καὶ δικάσειν μὲν αὐτοί, γενομένων δ' ἐκείνων ἐκπόδων δυνατώτερον ἔτι τῆς πόλεως ἐπάρξειν. Other passages cited in Rotondi, *Leges*, 339. List of defendants accused under the law in Broughton, II 27. On the law see also Haug, *art. cit.* 243.

121. According to Asc. p. 24, 24 Stangl, the hostility directed against the *nobilitas* derived in fact *ob sociis negatam civitatem*.

122. As is well-known, and as I have already said, motivation of this sort (*metus iudiciorum*) is found in Cic. *de Off.* II 75, and certainly posited there as a cause of the allies' revolt.

123. Fraccaro, *op. cit.* 189 = *Opuscula*, II 141.

124. E.g. by Klebs, *RE* s.v. 'Aemilius', col. 586 and by Niccolini, *Fasti*, 224.

125. Cf. the activity of Saturninus in 102 BC. Mithridates in 89 BC had informed the

Roman ambassadors of the sum total of monies spent at Rome to corrupt politicians to his cause (Cass. Dio, fr. 99 Boiss.: καὶ προσαποδείξας τοῖς πρέσβεσι τὸ πλῆθος τῶν χρημάτων ὧν τε κοινῷ καὶ ἰδίᾳ τισὶν ἀναλώκει κ.τ.λ.).

126. The fact is mentioned only in Asc. p. 24, 16 Stangl: cf. Pais, *Dalle Guerre Puniche*, I 96. Hill, *Middle Class*, 131, n. 5, is right to refer it to a year shortly before 92 BC (to 93 BC Broughton, II 15 and n. 6 on 16). The *legatio* of Scaurus must be dated about 96 BC: Badian, *Athenaeum* N.S. XXXIV 1956, 120 f.; *Studies*, 172; see also Gruen, *Historia* XV 1966, 56–9 and Luce, *Historia* XIX 1970, 169 f.

127. Cic. *pro Scauro* 5; cf. Fraccaro, 'Scauriana', 188 = *Opuscula*, II 140; Gruen, *Roman Politics*, 218.

128. E.g. Pais, *op. cit.* 97 f.; Fraccaro, 'Scauriana', 190 = *Opuscula*, II 142.

129. Cf. for this point the coin in Grueber, II 334 and 337; A. Pagani, *RIN art. cit.* 32 and Sydenham, *op. cit.* no. 632. But see *Es. e Soc.* 211, n. 46 [= 75, n. 46 above].

130. Fr. 36 Jacoby (*FgrH*. IIA, p. 246, 9): the context is a speech by Athenio inviting the Athenians to revolt (cf. W. S. Ferguson, *Hellenistic Athens*, 1911, 440 f. and J. Day, *An Economic History of Athens under Roman Domination*, 113 f.): πάρεισι γὰρ πρὸς αὐτὸν (Mithridates) πρέσβεις οὐ μόνον ἐκ τῶν Ἰταλικῶν ἐθνῶν, ἀλλὰ καὶ παρὰ Καρχηδονίων, συμμάχειν ἀξιοῦντες ἐπὶ τὴν τῆς Ῥώμης ἀναίρεσιν.
I cannot understand what lies behind the mention of the Carthaginians. The orthodox view, found in Mommsen (see A. Audollent, *Carthage Romaine (Bibl. Éc. franç. d'Athènes et de Rome*, LXXXIV) Paris 1901, 39) that it was a trick to persuade the Athenians seems to me improbable; perhaps it is a case of commercial relations between the Greek East and the countries of North Africa, especially Numidia; cf. A. Momigliano, 'I regni indigeni dell'Africa romana', in *Africa Romana* (Istituto di Studi Romani), 1935, 94 f. There is a clever if not wholly convincing attempt at explanation in C. Nicolet, 'Mithridate et les "Ambassadeurs de Carthage"', *Mélanges Piganiol*, II 807–14.

131. Diod. XXXVII 2, 11: ἐπικρατούντων δ' ἐπὶ μᾶλλον καὶ μᾶλλον τῶν Ῥωμαίων, πέμπουσιν οἱ Ἰταλοὶ πρὸς Μιθριδάτην τὸν βασιλέα Πόντου, ἀκμάζοντα τότε πολεμικῇ χειρὶ καὶ παρασκευῇ, ἀξιοῦντες ἐπὶ τὴν Ἰταλίαν κατὰ Ῥωμαίων ἄγειν τὰς δυνάμεις. οὕτω γὰρ ῥᾳδίως ἂν συναφθέντων τὸ Ῥωμαϊκὸν καταβληθήσεσθαι κράτος. ὁ δὲ Μιθριδάτης ἀπόκρισιν δίδωσιν ἄξειν τὰς δυνάμεις εἰς τὴν Ἰταλίαν, ἐπειδὰν αὐτῷ καταστήσῃ τὴν Ἀσίαν· τοῦτο γὰρ καὶ ἔπραττε.

132. Cf. Magie, I 207.

133. Th. Reinach, *Mithridate Eupator*, Paris 1890, 132.

134. Cic. *Phil.* XII 27.

135. With the reservations I shall indicate below, one should consult G. Niccolini, 'Le leggi *de civitate Romana* durante la Guerra Sociale', *RAL* ser. VIII 1, 1946, 110–24. See also Mommsen, 'Die röm. Tribuseintheilung nach dem marsischen Krieg', *GS* V, 262 f. On the problems treated in this chapter see Badian, *Studies*, 75–6; *Historia* XI 1962, 227–8; E. T. Salmon, 'Notes on the Social War', *TAPhA* LXXXIX 1958, 159–84; L. R. Taylor, *The Voting Districts of the Roman Republic*, Rome 1960, 101–17 with corrections by Brunt, *JRS* LV 1965, 108; Gabba, *Aufstieg und Niedergang*, I 792.

136. I quote the Appian passages for reference, I 49, 214: 'Ρωμαῖοι μὲν δὴ τούσδε τοὺς νεοπολίτας οὐκ ἐς τὰς πέντε καὶ τριάκοντα φυλάς, αἳ τότε ἦσαν αὐτοῖς, κατέλεξαν, ἵνα μὴ τῶν ἀρχαίων πλέονες ὄντες ἐν ταῖς χειροτονίαις ἐπικρατοῖεν, ἀλλὰ δεκατεύοντες ἀπέφηναν ἑτέρας, ἐν αἷς ἐχειροτόνουν ἔσχατοι. καὶ πολλάκις αὐτῶν ἡ ψῆφος ἀχρεῖος ἦν, ἅτε τῶν πέντε καὶ τριάκοντα προτέρων τε καλουμένων καὶ οὐσῶν ὑπὲρ ἥμισυ. I 53, 231: this was the Social War which devastated Italy ἕως Ἰταλία πᾶσα προσεχώρησεν ἐς τὴν Ῥωμαίων πολιτείαν, χωρίς γε Λευκανῶν καὶ Σαυνιτῶν τότε. δοκοῦσι γάρ μοι καὶ οἵδε τυχεῖν, ὧν ἐχρῇζων, ὕστερον, ἐς δὲ τὰς φυλὰς ὅμοια τοῖς προτυχοῦσιν ἕκαστοι κατελέγοντο, τοῦ μὴ

τοῖς ἀρχαίοις ἀναμεμιγμένοι ἐπικρατεῖν ἐν ταῖς χειροτονίαις, πλέονες ὄντες. On the passages of Appian see my Commentary.

On the question of the admission of the *dediticii* and of Lucanians and Samnites cf. the commentary of Strachan-Davidson, *Appian, Civil Wars; Book I*, Oxford 1902, 26; Salmon, *Samnium and the Samnites*, 360 f.

137. Niccolini, *Fasti*, 225. See, however, Haug, *art. cit.* 215 (Books II and III would have dealt with the summer of 90 BC). On the fragments of Sisenna there is an excellent treatment by G. Barabino in *Studi Noniani* (Univ. of Genoa: Ist. Filol. Class. e Medievale), 1967, 67–251.

138. G. Rotondi, *Leges*, 340; Münzer, *RE* s.v. 'Calpurnius', no. 98, col. 1396; E. Weis, *ibid.* s.v. 'lex Calpurnia', no. 1; Niccolini, *loc. cit.*; Carcopino³, p. 393; Broughton, II 33.

139. *ILS* 8888. The dating of the inscription to 89 BC is in Dessau, *loc. cit.*; Stevenson, *JRS* IX 1919, 95; Cichorius, *Röm. Studien*, 130 f.; Gelzer, 'Cn. Pompeius Strabo und der Aufstieg seines Sohnes Magnus', *APAW* 1941, 14, 9 (= *Kleine Schriften* II 112–13) and *Pompeius*, Munich 1949, 29. Arguments for 90 BC in Carcopino³, p. 395, n. 162, relying on Pais, *Dalle Guerre Puniche*, I 174 f. I note that V. Arangio-Ruiz, *Storia del diritto romano*⁶, 1950, 221, seems to hesitate to identify the law passed *de civitate* by the consul of 90 BC with the *lex Iulia* mentioned in the inscription (cf. *Scritti Carnelutti*, IV 60, n. 2). Cf. N. Criniti, *L'Epigrafe di Asculum di Gn. Pompeo Strabone*, Milan 1970.

140. Carcopino³, p. 393; this argument seems to have escaped A. Biscardi, 'La questione italica e le tribù soprannumerarie', *PP* VI 1951, 243. See Haug, *art. cit.* 247; the *lex Calpurnia* of 90 BC would be complementary to the *lex Iulia*.

141. *Das Zeitalter des Marius und Sulla*, 120.

142. *Art. cit.* 119–20.

143. Cf. Mommsen, *SR* III 132 and n. 3. That the grant in Dessau, *ILS* 8888, was *singillatim* is asserted by Dessau, comm. n. 6, and by Stevenson, p. 99: 'the *lex Iulia* conferred on generals certain powers of granting the *civitas* to individuals *de consilii sententia*'.

144. *Art. cit.* 121.

145. *Art. cit.* 248.

146. Sherwin-White, *The Roman Citizenship*, 133, widens the scope of the *lex Calpurnia* still further. R. Gardner's approach in *CAH* IX 195, n. 1, is very cautious.

147. *Art. cit.* 119, n. 2.

148. Mommsen, *SR* III 132–3.

149. *SR* III 135 and notes. Cf. also Gelzer, *APAW art. cit.* 9 = *Kleine Schriften* II 112–13.

150. Diod. XXXVII 17 (18).

151. In two passages of Livy's *Periochae*, LXXX and LXXXIV, the *civitas* appears to be given *ex S.C.* Mommsen, *SR* III 180, nn. 1 and 2 maintained that we have here inexactitudes due to the Epitomator himself. Willems, *Le Sénat de la République romaine*, II 685 and n. 2, defended the two passages (and also Gran. Lic. p. 20, 11 Flemisch) and supposed that the Senate had the power, when circumstances allowed, to give practical application to measures of a general character, as was the case with the *lex Iulia* and the *lex Plautia Papiria*.

Willems also cites Sisenna, fr. 17. However, as I have said above, the case is different here because a grant of the citizenship is not in question and above all we do not know what the passage of Sisenna said; in principle we can accept an argument which posits an increase in the number of tribes as much as one which posits a diminution, and for that matter many other hypotheses as well. In other words it is a matter once again – and the problem is insoluble – of the connexion between the *lex Iulia* of 90 BC and the *S.C.* of Sisenna, fr. 17. In this context Willems' idea could be accepted (without thereby going so far as Niccolini nor to the extremes of Biscardi) in the sense that the *lex Iulia* could have charged the Senate with applying the criteria governing the admission of *socii* to the citizenship and at least can have allowed it the power to make technical changes in the procedure; this latter suggestion, however, does not seem to me very probable.

152. *RA* III[2] 112. In that case it would no longer be possible to identify the Calpurnius of the fragment with no. 98 in *RE*, praetor in 74 BC. Lange, in fact, and before him Kiene, *Der röm. Bundesgenossenkrieg*, 1845, 229, identified him with Caesoninus (Münzer, *RE* s.v. no. 89). That the Calpurnius of the law and that of the *S.C.* are the same person is possible but not necessary.

153. *La costituzione romana dai Gracchi a Giulio Cesare*, 1928, 159; anticipated by Rice Holmes, *Roman Republic*, I 1923, 356.

154. *Art. cit.* 248.

155. Such as Rice Holmes and Levi, *loc. cit.* Other references in Niccolini, *Fasti*, 226 f. For proposed corrections of the word see my Commentary[2] on Appian, I, pp. 148 and 441. The explanation given by R. G. Lewis, *Athenaeum* N.S. XLVI 1968, 273–91, is unacceptable.

156. *Sylla ou la monarchie manquée*, Paris 1931, 33, n. 4; Carcopino[3], 394, n. 159.

157. *Athenaeum* N.S. XXVII 1949, 223 f.

158. Biscardi, *art. cit.* 247.

159. *Loc. cit.*

160. App. I 49, 215.

161. *Art. cit.* 247.

162. *Loc. cit.*

163. It is true that later Biscardi says that no one can explain how attention was focused on the *comitia centuriata*.

164. *Party Politics in the Age of Caesar*, 1949, 59.

165. Taylor, *op. cit.* 57. And these were distributed among many centuries.

166. See P. Fraccaro, *Studi Bonfante*, I 118 f. = *Opuscula*, II 171 f. and the remarks o A. Momigliano, *JRS* XXXI 1941, 159.

167. See the following chapter.

168. Cic. *pro Mur.* 47; cf. *Es. e Soc.* 76, n. 75 [= 30, n. 75 above].

169. Characteristically Biscardi, p. 250, comes out with the remark that the effect of Sulpicius' proposals was that he obtained a preponderance in the *comitia tributa*.

170. As P. Fraccaro ('La procedura del voto nei comizi tributi Romani', *AAT* XLIX 1913–14, 600 f., esp. 611–12 = *Opuscula*, II 244–6) has shown.

171. Lange, *op. cit.* 111, referred it to the *lex Iulia* and he is followed, clearly, by Rice Holmes and Levi. Badian (cited *Es. e Soc.* 250, n. 135 [= 89, n. 135 above]) was right to argue that the *lex Plautia Papiria* was of limited application.

172. Apparently this is usually deduced by giving the term *contribuere* the meaning of 'aggregate', and from this it clearly follows that the aggregation took place to something which already existed. In my opinion, however, one should understand *contribuere* here as 'to join together, to compress, to concentrate', used of putting several things into one: in this case all the *novi cives* into eight tribes only. This seems to be the meaning also in Just. XII 5, 8: *in unam cohortem eos, qui de rege durius opinati fuerant, contribuit*; Colum. IX 11, 1: *duas vel tres alveorum plebes in unum contribuere licebit*; and in Gaius, *Dig.* XXXV 2, 79: *quae . . . relicta sunt in unum contribuuntur* (see also Livy, XXXI 30, 6). In this case what results from the *contributio* is something new (cf. *ThLL* 4, 777, 47 f.).

173. See the remarks of Mommsen, *SR* III 179 and n. 1.

174. *Art. cit.* 242.

175. *Es. e Soc.* 265 f. [= 96 f. below]. Sherwin-White prefers, as we have seen, to interpret the demand for the citizenship rather as a desire for freedom from oppression by Roman magistrates than as a wish to share in political life (*op. cit.* 126 and 129), and claims that the question of *suffragium*, the right to participate in voting, was purposely exaggerated by writers of the Optimate tradition; for them that problem was connected with the maintenance of power and was therefore very important (p. 130). But just as the development of events rebuts his concept of the Social War, so the whole question *de novorum civium suffragiis* shows that this second claim, which is used to support his first concept of the causes of the war, will not do.

176. App. I 55, 242–3; Biscardi, *art. cit.* 250 and n. 1.

177. Livy, *Per.* LXXXIV.

178. Biscardi, *art. cit.* 252.

179. Biscardi, *art. cit.* 254–5, seems to assess these facts accurately.

180. Livy, *Per.* LXXXVI: see Levi, *Costituzione*, 163.

181. Rostovtzeff, p. 22.

182. 'Homo novus', *BJ* CXXXIV 1929, 54 f., esp. 66. Cf. *Das Zeitalter cit.* 193 f.

183. 'Caesar, the Senate and Italy', *PBSR* XIV 1938, 1 f.; *RR* 78 f. and also *JRS* XXVII 1937, 122 f.

184. The lengthy study of I. Suolahti, *The Junior Officers of the Roman Army in the Republican Period*, Helsinki 1955, has shown the profound change in the officer class which took place after 89 BC. See *RSI* LXIX, 1957, 278–9; also T. P. Wiseman, *New Men in the Roman Senate, 139 BC–14 AD*, Oxford 1971.

185. On this see, for example, the examples cited *Es. e Soc.* 242, n. 117 [= 86, n. 117 above]. We know that Italians were introduced at once and on a large scale into the equestrian order (as we shall see this also follows from the composition of the Sullan Senate); cf. S. J. De Laet, 'La composition de l'ordre équestre sous Auguste et Tibère', *RBPh* XX 1941, 509 f., esp. 519–20; Nicolet, *Ordre équestre*, 387 f.'. Since these Italians would certainly have belonged to the commercial class, whose economic and political interests I have already demonstrated, we can well understand their attitude in the years immediately after 89 BC; it is indicated, for example, by Asc. p. 69, 20 Stangl.

186. See Chapters XII and XIV.

187. On this cf. Willems, *Sénat*, 394.

188. *Es. e Soc.* 162 [= 61 above].

189. One of the sons of Minatus Magius, P. Magius (Münzer, *RE* s.v. no. 10), was tr. pl. in 87 BC (Cic. *Brutus*, 179). This leads me to call attention to the entire college of tribunes in that year (see the accounts of Niccolini, *Fasti*, 232 f. and Broughton, II 47, which are the basis of what follows). Six of the tribunes were pro-Cinna (Livy, *Per.* LXXIX; Gran. Lic. p. 15 Flemisch; the evidence of Appian, I 64, 290, seems in error); of these we know by name M. Vergilius (Cic. *Brutus*, 179; Οὐεργίνιος in Plut. *Sulla*, 10, 8); the Magius I have already mentioned and, in all probability, the Γάιος Μιλώνιος of App. I 65, 295 (C. Milonius in Gran. Lic. p. 17 and 19 Flemisch) and a Μάριος (Γάιος in App. I 65, 295) to be identified with M. Marius Gratidianus (Niccolini, *loc. cit.*). The other four were Sullans, of whom one, Sex. Lucilius (Vell. II 24, 2; in Plut. *Mar.* 45, 3 the reading is not certain), was murdered the year after (on the question see Niccolini, p. 236), while the others were able to escape. This composition of the college (6 Marians, 4 Sullans) is very interesting since we know that Sulla had interfered in the elections and had succeeded in getting Sertorius defeated (Plut. *Sert.* 4, 6). It is even possible that the nomination of P. Magius was due to Sulla: the Magii of this branch of the family, as is well-known, were loyal to Rome in the *Bellum Sociale* in which they fought alongside Sulla (Vell. II 16, 2) and

won the *civitas* as a reward. Sulla could not foresee that, once they became citizens, they would turn democrats. From the presence of Marius Gratidianus we may probably deduce that the tribunician elections in 88 had been held before the sedition of Sulpicius; it would be strange if Sulla had allowed a man to become tribune who was related to a declared *hostis*. This comes out clearly from the context of Plut. *Sert.* 4, 6. In any case, it seems that the Marian majority should be explained by the presence among the electors of *novi cives*; we know that in the consular elections, held when Rome was occupied by the legions from Capua, Sulla had to renounce the two candidates he preferred because of the electorate's hostility, and accept Cornelius Cinna of the opposite party (Plut. *Sulla*, 10, 4 f.). I am not convinced by the different interpretation offered by B. Scardigli, *Athenaeum* N.S. XLIX 1971, 229–37.

Evidence of a somewhat limited reform of the tribunate by Sulla on this occasion (App. I 59, 267), does not seem reliable (Carcopino, *Sylla*, 1931, 34, n. 2); Niccolini, *Il tribunato della plebe*, 1932, 145 and *Fasti*, 232, accepts Appian's statement. NB I have changed my view; see *Es. e Soc.* 407 f. [= 142 f. below].

190. I list here some of the democrats of the period 88–82 BC – apart from those mentioned in the two preceding notes and apart from the rebel chiefs – who appear to have become in all probability Roman citizens after 89 BC. In 82 (?) the tribunate (Niccolini, *Fasti*, 430 f.; Broughton, II 68) fell to Q. (?) Valerius Soranus (from Sora, Latin colony of 303 BC). He must be identified with the poet Valerius Aedituus (Fr. Della Corte, *RFIC* LXIII 1935, 68–70). The fact that he dared to pronounce the holy name of Rome has been rightly interpreted, taking into consideration his political views, as an act directed at breaking the Roman aristocracy's privileged position even on sacral and religious ground (so L. Alfonsi, *Epigraphica* X 1948, 81 f.; *ibid.* XI 1949, 47 f. I do not believe that his position as *aedituus* at Rome conflicts with his having been a Latin up to 89: Cichorius, *Hermes* XLI 1906, 64). Burrienus, *praetor urbanus* in 83, was by origin Etruscan or Picene (Syme, *JRS* XXVIII 1938, 123, n. 70); C. Carrinas, praetor in 82 (Broughton, II 67; Münzer, *RE* s.v. no. 1) was Etruscan or Umbrian (Syme, p. 90, n. 4). In 82 Sulla murdered a Lollius, probably Picene (Münzer, *RE* s.v. no. 2). There is evidence for the Lollii on Delos (Münzer, *RE* s.v. no. 7; cf. nos. 8, 9, 13, 14). They entered political life in the Sullan period and perhaps were not *cives* pre-89 (Münzer, *RE* s.v. col. 1375, is dubious: see however Passerini, *Athenaeum* N.S. XV 1937, 271, no. 48 apropos a Lollius mentioned in 129 BC in the *S.C. de agro Pergameno*). Also murdered by Sulla in 82 was a Venuleius (Oros. V 21, 8: cf. *BCH* XXXVI 1912, 89). Others from Campania (mentioned *Es. e Soc.* 155 f. [= 58 f. above]) were very probably already citizens. Cf. Badian, *FC* 245, n. 2.

191. *Loc. cit.*

192. *JRS* XXXIV 1944, 106.

193. The support of these local groups for the Marian faction needs to be analysed: in Etruria, Umbria and the Sabine country the lower classes were Marian, in Campania in general the upper classes. Syme's statement must therefore be accepted in the sense that Sulla would have favoured the anti-Marian social classes of those districts.

194. I rely, of course, on the list of Sullan senators which, following Hill, *CQ* XXVI 1932, 70 f., I have given *Es. e Soc.* 159 f. [= 59 f. above].

195. Cf. those which remain in the list *Es. e Soc.* 165, n. 29 [= 62, n. 29 above], after those which I have already mentioned have been removed: 61 L. Turius; 80 C. Fidiculanius Falcula; 85 L. Lartius; 89 M. Petreius; 94 Q. Rancius; 97 Sornatius; 98 P. Tadius; 102 L. Voluscius. Nos. 68–9 C. and L. Caepasius may also be added (in parenthesis I would also say here that we can enter in the list of Sullan senators (as no. 85 (a)) Licinius Bucco, on whom see Münzer, *RE* s.v. no. 39, and that

we should delete no. 78, L. Critonius, if he was, as appears to be the case, a Marian
moneyer in 83 or 82: Broughton, II 63).

196. Cf. nos. 65 C. Anneus; 95 M. Seius; for members of these *gentes* in the East Hatzfeld, *Trafiquants*, Index, s.v.

197. For an inquiry into the sources which on this point are at variance see *Es. e Soc.* 165
[= 62 above]. But see *Es. e Soc.* 407 [= 142 below].

198. On the significance of Sulla's Senate in this sense see Strasburger, *Concordia ordinum*
1931, 9 f. See also *Es. e Soc.* 407 [= 142 below].

199. Stein, *Röm. Ritterstand*, 207 f.

200. I would like to mention here the passage of Cic. *pro Mur.* 47 (63 BC) which shows
that in the face of Ser. Sulpicius Rufus' proposals made to reform the *comitia*
(certainly for electoral propaganda purposes) – see *Es. e Soc.* 76, n. 75 [= 30, n. 75
above] – opposition came not from the citizen body which was disillusioned and
sceptical, but from the *municipia: graviter homines honesti atque in suis vicinitatibus
et municipiis gratiosi tulerunt a tali viro esse pugnatum, ut omnes et dignitatis et
gratiae gradus tollerentur.*

201. This has been extensively documented and illustrated by Syme, *PBSR art. cit.* 18 f.
Cf. as a typical example Cic. *ad Att.* VIII 13, 2: *nihil prorsus aliud curant (municipales homines) nisi agros, nisi villulas, nisi nummulos suos* (49 BC).

202. As E. Lepore, *RSI* LXIII 1951, 565, has pointed out from evidence drawn from
Cicero's correspondence with Brutus (II 7, 1). In general on the desire for peace,
order and security cf. Wirszubski, *Libertas*, 91 f.

203. On the influx of Campanians into Caesar's faction see Syme, p. 90, n. 7 and 91, n. 1,
and *JRS* XXXIV 1944, 93 f. In general on the composition of the Caesarian faction
see Syme, *PBSR art. cit.* 20 f.

204. I append a list of Roman politicians who came in all probability from *municipia* and
who either held office in the post-Sullan decade or entered on their careers in this
period. It should be noted at once that this list is intended only to lend proof to
what has been frequently said concerning the entry into Roman political life of men
from the *municipia* after the Social War. It does not indeed pretend to be complete.
Of course I do not repeat here the names I have already set out above of Sullan
senators of Italian origin, though they naturally contribute to the same conclusion.

  1. Q. CAECILIUS NIGER, Münzer, *RE* s.v. no. 101; Syme, *PBSR* XIV 1938, 14,
     n. 68; Verres' quaestor, a Sicilian.
  2. L. COSSINIUS, Münzer, *RE* s.v. no. 2 (=1?); praetor 73. From Tivoli?
  3. M. CREPEREIUS, Münzer, *RE* s.v. no. 1; senator in 70; equestrian origin.
  4. Q. FUFIUS CALENUS, Willems, *Sénat*, 470; Münzer, *RE* s.v. no. 10; cf. nos. 8
     and 9.
  5. M. LOLLIUS PALICANUS, Willems, p. 457; Syme, *PBSR art. cit.* 25, n. 130; *id.
     RR* 31; tr. pl. in 70 BC. Picene. See Wiseman, *New Men in the Roman Senate*,
     237, no. 231.
  6. L. MARCILIUS, Münzer, *RE* s.v. no. 1: Samnite?
  7. C. ORCHIVIUS, Willems, p. 461; Münzer, *RE* s.v. no. 1; praetor in 66. From
     Praeneste?
  8. L. SAENIUS, Willems, p. 511; Münzer, *RE* s.v. no. 1; senator in 63. Etruscan?
  9. P. SATRIENUS, Willems, p. 502; Münzer, *RE* s.v. no. 1; Grueber, I 392;
     moneyer about 77 BC.
 10. SEX. TEIDIUS, Münzer, *RE* s.v. no. 2; Syme, *PBSR art. cit.* 24; id. *RR* 93 and
     94, n. 1. Senator in the Ciceronian period.
 11. M. TERPOLIUS, Willems, p. 488; Münzer, *RE* s.v.; Syme, *PBSR art. cit.* 23;
     tr. pl. in 77. From Praeneste? Cf. Wiseman, *op. cit.* 265, no. 424.

12. CN. TUDICIUS, Willems, p. 509; Münzer, *RE* s.v. Senator in 66.

13. C. URBINIUS, Willems, p. 505; Syme, *PBSR art. cit.* 22, n. 108; *id. RR* 193, n. 6. Metellus Pius' quaestor.

14. C. VIBIENUS, Willems, p. 539; Syme, *PBSR art. cit.* 24; *id. RR* 94, n. 1. Senator in Ciceronian period.

In the decade after Sulla we meet two senatorial Egnatii (Münzer, *RE* s.v. nos. 2 and 8; cf. no. 27) and a Herennius (Münzer, *ibid.* s.v. no. 7; cf. 6 and 9). If the former were related to the Egnatius who was leader of the Samnite rebels (Münzer, *ibid.* s.v. no. 10) and if the latter were related to Herennius the Picene (Münzer, *ibid.* s.v. no. 15: on M. Herennius cos. 93 see Syme, p. 94, n. 2), one would have to deduce that the Sullan and post-Sullan measures against the ex-rebels were not as serious as they are usually represented. Incidentally, Herennius, no. 7 in *RE*, if the evidence of the sources all refers to a single man, was certainly a Marian. Badian, *Hermes* LXXXIII 1955, 109–12, has shown convincingly that the episode of the tribune Herennius in Sall. *Hist.* II 21 Maur. must be referred to 88 BC: Herennius was perhaps a legate of Cn. Pompeius Strabo. We know, however, some citizen Herennii already by the second century BC (Passerini, *Athenaeum*, 1937, *art. cit.* 270, no. 40) whose relations with Marius were very close (Plut. *Mar.* 5, 7).

205. I cite the most important passages: *pro Sulla*, 22: *at hic etiam, id quod minime tibi necesse fuit, facetus esse voluisti, cum Tarquinium et Numam et me tertium peregrinum regem esse dixisti . . . illud quaero, peregrinum cur me esse dixeris . . . 'hoc dico', inquit, 'te esse ex municipio'. 23 . . . sed scire ex te pervelim quam ob rem qui ex municipiis veniant peregrini tibi esse videantur. non possunt omnes esse patricii . . . 24 ac si tibi nos peregrini videmur quorum iam et nomen et honos inveteravit et urbi huic et hominum famae ac sermonibus, quam tibi illos competitores tuos peregrinos videri necesse erit qui iam ex tota Italia delecti tecum de honore ac de omni dignitate contendent!* (Cf. Syme, *PBSR art. cit.* 5 f. and Schur, *art. cit.* 62). One recalls the invective of Catiline in Sall. *BC* 31, 7: *M. Tullius, inquilinus civis urbis Romae.* On Cicero's municipal origin being thrown in his face see the other evidence in R. Gnauck, *Die Bedeutung des Marius und Cato Maior für Cicero*, Diss. 1935, 33, n. 37. For the defence of the *homo novus*, the object of attack or hostility from the Roman *nobilitas*, cf. *pro Mur.* 15 f., 17. Vittinghoff, *Röm. Kolonisation und Bürgerrechtspolitik (Abh. Akad. Mainz)* 1951, 14, 1310 (=94), brings out the point that Cicero himself on certain occasions was the prisoner of his own outlook. See also the case of Decidius Saxa who was dubbed Celtiberian in mockery: Syme, *JRS* XXVII 1937, 122 f.

206. Cic. *pro Planc.* 18–24.

207. Cic. *Phil.* III 15.

208. *Bell. Afric.* 57, 4.

209. Cf. Wirszubski, *Libertas*, 69 f. This is the significance which *civitas* has also in Cic. *Phil.* XII 27: *Cn. Pompeius Sexti filius, consul me praesente, cum essem tiro in eius exercitu, cum P. Vettio Scatone, duce Marsorum, inter bina castra collocutus est: quo quidem memini Sex. Pompeium, fratrem consulis, ad colloquium ipsum Roma venire, doctum virum atque sapientem. quem cum Scato salutasset 'quem te appellem?' inquit. at ille 'voluntate hospitem, necessitate hostem'. erat in illo colloquio aequitas: nullus timor, nulla suberat suspicio, mediocre etiam odium. non enim ut eriperent nobis socii civitatem, sed ut in eam reciperentur petebant.* The passage is also important because it shows that the ties linking the Roman and allied nobility were not such as to make the latter always line up with Rome, as most scholars suggest.

210. On Campania see *Es. e Soc.* 151 f. [= 56 f. above]. The outburst of Pontius Telesinus at the battle of the Colline Gate (82 BC) is well-known: Vell. II 27, 2 *dictitansque adesse Romanis ultimum diem vociferabatur eruendam delendamque*

urbem, adiciens numquam defuturos raptores Italicae libertatis lupos, nisi silva, in quam refugere solerent, esset excisa (cf. Horace, *Od.* IV 4, 50 (Hannibal speaking) and also Livy, III 66, 4. See H. Fuchs, *Der geistige Widerstand gegen Rom in der antiken Welt*, 1938, 46 f.). The Sabine bull which rages against the wolf of Rome is a recurrent theme in coin types of the Italian rebels: Grueber, II 327 and n. 2, and 333; Sydenham, *op. cit.* no. 628. See 'Italia e Roma nella "Storia" di Velleio Patercolo', *CS* I 1962, 9 = *Es. e Soc.* 359 f.

211. As the intentions of Telesinus show. Cf. also *Es. e Soc.* 158 [= 59 above].

212. Cf. Strabo, V 4, 2, which refers, however, just to the Samnites: δεόμενοι τυχεῖν ἐλευθερίας καὶ πολιτείας. . . .; cf. Wirszubski, *Libertas*, 67 and Momigliano's review, with reservations expressed, in *JRS* XLI 1951, 147. The legend *Safinim* (=*Samnium*) on some coins of C. Papius Mutilus (Grueber, II 332 and n. 1) must probably be understood as a pointer to a policy of autonomy, and be referred presumably to the final period of the revolt. See A. Rocco, *Samnium* XIX 1946, 47 f.; Bernareggi, *RIN* V 14, 1966, 85; Salmon, *Samnium and the Samnites*, 75. This conflict between social classes is already strong in allied communities in the second century BC as A. H. McDonald, *JRS* XXXIV 1944, 11 f. has shown. Cf. Devoto, *Gli antichi Italici²*, Florence 1951, 377.

213. Cf. Sherwin-White, *Roman Citizenship*, 129. What we know of the constitution of the rebels (see Carcopino³, p. 380 f.) derives from the well-known passage of Diod. XXXVII 2, 5. Cf. H. D. Meyer, 'Die Organisation der Italiker im Bundesgenossenkrieg', *Historia* VII 1958, 74–9.

214. It is again from Diod. XXXVII 11, that we know the text of this ὅρκος φιλίας (so, it seems, one should read with O. Hirschfeld, *Kleine Schriften*, Berlin 1913, 288 f. instead of the φιλίππου of the MSS): . . . πατρίδα ἡγήσομαι τὴν 'Ρώμην . . . The authenticity of the document is notoriously controversial (most recently in favour of authenticity L. R. Taylor, *Party Politics, op. cit.* 46 and 198, n. 67, and Devoto, *op. cit.* 334). Rose, in his thorough study in *HThR* XXX 1937, 165–81, concluded, on the basis of his examination of the divinities invoked there and of their order in the text, that a Latin origin for the entire formula should be rejected; it is traceable, perhaps, to the work of a Hellenistic rhetorician. It is a fact, however, that the oath is certainly contemporary with the events of the Social War and that it may emanate from allied circles, possibly Greek in their outlook, interested in the *civitas* and in little sympathy with Roman religion. Its possible authenticity is not weakened by some scholars' view that the document was brought to the knowledge of public opinion or directly invented by Drusus' enemies; hence the possibility of an alternative explanation for the reading φιλίππου given by the source. A coin, possibly of 72 BC, with the names of the moneyers KALENI and CORDI (Grueber, I 415; K. Pink, *The Triumviri Monetales* (*Numismatic Studies* VII) 1952, 38, no. 71; Sydenham, *op. cit.* no. 797) seems to allude to peace between Rome and Italy after the *Bellum Sociale. Contra*, J-Cl. Richard, *MEFR* LXXV 1963, 313 f.

215. Cf. the remarks of Mommsen, *SR* III 780–1. Note also what is said by G. Vitucci, in De Ruggiero, *Diz. Epig.* s.v. 'Latium', 442–3.

216. Cf. De Ruggiero, *La patria nel diritto pubblico romano*, 1921, 16 f., 70. On the concept of *patria* see L. Krattinger, *Der Begriff des Vaterlandes im republikanischen Rom*, Diss. Zurich, 1944, esp. p. 25; M. Hammond, '*Germana Patria*', *HSPh* LX 1951, 147 f.

217. *de Leg.* II 5.

218. So M. Pohlenz, 'Der Eingang von Ciceros Gesetze', *Philologus* XCIII 1938, 105.

219. On all this see Sherwin-White, *op. cit.* 134 f. F. Sartori, in the course of some interesting research (*Problemi di storia costituzionale italiota*, Rome 1953) comes to conclusions which, with certain reservations, can confirm all that we have said. He

has illuminated, as far as the evidence allows him, the survival of Greek and Oscan constitutional forms in municipal organization subsequent to the Social War. This, of course, is only one aspect of that singular capacity to adapt which is continually demonstrated by the Roman political organization when confronted with pre-existing conditions. However, I cannot agree with much of what Sartori says in the concluding summary of his work (esp. pp. 160–3) where it seems to me that neither the historical development which led to the concession of the *civitas* to the *socii* nor the varied forms of the demands and purposes of the allies themselves are very clear. See my review in *Athenaeum* N.S. XXXII 1954, 285 f. = *Es. e Soc.* 600 f.

220. 'Sertorio', *Athenaeum* N.S. X 1932, 127 f., esp. 127–31.

221. A. Schulten, *Sertorius*, 1926. For earlier studies *id.* 'Viriathus', *NJA* XXXIX–XL 1917, 209 and 235–6 (parallel between Viriathus and Sertorius).

222. 'Sertorius', *Hermes* LXIV 1929, 199 f. A lengthy treatment and a shrewd assessment of the Sertorian episode are provided by L. Pareti, *Storia di Roma*, III 649–87. The ancient sources and their prejudices are dealt with on p. 649, n. 6. I note that Pareti, who follows Sallust's version for the pact with Mithridates (p. 677 f.), picks up the connexion with the negotiations which took place previously between Mithridates and the Italian rebels (see below, Chaps. XII and XIV). Also Pareti (p. 683) places the *lex Plautia de reditu Lepidanorum* in 73 BC and seems to assign it the same significance as that attributed to it by Treves (see following note).

223. Treves' view that Sertorius at the peak of his fortunes made efforts to obtain from his contacts among Roman politicians an amnesty granting him and his followers the right to return to Rome (p. 144) is, if I am not mistaken, based on a date of 73 BC for the *lex Plautia de reditu Lepidanorum*; this, on Treves' view, excluded the Lepidani of Sertorius and would have entailed the collapse of their hopes and as a consequence the conspiracy of Perperna. But the *lex Plautia* dates to 70 and applied to the Lepidani of Sertorius; there is no question that this follows from Suet. *Caes.* 5, a passage which Treves, p. 144, n. 3, has to explain away with an unconvincing argument. On the dating to 70 see H. Last, *CAH* IX 896 and L. R. Taylor, *CPh* XXXVI 1941, 121 n. 32, and *Es. e Soc.* 443 f. [= 151 f. below]. See Broughton, II 128. For a date of 73 or 72 see Gelzer, *Pompeius*, 72; A. Berger, *RE* Suppl. VII, s.v. 'lex Plautia', col. 403, and R. Grispo, *NRS* XXXVI 1952, 221 and n. 1.

224. W. Schur, *Sallust als Historiker*, 1934, 222–56.

225. App. I 2, 7; 34, 151; 55, 240; 60, 269.

226. V. Ehrenberg, *Ost und West. Studien zur geschichtlichen Problematik der Antike*, 1935, 177–201.

227. H. Berve, *PhW* LVII 1937, col. 650 f.

228. On a point of method one cannot accept Berve's assertion (that, even admitting the 'Roman' purpose and feeling of Sertorius, he is to be seen merely as a forerunner, a ghost-figure of Roman history, and this can have no effect on our historical judgement of Sertorius which does not depend on his plans but on his deeds which remain those of a traitor) since in that case any judgement on Sertorius is *a priori* negative in that he could establish nothing in the ten-year struggle – hence the negative evaluation of De Sanctis, *RFIC* N.S. V 1927, 147. The only way of understanding this struggle is to try to uncover the designs which dictated it.

A recent article by R. Grispo, cited *Es. e Soc.* 285, n. 223 [= 103, n. 223 above] is largely devoted to a re-examination of the military successes and defeats of the Sertorian decade without affecting to any important degree the work of Schulten. On the policies of Sertorius and the causes of the struggle, Grispo denies that evidence of continued contacts between Sertorius and democrats in Rome has any validity and thinks that the exile was aiming at dictatorship (p. 192, n.; 197 and n. 1; 215 f.).

229. Different views in Schulten, p. 106; Berve, p. 205 f.; M. Gelzer, 'Hat Sertorius in seinem Vertrag mit Mithridates die Provinz Asia abgetreten?' *PhW* LII 1932, col. 1129 f. = *Kleine Schriften*, II 139–45; Schur, p. 238 f.

230. *FHA* III p. 175 with the evidence. The passage of App. *Iber.* 38, 152–3 (206 BC) must be interpreted in the sense explained by *FHA* III, p. 163.

231. App. *Iber.* 38, 153 (*FHA* III p. 163): cf. *Es. e Soc.* 105, n. 153 [= 40, n. 153 above] and Fr. Vittinghoff, 'Röm. Kolonisation', *cit.* 1288 (=72) and n. 5. The most recent, to my knowledge, and the most exhaustive contribution on the subject of the Romanization of Spain is that of C. Sánchez-Albornoz, 'Proceso de la romanizacion de España desde los Escipiones hasta Augusto', *AHAM* 1949, 5–35.

232. A. Piganiol, *Histoire de Rome*, 1949, 121, makes this emigration begin about 175 BC; cf. *Es. e Soc.* 290, n. 236 [= 106, n. 236 below].

233. Cf. Livy, XXXIV 9, 12 (*FHA* III p. 179).

234. Cf. T. A. Richard, 'The Mining of the Romans in Spain', *JRS* XVIII 1928, 129 f.; O. Davies, *Roman Mines in Europe*, Oxford 1935, 116 f.

235. The well-founded view of T. Frank, 'The Activities of the Equestrian Corporations', *CPh* XXVIII 1933, 7 and n. 1 (with sources).

236. Frank, *art. cit.* 8. The famous passage of Polyb. VI 17, 2–4, was written about 150 BC.

237. Polyb. XXXIV 9, 9 = Strab. III 2, 10.

238. Diod. V 36, 3: ὕστερον δὲ τῶν ῾Ρωμαίων κρατησάντων τῆς ᾿Ιβηρίας, πλῆθος ᾿Ιταλῶν ἐπεπόλασε τοῖς μετάλλοις, καὶ μεγάλους ἀπεφέροντο πλούτους διὰ τὴν φιλοκερδίαν. The passage (derived from Posidonius) is also in Jacoby, *Fgr Hist.* IIA p. 308, F 117; cf. IIA Comm. p. 190 (note on F 47); see also Sánchez-Albornoz, *art. cit.* 14. There must have been much discussion in Roman circles about the middle of the second century BC of the possibilities of exploiting Spain if the embassy of Judas Maccabeus in 161 BC returned with the impression that it was only to get their hands on the wealth of that region that the Romans had undertaken the conquest of the country: *I Macc.* 8, 3 (*FHA* IV p. XII). On the impression given by this part of *I Macc.* see M. Sordi, *Acme* V 1952, 509 f.

239. Frank, *art. cit.* 10 f.

240. I have listed them *Es. e Soc.* 105, n. 153 [= 40, n. 153 above].

241. Livy, *Per.* XLI; Fest. p. 86, 5 Lindsay; cf. App. *Iber.* 43, 175–9 and the comm. of Mommsen on *CIL* II 2857. On the dedication of Iliturgis to Gracchus see A. Degrassi, *MAL* ser. VIII, XIII 1 1967, 34–8.

242. Livy, XLIII 3.

243. Strabo, III 2, 1; cf. Vittinghoff, p. 1289 (=73) and n. 1, and *FHA* VI p. 153 f.

244. *FHA* IV p. 140.

245. Cf. *Es. e Soc.* 114, n. 172 [= 43, n. 172 above] and *FHA* IV p. 139; also Vittinghoff, p. 1289 (=73), n. 2: Wilson, *Emigration from Italy*, 40–2.

246. *Es. e Soc.* 105, n. 153 [= 40, n. 153 above].

247. Strabo, III 5, 1: εἰσήγαγε (Metellus) δὲ ἐποίκους τρισχιλίους τῶν ἐκ τῆς ᾿Ιβηρίας ῾Ρωμαίων (the source seems to be Posidonius or Artemidorus: *FHA* IV p. 143; VI p. 273).

248. There are various signs that these foundations developed and grew in importance in a short space of time: Italica received part of the Corinthian booty of Mummius after 146 BC (*CIL* I² 630 = II 1119 = *ILLRP* 331); a Γάιον Μάρκιον . . . ἄνδρα ῎Ιβηρα ἐκ πόλεως ᾿Ιταλικῆς, certainly a Roman of Spain (here ῎Ιβηρα must mean *Hispaniensem*), had a command in 143 BC under a Quinctius (App. *Iber.* 66, 282 = *FHA* IV p. 116; on Marcius see Münzer, *RE* s.v. no. 10; on Quinctius see E. Kornemann, *Die neue Livius-Epitome* (*Klio, Beiheft* II) 1904, 100). Near New Carthage some of the oldest Latin inscriptions of Spain are found with names of citizens (e.g. *CIL* I² 2269 = II 3408 = *ILLRP* 117; II 3439 = 6247, 4 = I²

2397 = *ILS* 8706 = *ILLRP* 1262; II 3433 = I² 2270 = *ILLRP* 777; II 3434 = 5927 = I² 2271 = *ILLRP* 778); Kornemann (*RE* s.v. 'conventus', col. 1183) speaks therefore of *conventus civium Romanorum. Conventus c. R.* were also at Corduba, Hispalis and Tarraco (Kornemann, *ibidem*). As E. Albertini, *Mélanges Cagnat*, 1912, 312, pointed out, the Romans were grouped together at points where natural resources were greatest, permitting the establishment of a centre of trade and commerce.

249. Attested by milestones of Q. Fabius Q. f. Labeo Procos. (*CIL* I² 823 = II 4924–5 = *ILS* 5813 = *ILLRP* 461; cf. Mommsen, *SR* II³ 647, n. 2 and Münzer, *RE* s.v. 'Fabius', no. 92) and of M'. Sergius M'. f. Procos. (*CIL* I² 840 = II 4956 = *ILS* 5812 = *ILLRP* 462; cf. Münzer, *RE* s.v. 'Sergius', no. 17; for both see also *FHA* IV p. 144). As Mommsen, *RG* V² 1885, 67 pointed out, such ancient milestones are not found in any other Western province (see now, however, the milestone of Cn. Domitius Ahenobarbus, found in Narbonensis, dating to 120–118 BC: P.-M. Duval, *Gallia* VII 1949, 207 f. = *ILLRP* 460a; for the Sicilian milestone of an Aurelius Cotta see A. Degrassi, *Scritti vari di antichità*, III 1967, 195–204). The well-known passage of Strabo, III 4, 20, on the *togati* of the Ebro valley refers therefore to a development already mature well within the second century BC (cf. J. Caro Baroia, *Los Pueblos del Norte de la Península Ibérica*, Madrid 1943, 75 f. and C. H. V. Sutherland, *The Romans in Spain*, *217 BC–AD 117*, London 1939, 71).

250. See R. Thouvenot, *Essai sur la province romaine de Bétique (Bibl. Éc. franç. d'Athènes et de Rome* CXLIX) 1940, 135, n. 4 and Sánchez-Albornoz, *art. cit.* 13, n. 37. See also J. de C. Serra-Rafols, *Ampurias* XI 1949, 200 f. (coins of 268 and 217 BC; I have obtained this information from *Fasti Archaeologici* IV 1951, no. 2173).

251. Cf. Schulten, *RE* s.v. 'Hispania', col. 2035; Sutherland, p. 11 f. On the *argentum oscense* mentioned in Livy, XXXIV 10, 4 and 7, see, in addition to Schulten, *RE* s.v. 'Osca', Thouvenot, p. 228 and C. Seltman, *NC* ser. VI, 4, 77 f. In general on the emigration to Spain see Wilson, *Emigration from Italy*, 22 f. and 29 f.

252. See the following Chapters, and also 'Aspetti della lotta di Sesto Pompeio in Spagna', *Legio VII Gemina*, León 1970, 133 f. = *Es. e Soc.* 473 f.

253. At the battle of Munda *equites Romani partim ex urbe, partim ex provincia ad milia tres* were killed (*Bell. Hisp.* 31, 9. In *FHA* V p. 102 f. Klotz's edition of the *Bell. Hisp.* is reproduced with a limited app. crit.). Three *equites Romani Hastenses* are mentioned in *Bell. Hisp.* 26, 2 (A. Baebius and C. Flavius: cf. Münzer, *RE* s.v. 'Flavius', no. 12; A. Trebellius: Münzer, *ibid.* s.v. no. 1). An *eques Romanus* of Italica also occurs in *Bell. Hisp.* 25, 4 (Q. Pompeius Niger). The Roman citizens of Italica and Corduba who were implicated in the attack on Q. Cassius Longinus in 48 BC certainly belonged to the provincial nobility if not to the equestrian class (*Bell. Alex.* 48–64 = *FHA* V p. 81 f.; cf. Thouvenot, p. 143): L. Munatius Flaccus (Münzer, *RE* s.v. no. 19); T. Vasius; L. Mercello (Münzer, *RE* s.v.); L. Licinius Squillus (Münzer, *RE* s.v. no. 160); Manilius Tusculus (Münzer, *RE* s.v. no. 28); Annius Scapula, *maximae dignitatis et gratiae provincialis homo* (*Bell. Alex* 55, 2). See 'Aspetti della lotta', *art. cit.* Section 7 = *Es. e Soc.* 494 f.

On the number of citizens with the equestrian census at Gades in the Augustan period see the well-known remark of Strabo, III 5, 3. A Q. Iunius *ex Hispania* appears in Caes. *BG* V 27, 1 = *FHA* V p. 29; cf. Münzer, *RE* s.v. no. 31.

254. M. Aemilius Scaurus in Asc. p. 25, 5 Stangl, calls him *Hispanus; Sucronensis* is the term used by *auct. de vir. ill.* 72, 11; Quint. V 12, 10 and Val. Max. III 7, 8 (cf. VIII 6, 4). It may be conjectured that Asconius substituted *Hispanus* for *Sucronensis* as being the clearer term (Fraccaro, 'Scauriana', *RAL* ser. V 20, 1911, 191 = *Opuscula*, II 143). Cf. also Syme, *PBSR* XIV 1938, 14, n. 68. A L. Fabius Hispaniensis was quaestor in 81 BC: Grueber, II 352. He later joined Sertorius: see below. On the

242 *Notes*

Fabii of Saguntum, made Roman citizens by Metellus Pius and Pompey, see *FHA* V p. 19.

L. Decidius Saxa was a Roman citizen of Spain who made a career for himself with Caesar: cf. R. Syme, *JRS* XXVII 1937, 121 f. and *id. RR* 80, n. 1. An Egnatius is contemptuously called Celtiberian by Catullus, 39, 17: see Syme, *JRS art. cit.* 133 and n. 46. Spanish origin is suspected by some for the Caesarian senator Titius Hispanus (*Bell. Afric.* 28, 2); Willems, *Le Sénat*, I 596; Münzer, *RE* s.v. no. 13, col. 1557; Syme, p. 80, n. 2.

255. R. Menéndez Pidal, *Orígenes del Español*, 1926, 485 f.
256. V. Bertoldi, *Colonizzazioni nell' antico Mediterraneo*, Naples 1950, 130 f.
257. This last hypothesis of Menéndez Pidal met opposition when it appeared, and Pidal replied with some interesting observations in the second edition of his work, 1929, 303 f. and 582 f. (*inter al.* see W. v. Wartburg, *ZRPh* XLVIII 1928, 460). If the name Osca derives from Osci it is clear that this colonization is much earlier than the time of Sertorius, since *argentum oscense* is already in Livy in 197 BC (Menéndez[2], p. 582, against Wartburg). For the third edition of Menéndez see L. Terracini, *AGI* XXXVI 1951, 80.

On the whole question see the cautious notes of A. Kuhn, *Romanisches Philologie, I, Die romanischen Sprache*, Berne 1951, 355 f. and 386. See N. Lamboglia, *RSL* XVIII 1952, 108; R. Menéndez Pidal, *Boletín R. Academia Española* XXXIV May–August 1954, 165–216 and esp. in *Enciclopedia Lingüística Hispánica*, I, Madrid 1960, LIX–LXXXVI.

258. Thouvenot, p. 183.
259. *Scriptores Historiae Augustae, Vita Hadriani*, 1, 1 (see O. Th. Schulz, *Leben des Kaisers Hadrian*, Leipzig 1904, 17); W. Weber, *Rom. Herrschertum und Reich im zweiten Jahrhundert*, 1937, 13 and 125 (see Syme, *HZ* CLVIII 1938, 557). For other Aelii from Osca cf. M. Grant, *From Imperium to Auctoritas*, 1946, 167. Trajan, the *consobrinus* of Hadrian and therefore also *Italicensis* (App. *Iber.* 38, 153), is, according to Aur. Vict. *Epit. de Caes.* 13, 1, *ex urbe Tudertina*, i.e. of Umbrian origin.
260. See above.
261. Münzer, *RE* s.v. 'Mercello'; Schulze, *LE* 301 and Hübner on *CIL* II 2226. For the *gentilicium* Vasius cf. Schulze, *LE* 425 and 450.
262. A. Vives, *La moneda hispánica*, IV 1924, 21 f.; Grant, p. 473. Raius is perhaps Etruscan (Schulze, *LE* 217), Opsilius Oscan (Schulze, *LE* 335, n. 1 and 522, n. 7). Cf. also the *gentilicia* of Carteia (see Vives, *ibid.*): Ninius (Schulze, *LE* 311, n. 7 and 594); Falcidius (Schulze, *LE* 272); Minius (Sculze, *LE* 595 and 467); Arcius (Schulze, *LE* 126 and n. 6).
263. Vives, p. 44; Grant, p. 472, n. 24; Schulze, *LE* 380.
264. Vives, p. 33; *CIL* II 3508; Schulze, *LE* 160.

In an inscription of New Carthage prior to 45 BC (*CIL* I[2] 2269 = II 3408 = *ILLRP* 117) are mentioned L. Baebius, L. Cati(us), L. Taurius and Ser. Aefolan(us). On Catius, probably an Etruscan *gentilicium*, see Schulze, *LE* 76; on Taurius see Münzer, *RE* s.v.; on Aefolanus see Hübner, *Hermes* I 1866, 426; an A. Baebius in *Bell. Hisp.* 26, 2 (*eques Hastensis*).

The two brothers Rosci of *CIL* I[2] 2397 = II 3439 = *ILS* 8706 = *ILLRP* 1262 are perhaps originally from Lanuvium.
265. Vives, pp. 15–16; Grant, p. 472, nn. 20 and 22; Schulze, *LE* 105 and 163.
266. Vives, pp. 15–16; Grant, p. 472, nn. 21 and 23; Schulze, *LE* 355, 246, 550.
267. See *Es. e Soc.* 294, n. 254 [= 107, n. 254 above].
268. Cf. A. Afzelius, *Die röm. Kriegsmacht*, 1944, 66 f.
269. The *legiones vernaculae*, mentioned for example in *Bell. Alex.* 53, 5; 57, 1; *Bell. Hisp.*

7, 5; Caes. *BC* II 20, 4, are legions composed of natives (*in provincia nati: Bell. Alex. loc. cit.*): cf. Passerini, in De Ruggiero, *Diz. Epig.* s.v. 'legio', 552. For an analysis of the problem in greater depth see 'Aspetti della lotta', *art. cit. = Es. e Soc.* 473 f.

270. Caes. *BC* II 19, 3; cf. II 18, 1.
271. Caes. *BC* II 18, 1; *Bell. Alex.* 50, 3; 56, 4. On the knights killed at Munda see *Bell. Hisp.* 31, 9.
272. Caes. *BC* II 18, 4.
273. Gran. Lic. p. 16 Flemisch; cf. Münzer, *RE* s.v. 'Iunius', no. 51.
274. Plut. *Crass.* 6, 1.
275. Plut. *Sert.* 6, 9: 'Ρωμαίων δὲ τῶν αὐτόθι μετοικούντων τοὺς ἐν ἡλικίᾳ καθοπλίσας.
276. Grueber, II 352; see also G. Pierfitte, *Mélanges de la Société Toulousaine d'Études Classiques* I 1946, 121; and cf. Münzer, *RE* s.v. 'Fabius', no. 84.
277. Grueber, *loc. cit.* note.
278. Sall. *Hist.* III 83 Maur.
279. Of course, there were also those who showed opposition: we know about one of them, a Vibius Pac(c)iaecus, a wealthy latifundist of southern Spain near Malaca (cf. *FHA* IV p. 149). He helped Crassus in 85 BC and participated in 80 BC in the struggle against Sertorius by whom he was conquered and killed. The sources, especially those written in Greek, give discrepant spellings of his name, but the question has been clarified in an exemplary fashion by Münzer, *RE* s.v. 'Pac(c)iaecus' and 'Paccianus', nos. 1 and 2. A son of his who was a Caesarian is called *homo eius provinciae notus* in *Bell. Hisp.* 3, 4 (Wiseman, *New Men in the Roman Senate*, 248, no. 300). The case of the father Pac(c)iaecus is interesting because it appears to confirm the statement (see below) that the Roman citizens resident in southern Spain were rather opposed to Sertorius.
280. Οὓς ὠνόμαζε 'Ρωμαίους: Plut. *Sert.* 12, 2. See B. Scardigli, *A & R* N.S. XV 1970, 177–81.
281. App. I 108, 505–6; 109, 511; 112, 520; 114, 530; Plut. *Sert.* 15, 1.
282. App. I 107, 504; 113, 527; Plut. *Sert.* 15, 2.
283. Plut. *Sert.* 15, 5. Grispo, *art. cit.* 203, is mistaken when he translates 'maniples'.
284. See Treves, *art. cit.* 134 and n. 7.
285. Cf. e.g. Oros. V 23, 9.
286. Drumann-Groebe, *Geschichte Roms*, IV 369; G. Stahl, *De bello Sertoriano*, Erlangen 1907, 52, n. 7.
287. A. Schulten, *Sertorius*, 79, n. 394.
288. Livy, fr. 18 (from Book XCI). The calculation is based on 400 men to a cohort.
289. Treves, *loc. cit.*
290. Strabo, III 4, 10.
291. On the attitude of Corduba see Sall. *Hist.* II 28 Maur.; Cic. *pro Archia*, 26 and the comments of Schulten, *Sertorius*, 128. On the terror which the news of Sertorius' landing in 80 BC inspired in Baetica cf. Sall. *Hist.* I 107 Maur. It appears that this reaction is reflected in coin hoards of 79 BC: see Thouvenot, p. 135, n. 4. Cf. also J. L. Monteverde, 'El Tesorillo ibérico de Roa', *AEA* XXII 1949, 377 f. I have not been able to consult F. Mateu y Llopis, *Los tesoros monetarios de la época Sertoriana*, Barcelona 1949, which has also been published as an appendix to the Spanish translation of A. Schulten, *Sertorius*, by M. Carrenas, Barcelona 1949.
292. Cic. *pro Balbo*, 5.
293. See the case of Pacciaecus cited above.
294. Sall. *Hist.* II 54 Maur.; Plut. *Pomp.* 18, 5. Sutherland, *Romans in Spain*, 233, n. 12, emphasizes the significance of Valentia's support for Sertorius since he holds that it was a *colonia civium*. But it is more likely that it was not; the various views are

collected *Es. e Soc.* 114, n. 172 [= 43, n. 172 above]; cf. also F. Hampl. *RhM* XCV 1952, 63 and 69.

295. A. Piganiol, *Histoire de Rome*, 166. Cf. *id. La conquête romaine²*, 338.

296. See above, esp. Chap. VIII.

297. Sall. *Hist.* I 96 Maur.; Plut. *Sert.* 7, 1–3; cf. C. Cichorius, *Röm. Studien*, 256; Münzer, *RE* s.v. 'Livius', nos. 30 and 31.

298. App. I 114, 533; of course these three τῶν ἐκ 'Ρώμης αὐτῷ συμφυγόντων ἐπιφανῶν could be identified with some of the leaders known to us otherwise by name.

299. Suet. *Caes.* 5; cf. Münzer, *RE* s.v. 'Cornelius', no. 107.

300. Plut. *Sert.* 24, 4: τῶν ἀπὸ βουλῆς πεφευγότων πρὸς αὐτόν; cf. Münzer, *RE* s.v. no. 23.

301. Sall. *Hist.* II 98, 6 Maur.; Plut. *Pomp.* 18, 5; cf. Münzer, *RE* s.v. 'Herennius', no. 7. See *Es. e Soc.* 275, n. 204 [= 99, n. 204 above].

302. The same can be said of M. Antonius, another lieutenant of Sertorius (Sall. *Hist.* III 83 Maur.; Plut. *Sulla*, 26, 1; cf. Klebs, *RE* s.v. no. 2), very probably connected with Q. Antonius Balbus, democratic praetor in 82 BC and killed in that year in Sardinia (Klebs, *ibid.* no. 41; Grueber, I 344; H. Mattingly, *JRS* XII 1922, 235; Pink, *The Triumviri Monetales*, 35, n. 44).

303. Münzer, *RE* s.v. no. 8; for a different identification see most recently Wiseman, *New Men in the Roman Senate*, 264, no. 420.

304. Münzer, *RE* s.v. no. 4. Also his brother Lucius (*ibid.* no. 3; cf. nos. 1 and 2) was an officer of Sertorius, even more famous than Quintus (see Gelzer, *Pompeius*, 53).

305. Münzer, *RE* s.v. no. 2; his brother Caius was also a Sertorian (Münzer, *ibid.* no. 1).

306. Cichorius, *Röm. Studien*, 167 f.; Gelzer, *APAW art. cit.* 18 = *Kleine Schriften*, II 122–3; it could be that Νώνιος, a member of Fimbria's *consilium*, in App. *Mithr.* 59, 243 (cf. Münzer, *RE* s.v. 'Nonius', no. 1) is to be identified with one of the two brothers mentioned in the Asculan inscription (see Cichorus, *Röm. Studien*, 170).

307. *Es. e Soc.* 156 [= 58 above]; Schulze, *LE* 358.

308. Sergia: cf. *ILS* 8888.

309. Kubitschek, *De rom. tribuum* . . . 69; Cic. *in Vatin.* 36 and Schol. Bob. p. 151, 10 Stangl. The Asculum inscription dates to 90 or 89 BC.

310. Schulze, *LE* 96.

311. *Es. e Soc.* 90, n. 114 [= 36, n. 114 above].

312. See Münzer, *RE* s.v. no. 2. I am not certain whether – as Syme, p. 129, n. 4, inclines to believe – this Maecenas belonged to the well-known family of the friend of Augustus. In that case one would have to believe that the Sertorian Maecenas changed his political affiliation, since the grandfather of the Augustan knight was an enemy of M. Livius Drusus (Cic. *pro Cluentio*, 153; cf. Münzer, *RE* s.v. no. 3), and one would therefore have to see him as an exception to the generally oligarchic outlook of the Etruscan nobility: he could, however, be compared with Perperna. In Sall. *Hist.* III, 83 Maur. Maecenas is a *scriba*. We do not know whether the Sextilius who betrayed C. Julius Caesar Strabo in 87 BC was an Etruscan or merely possessed estates in Etruria (Val. Max. V 3, 3). Cf. Münzer, *RE* s.v. 'Sextilius', no. 1 and 'Iulius', no. 135, col. 429, 39; Drumann-Groebe, *GR* III 123.

313. Sall. *Hist.* III 83 Maur.; Schulze, *LE* 253.

314. See above, Chaps. I and II *passim*.

315. Other known Sertorian leaders carry names of Roman *gentes* and there is little that can be said about them: Octavius Graecinus, who was perhaps of Tiburtine origin (Münzer, *RE* s.v. 'Octavius', no. 55); Aufidius (Klebs, *RE* s.v. no. 1); Mallius (Münzer, *RE* s.v. no. 1 = 'Manlius', no. 5). I have not been able to take into account the various hypotheses of H. Mattingly, *JRS* XII 1922, 235; *id. NC* ser. V 4, 1924, 31 f.; *id. Roman Coins*, 1928, 62, 65, 80. From an examination of the

various denarius types of this period he believed it possible to arrive at the political views of the people named on the coins, and hence in our case to designate a number of men as Marian, democratic or Sertorian. Sometimes these hypotheses lead to conclusions that conflict with other source-data which are certain (see on these lines Ehrenberg, *op. cit.* 194). Moreover, one of the foundation-stones of Mattingly's view – his connexion of the issues of *serrati* with the democrats – has been shown to be fallacious by Sydenham, *NC* ser. V 15, 1935, 209 f. Cf. *id. The Coinage . . . Republic*, XL. List of Sertorian officers in Broughton, II 120–1.

316. We know from various sources that it was Mithridates who started the negotiations for a treaty with Sertorius, and that he was prompted by Magius and Fannius; see not only Plut. *Sert.* 23, 4 (who mentions only πρέσβεις) and Sall. *Hist.* II 78 and 79 Maur., but also Cic. II *Verr.* 1, 87 and *id. de imp. Cn. Pomp.* 46 (on which see Gelzer, *PhW art. cit.* col. 1134 = *Kleine Schriften*, II 144); cf. ps.-Asc. p. 244, 1–5 Stangl and Oros. VI 2, 12. App. *Mithr.* 68, 287, however, has something slightly different: Magius and Fannius are presented as inciting Mithridates to enact a treaty with Sertorius and they negotiated it (see also ch. 72) but the two exiles with Mithridates are called δύο δ' αὐτοῦ τῶν στασιωτῶν, where αὐτοῦ is Sertorius. Indeed, the account of the treaty negotiations is preceded by Sertorius' creation of a senate of 300 members. Now Magius and Fannius could be considered members of the Sertorian faction only through the common link with the Marian democrats, but Sertorians they were not; they later returned to Asia and remained there. It seems, then, bearing in mind the wholly anti-Sertorian tone of the chapter, that this inaccurate detail was also intended to aggravate Sertorian responsibility by tracing the initiative for the affair to members of his circle and *ipso facto* to Sertorius: this was a fiction. See also B. Scardigli, *Athenaeum* N.S. XLIX 1971, 252–8.

317. Münzer, *RE* s.v. 'Fannius', no. 12 and 'Magius', no. 6.

318. Vell. II 16, 3.

319. *Es. e Soc.* 155 [= 58 above].

320. Grueber, I 314; Münzer, *RE* s.v. 'Fannius', no. 15; Pink, p. 35.

321. App. I 108, 507. Plut. *Sert.* 22, 5, says that they were φεύγοντας ἀπὸ 'Ρώμης βουλευτάς. See 'Senati in Esilio', *BIDR* III 2, 1960, 221 f. = *Es. e Soc.* 427 f.

322. App. I 115, 537; Plut. *Sert.* 27, 3; *Pomp.* 20, 7–8.

323. Plut. *Sert.* 23, 2.

324. Cic. II *Verr.* 5, 72; 146; 151; other passages in the notes which follow. Cf. E. Ciccotti, *Il processo di Verre*, 1895, 227 and 230, and above all J. Carcopino, 'Observation sur la *De Suppliciis*', *RIDA* IV 1950 (= *Mélanges De Visscher* III), 229 f. See also Sall. *Hist.* IV 32 Maur. and Cic. II *Verr.* 5, 2.

325. Cic. II *Verr.* 5, 154.

326. Münzer, *RE* s.v. no. 5.

327. *Es. e Soc.* 155 [= 58 above].

328. Cic. II *Verr.* 5, 155.

329. Münzer, *RE* s.v. no. 9; Carcopino, *art. cit.* 256; cf. also 258 f., esp. 264 (interesting remarks on P. Gavius, a Hirpine from Compsa. I note, however, that although in Cic. II *Verr.* 5, 158 *Consanus* is the generally accepted reading (e.g. by Münzer, *RE* s.v. 'Gavius', no. 6), the tradition indicated by β in the Teubner edition of A. Klotz, 1923, has *cosanus* (also at 160 and 164). In that case he would be a citizen of Cosa, *colonia Latina* of 273 BC, *municipium* after the Social War. The *gentilicium* Gavius occurs in the Republican period at Firmum (*RE* no. 1), at Arpinum (no. 7), at Fundi (no. 10) and in the Augustan period at Arretium (no. 2). It would indicate relationships between Sertorius and Etruria. However, following Frank, *AJPh* LVI 1935, 61 f., it seems preferable to maintain that he came from Compsa). See Salmon, *Samnium and the Samnites*, 327, n. 1.

330. There is no need to do more than refer to the work of L. R. Taylor, *Party Politics*, *passim*.
331. See *Es. e Soc.* 82 f. [= 32 f. above].
332. Cf. *Es. e Soc.* 67, n. 53 [= 27, n. 53 above].
333. Niccolini, *Il tribunato della plebe*, 145 f. On this period of history see U. Laffi, 'Il mito di Silla', *Athenaeum* N.S. XLV 1967, 177–213, 255–77; R. F. Rossi, *PP* XX 1965, 133–52.
334. Gran. Lic. p. 33 Flemisch.
335. Sall. *Hist.* I 77, 14 Maur. See N. Criniti, 'M. Aemilius Lepidus', *Memorie Ist. Lombardo* XXX 4, 1969, 319–460.
336. Whether he was in this respect *primus* (Sall. *Hist.* III 48, 8 Maur. and ps.-Asc. p. 189, 8 Stangl) it is impossible to tell. Cf. Niccolini, *Fasti dei tribuni della plebe*, 240; Münzer, *RE* s.v. no. 9.
337. Asc. p. 61, 20 Stangl; cf. p. 53, 24.
338. Sall. *Hist.* III 48, 8 Maur.: *ex factione media*; cf. Taylor, p. 20; F. E. Adcock, *JRS* XL 1950, 139 and M. I. Henderson, *JRS* XLII 1952, 115. Sources on the *lex Aurelia* in Niccolini, *Fasti*, 242. See A. La Penna, *Sallustio e la rivoluzione romana*, Milan 1968, 287.
339. Cic. *pro Cluentio* 77.
340. Plut. *Lucull.* 5; cf. ps.-Asc. p. 189, 8 Stangl; Sall. *Hist.* I 77, 11 Maur.
341. Cf. Reinach, *Mithridate*, 320; Carcopino, *Caesar*, 527; Niccolini, *Fasti*, 429. Broughton, II 103, does not think he was a tribune.
342. Cf. Münzer, *RE* s.v. 'Cornelius', no. 97.
343. Sall. *Hist.* III 48, 21 and 23 Maur.; cf. L. R. Taylor, *TAPhA* LXXIII 1942, 11.
344. Licin. Macer, fr. 26 Peter. On Sulla's confiscations see *Es. e Soc.* 121 f. [= 45 f. above].
345. Plut. *Pomp.* 21 and 22; App. I 121, 560; ps.-Asc. p. 189, 8 Stangl.
346. Evidence in Rotondi, *Leges publicae*, 369, and Niccolini, *Fasti*, 248.
347. The latter had been moneyer in 85 BC with the Marians; see Münzer, *RE* s.v. 'Licinius', no. 112, col. 420.
348. It may help here to mention that we can in all probability infer from the historical references and the judgements contained in the so-called *Rhetorica ad Herennium* what was the democratic view at this period of events prior to the civil war. Especially relevant is IV 9, 13, on the motives which induced the allies to revolt (apparently the passage cites an example of a speech for the *quaestio* set up under Varius' law); it is interesting for its complete lack of hostility and for its recognition, in the last analysis, that the allies had noble motives. The traditional dating for the *Rhetorica* used to be between 86 and 82 BC. (W. Warde Fowler, *Roman Essays and Interpretations*, 1920, 91 f.) and was based on the well-known passage IV 54, 68. But of the two historical examples mentioned there only the second can be used to determine the chronology of the work; this contains an allusion to Marius' seventh consulship (86 BC) and is valid therefore as a *terminus post quem*. It seems clear that the first example of *brevitas* (*Lemnium praeteriens cepit* etc.) does not refer to the Asiatic operations of Lucullus in 86–85 BC (so W. Kroll, *Mélanges Bidez*, II 555 f.), but must concern the exploits of Philip in about 200 BC (F. Münzer, *Philologus* LXXXIX 1934, 215 f.; the passage would be an example derived from Rhodian oratory: some of its greatest exponents were well-known at Rome in the Sullan period). M. I. Henderson, *JRS* XLI 1951, 73, on the basis of I 11, 20, where the survival of *damnati de repetundis* is mentioned, says that the author certainly wrote in the Sullan period. (On the *poena legis repetundarum*, however, different conclusions are reached by A. N. Sherwin-White, *PBSR* XVII 1949, 25). Mrs. Henderson accepts as the *terminus ante quem* 75 BC, the year of C. Herennius' death

(Sertorian leader in Spain; Sall. *Hist.* II 98, 6 Maur.; Plut. *Pomp.* 18, 5. We should note that the identification of the person to whom the work is dedicated with the Sertorian Herennius is not in fact certain: Münzer, *RE* s.v. 'Herennius', nos. 6, 7, 8). Mrs. Henderson sets out at p. 73, n. 18, excellent arguments against 82 BC as the *terminus ante quem.* An argument in favour of her view could be that in the *Rhetorica* the term *Bellum Italicum* is used (II 2, 2) to refer to the Social War, and this seems to take us on to a time later than that of other authors – certainly contemporary with the war – who use the term *Bellum Marsicum* (cf. the review of W. Ensslin, *PhW* XLV 1925, col. 365). See G. Calboli, 'Cornificiana 2. L'autore e la tendenza politica della *Rhetorica ad Herennium*', *Mem. Acc. Sc. Ist. Bologna* Cl. Sc. Mor. LI–LII 1963–4.

349. See above, Chaps. VII and VIII.
350. *Es. e Soc.* 67, n. 53 [= 27, n. 53 above].
351. *Es. e Soc.* 67 [= 27 above].
352. Syme, p. 17: 'But even Sulla could not abolish his own example and preclude a successor to his domination.'
353. As H. Last, *CAH* IX 314, emphasizes, the movement in favour of the tribunes' power and the interventions of the military leaders were reinforced at a certain point by the renewed pressure of economic interests. I believe that these latter became more acutely felt after 75 BC in the context of the Mithridatic War and perhaps because of the attitude of Lucullus in the East (M. Villoresi, *Lucullo,* Florence 1939, 85 and 152; Hill, *Middle Class,* 69 and 157). This coalition of those opposed to the oligarchs and of those with economic interests led to the *lex Aurelia* of 70 BC dealing with the reorganization of the jury courts in the *quaestio de repetundis* (Hill, *Middle Class,* 154 f.).
354. On this see W. Schur, *Sallust als Historiker,* 281.
355. This is Schur's interpretation, which I fully accept, of the problem of Pompey's role in Sallust: the title of the chapter (p. 256 f.) anticipates the conclusion.
356. Sall. *BC* 38, 3; cf. L. R. Taylor, *TAPhA art. cit.* 3 f.
357. Cic. *ad Att.* VIII 11, 2.
358. Gelzer, *Pompeius,* 46 f.
359. Sall. *Hist.* II 98 Maur.
360. Schur, *Sallust,* 266 f., esp. 269–70.
361. Schur, *Sallust,* 259; Gelzer, *Pompeius,* 59.
362. Cic. II *Verr.* 5, 153.
363. Sall. *Hist.* I 12 Maur.; cf. Schur, *Sallust,* 284.
364. M. I. Henderson, *JRS* XXXI 1941, 177.
365. Henderson, *loc. cit.*
366. Cf. A. Momigliano, *JRS* XXX 1940, 78.
367. Schur, *Sallust,* 222–56.
368. From Cic. II *Verr.* 1, 87 (cf. Ciccotti, *Il processo di Verre,* 90 f.) it is clear that the negotiations began in 79 BC; see also Magie, II 1209.
369. The presence of Italians in Archelaus' army in Greece (86 BC) is attested by Front. *Strat.* II 3, 17; *mixtis fugitivis Italicae gentis, quorum pervicaciae plurimum fidebat* (Archelaus). It is uncertain whether the passage should be referred to the battle of Chaeronea (see Mommsen, *RG* II⁵, 1869, 293; Reinach, *Mithridate,* 173; Carcopino³, p. 435, n. 120) or to that of Orchomenus (Kromayer, *Antike Schlachtfelder,* II 1907, 370, n. 1; Ormerod, *CAH* IX 253, n. 1; Ferrabino, *MAT* LXV 1916, 5, p. 1, n. 1).
370. See above, Chap. XII.
371. The fact that some members of the commercial class opened negotiations and begged Mithridates for help immediately after the massacres of 88 BC had destroyed

so many lives and such great fortunes among the Italian *negotiatores* makes it less strange that the pressure to give up dominion in Asia came from persons close to, and even belonging to, the very class whose interests had been, and were bound still to be, tied to a policy of expansion. A testimony to the exasperation which dominated these heirs to the allied revolt!

372. This can, perhaps, be deduced from the case of C. Appuleius Decianus, the first *Roman* politician to take refuge with Mithridates. He was tribune in 98 BC and, after being successfully prosecuted, *in Pontum se et ad partes Mithridaticas contulit* (Schol. Bob. p. 95, 14 Stangl; cf. Klebs, *RE* s.v. no. 21 and Pais, *Dalle Guerre Puniche*, I 59 f.). A son of his appears as a businessman in Asia (Klebs, *loc. cit.* no. 22; Hatzfeld, *Trafiquants*, 120) and one may hazard the guess that the tribune of 98 took himself off to the East because his contacts there, including those with Pontus, could be useful to him. On the Magii in the East see Hatzfeld, *Trafiquants*, 88 and n. 2. It is worth mentioning here that business relationships continued between Spain and the East during the war against Sertorius: Plut. *Sert.* 23, 2. An Ἀττίδιος, ἀνὴρ Ῥωμαῖος, ἀπὸ βουλῆς, διὰ δίκην φυγὼν ἐκ τῆς πατρίδος ἐς Μιθριδάτην . . . (App. *Mithr.* 90, 140; Klebs, *RE* s.v. 'Atidius', no. 2) was killed in 67 BC.

373. For the whole problem see Gelzer, *PhW art. cit.* col. 1129 f. = *Kleine Schriften*, II 139–45. Magie, I 322, follows Appian's version.

374. Sall. *Hist.* II 98, 10 Maur.; Plut. *Sert.* 21, 8 and 9; App. I 108, 508 and *id. Iber.* 101, 439.

375. Plut. *Pomp.* 20, 7.

376. Cf. Treves, *art. cit.* 133.

377. Plut. *Sert.* 22, 8.

378. Plin. *NH* VII 26 (27), 96; Flor. II 10, 22, 1; cf. Gelzer, *PhW art. cit.* col. 1133 = *Kleine Schriften* II 143; a different view in Berve, *art. cit.* 122.

379. Plut. *Sert.* 6 and 22.

380. Treves, *art. cit.* 135 f. On the Sertorii in Spain, attesting grants of the *civitas*, see Schulten, *Sertorius*, 136. See Badian, *FC* 319–20.

381. Plut. *Sert.* 23, 7.

382. Gelzer, *PhW art. cit.* col. 1135 = *Kleine Schriften*, II 144.

383. It is true that according to the sources M. Marius later fought for Mithridates: App. *Mith.* 77, 338 (see the app. crit. in the edition of Viereck-Roos², p. 479); Plut. *Lucull.* 12, 5; Oros. VI 2, 21; cf. Reinach, *Mithridate*, 332. That Sertorius also sent troops to Mithridates is said by Plut. *Sert.* 24, 3 and *id. Lucull.* 8, 7.

384. Cf. Plut. *Sert.* 18, 8.

385. Momigliano, *JRS* XXX 1940, 78.

386. Cic. II *Verr.* 5, 153.

387. Cf. above, Chap. IX.

388. Cic. II *Verr.* I, 87.

389. App. *Mithr.* 72, 308 and Cass. Dio, XXXVI 8, 2.

390. Diod. XXXVII 2, 14: εἶτα τῆς περὶ Σύλλαν καὶ Μάριον ἐμφυλίου στάσεως ἀναρριπισθείσης Ῥωμαίοις, οἱ μὲν (of the Italians) Σύλλᾳ οἱ δὲ Μαρίῳ συνεμάχησαν. καὶ τὸ μὲν πλέον αὐτῶν ἔπεσε τοῖς πολέμοις, τὸ δ' ὑπόλοιπον ἐπικρατήσαντι Σύλλᾳ προσεχώρησε. καὶ οὕτω τέλεον τῇ ἐμφυλίῳ συναπέσβη στάσει μέγιστος γεγονὼς καὶ ὁ Μαρσικὸς ἐπικληθεὶς πόλεμος. For Tacitus, *Ann.* VI 12, 4, cf. Kiene, *Bundesgenossenkrieg*, 311 and the note in Furneaux's edition², *ad loc.*

391. *Es. e Soc.* 143 [= 52 above].

392. App. I, 34 151; cf. *Es. e Soc.* 67, n. 53 [= 27, n. 53 above]; also M. Hammond, *City-State and World-State in Greek and Roman Political Theory*, Cambridge 1951, 84 f.

393. *Es. e Soc.* 67 f. [= 27 f. above].

Notes to Appendix

1. On the recent publication by H. Hill, *The Roman Middle Class in the Republican Period*, Oxford 1952. Hill replied to my comments in *Athenaeum* N.S. XXXIII 1955, 327–32: but see *Es. e Soc.* 419, n. 35 [= 147, n. 35 below].
2. Cic. *pro Rosc. com.* 42; Schol. Juven. III 155. Cf. Kubitschek, *RE* s.v. 'census', col. 1923, 61.
3. See e.g. Ernst Meyer, *Röm. Staat und Staatsgedanke*, Zurich 1948, 85 f.; 436, n. 91. See also Nicolet, *L'ordere équestre*, 48 f.
4. *Es. e Soc.* 149 f. [= 55 f. above].
5. *Middle Class*, 88 and *passim*.
6. *Der römische Ritterstand*, 1927, 22.
7. This, of course, holds for a social unit which already existed; it is another matter, as we shall see, in the case of the Latin colonies.
8. See on the question Rice Holmes, *Roman Republic*, I 391 f. and Hill, *Middle Class*, 212 f.
9. Rice Holmes, p. 391; cf. however Last, *CAH* IX 338 f.
10. So Stein, *op. cit.* 22.
11. Cf. Plin. *NH* XXXIII 2 (8), 34 and Last, p. 895.
12. *Op. cit.* 51.
13. *Middle Class*, 18 f.
14. *SR* III 258 and 479–80. Cf. *Es. e Soc.* 149 and n. 24 [= 55 and n. 24 above].
15. The so-called *equites equo privato*: although this term is used only in Livy, XXVII 11, 14 apropos the cavalry of Cannae, Hill's claim (*AJPh art. cit.* 358, n. 3) that it has validity only in this specific case does not seem legitimate: *contra*, Nicolet, *L'ordre équestre*, 66.
16. It is more likely that all the examples where there is a mention of *census equester* for the period prior to the third century BC are to be explained rather as annalistic anachronisms than, with Hill, by supposing that the authors wanted by that term to indicate the census of the first class to which undoubtedly the *equites equo publico* and, *a fortiori*, the *equites equo privato* belonged.
17. Cf. Kübler, *RE* s.v. 'equites Romani', col. 284, 10–15. I do not think, therefore, that we can say (with A. N. Sherwin-White, *PBSR* XVII 1949, 7, n. 14) that Polybius is not aware of the equestrian class.
18. On the question when this type of levy was introduced cf. *Es. e Soc.* 144 f. [= 53 f. above].
19. Cited in detail *Es. e Soc.* 147 [= 54 above].
20. Cf. also A. Alföldi, *Der frührömische Reiteradel und seine Ehrenabzeichen*, 1952, 105 f.
21. *AJPh art. cit.* 360.
22. Asc. p. 12, 22 Stangl. The verses of Pomponius, 154–5 Ribbeck[3], show that the terminology *equites* and *pedites*, used to indicate social classes, was in current use, whether the poet is remembering his native Bononia (Livy, XXXVII 57, 8) or is reflecting a situation in Campania (P. Frassinetti, *Fabula atellana*, 1953, 140).
23. This alone is envisaged by Hill, *Middle Class*, 24.
24. Cf. Mommsen, *SR* III 258; Hill, *Middle Class*, 18, n. 1.
25. *Middle Class*, 33.
26. *SR* III 259, n. 1; see, however, Alföldi, *op. cit.* 113, n. 293.
27. See especially Cic. *de Rep.* IV 2: . . . *equitatus, in quo suffragia sunt etiam Senatus.*
28. Cf. e.g. P. Fraccaro, 'Ricerche storiche e letterarie sulla censura del 184/83', *St. Storici per l'antichità classica* IV 110 f. = *Opuscula*, I 490–1; Hill, *Middle Class*, 15; 42 f.

29. Cf. Kubitschek, *art. cit.* coll. 1922–3.
30. This is the usual interpretation of Cicero, *de Rep.* IV 2: cf. Hill, *Middle Class*, 105 f.
31. Apparently it was Sulla who limited the right of admission into the eighteen centuries to sons of senators (Mommsen, *SR* III 486).
32. See Last, *CAH* IX 894 f.
33. Cf. for the first century BC Q. Cicero, *de pet. cons.* 8, 33 (Stein, p. 3, n. 1).
34. *Mélanges historiques et littéraires*³, 1876, 270 f.
35. Hill, *Middle Class*, Preface, p. 114.
36. Cf. Pliny, *NH* XXXIII 1 (7), 29.
37. Referred to in Stein, *op. cit.* 49, n. 3; 50, n. 1.
38. Cf. Friedlander-Wissowa, *Sittengeschichte Roms*¹⁰, I 114 f.
39. The assumption of political functions by the *ordo equester* led – see Pliny, *NH* XXXIII 2 (8), 34 – to the association of the equestrian class with Senate and people in the formulas of official documents: cf. Stein, *op. cit.* 57, n. 4 and 58, nn. 1–2; cf. also Kübler, *RE* s.v. 'ordo', col. 932.
40. I think we should bear in mind here the personality of M. Aemilius Scaurus.
41. Cf. Suet. *Vesp.* 9, 2 and App. I 22, 91; II 13, 47 (ἀξίωσις).
42. See Pliny, *NH* XXXIII 1 (7), 29.
43. *Middle Class*, 47.
44. Hill, *Middle Class*, 50 f. and also P. Fraccaro, *Enc. Ital.* IX 537.
45. *Op. cit.* 270 f. Mérimée was inclined to accept Merivale's guiding principle, that the trend towards unity in the Roman world of the Caesarian period was connected with the rise of the middle classes, but limited very strictly the extent to which we should admit the theory of the existence of these middle classes in the last century of the Republic. Even though he represents Caesarian society in an out-of-date moral cliché, he is quite right to observe that one cannot identify the *equester ordo* with a politically independent middle class.
46. See on this W. Kroll, *Die Kultur des Ciceronischen Zeit*, I 1933, 15 and 72.
47. Cf. also J. Bayet, *REL* XXX 1952, 494, and the reviews by H. H. Scullard, *EHR* LXVIII 1953, 297, and by M. Gelzer, *Gnomon* XXV 1953, 319–23, which on some points agree with my comments.

Notes to *IV*

* *ASNP* XXXIII 1964, 1–15. See Badian, *Historia* XI 1962, 228–33, and *id. Lucius Sulla, The Deadly Reformer* (7th Todd Memorial Lecture) Sydney 1970; U. Laffi, 'Il mito di Silla', *Athenaeum* N.S. XLV 1967, 177–213; 255–77; and my article in *Aufstieg und Niedergang der römischen Welt*, I Berlin–New York 1972, 794–805. This paper was read to the Fourth Congress of Classical Studies (Philadelphia, August 24–9, 1964) at the Concurrent Session devoted to *The Age of Marius and Sulla* (August 26, 1964).

1. E. Gabba, *Appiano e la storia delle Guerre Civili*, Florence 1956, 13 f. Cf. E. J. Weinrib, 'The Judiciary Law of M. Livius Drusus', *Historia* XIX 1970, 414–43; Chr. Meier, *Res Publica Amissa*, Wiesbaden 1966, 208–16. Also important is T. J. Luce, 'Marius and the Mithridatic Command', *Historia* XIX 1970, 161–94.
2. E. Badian, *Foreign Clientelae, 264–70 BC*, Oxford 1958, 216 f.; see *Es. e Soc.* 576 f. [= 168 f. below].
3. See also E. Lepore, *Il princeps ciceroniano e gli ideali politici della tarda repubblica*, Naples 1954, 25.
4. App. *BC* I 35, 157–61 with my Commentary² (*Appiani Bell. Civ. lib. I*, Florence 1967) and 'Osservazioni sulla legge giudiziaria di M. Livio Druso (91 a.C)', *PP* XI

1956, 363–72 = *Es. e Soc.* 369 f. It therefore differed from the law of the consul Q. Servilius Caepio of 106 BC: Broughton, *The Magistrates of the Roman Republic*, I 553; G. Tibiletti, *Athenaeum* N.S. XXXI 1953, 73–5 and 83.

5. *pro Cluentio*, 153–4; *id. pro Rab. Post.* 16–17; cf. Gabba, *PP* XI 1956, 370–1 = *Es. e Soc.* 379 f.
6. Though this is exaggerated by C. Lanzani, *RFIC* XL 1912, 276–7.
7. In general see *Es. e Soc.* 193 f. [= 70 f. above].
8. Evidence in my Commentary on Appian, *BC* I 36, 162 (pp. 121–2).
9. Ascon. p. 54, 17–18 Stangl.
10. See *Es. e Soc.* 208 f. [= 74 f. above] and Gabba, 'Italia e Roma nella Storia di Velleio Patercolo', *CS* I 1962, 1–9 = *Es. e Soc.* 347 f.; E. T. Salmon, 'The Causes of the Social War', *Phoenix* XVI 1962, 107 f.
11. App. *BC* I 35, 156 and 36, 162, with my Commentary. Cf. also J. Heurgon, 'The Date of Vegoia's Prophecy', *JRS* XLIX 1959, 41–5.
12. See *Es. e Soc.* 577 [= 168 below].
13. Münzer, *RE* s.v. 'Licinius', no. 55, col. 262.
14. Badian, *FC* 213–14.
15. Münzer, *loc. cit.*
16. The article of E. Badian, 'Caepio and Norbanus', *Historia* VI 1957, 318–46, re-published in *Studies in Greek and Roman History*, Oxford 1964, 34–70 (from which I quote), is fundamental for the decade 100–90 BC.
17. Cic. *de domo*, 50; Asc. p. 24, 20 Stangl; cf. Badian, *Athenaeum* N.S. XXXIV 1956, 122–3.
18. Cic. *pro Scauro*, 5; Asc. p. 24, 24 Stangl.
19. App. *BC* I 37, 165 f., with my Comm. Cf. E. Badian, 'Quaestiones variae', *Historia* XVIII 1969, 447–91.
20. App. *BC* I 37, 166.
21. App. *BC* I 37, 167; Cic. *de Orat.* III 11; *id. Brutus*, 205.
22. Cic. *de Orat.* I 25; he was probably connected with the Metelli: Badian, *Studies*, 36–9.
23. App. *BC* I 37, 168 and my Comm., though others see a confusion with Memmius: A. Biedl, '*De Memmiorum familia*', *WS* XLVIII 1930, 102.
24. App. *BC* I 37, 167 and my Comm.
25. Cic. *Tusc. Disp.* II 57: according to Badian, *Studies*, 57–8, M. Antonius broke away from Marius after 95 BC.
26. Badian, *FC* 212 f.
27. Cic. *Brutus*, 304; Miltner, *RE* s.v. 'Pompeius', no. 39.
28. Sisenna, fr. 44 Peter: *Lucium Memmium, socerum Gai Scribonii tribunum plebis, quem Marci Livi consiliarium fuisse callebant et tunc Curionis oratorem.* The passage is not entirely clear: we should certainly correct *tribunum* to *tribuni* (Biedl, *art. cit.* 100 and 103). Biedl's reconstruction (*art. cit.* and also *WS* XLIX 1931, 112) seems preferable to that of Münzer, *RE* s.v. 'Memmius', no. 14, coll. 620–1. Cf. T. P. Wiseman, 'Lucius Memmius and His Family', *CQ* XVII 1967, 164 f.
29. Cic. *Brutus*, 304; Malcovati, *ORF*³, p. 267; Münzer, *RE* s.v. 'Marcius', no. 75, col. 1565. M. Gelzer, 'Cn. Pompeius Strabo und der Aufstieg des Sohnes Magnus', *APAW* 1941, no. 12 = *Kleine Schriften*, II Wiesbaden 1963, 118, is wrong in thinking that he testified for the defence.
30. Broughton, *MRR* II 26; Niccolini, *Fasti dei tribuni della plebe*, 225.
31. A possibility tentatively suggested by Münzer, *RE* s.v. 'Scribonius', no. 10, col. 862, comparing the passage cited from Sisenna with the obscure evidence of Asc. p. 58 Stangl, and accepted by Biedl, *loc. cit.* Scribonius later followed Sulla to the East (Cic. *Brutus*, 227) and returned to Italy with him in 83 BC.

32. III 11: *qui in eadem invidiae flamma fuisset*; Münzer, *RE* s.v. 'Sulpicius', no. 92, col. 846.
33. Cic. *de Orat.* I 25.
34. Cic. *Lael.* 2.
35. Plut. *Cato Minor*, 3, 2. For the son staying at his uncle's house see Plut. *Cato Minor*, 1, 1 and 2, 1. But see Münzer, *RE* s.v. 'Porcius', no. 16, coll. 168–9.
36. Gabba, Comm. on App. *BC* I 30, 133 (p. 105): usually assigned to 99 BC (Broughton, *MRR* II 2). See Gabba, 'Politica e cultura in Roma agli inizi del I secolo a.C.', *Athenaeum* N.S. XXXI 1953, 259 n. 1 = *Es. e Soc.* 175, n. 1.
37. Badian, *Studies*, 41–3.
38. Badian, *Historia* XVIII 1969, 461–75, has re-established the traditional date (Asc. p. 61 Stangl) and rejected the shift to 88 BC suggested by Pareti, *Storia di Roma e del mondo Romano*, III 551 f. and by Badian himself, *Studies*, 75–6, and accepted by myself [in the original version of this article in *ASNP* XXXIII 1964, 6]. A summary of the explanation is to be found in *Aufstieg und Niedergang*, I 791, n. 161.
39. Asc. p. 61, 28 f. Stangl: Badian, *Historia* XI 1962, 208 and n. 45.
40. Cic. *Brutus*, 305; he was judged, therefore, by a senatorial jury.
41. In Greenidge-Clay, *Sources for Roman History*[2], Oxford 1960, 151.
42. Badian, *Historia* XVIII 1969, 474. Hence the traditional theory that Cn. Pompeius Strabo was accused under the *lex Varia* must be abandoned. For this see M. Gelzer, *art. cit. Kleine Schriften*, II 117–18; Miltner, *RE* s.v. 'Pompeius', no. 45, col. 2258; Badian, *Studies*, 55–6; N. Criniti, *L'Epigrafe di Asculum di Gn. Pompeo Strabone*, Milan 1970, 70–1.
43. Badian, *FC* 231 f.; Pareti, III 556; A. W. Lintott, 'The Tribunate of P. Sulpicius Rufus', *CQ* N.S. XXXI 1971, 442–53.
44. Cic. *de Har. Resp.* 43; cf. *id. Lael.* 2: *cum is* (Sulpicius Rufus) *tribunus plebis capitali odio a Q. Pompeio, qui tunc erat consul, dissideret, quocum coniunctissime et amantissime vixerat.* To this effect, but with different opinions on the timing of the events, H. Last, *CAH* IX 201 f.; Münzer, *RE* s.v. 'Sulpicius', no. 92, col. 846–7; Badian, *FC* 231–3; Luce, *Historia* XIX 1970, 192–3. *Rhet. ad Herenn.* II 45 mentions the initial opposition by Rufus to the recall of those exiled under the *lex Varia*, which he himself later advocated, introducing a formal proposal to that effect (Niccolini, *Fasti*, 229–31). There may be a reference to the consequences of the *lex Licinia Mucia*: Badian, *Historia* XVIII 1969, 487–90. We are in any event still in his pro-Senate phase, and to this also belongs his opposition to the illegal candidature of C. Caesar Strabo for the consulship (perhaps December 89: Badian, *FC* 230).
45. Thus, e.g., Badian, *FC* 232; I am in agreement with the rest of his account there. Cf. *id. Historia* XVIII 1969, 485.
46. For his intimate connexion with Atticus see Cic. *Lael.* 2, and Nep. *Att.* 2, 1.
47. For the knights' support of Sulpicius see Plut. *Mar.* 35, 2, and *id. Sulla*, 8, 3.
48. App. *BC* I 59, 265 f.
49. App. *BC* I 57, 255 f. and esp. 59, 265 f.; Miltner, *RE* s.v. 'Pompeius', no. 39.
50. App. *BC* I 59, 265–6, and my Comm., with improvements in *Athenaeum* N.S. XXXVIII 1960, 212–16: L. R. Taylor, *The Voting Districts of the Roman Republic*, Rome 1960, 104 and n. 9.
51. Vell. II 16, 2.
52. See *Es. e Soc.* 268, n. 189 [= 97, n. 189 above].
53. App. *BC* I 59, 267; cf. *Es. e Soc.* 407 f. [= 142 f. below], and my Comm., pp. 343–5.
54. *L. Sulla civitatis statum ordinavit, exinde colonias deduxit.*
55. See *Es. e Soc.* 420 f. [= 148 f. below].
56. See *Es. e Soc.* 265 f. [= 96 f. above], and the discussion of the bibliography.

57. App. *BC* I 77, 350–2.
58. Livy, *Per.* LXXXVI.
59. App. *BC* I 86, 393; perhaps the two pieces of evidence allude to the same point: see Taylor, *VDRR* 118–19.
60. Cic. *Phil.* XII 27.
61. App. *BC* I 100, 465–8, and my Comm.; cf. *Aufstieg und Niedergang*, I 800–3.
62. In general on the Sullan senate see *Es. e Soc.* 159 f. [= 59 f. above] and *ibid.* 407 f. [= 142 f. below]; Badian, *FC* 245–7. Cf. C. Nicolet, *L'ordre équestre à l'époque républicaine*, I, Paris 1966, 573–80; J. R. Hawthorn, *G & R* IX 1962, 50–60.
63. App. *BC* I 100, 468; Taylor, *VDRR* 292.
64. G. Tibiletti, *SDHI* XXV 1959, 121–2.
65. Badian, *Historia* XI 1962, 232, with bibliography on the problem.
66. *Sylla ou la monarchie manquée*[4], Paris 1931, 147 f.
67. Cf. the review of M. Gelzer, *Gnomon* VIII 1932, 605–7 = *Kleine Schriften*, II 103–5.
68. A. Krawczuk, *Eos* 1954–5, fasc. 2, 121 f.; Badian, *Historia* XI 1962, 230, n. 117, and *id. FC* 297, note U. Cf. T. E. Kinsey, *Mnemosyne* XX 1967, 61–7; cf. E. S. Gruen, *Roman Politics and the Criminal Courts, 149–78 B C*, Cambridge (Mass.) 1968, 265.
69. See especially 139; Badian, *Historia* XI 1962, 230 (a similar view earlier, apparently, in G. Beloch, *Le monarchie ellenistiche e la repubblica romana*, Bari 1933, 134). In that case the supplement in *TAM* II 899, l.2, is erroneous. Cf. R. K. Sherk, *Roman Documents from the Greek East*, Baltimore 1969, no. 19, p. 112 f. In my Comm. on App. p. 282 I took the view that the abdication occurred at the end of 80, coinciding with the end of Sulla's second consulship: so also R. Syme, *HSPh* LXIV 1959, 33.
70. *FC* 249 f.
71. Cf. earlier A. Afzelius, 'Zwei Episoden aus dem Leben Ciceros', *C & M* V 1942 (pub. 1943), 213–17. He roundly denies there was any danger for Cicero since it was the unimportance of the case that accounts for the lack of interest shown by the *nobiles*, who entrusted it to *adulescentes*. According to Afzelius, Sulla was fully in accord with the *nobilitas* friendly to Roscius (so also J. Humbert, *Les plaidoyers écrits et les plaidoiries réelles de Cicéron*, Paris undated, 100–1).
72. Plut. *Cic.* 3, 3–6, and commentary by D. Magnino, Florence 1963: Afzelius, p. 217; cf. also *auct. de vir. ill.* 81, 2.
73. *de Off.* II 51.
74. II *Verr.* 3, 81; cf. E. Ciaceri, 'L'atteggiamento politico di M. Tullio Cicerone di fronte a L. Cornelio Silla', *AIV* LXXIX 1919–20, 556–7 (and in general 541–62, recast with some variations in *Cicerone e i suoi tempi*) and also V. M. Smirine, *VDI* IV 1958, 88–103.
75. Drumann-Groebe, *Geschichte Roms*, V 258 and esp. n. 3; Ihne, *Röm. Geschichte*, VI 128. *Contra*, Ciaceri, *Cicerone e i suoi tempi*, I 1926, 24, n. 8.
76. *Op. cit.* 100–11.
77. 6; 21 (Humbert, p. 100); 22; 25; 91; 109–10; 127; 130–1.
78. 131: A. Haury, *L'ironie et l'humour chez Cicéron*, Leiden 1955, 114–15, has shown how this tone is prevalent in the speech (but he does not appear to cite this specific passage).
79. 22: Haury, p. 76.
80. E.g. 22; 131; 139.
81. 1; 9; 11; 14; 28; 31; 80; 150; 154.
82. 80; 89; 125; for the reticence of 137 cf. R. Heinze, 'Ciceros Politische Anfänge' (*Sächsische Akademie der Wissenschaften* 1909), now in *Vom Geist des Römertums*[2], Leipzig and Berlin 1939, 65.
83. 1; 3; 5; 7 etc.
84. 1–3; 5; 148.

85. So rightly Heinze, pp. 63–5.
86. 16.
87. 135–9.
87[a]. *quapropter desinant aliquando dicere, male aliquem locutum esse, si qui vere ac libere locutus sit, desinant suam causam cum Chrysogono communicare, desinant, si ille laesus sit, de se aliquid detractum arbitrari, videant ne turpe miserumque sit eos, qui equestrem splendorem pati non potuerunt, servi nequissimi dominationem ferre posse.*
88. T. A. Dorey, 'A Note on the *Pro Roscio Amerino*', *Ciceroniana* II 1960, 147–8. See also Heinze, pp. 78–9.
89. 153.
90. Plut. *Sulla*, 31, 1–4: identified by Münzer, *RE* s.v. 'Caecilius', no. 71, with a son of Caprarius.
91. Plut. *Sulla*, 31, 4: οὐδενὶ τῶν ἐν τέλει κοινωσάμενος. As is known, the proscriptions were permitted by a *lex Cornelia* (see my Comm. on App. *BC* I 95, 442 f.). Cic. *pro Rosc. Am.* 123, is surely ironic, and so the hypothesis of T. E. Kinsey, *Mnemosyne* XXI 1968, 290–2, is pointless. In spite of the place in which Appian, in his narrative, puts the account of the proscriptions, they clearly come after the nomination of Sulla as dictator.
92. One tradition mentions L. Fufidius as suggesting the compiling of the lists (Plut. *Sulla*, 31, 3: Oros. V 21, 2–3; Flor. II 9, 25) but in any case it was certainly before his admission to Sulla's senate. See *Es. e Soc.* 167 [= 64 above]. See also C. Nicolet, *REL* XLV 1967, 297–304.
93. Plut. *Sulla*, 10, 4.
94. App. *BC* I 57, 253: Badian's suggestion (*Studies*, 220), that the quaestor who alone stayed with the consul is to be identified with Lucullus, is also advanced by T. F. Carney, *A Biography of C. Marius* (*PACA* Suppl. I), 1961, 33, n. 165.
95. E. Badian, 'Waiting for Sulla', *JRS* LII 1962, 47–61 = *Studies*, 206–34 (reservations expressed by E. Candiloro, *SCO* XII 1963, 224–6: Badian replied in *Athenaeum* N.S. XLII 1964, 422–31): see also Ch. M. Bulst, '*Cinnanum Tempus*', *Historia* XIII 1964, 307–37 (not completely acceptable).
96. 33.
97. 136.
98. Cic. *Phil.* XII 27.
99. As is clear from the fact that Sulla later considered the day of the breach as the real beginning of the civil war: App. *BC* I 95, 441 and my Comm.
100. App. *BC* I 85, 383–7 and my Comm. The opposing tradition emphasized the cunning of Sulla.
101. *Inscr. Italiae*, XIII 1, pp. 55 and 130.
102. App. *BC* I 98, 459 f.
103. Livy, *Per.* LXXXIII; App. *BC* I 77, 350–3. Cf. J. Jahn, *Interregnum und Wahldiktatur*, Kallmünz 1970, 161–5, and Meier, *Res Publica Amissa*, 248–53.
104. Fr. 132 Peter.
105. E. Candiloro, *SCO* XII 1963, 212–26. The pro-Optimate Posidonius was a supporter of Sulla in his account of the events of the Mithridatic War (Jacoby, *Fgr Hist.* IIC 158) but we cannot tell how, or even whether, he passed judgement on Sulla's domestic policy, since it is not even known at what point he concluded his *Histories* (Jacoby, p. 156).
106. Gabba, *Athenaeum* N.S. XXXVIII 1960, 175–225.
107. La Penna, *Athenaeum* N.S. XLI 1963, 212–19.
108. *Oratio Lepidi*, 2.
109. Cic. *de Rep.* VI 12; see App. *BC* I 16, 67, and Pareti, *Storia di Roma*, III 326–7. Cf. Nicolet, *REL* XLII 1964, 212–30.

110. App. *BC* II 107, 448.
111. Plut. *Cic.* 10, 2, is important here.
112. Plut. *Crass.* 15, 7.
113. Plut. *Pomp.* 15, 1–2: Sall. *Oratio Lepidi*, 16 and 18. Lucullus, perhaps the closest of Sulla's followers and the nearest to his political position, won the confidence of the provinces of the Greek East by his correct and law-abiding attitude, and thereby gained a balanced assessment in Sallust's historical writings: La Penna, *Athenaeum* N.S. XLI 1963, 246–54. Cf. *id. Sallustio e la rivoluzione romana*, Milan 1968, 287 f.
114. Cicero's observation (146) that Chrysogonus had no confidence in Sulla's settlement is noteworthy.
115. La Penna, *Athenaeum* N.S. XLI 1963, 210–12.
[115ª. Napoleon III: 'La France a compris que je n'étais sorti de la légalité que pour rentrer dans le droit'.]
116. *The Roman Revolution*, Oxford 1939, 17.
117. This very widespread theory also serves to support 'political' interpretations of Roman portraiture by archaeologists; the well-known 'realism' derived from the *imagines* of the great noble families allegedly originated in the Sullan period, and represented in sculpture the Sullan reaction, which extolled the Roman social system of the early Republic and was directed against the forces of the Plebs: R. Bianchi Bandinelli, 'Sulla formazione del ritratto romano', *Archeologia e Cultura*, Milan–Naples 1961, 172 f.
118. The thesis of Carcopino to which I have referred has often been taken up and in various degrees accepted. Recently, F. Altheim, 'Das Ende der röm. Kolonialreiches', *WZ* Berlin IX 1959–60, 161–6, has emphasized the importance of Sulla's precedent for Augustus. Concerning the significance of the Sullan model, and its conscious or unconscious imitation in the politics and civil wars of the first century BC, much material has been collected – although rather erratically – in the work of P. Jal, *La guerre civile à Rome, Étude littéraire et morale*, Paris 1963, *passim*, where there is also a copious bibliography; particularly important are the many works of A. Alföldi, to which should now be added his article in *JBM* XLI–XLII 1961–2, 275–88.

Notes to V

* *Athenaeum* N.S. XXXIV 1956, 124–38. See also my Commentary², *Appiani Bell. Civ. lib. I*, Florence 1967, 343–5; P. A. Brunt, 'Sulla and the Asian Publicans', *Latomus* XV 1956, 17–25; C. Nicolet, *L'ordre équestre à l'époque républicaine*, I, Paris 1966, 581–91, with a list of Sullan senators who offer some points of interest concerning the equestrian class; J. R. Hawthorn, 'The Senate after Sulla', *G & R* IX 1962, 50–60; E. S. Gruen, *Roman Politics and the Criminal Courts*, Cambridge (Mass.) 1968, 257–8; U. Laffi, 'Il mito di Silla', *Athenaeum* N.S. XLV 1967, 177–213. For Sulla and the censorship see L. R. Taylor, *The Voting Districts of the Roman Republic*, Rome 1960, 119. See also T. P. Wiseman, *New Men in the Roman Senate, 139 BC–14 AD*, Oxford 1971. I would like to express my deepest gratitude to Miss Lily Ross Taylor, formerly Director of Classical Studies at the American Academy in Rome, with whom I had the good fortune to be able to discuss these problems during my residence at the Academy (1955). Of course I alone am responsible for the views expressed here.
1. Cf. H. Bennett, *Cinna and his Times*, Menasha 1923, 35, n.
2. Cf. Willems, *Le Sénat de la république romaine*, I² 394 and 403–4; R. Syme, *PBSR* XIV 1938, 10 with n. 38.

3. This is the implication of M. Gelzer, *Caesar. Der Politiker und Staatsmann*[3], Munich 1941, 38.
4. Mommsen, *SR* III 487; Willems, I[2] 404 f.; R. Syme, *JRS* XXXIV 1944, 102.
5. Some scholars, however, think that they can be reconciled: see e.g. L. Pareti, *Storia di Roma e del mondo Romano*, III 620.
6. Cf. H. Hill, 'Sulla's New Senators in 81 BC', *CQ* XXVI 1932, 170 f.; see *Es. e Soc.* 159 f. [= 59 f. above].
7. See *Es. e Soc.* 161 [= 60 above].
8. Cf. E. G. Hardy, 'The Number of the Sullan Senate', *JRS* VI 1916, 59 f.
9. See Willems, I[2] 394.
10. Which would lead one to suppose that in 92 BC the *lectio* had been held.
11. Leaving aside for the moment the problem that in the first instance they were chosen ἐκ τῶν ἀρίστων ἀνδρῶν, in the second ἱππέων.
12. Cf. Willems, I[2] 242 and n. 5.
13. Willems, I[2] 406.
14. Livy, XXIII 23, 6 (I follow the reading of Sigonius: Conway supplies [*non*] before *magistratus*; Stroth less probably reads *qui* [*minores*] *mag.*): Willems, I[2] 285 f. It is worth noting that the corresponding passage in the *Periocha* says that the Senate *ex equestri ordine . . . suppletus est.*
15. So Hill, *The Roman Middle Class in the Republican Period*, Oxford 1952, 147, though he is wrong in thinking of the eighteen centuries *equites equo publico*.
16. Cf. e.g. E. G. Hardy, *art. cit.* 61–2.
17. Willems I[2] 408; J. Carcopino, *Des Gracques à Sulla*[3], 469; Pareti, III 620.
18. Cf. also A. H. J. Greenidge, *The Legal Procedure of Cicero's Time*, Oxford 1901, 43.
19. Cic. *pro Corn*. I. fr. 54 Schoell says: *memoria teneo, cum primum senatores cum equitibus Romanis lege Plotia iudicarent, hominem dis ac nobilitati perinvisum, Cn. Pompeium, causam lege Varia de maiestate dixisse.* For this episode cf. M. Gelzer, 'Cn. Pompeius Strabo und der Aufstieg seines Sohnes Magnus', *APAW* 1941, no. 14, p. 13 = *Kleine Schriften*, II, Wiesbaden 1963, 117; Hill, *Middle Class*, 137–8. Badian, *Historia* XVIII 1969, 465–75, has shown that an allusion to a trial of Pompeius Strabo is impossible, and that the correction *Pomponium* should be made in the Ciceronian passage.
20. Cf. G. Niccolini, *Fasti dei tribuni della plebe*, Milan 1934, 228. Mommsen, *SR* II[3] 231, points out that in the *lex repetundarum* of the Bembine tablets, line 14, the 450 jurors have to be *tributim discriptos*. Note also the organization of the jurors by tribes required by the *lex Licinia de sodaliciis* of 55 BC (J. Lengle, *Röm. Strafrecht bei Cicero und den Historikern* (*Neue Wege zur Antike*, I, 11) Leipzig 1934, 33, and S. Accame, *BMIR* XIII 1942 (Appendix to *BCAR* LXX 1942), 36–7). It may also be pointed out that by the *lex Aurelia* of 70 BC the juries came to be composed of three equal groups – senators, knights and *tribuni aerarii* (evidence in Hill, p. 155, n. 2.); the last-mentioned were probably elected by each individual tribe in equal numbers (Hill, pp. 155–6). Finally, as a result of the modifications made by Pompey in 55 BC to the *lex Aurelia*, the origin of the jurors remained unchanged, though it seems that their selection was no longer left to the judgement of the urban praetor (cf. Cicero, *pro Cluentio*, 121, and Lengle, *RE* s.v. 'tribunus', no. 1, col. 2434; Cic., *in Pis*. 94: *neque legetur quisquis voluerit, nec quisquis noluerit non legetur, . . . iudices iudicabunt ii quos lex ipsa, non quos hominum libido delegerit*); their selection was handed over, though it is not very clear how, to election by the *comitia centuriata*; Asc. *in Pis*. p. 21, 15 f. Stangl: *rursus deinde Pompeius in consulatu secundo . . . promulgavit ut amplissimo ex censu ex centuriis aliter atque antea lecti iudices, aeque tamen ex illis tribus ordinibus, res iudicarent.* In my opinion A. Momigliano, *BCAR* LIX 1931, 175–6, was right in emphasizing the alterations made by Pompey in the

selection of jurors; yet it is also possible that in the words *amplissimo ex ordine* there is a reference to some new detail introduced by Pompey (Hill, p. 212). Although we know that the reform of the *comitia centuriata* made the relationship between tribes and centuries very close, I am not sure whether it is right to speak, as Hill, p. 178, does, of a 'selection . . . by tribes' instituted by Pompey.

21. For a comparison with the organization of the first Senate of Romulus which is described in Dion. Hal. II 12, see Gabba, *Athenaeum* N.S. XXXVIII 1960, 216–18.

22. Cf. W. Ensslin, 'Appian und die Liviustradition zum ersten Bürgerkrieg', *Klio* XX 1925–6, 415–65.

23. See H. Last, *CAH* IX 894 f.: *Es. e Soc.* 340 f. [= 127 f. above].

24. If Pareti, III 551 and n. 1, were right in redating the tribunate of Plautius and Papirius to the year 88 BC, it would be a serious matter, but I do not see any adequate reason for abandoning the traditional date. After earlier doubts the traditional dating in 89 BC is re-established, in my view decisively, by Badian, *Historia* XVIII 1969, 461–75.

25. Cass. Dio, XLIII 25, 1, says that the *tribuni aerarii* of the *lex Aurelia* of 70 BC came ἐκ τοῦ ὁμίλου, but cf. Cic. *pro Planc.* 21, and in general Hill, p. 212 f.

26. Cf. also the proposals made by Sallust to Caesar: *iudices a paucis probari regnum est, ex pecunia legi inhonestum: quare omnes primae classis iudicare placet, sed numero plures quam iudicant* (ps.-Sall., *ad Caes.* II 7, 11, to be taken in conjunction with II 3, 2–3).

27. Cf. Livy, I 43, 10; Cic. *de Rep.* II 39; Dion. Hal. IV 20, 3–4. I believe that on this section of Appian (59, 266) we should accept the interpretation of Mommsen, *SR* III 270, which is that given in the text above. The different view of Meyer, 'Die angebliche Centurienreform Sullas', *Hermes* XXXIII 1898, 652–4, which has often been adopted (e.g. recently by Pareti, III 559), maintains rather that Sulla took all legislative power from the *comitia tributa*. However, the natural interpretation of the first phrase of 59, 266, seems to be that Sulla made the *auctoritas patrum* obligatory for the *comitia tributa*, a measure which he renewed in 81 BC. For a fuller discussion of the problem and for bibliography I refer to my Comm.[2] on 59, 266–7, and on 100, 466–7 (pp. 171–2 and pp. 273–5). For some theories of C. Nicolet, *MEFR* LXXI 1959, 211–25, in my opinion unacceptable, I refer to my arguments in *Athenaeum*, N.S. XXXVIII 1960, 213, n. 108.

28. It is impossible to say whether Cicero, *pro Rosc. Am. 8*, refers to the equestrian origin of the Senatorial jurors: *qui* (you, the jurors) *ex civitate in Senatum propter dignitatem, ex Senatu in hoc consilium delecti estis propter severitatem*; for the view that it does so refer see H. Strasburger, *Concordia ordinum*, Leipzig 1931, 10.

29. See, e.g., Cic. *pro. Rosc. Am.* 146; Q. Cic. *de pet. cons.* 9; Asc. *in orat. in toga cand.* p. 69, 20–2 Stangl; App. I 95, 442 and 103, 482; Livy, *Per.* LXXXIX; Flor, II 9, 5. Cf. Rice Holmes, *The Roman Republic*, Oxford 1923, I 59 and Hill, *Middle Class*, 146–7.

30. Hill, *CQ* XXVI 1932, *loc. cit.* and *id. Middle Class*, 170.

31. R. Syme, *PBSR* XIV 1938, 22–3, anticipated by W. Schur, 'Homo novus', *BJ* CXXXIV 1929, 54 f. and H. Strasburger, *Concordia ordinum*, 9–10.

32. See *Es. e Soc.* 270 f. [= 98 above].

33. For Atticus see A. H. Byrne, *T. Pomponius Atticus*, Bryn Mawr 1920, 52–3; for the emigration see Bennett, *Cinna and His Times*, 58–9.

34. Cf. the exhaustive discussion of D. Magie, *Roman Rule in Asia Minor*, Princeton 1950, II 1116–18.

35. This seems an appropriate occasion to reply briefly to the points made against me by H. Hill, *Athenaeum* N.S. XXXIII 1955, 327–32, about my remarks on his use of the term 'Middle Class' to indicate the Roman equestrian class (*Es. e Soc.* 341–5

[= 128 f. above]). I never dreamt of saying that the equestrian class did not exist in the Republican period as an *ordo* whose *dignitas* was distinct from that of the Senate (see also my remarks on the equestrian census: *ibid.* 335–9 [= 125 f. above]), nor that the remarks of Plin. *NH* XXXIII 1 (7), 29 and 2 (8), 34, were erroneous. I would simply repeat that for the Republican period we cannot, in my view, speak of the equestrian class as a 'middle class' in the normal economic and social use of the term as we find it today; Pliny in fact refers to a tripartite division of the Roman citizen body which is solely *political* in character and which applies to the Imperial period, although, obviously, there are references to Senators, Equites and Plebs earlier than that. Indeed, under the Empire the equestrian order is found side by side with Senate and people on Roman documents (Stein, *Der römische Ritterstand*, Munich 1927, 57–8). Finally, I repeat that the term 'middle class' for the *ordo equester* is acceptable only with the meaning it bears in the ancient sources, viz. without any reference to the economic and social structure of the Roman state (*Es. e Soc.* 342 f. [= 128 f. above] and more recently T. R. S. Broughton, *CPh* L 1955, 275–6).

36. Cf. Gabba, 'Note Appianee', *Athenaeum* N.S. XXXIII 1955, 218 f. = *Es. e Soc.* 537 f.

37. See most recently to this effect, with some reservations of varying importance, L. R. Taylor, *Party Politics in the Age of Caesar*, Berkeley: Los Angeles 1949, 52, and Pareti, III 620. The passage of Schol. Gron., p. 326, 20 Stangl, is worthless: see Willems, I² 409.

38. Niccolini, *Il tribunato della plebe*, Milan 1931, 105; Hill, *Middle Class*, 148; Pareti, III 722.

39. For Cicero, *div. in Caec.* 8, see Willems, I² 415; and see also the latter's excellent discussion at p. 409 f.

40. See Cic. *pro Archia*, 11: Cicero's argument would have been greatly helped by a mention of the abolition of the censorship.

41. Mommsen, *SR* II³ 336–7 and notes.

42. Cf. Mommsen, *SR* II³ 426–7 and III 1219–20; Hill, *Middle Class*, 148.

43. Following the reading of C. Pietrangeli, 'La scoperta di nuovi frammenti del *Senatusconsultum de Asclepiade*', *BIDR* LI–LII 1948, 284 and 291; cf. R. K. Sherk, *Roman Documents from the Greek East*, Baltimore 1969, no. 22, pp. 124–32.

44. Cf. also L. Gallet, *RD* VI 1937, 393. For Sulla's censorial powers see G. Tibiletti, *SDHI* XXV 1959, 121–2.

45. Cf. J. Carcopino, *La Loi de Hiéron et les Romains*, Paris 1914, 102 f.

46. Willems, I² 225 f.

47. Willems, I² 411.

48. The passage of Cicero, *div. in Caec.* 8, on the popular desire for the censorship seems to confirm my explanation: T. P. Wiseman, *JRS* LIX 1969, 65.

49. Cf. R. Syme, *The Roman Revolution*, Oxford 1939, 66; Broughton, *The Magistrates of the Roman Republic*, II 126.

50. Cf. L. R. Taylor, *TAPhA* LXXIII 1942, 13, n. 23.

51. See especially Cic. *pro Cluentio* 117 f. and Willems, I² 412 f., 417–20.

52. For a different interpretation cf. Carcopino, *Des Gracques à Sulla³*, 443, n. 151.

53. Cf. T. Frank, *CPh* XIX 1924, 332 f.

54. See my Commentary on Appian for details.

55. That the laws *de civitate* found application in successive *senatus consulta* is clear from Livy, *Per.* LXXX and LXXXIV; Sisenna, fr. 119 Peter (perhaps referring to the *lex Iulia* of 90 BC). Cf. Gran. Lic. p. 21, 9 Flemisch and Willems, II 685 and n. 2.

56. Cf. Taylor, *Party Politics*, 52 and n. 10 (p. 200).

57. Cf. *Es. e Soc.* 250 f. [= 89 f. above].

Notes to VI

* PP V 1950, 66–8. See R. E. Smith, 'The *lex Plotia agraria* and Pompey's Spanish veterans', *CQ* N.S. VII 1957, 82–5, rightly linking the passage of Plut. *Lucull.* 34, 4 with the law.

1. On the contents of the *lex Flavia* see esp. Cic. *ad Att.* I 19, 4.

2. *Röm. Alterth.* III² 115. According to G. Humbert, in Daremberg-Saglio, *Diction. des Ant.* I 164, the law in question was the same as the *lex Plautia de civitate*.

3. *Leges publicae populi Romani*, Milan, 1912, 342.

4. *Histoire romaine*, II 390 f. Cf. *Des Gracques à Sulla³*, Paris 1952, 402–3.

5. *Das Zeitalter des Marius und Sulla (Klio, Beiheft* 46), Leipzig 1942, 125 and n. 2. Cf. also Vancura, *RE* s.v. 'leges agrariae', col. 1155.

6. *Commentationes epigraphicae*, I, Berlin 1850, 362 (thence E. De Ruggiero, 'agrariae leges', *Encicl. Giurid. Ital.* 856). However, many reservations had already been raised both by A. Macé, *Les lois agraires chez les Romains*, Paris 1846, 415, n. 1, who wanted to place it in a year between 64 and 61 BC, and by Ed. Laboulaye, 'Des lois agraires chez les Romains', *Revue de Législation et de Jurisprudence* XII 3, 1846, 46.

7. *Fasti dei tribuni della plebe*, Milan 1934, 346 (tribunes of uncertain date). See also P. Terruzzi, 'agrarie leggi', *Encicl. Ital.* 936.

8. Niccolini, *op. cit.* 251, places Plautius in the college of 69, rightly rejecting the traditional dating which put him in 73–72 BC. The date of 70 BC was earlier advanced by Ed. Meyer, *Caesars Monarchie und das Prinzipat des Pompeius³*, 1922, 341, and is now accepted by L. R. Taylor, 'Caesar's early career', *CPh* XXXVI 1941, 121 and n. 32 (cf. also 'Caesar and the Roman nobility', *TAPhA* LXXIII 1942, 11): as we shall see, there are some factors which make the latter date preferable.

9. 'Véritable harangue' Carcopino calls it, *Hist. rom.* II 682 (cf. *César*, Paris 1950, 722). It is missing in the collections of fragments of *Oratores Romani* by H. Meyer and E. Malcovati.

10. *Cassii Dionis Historiae Romanae quae supersunt*, I, Hamburg 1750, 152, § 15: followed, in his identification of Metellus, by H. Smilda, in U. P. Boissevain, *Cassii Dionis Hist. Rom. quae supersunt*, IV *Index Historicus*, 1926, 110.

11. Carcopino, *op. cit.* II 625 (cf. *César* 665).

12. Cf. Plut. *Pomp.* 45.

13. *Op. cit.* 53, n. 5. See M. Gelzer, *Pompeius*, Munich 1949, 143.

14. Sall. *Hist.* IV 49 Maur.; Vell. II 30, 2.

15. See A. Garzetti, *Athenaeum* N.S. XX 1942, 20 and notes.

Notes to Review of Badian

* *RFIC* LXXXVII 1959, 189–99.

1. The dedication with which Badian has prefaced his book is a fine testimony to the position held by Italian scholarship in the field of ancient history and must be a matter of great satisfaction to all Italian readers.

2. More generally it may be said that the attention given to the salient moments in the history of Rome's foreign relations has led to some neglect of the principles which underlay the Roman attitude in the third and second centuries BC; these have been outlined by Fraccaro in *Opuscula* I 27 f. ('Il corso della storia romana') and p. 103 f. ('L'organizzazione politica dell'Italia romana') and in my view are amply confirmed by B.'s study.

3. In the Verrines Cicero calls them *liberae et immunes* but this formula probably goes back to the *lex Rupilia*, i.e. to a time when the concept of *libertas* was changed and it was felt necessary to make explicit the point that the cities enjoyed *immunitas* also (see Badian, pp. 87–9).

4. Cf. also Pareti, *Storia di Roma e del mondo Romano*, II 181 f.

5. He stresses this opinion in Part II as well, e.g. at p. 287 f., but I cannot persuade myself that he is right.

6. On this point it would be possible to enlarge by consulting the fine work of H. H. Schmitt, *Rom und Rhodos*, Munich 1957, 129 f., 151 f. We must remember that the dedications of the Lycians, attesting gratitude to the Roman people for the freedom obtained, are to be dated around 167 BC (Degrassi, *BCAR* LXXIV 1951–2 (pub. 1954), 19 f. = *Scritti vari di antichità*, I 1962, 415 f.; *ILLRP* 174–5), and in one of these (Degrassi, *BCAR cit.* p. 21 = *ILLRP* 175) the Roman people is called *cognatus* of the Lycians, a nice parallel with the case of Segesta (Badian, p. 37).

7. The same can be said for the Senate's opposition to transmarine colonization (p. 163), on which see Fraccaro, '*Lex Flaminia*', *Opuscula*, II 204–5.

8. Badian, p. 171, n. 1. Badian's argument on the βιβλίον of Caius (Plut. *Gracchi* 8, 9) is hypothetical and in fact does not allow for the way in which the speeches of the two Gracchi were transmitted. In the same way his remarks on Vettius (p. 170) do not seem to be valid since they rest on the fragile suggestion of Münzer that he belonged to the Vettii Sabini. See Badian, *Historia* XI 1962, 201, n. 19.

9. He should also have discussed App. I 10, 41 (cf. my Commentary[2] on *Appiani Bell. Civ. lib.* I, Florence 1967, 29) which attests the existence in allied communities of the same class distinctions as at Rome (see also I 21, 86–7 and Commentary, 67). I agree with Badian, p. 170, n. 2, that Velleius' tone is rhetorical, but I note that the evidence of II 6, 2, about Caius Gracchus has been explained, if somewhat tentatively, by Fraccaro, *Studies Robinson*, II 892 f. = *Opuscula*, II 85 f., as an allusion to the colonization of Cisalpine Gaul by Fulvius Flaccus.

10. Cf. his note Q on p. 296. I will not refute his comments made there, which I cannot accept at all, and I refer the reader to my Commentary on the passages concerned. Badian's comment on App. I 18, 73 f. (p. 175, n. 8) is not clear to me.

11. So p. 186, but at p. 301 'interposed a single veto': why, if the *rogatio* had not even been promulgated?

12. If events had followed Badian's chronology, it would be difficult to see what Caius was doing from July 122 (failure in third election) to *c.* June 121, the date of the vote on the *rogatio Minucia*.

13. Badian's interpretation (repeated in *Historia* XI 1962, 226 and n. 104) is accepted also by Brunt, *JRS* LV 1965, 94 and by E. J. Weinrib, *Historia* XIX 1970, 442: wrongly in my opinion (see *Aufstieg und Niedergang der römischen Welt*, I, Berlin–New York 1972, 787–9).

14. So rightly G. Samonati, *GIF* XI 1958, 111, though I find his proposal to correct the *Faesulae* of Florus, II 6, 11 unacceptable. In spite of Badian's objections (*Historia* XI 1962, 226, n. 103) this interpretation is also accepted by Brunt, *JRS* LV 1965, 94 and by Heurgon, 'L'Ombrie à l'époque des Gracques et de Sulla', *Atti del primo Convegno di Studi Umbri*, Perugia 1964, 122.

15. Badian's argument from Plut. *Mar.* 41, 4 (p. 222) is not, I think, acceptable; it is not easy to believe that the farmers and the free shepherds mentioned there as following Marius in 87 BC (he also called the slaves to freedom) are to be identified with small proprietors. On the contrary, they must correspond to the freedmen, *coloni* and *pastores*, who, along with slaves, made up the troops enrolled by Domitius Ahenobarbus on his estates according to Caesar, *BC* I 34 and 56. On their status see R. M. Haywood, *AJPh* LIV, 1933, 149–50. Moreover, what is said by B. at p. 297 (note

S) is not convincing: the Marian soldiers who supported Saturninus in the voting of 100 BC and who came in from the fields (App. I 29, 132) are clearly citizens, and I do not see how they can have come, as B. believes, from Etruria, or at least from those districts of Etruria which later sided with Marius in the civil war. B.'s hypothesis (pp. 234–5) that in 91 BC Marius had incited the Etruscans and Umbrians against Drusus' laws thus falls to the ground.

16. Certainly the anti-Roman outbreak at Asculum must have had a popular character. B. does not seem to have considered App. I 38, 170: when the Romans got to know (of the secret agreements of the *socii*) περιέπεμπον ἐς τὰς πόλεις ἀπὸ σφῶν τοὺς ἑκάστοις μάλιστα ἐπιτηδείους, ἀφανῶς τὰ γιγνόμενα ἐξετάζειν. I think we can infer from this that Servilius, for example, must have had connexions with the district of Asculum. The case of Servilius is mentioned in Diod. XXXVII 13, in connexion with an obscure episode in which the protagonists are a C. Domitius (identified by Münzer with the consul of 96 BC: *RE* s.v. 'Domitius', no. 21, col. 1327) and Poppaedius Silo (for the chronology see also my Commentary on Appian, p. 122). If Domitius had functions analogous to those of Servilius in this episode but in the territory of the Marsi, might one conclude that he had *clientelae* in that district? One could link this suggestion with the enrolments of Marsi and Paeligni in 49 by L. Domitius Ahenobarbus. As is known, he promised his soldiers allotments from his own estates (Caesar, *BC* I 15, 7, and 17, 4); these allotments should have been in that district since it seems difficult to believe that he promised them land in Etruria. Note also the Augustan poet Domitius Marsus.

17. On the Domitii (p. 313) B. is right to reject the view of Duval (*Gallia* VII 1949, 216 f.) that the proconsulship of Cn. Domitius Ahenobarbus in Narbonensis lasted until 118 BC and later (so also Degrassi, *ILLRP* I p. 259). The basis for this view – i.e. that since the milestone of Ahenobarbus recently discovered reckons the miles from Narbo, it must be later than the foundation of the colony (118 BC) – will not do, as is now shown by the milestone of C. Aurelius Cotta of 252 BC found in Sicily (De Vita, Κώκαλος I 1955, 10 f.: the dating is not certain; Degrassi, *Scritti vari di antichità*, III 1967, 195–204), on which the miles are reckoned from Agrigentum. Narbo was an important city even before the foundation of the colony. On the vexed problem of the date of Narbo Martius see Badian, *Roman Imperialism in the late Republic*², Oxford 1968, 98, n. 32, and B. Levick, *CQ* XXI 1971, 170–9.

18. I should like to make it clear that I have never tried to show Sertorius as the champion of the Italians in Spain (B. p. 269, n. 7): this is only a suggestion of Piganiol's, *Histoire de Rome*, Paris 1949, 166. It was rather my intention to depict the struggle of Sertorius as the continuation of the war fought by the Marians in Italy: see *Es. e Soc.* 312 f., 325 f. [= 114 f., 120 f. above]. Whether for this purpose Sertorius used the support of elements that had recently or in earlier times come to Spain from southern Italy is another question.

Index

Roman names appear under the *nomen* (except for the familiar Augustus). The notes have been indexed as if they had appeared at the foot of the page. All dates BC.

Index of Passages

INSCRIPTIONS

INSCRIPTIONES ITALIAE
(ed. Degrassi)

DATE DUE

GAYLORD			PRINTED IN U.S.A.